MAGAZINES

IN THE

UNITED STATES

JAMES PLAYSTED WOOD

SECOND EDITION

THE RONALD PRESS COMPANY ⟋ NEW YORK

Library of Congress Catalog Card Number: 56-10175
PRINTED IN THE UNITED STATES OF AMERICA

For W. T. W.

PREFACE

Moore than 7,000 periodicals are published in the United States. Some 3¾ billion copies are sold every year. American magazines are read regularly by many millions, and to some extent by almost everyone in this country who can read.

This book attempts to show, from general magazines that were important in their time and from important nationally circulated magazines of today, what magazines are and in what directions they exert their social and economic influence. It traces and gauges the force of periodicals from Benjamin Franklin's *General Magazine* to the weeklies and monthlies of the present. It shows how magazines have both reflected and helped to mould American tastes, habits, manners, interests, and beliefs; how they have shaped opinion on public questions; how they have crusaded effectively for social and political reforms; and how magazine advertising, as well as magazine editorial content, has affected the American home and standard of living.

This new edition has been prompted by several circumstances. Social historians, students of contemporary culture and opinion, publishers, editors, advertisers, and others to whom what magazines are and do is a matter of material and daily concern, have accorded the book a gratifying reception since its first appearance in 1949. Television has had its effect on magazine editorial content, magazine reading, and magazine advertising. There is an increasing general awareness of the importance in our time of public communications of every kind. There have been marked changes of many kinds in American magazines.

There is more factual, less imaginative, material in most of the big general magazines. Throughout, there is less literature, more journalism. The feature article has replaced the familiar essay. Fiction in many magazines has given way to the exploitation of "personalities" in biographies or ghost-written autobiographies. In editorial content the once valid distinction between class and mass magazines has virtually disappeared. Similarity of subject choice and treatment is more and more apparent.

New magazines have come since 1949 and some of them have already gone. *Flair* lasted less than a year. *Quick* reached the logical limits of condensation and disappeared not once but twice. In its 103d year of publication *Country Gentleman* was absorbed by its chief competitor. *Sports Illustrated* was born in 1954. Harold Ross died, but *The New Yorker,* which he founded in 1925 and edited until his death, is still fulfilling its avowed purpose of making sense and making money. *Collier's* went biweekly in 1953. *The Saturday Evening Post* appeared in new type and layout in 1955. *The Reader's Digest,* which broke its own precedent when it began to accept advertising in 1955, flourishes like the green bay tree. Despite concerted attack, the comic magazines, their circulations astronomical, still flourish like weeds. *The Saturday Review* has dropped *of Literature* from its title but seems, in the larger sense, more "literary" then ever.

Completely new sections have been added in this edition on the grocery-distributed magazines and on the comics. The sections dealing with the farm magazines, with *The Reader's Digest, The New Yorker, Time, Life, The Saturday Evening Post,* and other large-circulation magazines, have been enlarged and brought up to date. Discussion of additional magazines of varied significance has been included and, where the facts dictated, new data and interpretations have been inserted throughout the chapters on current magazine publishing.

The original idea for this book was suggested by Donald M. Hobart, and his advice and encouragement contributed essentially to the book's development. For research assistance in the preparation of this new edition the author's sincere thanks go to Mrs. Bernice Read and to Elizabeth Craig Wood.

JAMES PLAYSTED WOOD

Philadelphia, Pa.
May, 1956

CONTENTS

ILLUSTRATIONS

MAGAZINES
IN THE
UNITED STATES

Chapter 1

ENGLISH MAGAZINE ORIGINS

THE ENGLISH newspaper developed in the late seventeenth century out of the political pamphlet and the newsletter. The English magazine developed out of the newspaper within less than fifty years after the first newspaper was founded.

The first newspaper was the *London Gazette*, which had been founded as the *Oxford Gazette* in 1665. What is usually, and with considerable justification, described as the first magazine in English was started when an outspoken Nonconformist with too skillful a pen was sent to jail in 1703. The writer, described in the advertisements for his arrest as "a middle-sized spare man about forty years old of a brown complexion and dark brown-coloured hair, but wears a wig; a hooked nose, a sharp chin, grey eyes, and a large mole near his mouth," was pilloried for three days and then imprisoned for the ironic opinions he had expressed against the extreme position of the established Church of England in his *Shortest Way With Dissenters*. Daniel Defoe, who had not yet written *Robinson Crusoe* or his other picaresque novels, thereupon began to issue in February, 1704, from Newgate Prison or immediately after his release from it, a weekly periodical which he called *The Review*.

The journalistic idea, the idea of periodical publication, was still new. It is not always possible to distinguish absolutely between the newspaper and the magazine of this time. The form of neither was fixed. The provinces of both media for public communication overlapped as, to a lesser extent, they still do, but the *Gazette* and its rivals and imitators were con-

3

cerned almost solely with the news. *The Review*, written in Defoe's accurate, straightforward style, printed the news, too, but it also printed articles on domestic affairs and on national policy. Defoe was *The Review's* sole editor and contributor during its nine-year history. In its four small pages, which appeared usually three times a week, he expressed and forcefully defended his views on all matters of public concern. He instituted a department, run monthly at first, called "Advice from the Scandalous Club," in which he discussed literature, manners, and morals. He made *The Review* recognizably a magazine. It was Defoe's "Advice from the Scandalous Club," turned after 1705 into the semi-weekly *Little Review*, which suggested theme and treatment to the famous periodical writers who followed Defoe. Before *The Review* ceased publication in 1712, Richard Steele had started *The Tatler*.

The first *Tatler* appeared in April, 1709. Ostensibly by Isaac Bickerstaff, a name which Swift had made famous, it contained political news. More varied material soon followed. In imitation of *The Review*, Steele, motivated by the desire of financial gain and by the equally strong wish to influence the men and women of his day—twin desires which still motivate magazine editors—began his characteristic essays. He printed foreign intelligence and theatrical news, but he wrote and published short articles attacking the fads and follies of the day. "Poor Dick Steele," as Thackeray describes him in one of the finest of his essays in *The English Humorists*, might stumble, fall, and get up again in his own life, but his intent was moral and so were the principles of conduct he preached. *The Tatler* spoke out against gambling, drinking, and dueling. It also gave the gossip of the coffeehouses; and gossip about people and places is still a characteristic of the magazine. As Jenny Bickerstaff—for magazines from the first have wooed women readers as well as men—Steele wrote on subjects of interest to women. These, with advertising, were the contents of *The Tatler*.

Advertising, a feature destined to become so characteristic of modern magazines, not only served its usual purposes but even provided the subject of a *Tatler* essay. In Number 224 of *The Tatler*, September 14, 1710, Addison wrote:

> It is my custom, in a dearth of news, to entertain myself with those collections of advertisements that appear at the end of all our public prints. . . . But to consider this subject in its most ridiculous lights, advertisements are of great use to the vulgar. . . . A man that is by no means big enough for the Gazette may easily creep into the ads. . . . A second use . . . has been the management of controversy. . . . The inventors of "strops for razors" have written against one another in this way for several years. . . . The third and last use of these writings is to inform the world, where they may be furnished with almost everything that is necessary for life. If a Man has pains in his head, cholics in his bowels, or spots in his clothes, he may here meet with proper cures and remedies. If a man would recover a wife or a horse that is stolen or strayed; if he wants new sermons, electuaries, asses milk, or anything else, either for his body or his mind, this is the place to look for them in.

Advising copywriters of the day, Addison continued:

> The great art in writing advertising is the finding out the proper method to catch the reader, without which a good thing may pass over unobserved, or be lost among commissions of bankrupts. Asterisks or hands were formerly of great use for this purpose. Of late years the *N.B.* has been much in fashion, as also little cuts and figures, the invention of which we must ascribe to the author of spring trusses. . . .
>
> By the remarks I have here made, it plainly appears, that a collection of advertisements is a kind of miscellany; the writers of which, contrary to all authors, except men of quality, give money to the booksellers who publish their copy.

Joseph Addison had joined Steele in writing *The Tatler* after about its eightieth number. They continued to work together and in March, 1711, published the first issue of the famous *Spectator*. The humorous coffeehouse sketches which Steele had originated and Addison perfected became the new magazine's daily contents; all other material, except short advertisements, was dropped. Together the genial, very human Steele and the urbane, scholarly Addison created the English informal essay and made it the first magazine contribution to literature.

In *The Spectator* they almost gave form to the short story. Steele introduced Sir Roger de Coverley and the other characters of the most famous club in English literature in the second issue. The stories of Sir Roger, most whimsical of knights, and of Will Honeycomb, Sir Andrew Freeport, Captain Sentry, Will Wimble, and other delightful eccentrics of the club may be said to be the first magazine fiction. The pleasant, colloquial essays of *The Tatler* gave way to more serious essays. Addison, a fine critic, taught appreciation of literature and of classical learning at the same time that he and Steele discoursed humorously on the topics of the day.

The Spectator, 274 of its issues by Addison, 236 by Steele, the remaining 45 by occasional contributors, was read with delight by the literate and sophisticated of polite London to whom it was addressed. Its circulation reached 3,000 in a city of about a half million. Some numbers are said to have had a sale of 20,000 copies. Addison and Steele meant to entertain, but their serious purpose, as the essays show and Steele affirmed, was "to expose the false arts of life, to pull off the disguises of cunning, vanity, and affectations, and to recommend a general simplicity in our dress, our discourse, and our behavior." As *The Review* had been for practical, clear-spoken Defoe, *The Spectator* was a means of expression for these sharpest and most graceful of Queen Anne wits and moralists. More than a means of expression, it was a means of reaching and influencing public opinion. As such, *The Tatler* and *The Spectator* succeeded both in moulding the ideas and tastes of urban England in the early years of the eighteenth century, and in establishing the magazine as a journalistic and literary form of marked social force.

Numerous imitators of *The Tatler* and *The Spectator* sprang up. The coffeehouses of London were filled with wits and journalists eager to write for the newssheets and the new periodicals. Steele himself fathered half a dozen later and less successful periodicals, most of them Whig political organs or gossip sheets: the *Guardian,* the *Englishman, Town Talk,* the *Tea Table, Chit Chat,* the *Plebeian.* Alexander Pope used the *Grub Street Journal* (1730–1738), a magazine which he had in all probability founded though he consistently denied connection with it, to say that his many enemies were nasty people and to pour a little boiling oil on them in each issue.

In 1731 appeared the first number of the first monthly periodical to describe itself by the word "magazine." Under the name of Sylvanus Urban, Edward Cave, a London printer and bookseller, began publication of what was actually conceived as a *museum, depository,* or *magazine* which, while it paid some attention to current events, was more concerned with collecting in more permanent form the best of the material appearing in the journals. Cave's *Gentleman's Magazine* soon ceased to be merely eclectic. As did *Harper's New Monthly Magazine,* which was founded more than a century later in New York, and *The Reader's Digest,* founded almost two centuries later, both of which started purely as reprint periodicals, *The Gentleman's Magazine* soon began to publish more varied materials. It printed both prose and verse, historical and biographical material, and obituaries. It listed other publications. It printed songs with music, much as *Godey's Lady's Book* did in the nineteenth century and as Edward Bok's *Ladies' Home Journal* did as late as 1910. Some features of the first monthly magazine have lasted a long time. *The Gentleman's Magazine* even offered engravings and maps, as does the *National Geographic Magazine* today.

Perhaps the best, and certainly the best-known, feature of *The Gentleman's Magazine* was its reports of the debates in Parliament. The magazine had reported these from 1732.

Six years later this task was assigned to one of the most famous of all magazine contributors, Dr. Samuel Johnson, who was just beginning his London career. Johnson wrote voluminously for the magazine, but his chief job was to report activities in Parliament. From inaccurate and sketchy notes made by Cave's friends and from his own imagination he pieced together these reports for publication in the monthly. He really wrote the speeches he attributed to English statesmen of the day, and probably wrote them better than those who delivered them could have done. When the House of Commons declared that publication of its proceedings was illegal, Johnson reported them under the transparent disguise of "Reports of the Debates in the Senate of Magna Lilliputia." Names of the speakers were designated only by their initial and final letters.

Besides his political writing, Johnson wrote numerous essays, biographies, and literary notices for *The Gentleman's Magazine*. In the issue for August, 1743, he announced that his famous *Life of Richard Savage* was in preparation. It was published in 1744. The circulation of *The Gentleman's Magazine* was already a high 10,000 when Samuel Johnson became Cave's assistant. Johnson, the first important writer to ally himself with a popular monthly as a reporter, article writer, and editor, aided largely in pushing it up to an almost incredible 15,000. *The Gentleman's Magazine* had imitators, the most important of them the *London Magazine*, but it was the outstanding success of its time.

Dr. Johnson ceased to write for *The Gentleman's Magazine* in 1744, but his connection with magazines was to continue. From 1750 to 1752, he published *The Rambler*, a paper after the *Spectator* manner. Johnson's essays appeared in it regularly every Tuesday and Saturday. By this time England had about 150 periodicals. Later Johnson undertook another series of essays in *The Idler*, which, from 1758 to 1760, ran as a department of *The Universal Chronicle, or Weekly Gazette*.

By the mid-eighteenth century the magazine form had begun to crystallize and the magazine pattern to make itself clear. Some magazines, such as *The Tatler, The Spectator,* and *The Rambler,* were of the periodical essay type, and others, such as *The Gentleman's Magazine,* the *London Magazine,* and *The Monthly Review,* displayed more varied contents; but they all had magazine intents and features in common. Such periodical writers as Defoe, Steele, Addison, and Johnson developed a vehicle of literary quality meant to be more durable than the newspaper, to carry less ephemeral material, to comment as well as to inform, to communicate pleasure as well as fact, to provoke speculation, and to influence belief and conduct.

Before this time the magazine idea had spread to the British possessions in America. Inspired by the success of *The Gentleman's Magazine* and its rival, the *London Magazine,* Benjamin Franklin decided to establish in Philadelphia a monthly magazine for all the Colonies.

Chapter 2

MAGAZINE BEGINNINGS IN AMERICA

IN THE *Pennsylvania Gazette,* a weekly which Franklin had published since 1729, the reputed ancestor of *The Saturday Evening Post,* Franklin announced in November, 1740, his plans to publish *The General Magazine, and Historical Chronicle, for All the British Plantations in America.* Unfortunately Franklin offered the editorship of what was to be the pioneer American magazine to John Webbe, a Philadelphia lawyer, who quickly divulged his knowledge of the scheme to Andrew Bradford, son of Pennsylvania's first printer. Thereupon Bradford immediately announced a magazine of his own and, on February 13, 1741, with Webbe as editor, got out the first issue of his own *American Magazine, or a Monthly View of the Political State of the British Colonies.* Three days later, Franklin, acting now as his own editor, published the first issue of the *General Magazine.*

The *General Magazine* was what Franklin conceived a magazine to be, literally a magazine or storehouse of varied material, gathered mostly from books, pamphlets, newspapers, and political documents, and offered for edification and entertainment of his readers. His magazine contained seventy-five pages, twice as many as Bradford's, and sold for sixpence sterling the single copy. There were no subscribers, Franklin depending on single copy sales. The first issue, dated January, 1741, was typical of the six monthly numbers published. It contained a discussion of the currency, a vital subject in the Colonies; "Accounts of and Extracts from New Books and Pamphlets Published in the Plantation"; included sermons by Mathew

Byles and George Whitefield, the English evangelist whom Franklin admired;[1] ten pages of verse ("Poetical Essays"); and "The Historical Chronicle" or news section. The "Chronicle" in this first issue described the Grand Mogul's defeat by Thomas Koulikan, recorded events in Turkey and Russia, and revealed that the German Emperor had died the preceding October from "being poisoned by eating mushrooms stew'd in oil." A fire at Charleston was described, and the "Chronicle" gave the most vivid of the Philadelphia news.

Succeeding issues of the *General Magazine* described proceedings in Parliament that affected the American Colonies, the negotiations of New York with the Six Nations. They contained more discussions of the uncertain Colonial currency, offered more sermons—for this was the period of the Great Awakening, the religious revival led by Whitefield and by Jonathan Edwards in Northampton, Massachusetts, which swept the Colonies in the mid-eighteenth century—and more verse. An article in the February issue described life in an orphan asylum which Whitefield had founded in Georgia. A lead article in March was on "The Present State of Virginia"; another article, "Evolutions of the Foot," described infantry drill and maneuvers; and a third dealt with "A New Method of Making Molasses from the Summer Sweeting as Communicated to the Royal Society and Put in #374 of Philosophical Transactions." Franklin's scientific interests, which led him to found the American Philosophical Society in 1743, show in his magazine.

There were intimations of things to come in the April issue of the *General Magazine*. In that issue Franklin printed what

[1] The frugal Franklin was, at least temporarily, much moved by Whitefield's persuasive powers. In his *Autobiography* he writes: "I happened . . . to attend one of his sermons, in the course of which I perceived he intended to finish with a collection, and I silently resolved he should get nothing from me. . . . As he proceeded I began to soften and decided to give the coppers. Another stroke of his oratory made me ashamed of that, and determin'd me to give the silver; and he finished so admirably, that I empty'd my pockets wholly into the collector's dish, gold and all."

was, even then, a not very convincing attempt of the New York
Assembly to allay the suspicions of that Colony's nervous lieu-
tenant governor:

> To what is mentioned of a Jealousy in England, that the
> Plantations are not without Thoughts of throwing off their
> Dependence on the Crown of England, we shall say the less, as
> your Honour declares you hope and believe no Man in the
> Colony has such an Intention, and we dare vouch, that not one
> single Person in it has such an Intention.

Obviously Franklin was editing his magazine not for Philadelphia or for Pennsylvania, but for the Colonies as a whole.
Unformed as they were, and of short duration, the first American magazines were not merely local in content and appeal.
They showed from the first the magazine trend toward coverage
of all the Colonies that developed a century and a half later into
the nation-wide coverage of the national magazine.

From the beginning the magazine's intent was the widest
possible dissemination of important information, a basic intent
of today's national magazines. They were founded, too, with
the very definite intent of influencing public opinion, particularly on one crucial subject. Bradford, who had beaten Franklin to the street with his monthly American magazine, said that
one of his reasons for publishing the *American Magazine* was
"That the parliament and People of Great Britain may be truly
and clearly informed of the Constitution and Government in the
Colonies, whose Great Distance from the Mother-country seems
in some sense to have placed them out of her View."

The *American Magazine and Monthly Chronicle*, begun in
1757, was prefaced with:

> It has long been a matter of just complaint, among some of
> the best friends of our national commerce and safety, that the
> important concerns of these Colonies were but little studied and
> less understood in the mother-country, even by many of those,
> who have sustained the highest offices of trust and dignity in
> it. . . . The present war [the French war] has rendered this

country, at length, the object of a very general attention, and it seems now become as much the mode among those who would be useful or conspicuous in the state, to seek an acquaintance with these colonies, their constitutions, interests and commerce. . . . This favorable disposition, if duly cultivated, may have a happy influence. . . .

The earliest American magazines were out, then, to influence opinion in the Colonies and opinion in England. One of Franklin's purposes and accomplishments in the *General Magazine* was to present political information, knowledge of which he felt should be widespread among the thirteen Colonies. To this end he devoted about a third of the space in his magazine to the reprinting of state papers.

The shrewd Franklin was, of course, well aware of the wider audience he could reach and influence through the medium of his magazine. He was no stranger to journalism. As a printer's apprentice he had worked with his brother James in getting out in Boston the *New England Courant,* founded in 1721 as the second newspaper published in America, preceded only by the *Boston News Letter* in 1704.[2] By 1729 he was issuing weekly from his own press in Philadelphia the *Pennsylvania Gazette* purchased from Samuel Keimer, who had founded it as *The Universal Instructor in All Arts and Sciences and Pennsylvania Gazette* the year before, when he heard that the twenty-two-year-old Franklin was planning a similar weekly.

The *Gazette,* a reflection of its acute and ambitious publisher-editor, became perhaps the best paper in the Colonies. Besides the news, it contained in its early years some of Franklin's familiar essays, disputes with imaginary characters created by Franklin for the purpose, and weather reports which Franklin was the first to introduce as a journalistic feature. In 1754, at the time of the Albany Congress, the *Gazette* carried

[2] Franklin calls it the second newspaper in his *Autobiography.* Actually the *Boston Gazette,* printed but not edited by James Franklin, dating from 1719, intervened.

what is usually considered America's first cartoon, probably drawn by Franklin himself. The earliest plea for a United Colonies, if not a United States, it pictured a snake in eight parts and underneath the legend "Join or Die." Publication was suspended for two weeks in 1765 as a protest against the Stamp Act, but was only twice interrupted during the Revolution.

Only three numbers of Bradford's monthly were published, six of Franklin's, but the magazine, once established, quickly took root in American soil. About a hundred were founded before the end of the eighteenth century. William Beer in his *Checklist of American Magazines, 1741–1800,* (Worcester: 1923), lists 98. The figure varies according to the source used. Some of these "magazines" were really weekly newspapers. These magazines contained essays, poetry and fiction, political writing, literary and dramatic criticism, articles on economics and religion, comments on slavery, women's dress, dueling, swearing. They contained the best American writing of their time and reflected, as the best of our national magazines reflect today, the world in which their readers lived.

Notable editors succeeded Franklin and Webbe. Mathew Carey, Thomas Paine, Charles Brockden Brown, Hugh Brackenridge were all eighteenth-century Philadelphia editors, for Philadelphia was the center of the magazine-publishing industry. Noah Webster, whose *Spelling Book* and *Dictionary* were to be so basic in American education and in the standardization of American spelling, was a New York editor by 1787. Isaiah Thomas was Boston's best eighteenth-century editor.[3]

One of the most important American magazines of the eighteenth century was published only from January, 1775, to July, 1776, but none of its contemporaries exceeded it in social force at a crucial period in American history. Thomas

---

[3] Thomas was also a printer and publisher. His *A Specimen* (of the types he used), 1785, and his *History of Printing in America,* 1810, are valuable sources on early American printing. Thomas founded the American Antiquarian Society in 1812.

THE
GENERAL MAGAZINE,
AND
Historical Chronicle,
For all the *British* Plantations in *America.*
[To be Continued Monthly.]

JANUARY 1741.

VOL. I.

PHILADELPHIA:
Printed and Sold by B. FRANKLIN.

Benjamin Franklin conceived the idea of a monthly magazine for the American Colonies. The first issue of his *General Magazine* appeared on February 16, 1741.

Paine, whose electrifying pamphlet *Common Sense* did so much to crystallize the sentiment toward separation from England and whose letter *The Crisis* ("These are the times that try men's souls . . .") inflamed readers with his own fiery patriotism, had been in America only three months before Robert Aitkin made him editor of the *Pennsylvania Magazine*. Though it had been started by the milder Aitkin as a quieter periodical, there was soon no mistaking the sympathies of the *Pennsylvania Magazine*. The vignette of the magazine showed the goddess of Liberty holding a shield with the Pennsylvania arms emblazoned on it. A mortar labeled "The Congress," battle-axes and pikes, the word "Liberty" on a gorget hanging from a tree, surrounded the goddess.

Paine, who numbered David Rittenhouse, Benjamin Rush, Mathew Wilson, and President John Witherspoon of Princeton among his important contributors, gave the *Pennsylvania Magazine* its strong political bias and himself wrote much of the strongly revolutionary matter that made the magazine so powerful an instrument of the times. "Reflections on the Duty of Princes" and "On Liberty," the former signed only with initials, the latter with a classical pseudonym after the fashion of the time, which appeared in early issues were obviously written by Paine. His famous poem "The Liberty Tree" was published in June, 1775. Before that had appeared an Irish-dialect attack on the British troops in Boston and a poem in memory of the American volunteers killed at Lexington and Concord on April 19, 1775. Consistently there was non-political matter in the *Pennsylvania Magazine*—verse, essays, a series on "The Old Bachelor," and an "Occasional Letter on the Female Sex"— but the periodical took its color and gained its force from Thomas Paine's revolutionary ardor. A department called "Monthly Intelligence" recorded the war news each month, printed the letters of Washington and other Colonial leaders and the proceedings in Parliament and in the Continental Congress. "Substitutes for Tea" was run in February, 1775, and the "Dialogue on Liberty" in April, 1776. The war put an abrupt end to the *Pennsylvania Magazine*, but it went down defiantly, carrying in the issue of July, 1776, its last number, the Declaration of Independence which it had been a strong force in bringing about.

The Revolution was over when the same man founded four months apart what were to be the most successful American magazines of the late eighteenth century. Mathew Carey, jailed in Dublin for his pamphlets criticizing British policy, fled to France, where Benjamin Franklin employed him for a time as a printer at Passy. Returning to Ireland, he was again jailed for his militant anti-British editing of the *Volunteer's Journal*. This time Carey fled to America where, less than six months after his arrival in Philadelphia, he started the *Pennsylvania Herald*, with $400 borrowed from Lafayette. It came to a sudden end when Carey was wounded in a duel.

In August, 1786, the *Pennsylvania Gazette* carried an announcement of the first new magazine Carey was to edit and print. *The Columbian Magazine, or Monthly Miscellany* was to be started, according to the announcement, at a time "when the genuine spirit of liberty has extended its benign influence over these independent and highly favored republics." It was to be a monthly of forty-eight pages, with copperplate engravings, sold to subscribers at twenty shillings a year. The first number appeared in October, 1786. By March, 1787, Carey, having established the second of his magazines, *The American Museum*, hired Francis Hopkinson as editor and Jeremy Belknap as contributor. A paid editor and a paid contributor were startling magazine innovations. The *Columbian* introduced other changes. It stressed publication of original contributions and obtained capable men to write them. Most magazines of the period contained many items clipped from English magazines, other American magazines, newspapers, and pamphlets. There were no copyright laws to infringe. Ownership of writing was not as important as getting the material before the public.

The new *Columbian,* a new magazine for a new nation, paid particular attention to politics, agriculture, inventions, science, and business. Its writings were concerned with these subjects as well as with purely literary offerings. So were the copperplate engravings, most of them done by James Trenchard, one of the magazine's publishers. An important contributor was Dr. Benjamin Rush, who, after obtaining his medical degree at Edinburgh, returned to his native Philadelphia where he became a professor in the medical school of the University of Pennsylvania. Dr. Rush, a member of the Continental Congress and a signer of the Declaration of Independence, was a strong Federalist with decided ideas about slavery, capital punishment, the use of liquor and tobacco, education, and the proper treatment for yellow fever. About all of these subjects he wrote vividly and forcefully in the *Columbian.* He showed his hatred of slavery in several *Columbian* articles, one of them "The Paradise of Negro-Slaves"; his dislike of whisky in "A Moral and Physical Thermometer"; his belief in free schools in "The Benefits of Charity"; his medical interests in "An Inquiry into the Methods of Preventing the Painful and Fatal Effect of Cold upon the Human Body"; and his political beliefs in "Causes Which Produced the Ruin of States."

Reprinted items gave *Columbian* readers matter from the pens of Franklin, Washington, General Israel Putnam, and David Ramsay. There were selections from writers abroad: Johnson, Burke, Voltaire, Montesquieu, and Rousseau. At the same time the *Columbian* was running in 1787 and 1788 *The Forresters: An Historical Romance,* in which Jeremy Belknap, one of America's first paid magazine writers, through humorous allegory narrated the founding and growth of the British colonies in America.[4] Belknap also contributed a series of biogra-

[4] Jeremy Belknap was a Congregational clergyman and a historian of Boston and one of the founders of the Massachusetts Historical Society, the first society of its kind in America. He had been offered the editorship of the *Columbian* but refused it because a Boston church offered him a larger salary, 125 pounds a year.

phies of "Heroic and Virtuous Men" of the United States, including sketches of John Winthrop, Sir Ferdinando Gorges, and Captain John Smith. He even contributed an article, earlier printed in *The Boston Magazine,* which endeavored to determine whether the discovery of America had been a blessing or a bane to man. It was Belknap who promoted the sale of the *Columbian* in Boston and who persuaded the young John Quincy Adams to publish in the magazine his oration at the Harvard commencement of 1787.

The *Columbian* was good, but in some ways *The American Museum* was even better. Running from 1787 to 1792, when the *Columbian* also was discontinued, its issues are now invaluable as historical source material. This was not accidental. In contrast to the *Columbian,* which was to publish as much original material as possible, the *Museum* was planned by Carey as a repository of important American writing. It was to be a museum of American writing worthy of preservation—and a publishing bargain: one hundred pages a month at a "quarter dollar" a number, or eighteen shillings a year; $2.50 outside Pennsylvania. Few modern magazines give their readers as much solid worth for their money.

Carey sought out and reprinted the basic documents of the Revolution. His first volume contained Paine's *Common Sense,* Washington's *Circular Letter to the Army,* Humphreys' *Address to the Armies of America,* Trumbull's *M'Fingal.* Various issues of the *Museum* reprinted writing by Benjamin Franklin, Witherspoon, Hopkinson, Dr. Ladd, Noah Webster, Hancock, and many others eminent in statesmanship or literature. The *Museum* ran articles on scientific subjects by Rittenhouse, Benjamin West, James Bowdoin, John Winthrop of Harvard, Samuel Dexter, and many others. It published the poetry of Freneau, Trumbull, Hopkinson, Dwight, Godfrey. Paine's *Crisis,* Dickinson's *Letters from a Pennsylvania Farmer,* and Witherspoon's *Letters on Marriage* were all reprinted in the *Museum.*

Carey, an anti-Federalist himself, printed the writings on both sides of this central question of the day, including the *Federalist* papers. He published articles on industry, the currency, commerce, politics, science, education, agriculture, and many directed against slavery. Carey made perhaps no more important contribution to the thought of his time and the subsequent economic history of the United States than in his selection of writing dealing with American business. The articles he chose emphasized a conservative and practical approach to business problems. They stressed protection as necessary to assist the growth of American industry, advocated free trade among the states but a national tariff to combat tariffs imposed abroad on goods imported from America. Carey published the opinions on business of Dickinson, Franklin, Rush, and James M'Henry, but gave particular prominence to those of two Philadelphians, Coxe and Barton. Tench Coxe was president of the Pennsylvania Society for the Encouragement of Manufactures and the Useful Arts. His "Address to an Assembly of Friends of American Manufactures, Convened for the Purpose of Establishing a Society" emphasized the need for private enterprise and government to join forces in the encouragement of American industry. An address, arguing for the tariff, was read at Franklin's home and published in the *Museum*. Carey also printed an essay by William Barton, secretary of the Pennsylvania Society for the Encouragement of Manufactures, who expressed similar conservative business opinions on the powers of Congress to regulate trade.

With Carey the American magazine went beyond the mere proffering of entertainment and spreading of information. The ideas he placed before his readers helped them to form their opinions on social, political, and business affairs in the formative period of the new country.

The Massachusetts Magazine, founded by Isaiah Thomas in 1789, one of but two American magazines of the eighteenth century to live for eight years, made what was then a significant and prophetic departure in magazine publishing. Thomas, an experienced book and newspaper publisher, directed his new monthly not only to the cultured, at whom most magazines of the period were aimed, but also to the intelligent if less intellectual readers who had not yet been a recognized magazine audience. As do the best of modern magazines, it appealed to those with journalistic as well as those with erudite tastes. It was projected emphatically to entertain as well as to inform. The new magazine intended, its first issue stated, to "gratify and excite the natural inquisitiveness of the human mind . . . rouse and strengthen the native powers of the soul . . . give birth to literary emulation and effort . . . enforce and reward studious application . . . improve the taste, the language and the manners of the age . . . increase an acquaintance with natural and civil history, with arts, manufactures and commerce, with law, physick and divinity . . ." It was an ambitious program, and in reaching to tap the large potential magazine audience which publishers and editors had to this time neglected, Thomas offered excellent and varied fare.

Besides articles of most of the types printed by his contemporaries and competitors, Thomas published plays, essays, engravings, and sentimental fiction. Joseph Dennie, to become one of the most famous Philadelphia editors and essayists during the first quarter of the next century, made his magazine debut in *The Massachusetts Magazine*. Mrs. Sarah Wentworth Morton, wife of a Massachusetts attorney general and long thought to be the author of the first American novel, *The Power of Sympathy*, which Thomas had published in his *Royal American Magazine*, was a contributor of poetry. Sentiment and sentimentality, melodrama replete with villains and seductions, appeared in the tales carried by *The Massachusetts Magazine*, along with poetry, essays, serious discussions of contemporary problems and selections from the writings of the omnipresent Franklin, Jefferson, Jedidiah Morse, Dr. Rush, William Livingston, and others.

In 1778, only five years after his graduation from Yale, Noah Webster published *A Grammatical Institute of the English Language*, the first part of which became his famous *Spelling Book*. Four years later he left his teaching of English and mathematics in the Episcopal Academy at Philadelphia, where he had gone from his native Connecticut, to establish New York's first monthly magazine, *The American Magazine*. This was in 1787, almost half a century after the beginning of magazine publication in Philadelphia, when Webster, already well known as a philologist and a Federalist, was twenty-nine years old. Webster, by nature a writer and a disputant, made the *American* a bright and spirited magazine. The magazine, as Webster saw it, was meant to be a vehicle for the expression of ideas, and doing much of the writing himself, he used it to express his own ideas on the subjects in which he was most interested. Webster was a strong Federalist, largely because attempts to obtain copyrights for his *Spelling Book* from each of the thirteen states showed him the necessity for a central government to control such matters. He wrote much about the new Constitution, discussing governmental affairs in each issue. He wrote much, and sensibly, about education. He thought the teaching of English should be emphasized, the teaching of Greek and Latin minimized. One teacher should not teach a number of diverse subjects. There should be electives. He believed girls should be taught English, arithmetic, and geography. He felt that the teaching of religion, with government approval, was dangerous.

Webster printed the poetry of his fellow Yale men, John Trumbull, Joel Barlow, and Timothy Dwight. He even sprang to Dwight's defense when an English review harshly criticized Dwight's verse. "The London Reviewers Reviewed," which appeared in July, 1788, was one of the first American retorts to what was long seen as the consistently prejudiced criticism of American writing by English critics. In yet another important department the young Webster showed himself an astute editor.

He paid more attention to women as readers than any other magazine had done to this time. In the first issue of the *American* he promised that "his *fair readers* may be assured that no inconsiderable pains will be taken to furnish them entertainment," and he provided the kind of Gothic and sentimental fiction considered appealing to feminine taste. He also, and not too deftly, offered advice on female dress and behavior.

It was part of Webster's plan to make his magazine national in coverage and distribution. He planned at one time to have part owners in Boston, Connecticut, Philadelphia, Virginia, South Carolina, and in New Jersey, Maryland, or Georgia. These part owners were to serve also as correspondents, sending in material from their sections to the editor in New York. Copies of the magazine were to be sent out from New York to every part of the nation. He tried through Belknap to secure subscriptions in Boston, later projected a Boston-New York magazine with Isaiah Thomas of *The Massachusetts Magazine*. All of Webster's attempts at expansion failed. *The American Magazine*, for which its editor had once envisioned 5,000 subscribers, never obtained more than 500, and lasted only one year. Webster went back to Connecticut where he practiced law and continued his philological work, returning to become editor of the Federalist journals, the *American Minerva*, 1793, and the *Herald*, 1794.

A little more than a year after the demise of Webster's *American* came the *New-York Magazine* which, with the *Massachusetts Magazine*, was to last as long as eight years. It did not differ importantly from other magazines of the time except that it included a department of dramatic criticism by William Dunlap and had among its contributors, all of whose works appeared anonymously, Charles Brockden Brown and members of the Friendly Club, a group composed of New York business and professional men. Its importance in the development of American magazines lies in what was at the time its almost spectacular longevity.

The average life of the American magazines of the eighteenth century was only fourteen months. There was little advertising to support them; what there was appeared in most cases only on the covers, in supplements, and on the final pages. Publishers were almost wholly dependent upon subscriptions for the support of their ventures. With the price of most magazines about a shilling a copy, even when subscribers paid promptly, which they seldom did, there was barely sufficient income to keep the best of the magazines solvent. There were other hindrances.

Until 1794, the magazines were badly handicapped by postal regulations, though those were no handicap to Benjamin Franklin who used his position as Philadelphia postmaster to keep the *American Magazine* of his enemy, Bradford, out of the mails while he allowed postriders to carry his own *General Magazine*. The postal law of 1792, however, confused and inequitable in practice, operated to prevent mailing of the *Columbian* and the *Museum*, which thereupon suspended publication, while the *Massachusetts Magazine* and the *New-York Magazine* were not affected. The more liberal postal law of 1794, recognizing the importance which magazines had attained, ruled that a sixty-four-page magazine could be carried less than fifty miles for four cents, between fifty and one hundred miles for six, and more than one hundred miles for eight cents.

Magazines were never profitable ventures in these early days. It is proof of the earnestness of their publishers and editors and the eagerness of the colonial and early republican audiences that one magazine after another appeared and that many lasted as long as they did. Editors strove to make their magazines useful vehicles for the communication of ideas, repositories of writing that they thought should be preserved, and instruments that would affect the public mind and influence national decisions that had to be made.

These early magazines had a definite force in unifying the Colonies and in inciting, then sustaining, the Revolution. They fought effectively for the ratification of the Constitution, encouraged native literary and artistic expression, and helped to promote American industry and commerce. They discussed important national affairs, and by reprinting work which had first appeared in English periodicals they made Americans aware of thought and action abroad. They recorded the American political and social life of the period and offered their readers almost all of the most significant American writing of the second half of the eighteenth century.

Americans took a patriotic pride in their early magazines, knew their value, saw them as useful and pleasing, and felt that they were an important sign of America's dawning cultural as well as political independence, a concept that was to be emphasized in books and magazines through the first half of the next century. Lyon Richardson points out in his *A History of Early American Magazines* that a great many subscribers to American magazines in the eighteenth century considered themselves patrons of an instrument that spread knowledge, advanced culture in the United States, and supported the literary and practical arts developing in the country. Though subscription lists seldom attained to the more than 1,600 recorded for Mathew Carey's *American Museum*, running on an average nearer the 500 maximum of Webster's *American Magazine*, the figures hardly indicate the scope of magazine circulation and readership before the year 1800. As Frank Luther Mott says in his careful and thorough study, *A History of American Magazines, 1741–1850*, the influence of the early magazines was probably far greater than the number printed and circulated would indicate. Books and magazines were prized if only because comparatively few were available. Every page of every magazine was read carefully by a number of people. Thus the influence exerted by the early magazines was both intensive and extensive.

A mere list of a few of the contributors and subscribers to American magazines of Colonial, Revolutionary, and immediately post-Revolutionary years indicates something of the stature the first magazines could boast. Contributors included almost every eminent writer, poet, and statesman of the time: Washington, Franklin, Hamilton, John Jay, Fisher Ames, Tench Coxe, Benjamin Rush, John Witherspoon, Noah Webster, Francis Hopkinson, Thomas Paine, Philip Freneau, Charles Brockden Brown, Jeremy Belknap, Edward Shippen, Thomas Godfrey, Joel Barlow, John Trumbull, Edmund Randolph, John Hancock, Richard Henry Lee, Roger Sherman, Hugh Williamson, Timothy Dwight, William Barton, James M'Henry, Albert Gallatin, William Livington, Isaac Bartram, John Ewing, Hugh Brackenridge, David Rittenhouse. Paul Revere was perhaps the most famous magazine illustrator.[5]

Heading the list of subscribers to the *New-York Magazine* were George Washington and John Adams. Washington subscribed also to *The American Museum*, as did Franklin, Dickinson, Hamilton, Jefferson, Madison, Humphreys, Hopkinson, Pinckney, Rush, Webster, Edmund Randolph, Edward Shippen, Robert Morris, Rufus King, Robert Molyneux, and even the British consul, Phineas Bond.

To Mathew Carey,[6] editor of *The American Museum*, George Washington wrote a letter which Carey used as an advertisement in the *Pennsylvania Gazette* issues of July 16 and August 20, 1788, and which has since been quoted by most American literary and magazine historians. Washington expressed his delight in magazines, his strong approval, and his concern for their success. Of the *Museum* he wrote: ". . . I am of the opinion that this work is not only eminently calculated to dissiminate [sic] political, agricultural, philosophical

---

[5] Isaiah Thomas paid Paul Revere three pounds each for a series of twenty-two engravings for the *Royal American Magazine* of Boston.
[6] Mathew Carey is buried in Philadelphia, in the cemetery of St. Mary's Catholic Church on Fourth Street near Locust. A bronze plaque on the front of the church reads: "Matthew Carey, the leading publisher of the early years of the Republic and the chief force in the creation of early American literature."

and other valuable information; but that it has been uniformly conducted with taste, attention, and propriety."

Of magazines in general Washington said: "I consider such easy vehicles of knowledge, more happily calculated than any other, to preserve the liberty, stimulate the industry and meliorate the morals of an enlightened and free people."

Chapter 3

MAGAZINES AS NATIONAL EDUCATORS: *THE PORT FOLIO* AND ITS CONTEMPORARIES

THE ADAMSES, four generations of them—presidents, diplomats, lawyers, historians, educators, businessmen—were all writers. In 1794, George Washington appointed John Quincy Adams as minister to Berlin, largely because of a series of pamphlets he had written in support of this country's neutral position toward France and England. Later, President John Adams sent his son as minister to Berlin, where he completed a business treaty with Prussia in 1799. On Jefferson's election to the Presidency in 1800, Adams recalled his son who came back to the United States determined to be a professional writer. The low opinion Europeans had for American literary performance led John Quincy Adams to feel that he would be doing his country a service as well as following his own inclination and talents. Though he became a statesman instead, he was all his life a voluminous and capable writer of prose and verse. When he returned to the United States in 1801, his Harvard friend Joseph Dennie was just starting the brightest and most important magazine of the new century. In pursuit of his chosen career, Adams became one of the chief contributors to *The Port Folio* during its first year.

Joseph Dennie, bohemian, bibulous, a wit, a dandy, an Anglophile, a reactionary, a writer of sharp and polished prose, was called the "American Addison." Usually described as the second professional man of letters in America, he had already edited the *Tablet* in Boston and the *Farmer's Weekly Museum* in Walpole, New Hampshire, for which he wrote his characteristic "Lay

28

Preacher" essays. Coming to Philadelphia first as a clerk to Timothy Pickering, who was then Secretary of State, he was soon one of the most colorful and most skillful magazine editors of his time.

J. T. Buckingham, later editor of *The New-England Magazine*, who had been a boy in Walpole during Dennie's editorship of the *Farmer's Weekly Museum*, described him as slipping along Chestnut Street in Philadelphia to the *Port Folio* office "in a pea-green coat, white vest, nankeen small-clothes, white silk stockings and pumps, fastened with silver buckles which covered at least half the foot from the instep to the toe." A determined individualist, perverse from the start—he had been rusticated from Harvard where he had studiously read everything he could find except the books assigned by his instructors—Dennie defiantly, perhaps artfully, for the flattery must have been irresistible, addressed his prospectus of *The Port Folio* to one class of readers only. It was, in large type, "Submitted to Men of Affluence, Men of Liberality, and Men of Letters." The brilliant literary weekly that he put out was a success from its first issue of January 3, 1801. Most of that first issue was written by two men, John Quincy Adams and the colorful Joseph Dennie himself.

Adams' *Tour Through Silesia*, afterward printed as a book in two volumes, ran through most of 1801. The first *Port Folio* also carried Adams' version of the thirteenth satire of Juvenal. Dennie's essays began in the first number with the first of a series called "An Author's Evenings" (from the shop of Messrs. Colon and Spondee); these were reviews and criticism with lengthy selections culled from his wide reading. During 1801 he began again with his "Lay Preacher" essays and with another series, "The Farrago," all satirical and witty essays modeled after Addison and Goldsmith. There was a theatrical review but no political article in the first issue of *The Port Folio*. There were many political articles in succeeding numbers.

Dennie stated that one reason for founding his magazine was to combat revolutionary doctrines. He believed and said that the separation of the Colonies from England was a historical mistake. He was soon attacking President Jefferson, especially his literary pretensions, in almost every issue. The Declaration of Independence, he wrote, was filled with mistakes of grammar and diction. It was a "false and flatulent and foolish paper." In April, 1803, he declared in *The Port Folio* that democratic government itself was a mistake. Out of it could come only "civil war, desolation, and anarchy." As a result of this attack, Dennie was indicted on July 4 of the same year for seditious libel. Brilliantly defended by Joseph Hopkinson, he was acquitted in December, and Oliver Oldschool, Esq., as Dennie editorially called himself, went on with his attack. Most things American were bad; all things English were good. Next to Jefferson he seems most to have detested Noah Webster, whose effrontery in Americanizing the English language in his dictionary he saw as blasphemous—". . . let then the projected volume of *foul and unclean* things bear his own Christian name and be called NOAH'S ARK!" Dennie would have none of the *Republic* of letters. It was the *Monarchy* of letters to Oliver Oldschool, Esq. For their apparent lack of convictions, he would have despised many modern editors.

But there was more to this editor and more to his magazine than the prejudices and idiosyncrasies of Joseph Dennie. He made *The Port Folio* a force in American letters, an urbane magazine for an urbane and literate audience. He abused the freedom of the press in his political articles, but, as John Quincy Adams said in his epitaph, which is all but illegible now on Dennie's monument in the churchyard of St. Peter's in Philadelphia, "he contributed to chasten the morals, and to refine the taste of this nation." He made the magazine in this country the equal of similar productions in England at the time, and educated the most cultured section of the American public to look to magazines for the best writing of the day. He made the magazine an educational as well as a political force, gave it form, finish, variety, and literary excellence.

The Port Folio, well printed, well leaded, as readable and entertaining today as when its Saturday numbers appeared, published essays, travel articles, scholarly criticism of classical, English, and American writing, biographies of English authors and statesmen and of eminent Americans, much original poetry, and letters to Mr. Oldschool. At the bottom of the third column on page eight of each of the weekly eight-page issues the epigram was a regular feature,[1] and there were jokes, often risqué, in most numbers. The whole was well issued and well edited.

Dennie's own ironic style set the tone of his magazine. His "Lay Preacher" essay in the third number of 1801 was "A Lesson for Loungers." In it, writing as though he lived in Queen Anne's London, he advised: "If a coffee room be crowded, endeavour to fix yourself in a corner at the table, in such a manner that you prevent anyone from passing you to get seated on any other part of the bench; or, if that cannot conveniently be done, put one or both your legs, at full length upon the seat, lean back, whistle or pick your teeth. This will shew your consequence."

In 1804, there was much by and about Tom Moore who, visiting the United States after leaving his Bermuda post as

---

[1] Typical:

> "Says a parson to Tipsey, 'I'm shocked at the sight,
>   So often your spirits are sinking;
> In riot and folly so much you delight,
>   And still take such pleasure in drinking.'
>
> "Says Tipsey to Parson, 'I'll puzzle you quick,
>   Of this paradox shew me the merits;
> Gin now is so *cheap,* that though sometimes I'm sick,
>   I'm gayest when full of *low spirits.*"

And, from the issue of March 13, 1802: "A gentleman, informed by a bill on a window of a house that *apartments were to let,* knocked at the door, and, attended by a pretty female took a survey of the premises. Pray, my dear, said he smiling, are you to be *let* with the lodgings?—No, replied the Fille de Chambre with vivacity, but I am to be *let alone.*"

Admiralty registrar, spent much time with Dennie and his coterie of Philadelphia wits. There was also one issue in which a black rule bordered every column on every page. "This paper," read a notice on the front page, "is consecrated to the Memorial of Alexander Hamilton." In it Dennie, the Federalist, published all the Burr-Hamilton correspondence which led to the Weehawken duel, the full text of the funeral oration at Trinity Church in New York, a letter from Bishop Benjamin Moore, and all of the various newspaper tributes to Hamilton.

Contributions to *The Port Folio* were signed only with such pseudonyms as Amicus, Crito, Lucius Crassus, or with initials. Anonymity was the common magazine practice; the concept of the "name" writer had not yet arrived. Most of Dennie's contributors were members of the convivial Tuesday Club. These were university graduates, wits, Federalists, all of them men with literary tastes and abilities who met most often at the home of Joseph Hopkinson, author of "Hail Columbia," at Fourth and Chestnut Streets in Philadelphia. Prominent in the group, which Albert H. Smyth lists in *The Philadelphia Magazines and Their Contributors, 1741–1850*, were Charles Brockden Brown, Hopkinson, Thomas Cadwalader, Richard Rush, Philip Hamilton, Samuel Ewing, John Dorsey, Charles J. Ingersoll, William Meredith, and Thomas I. Wharton. Out-of-town contributors in Boston and New York included Royall Tyler, J. S. J. Gardner, Condy Raquet, Alexander Wilson, Thomas Fessenden, and William Dunlap, portrait painter, novelist, playwright, and biographer of Charles Brockden Brown.

But it was the lively Dennie himself who gave the weekly issue of *The Port Folio* from 1801 to 1809 its characteristic dash and brightness. His "To Readers and Correspondents" was always brisk and to the point. "We must earnestly caution our correspondents against *prolixity* a *deadly* sin. It is for the *interest* of all who wish to contribute to the Port Folio to be as *succinct* and *brief* as possible," he wrote in an early issue.

THE PORT FOLIO.

BY OLIVER OLDSCHOOL, ESQ.

"VARIOUS, THAT THE MIND
OF DESULTORY MAN, STUDIOUS OF CHANGE,
AND PLEAS'D WITH NOVELTY, MAY BE INDULGED."
COWPER.

VOL. I.]

PHILADELPHIA, SATURDAY, JANUARY 3d, 1801.

[No. 1.

TRAVELS.

FOR THE PORT FOLIO.

The subsequent letter is the commencement of a series, which will be regularly published in this paper. It is unnecessary to dwell upon the general excellence of the following tour. It will be obvious to every intelligent reader that it has been made by no vulgar traveller, but by a man of genius and observation, who, in happy union, combines the power of selecting the most interesting and picturesque objects, and of describing them gracefully.]

JOURNAL OF A TOUR THROUGH SILESIA.

LETTER I.

Frankfort, on the Oder, 20th July, 1800.

As I have bespoken your company, upon our journey into Silesia, I begin this letter at our first resting station from Berlin. Hitherto, we have indeed seen little more than the usual Brandenburg sands, and perhaps you will find our tour as tiresome, as we have found it ourselves. I cannot promise you an amusing journey, though I hope it will prove so to us. My letters to you, on this tour, will be in the form, and serve as the substitute of a journal. They will, of course, be fragments, written at different times and places; nay, perhaps in different humours. Therefore, make up your account, to receive patiently all my tediousness.

On Thursday, the 17th inst. we left Berlin, just after three in the morning, and arrived here at about nine the same evening. The distance is ten German miles and a quarter; which you know is a very long day's journey in this country. In the course of a few years, it will be an easy journey of eight hours; for the present king, who has the very laudable ambition of improving the roads through his dominions, is now making a turnpike road, like that to Potsdam, the whole way hither; as yet, not more than one German mile of it is finished, and the rest of the way, is like that, which on every side surrounds the *Todoux* of modern times. As we approach within a few miles of Frankfort the country becomes somewhat hilly, and of course more variegated and pleasant than round Berlin; but we could perceive little difference in the downy softness of the ground beneath us, or in the *needles* of the places within our view. Part of the country is cultivated, as much as it is susceptible of cultivation, and here and there we could see scattered spires of wheat, rye, barley, and oats shoot from the sands, like the hairs upon a head almost bald. We came through few villages, and those few had a miserable appearance. A meagre composition of mud and thatch composed the cottages, in which a ragged and pallid race of beggars reside; yet we must not be unjust, and confess, that we passed by one nobleman's seat, which had the appearance of a handsome and comfortable house.

We arrived here just in time to see the last dregs of an annual *fair*, such as you have often seen in the towns of Holland, and as you know are customary in those of Germany. But we hear great complaints against the minister Struensee, for having ruined the value of the *fair*, by prohibiting the sale of foreign woollen manufactures, which have heretofore been the most essential articles of sale at this fair. This prohibition is for the sake of encouraging the manufactures of this country, a principle, which the government pursue on all possible occasions. They are no converts to the opinions of Adam Smith and the French economists, concerning the balance of trade, and always catch with delight at any thing which can prevent money from going *out of the country*. Of this disposition we have seen a notable instance in the attempts lately made here of producing sugar from beets, of which I believe you heard something while you were here, and about which much has been said and done since then. At one time we were assured beyond all question, that one mile square of beets would furnish sugar for the whole Prussian dominions. The question was submitted to a committee of the Academy of Sciences, who, after long examination and deliberation, reported, that in truth, sugar, and even brandy, could be produced from beets, and in process of time might be raised in great quantities; but that, for the present, it would be expedient to continue the use of sugars and brandies, such as had been in use hitherto. Since this report, we have heard little or nothing of beet sugar.

This is an old town, pleasantly situated, and containing about twelve thousand inhabitants, of which a quarter part are Jews. It is therefore distinguished by those peculiarities, which mark all European towns where a large proportion of Israelites reside, and to express which, I suppose resort must be had to the Hebrew language. The English at least is inadequate to it; for the word *filth* conveys an idea of spotless purity, in comparison to the Jewish nastiness. The garrison of the town consists of one regiment. There is here likewise an university; and by the introduction of a letter from Berlin, we have become acquainted with two of the professors. The number of students is less than two hundred; and of them, one hundred and fifty are students of law; ten or fifteen of divinity; and not more than two or three of medicine. The library, the museum, and the botanical garden, the professors tell me, are all so miserable, that they are ashamed to show them.

The banks of the Oder, on one side, are bordered with small hills, upon which at small distances, are little summer-houses with vineyards, at which, during summer, many inhabitants of the town reside. On the other side, the land is flat, and the river is restrained from overflowing only by a large dyke, which has been built since the year 1785. At that time the river broke down the smaller dyke, which had, until then, existed, and overflowed the country to a considerable ex-

tent. Prince Leopold of Brunswick, a brother of the present reigning duke, was then colonel of the regiment in garrison here, and lost his life in attempting to save some of the people, whom the inundation was carrying away. You have probably seen prints of this melancholy accident, and there is an account of it in the last editions of Moore's *Travels*. (I mean his first work.) There is a small monument erected in honour of the prince, upon the spot where his body was found. It was done by the free-masons of this place, of which society he was a member. But there is nothing remarkable in it. There is likewise in the burying ground a little monument, or rather tomb-stone, to Kleist, one of the most celebrated German poets, whom his countrymen call their Thomson. He was an officer in the service of Frederick the second, and was killed at the battle of Cunersdorf, a village distant only a couple miles from this place.

Just at the gate of the town, there is a spring of mineral water, at which a bathing house has been built, with accommodations for lodgers. This bath has been considerably frequented for some years past, and the physicians of the town say, that the waters are as good as those of Freyenwalde. I am willing to believe them as good as those of Toeplitz; for my faith in mineral waters in general, was not much edified by the success of our tour there last summer.

22d July. Still at Frankfort. We had left Berlin without being fully aware of the precise nature of the journey we had undertaken; and had not thought of taking with us furs, and winter-cloathing for a tour in the dog-days. But one of the professors, whose acquaintance we have made here, had formerly gone the same journey; and from his representations, we have been induced to send back to Berlin for thick cloathing, and this circumstance has prolonged our stay here a couple of days more than we at first intended. Yesterday we took a ride of three or four miles, to the country seat of a Mr. Schoening, the *landrath* of the *circle*. The functions of his office are to collect the territorial taxes within a certain district called a *circle*, which is a subdivision of the province. You know the importance and extent of this title of *rath* or *counciller*, in the constitutions of the German states. It is a general name, designating every officer in all the subordinate parts of the administration; and sometimes a mere honorary title, which Frederic the second, by way of joke, once granted to a person, upon *condition* that he should never presume to give any *counsel*. For the principle upon which the name is founded is, that the person holding the office gives the king occasionally counsel, and the first part of it usually designates the particular department in which he gives it.

Mr. Schoening and his lady received us with great kindness and hospitality. From the neighbourhood of their house, and on our return, we had the pleasure of agreeable prospects of the

"Write it in English" was repeated Dennie advice. Using the technique of the modern semanticist, he translated the Constitution into what he considered clear, logical English. In May, 1801, Oliver Oldschool took his public to task for its lack of interest in political affairs. "We regret that we have had such imperfect assistance in the *political* department of the *Port Folio*. We had confidently expected *more* from *principals*. It is to be deplored that such supineness continues, that such a political palsy deadens the better half of our countrymen."

Dennie had started with a large circulation of 2,000. It mounted steadily, but in December, 1803, he was forced to write the type of appeal that all editors had to use in the days before advertising, when magazines were entirely dependent upon their income from subscriptions to continue publishing:

To Subscribers

In the course of the current and ensuing month every journalist has a right to remind his readers, that his claims must be cancelled. The Editor of the Port Folio has, for three years, conducted the miscellany, with an assiduity of labor, which deserves its stipulated price, and with a liberality of expense for the establishment that calls for a candid consideration. For some time his subscription list has been augmenting, and the circulation of his paper widens every week. But he is obliged to add that applications for his journal are, at some seasons, more frequent than payments, and that, though many are considerate and punctual, others are negligent.

The Port Folio, the best American magazine of its time and fascinating to read now, became a quieter monthly in 1809. Dennie died in 1812 at the age of forty-four. One of his assistants, Nicholas Biddle, later president of the Bank of the United States, succeeded him and made the magazine more and more a literary review. Politics were excluded now, and *The Port Folio* became patriotic in tone during the War of 1812. Biddle, who remained as editor only two years, was succeeded by others, and *The Port Folio* lasted until 1827.

The truth of Ralph Waldo Emerson's remark that an institution is but the lengthened shadow of a man is well illustrated by Joseph Dennie and *The Port Folio*, and throughout the whole story of American magazines. There is a corollary. A strong editor, even a strongly wrongheaded editor, has usually meant a strong and influential magazine; whereas intelligent editors of moderate views and no firm opinions have often produced colorless and comparatively ineffective magazines. Magazines have sickened and declined, sometimes disappeared, when an editor with a strongly marked character has been succeeded by someone as capable but not as distinct. *The Atlantic Monthly* has had a remarkable succession of able editors, but the magazine assumed a different character under such editors as James Russell Lowell, James T. Fields, William Dean Howells, Thomas Bailey Aldrich, Horace Scudder, Bliss Perry, and Ellery Sedgwick. Propriety and dullness almost accomplished its extinction at the beginning of this century. Such disparate individuals and editors as Sarah Josepha Hale of *Godey's*, S. S. McClure of *McClure's*, Harold Ross of *The New Yorker*, and Henry Luce of *Time* and *Life* are other cases in point.

There were other magazines and magazine editors contemporary with Joseph Dennie and his *Port Folio*. One, edited by a *Port Folio* contributor, is of interest for the stature of its editor and for his distinctive conception of what a magazine should be.

Charles Brockden Brown is always called the first professional man of letters in America, as he was the first to devote himself wholly to writing as a profession. Born in Philadelphia in 1771, he had his first writing published in the *Columbian Magazine* in August, 1789. He studied law, but went to New York where he undertook the then risky experiment of earning his living by authorship. In rapid succession he produced five sentimental melodramas, important now because their author used American scenes and characters for the first time in native American fiction. The novels were *Wieland* (1798), *Arthur Mervyn* (1799), *Ormond* (1799), *Edgar Huntley* (1799), and *Clara Howard* (1801). In 1803, Brown returned to Philadelphia where he founded the *Literary Magazine and American Register*.

In the very long prospectus which filled the first three pages of this magazine's first issue, September, 1803, Brown said that he had gathered a group of friends who possessed literary talents and that, as editor, "my province shall be to hold the mirror up so as to assemble all their wit in its verge, and reflect them on the public in such manner as to warm and enlighten." Many magazines, he knew, had been started, had run for a number of issues, then had disappeared. This was not always because of lack of public interest and support. ". . . The public is always eager to encourage one who devotes himself to their rational amusement." Magazines disappeared usually because "those who managed the publication have commonly either changed their principles, remitted their zeal, or voluntarily relinquished their trade, or last of all, and like other men, have died."

Enlightenment and rational amusement were, then, prime purposes of a magazine. The magazine would also offer varied fare. The editor, Brown wrote, "will not forget that a work which solicits the attention of many readers, must build its claim on the variety as well as copiousness of its contents." The *Literary Magazine and American Register* would speculate and comment on foreign affairs, merely record domestic matters. It would contain materials from the newest foreign publications, but it would pay particular attention to American writing. "As to domestic publications, besides extracting from them anything serviceable to the public, he will give a critical account of them, and in this respect, make his work an American Review, in which the history of our native literature shall be carefully detailed." Magazines were intent, from the founding of the United States, on developing and encouraging a native literature. Brown thus echoed a general magazine editorial concept. He was also careful to point out one significant distinction between the magazine and the newspaper. Each month he would give foreign and domestic news, but in magazine not in newspaper fashion. The *Literary Magazine and American Register* would handle "in a precise and systematic order, that intelligence which the common newspapers communicate in a vague and indiscriminate way." The magazine, he realized, has the time to judge and to comment on the news.

The *Port Folio* was still appearing, but Brown's *Literary Magazine and American Register* had disappeared and a flood of new weekly and monthly magazines had been started when, on August 4, 1821, the first issue of *The Saturday Evening Post* was published in the office once occupied by Benjamin Franklin behind 53 Market Street, Philadelphia.[2] The paper, edited by Thomas Cottrell Clarke and printed once a week on "a large royal sheet" folded to make four pages, was published by Atkinson & Alexander on Market Street "four doors below Second, where Subscriptions and Advertisements will be thankfully received." The cost of a year's subscription was a modest two dollars—in contrast to six dollars for *The Port Folio*—but the editors prudently made a condition that half the sum was payable in advance.

The issues of *The Saturday Evening Post* in 1821 contained essays, poetry, obituaries, a "Moral and Religious Column," a department called "The Ladies' Friend" which offered verse and

[2] Until its 1897 purchase by Cyrus H. K. Curtis, who had for some time been interested in the history and tradition of the *Post,* the magazine carried "Founded A.D. 1821" in large type on its first page. After purchase, a box was inserted which read in bold-face type: "In 1729 this paper was purchased by Benjamin Franklin and published by him as 'The Pennsylvania Gazette.' On August 4, 1821 the present title was adopted, and the office of publication was the one occupied by Benjamin Franklin in the rear of 53 Market Street Philadelphia."

articles deemed particularly appropriate to feminine taste, marine intelligence, editorials, an "Almanack," and news. The first issues ran two columns of short advertisements on the front page, two columns on the back, and a scattering of advertisements and notices on the inside pages. By 1822 poetry, both moral and sentimental, had replaced the advertisements on the front page, while page four was almost solid advertising. By the 1830's, *The Saturday Evening Post* was a larger and better periodical, more magazine and less newspaper, though the legend spread as a banner underneath the logotype read: "A Family Newspaper, Devoted to Literature, Morality, Science, News, Agriculture and Amusement." [3] It was still a four-page sheet, but seven columns wide and illustrated. The subscription price in 1833 was "$2.50, if paid during the year; $2.00 if paid in advance; $3.00 if not paid during the year."

The *Post* quickly became, and remained for the next forty years, one of the most important weeklies in the United States. The issue of April 2, 1836, carried one of William Cullen Bryant's poems, "The Legend," on the front page. Edgar Allan Poe wrote his famous "The Black Cat" for its pages. Harriet Beecher Stowe, James Fenimore Cooper, Bayard Taylor, N. P. Willis, Emerson, James Russell Lowell, and Hawthorne were *Post* authors. Circulation before the Civil War mounted to an impressive 90,000. Other literary journals, *The Saturday News*, the *Saturday Bulletin*, and the *Saturday Chronicle*, were merged with the magazine. Among its early editors were

---

[3] By 1848, when it was one of the strongest weeklies of the day, *The Saturday Evening Post* described itself as "Neutral in Politics; Devoted to General News, Literature, Science, Morality, Agriculture, and Amusement." During the year a different order of importance was recognized; morality came first and business was included. Beginning with the issue of March 4, 1848, the legend read: "Devoted to Morality, Pure Literature, Foreign and Domestic News, Agriculture, The Commercial Interests, Science, Art and Amusement." By 1874, the *Post* was simply "The Great Family Paper for Half a Century." In 1889, the magazine described itself as "The Great Pioneer Family Paper of America."

Benjamin Mathias, Charles J. Peterson, Rufus W. Griswold,[4] H. Hastings Weld, and Henry Peterson.

Only three years after appearance of *The Saturday Evening Post,* magazines had become so numerous in the United States that a writer in the *Cincinnati Literary Gazette* was moved to express his amazement in verse:

> "This is the age of Magazines
> Even Skeptics must confess it:
> Where is the town of much renown
> That has not one to bless it?"

Magazines were numerous, and they were read. Emanating from Philadelphia, until past the middle of the century the undisputed "magazine city," they were read eagerly by a busy people concerned necessarily with the practical problems of agriculture, commerce, industry, and geographical expansion. Readers looked to magazines for information, for news and intelligent comment on the news, for guidance in their political thinking, and for entertainment.

The Port Folio, intellectual, satirical, almost wholly literary and political in content, appealed to the educated and cultured. The less aristocratic *Saturday Evening Post* and the other weeklies and monthlies of its kind undertook and accomplished a different service for a far wider audience. Their pages were devoted to a wide range of subjects—to any and every subject conceivably of interest to their readers, and almost everything was. Unlike the intellectual reviews, their purpose was not critical but educational in the widest sense. They popularized art and literature, instructed in matters of morals, manners,

[4] Rufus Griswold was the most important of these men. He became editor, 1842–1843, of the splendid *Graham's Magazine,* of which Charles J. Peterson and Poe had also been editors. He later edited the *International Magazine* in New York which, in 1852, was merged into *Harper's Magazine.* His greatest service to American letters was in compiling and editing the first important anthologies of American writing: *Poets and Poetry of America* (1842) and *The Prose Writers of America* (1847). Charles Peterson in 1842 founded, in imitation of *Godey's,* the very popular *Peterson's Magazine* which lasted until 1898.

and taste. There were no public libraries in the United States of the 1820's and 1830's. The country's few colleges along the Eastern seaboard were for the very few. Even ordinary schooling, when obtainable, was limited in scope. Magazines served as schools and mentors, as instructors and advisers, for those who could obtain and read a copy.

News and analysis of the news were, as they are today, important features of these magazines. Newspapers were local only in their circulation. Books, less common then than now, were read by comparatively few. The magazine had become, as the *Pennsylvania Gazette* originally described itself, the "universal instructor."

Europe was experiencing in the 1820's the liberal impulses that were to result in England in the Reform Bill of 1832. Greece was struggling toward nationalism. In Germany and the Italian Peninsula were already apparent the stirrings of liberal thought that were to culminate in the revolutions of 1848. The Industrial Revolution was beginning to make itself felt in England. In English poetry this was the Romantic period of Wordsworth—disapproved by Joseph Dennie for his revolutionary and democratic tastes, but admired as a poet—Coleridge, Byron, Shelley, and Keats. America's was still a primarily agrarian economy, with commerce brisk but industry hardly beginning to expand toward a dominant position. Rough Jacksonian democracy displaced aristocratic federalism and the milder Jeffersonian democracy when Andrew Jackson became President in 1828.

All the ferment in Europe, all the events and tendencies in political, social, and economic life in the early nationalistic period of the United States, were reported directly to its people in the magazines. The magazines did more. Editors of both the intellectual and the popular magazines resented the imputations, more often the loud declarations, of European, particularly English, writers and travelers that the United States was a barbaric region whose people were devoid of culture, taste, intelligence, or any semblance of good manners. Determined to give the lie to such English magazine writers as Sidney Smith, who had expressed his scorn of American writing, and to such travelers in the United States as Mrs. Frances Trollope whose *Domestic Manners of the Americans* (1832) was merely the most notorious of many such attacks, they filled their magazines with didactic and sentimental verse [5] and with essays designed to improve the taste of their readers as well as to inculcate approved morals and manners.

"Neutral in politics" as was *The Saturday Evening Post*, it and its contemporaries could leave factional disputes to the newspapers while they carried out their more fundamental informational and educational programs. They could offer, too, in quantity and quality, what the newspaper medium could not supply—entertainment. They were the great and, for a great part of the population, the sole source of literate entertainment. Their verse, humor, lighter essays, and tales were directed at the little leisure that Americans had in the first part of the nineteenth century. It was because of these accomplishments that the "dean of American magazine editors," Henry Mills Alden, editor of *Harper's Magazine* from 1869 to 1919, could say: "Periodical literature has done more for the American people than for any other. It had a considerable development before there was an American literature, meeting the intellectual needs of a sturdy race which, while its energies were engaged in the solution of difficult practical problems . . . was yet intelligent and keenly curious." [6]

By the mid-1830's, magazines were a dominating force in American life. Edgar Allan Poe, magazine editor and magazine writer all his life, wrote in *Marginalia* No. XXV:

> The whole tendency of the age is Magazineward. The magazine in the end will be the most influential of all departments

[5] It must be remembered that poetry was the popular literary form. The novel was still fairly new. The short story had not been developed.

[6] Henry Mills Alden, *Magazine Writing and the New Literature* (New York: Harper & Bros., 1908), p. 49.

of letters. . . . In a few years its importance will be found to have increased in geometrical ratio.

We now demand the light artillery of the intellect; we need the curt, the condensed, the readily diffused—in place of the verbose, the detailed, the voluminous, the inaccessible. On the other hand, the lightness of the artillery should not degenerate into pop-gunnery—by which term we may designate the character of the greater portion of the newspaper press—their sole legitimate object being the discussion of ephemeral matters in an ephemeral way.

Examination of several other magazines founded between 1800 and the Civil War may help to validate Poe's opinion and prophecy.

Chapter 4

EARLY GENERAL MAGAZINES AS A LITERARY AND CRUSADING FORCE

CHARLES FRANCIS ADAMS, son of John Quincy Adams, graduated from Harvard, spent three years in Washington while his father was President, studied law in the Boston office of Daniel Webster, then turned to writing. Like his father, he wrote for the magazines, publishing articles on American history in *The North American Review*. He later edited the ten-volume *Works of John Adams,* wrote a sound biography of his grandfather, and edited the unique letters of his unique grandmother, Abigail Adams, and the very important *Memoirs of John Quincy Adams*. He published other writing, but his greatest service was as a capable minister to Great Britain during the Civil War, when his diplomacy prevented recognition of the South by England and stopped Britain's supplying ironclad vessels to the South. One son, Henry Adams, served as his secretary in London. Another son, three years older, a second Charles Francis Adams, served as colonel of a regiment of Negro cavalry and emerged from the war a brevet brigadier general. When at the close of the war the two young Adamses looked about for a place to start their war-interrupted careers, it was to magazines that both turned, and they turned first to the same *North American Review* which had published their father's first efforts.

John Gorham Palfrey, its editor, suggested that Henry Adams write for the *North American* an article on Captain John Smith's relations with Pocahontas. It appeared in 1867, and the future historian of the administrations of Jefferson and

Madison, the autobiographer whose *Education of Henry Adams* has become an American classic, was pleased because "for fifty years *The North American Review* had been the stage coach which carried literary Bostonians to such distinctions as they had achieved." He was soon writing more *North American* articles and articles for the powerful English magazines. Within a few years Henry Adams became the editor of the *North American,* which he was proud to be able to describe as "the first literary power in America."

Henry's brother, Charles Francis Adams, was also successful in his own magazine venture. After separation from the army, he considered various occupations, selected what he thought the most important activity of his day, and started to make his place in it by writing an article on railroads for the *North American.* He wrote more articles on railroads, and in July, 1869, his "Chapter of Erie" appeared in the *North American.* That same month, largely because of his magazine articles, the Massachusets Railroad Commission was formed, and he was appointed one of the commisioners, later its chairman. The Massachusetts Commission, as Henry Cabot Lodge points out in the Memorial Address prefixed to Charles Francis Adams' *Autobiography,* was the first effective railroad commission. It served as a model for the system of similar commissions adopted by other states and eventually culminated in the Interstate Commerce Commission.

The North American Review started the two outstanding members of the fourth generation of the Adams family on their important careers. It is indicative of the force of this magazine that two such men could use it as a vehicle for their ideas, and that the articles which one of them published in it had a deep political and economic effect at a time when direction and regulation of railroad enterprise in this country were badly needed.

The North American Review, one of the longest-lived and most distinguished of American magazines, was founded in

1815 with the deliberate purpose of achieving greater national scope than any previous American magazine. Never a popular magazine, it was largely a literary, historical, and critical review from the time of its founding until it ceased publication in 1939. Though national in editorial coverage, it was a parochial Boston-Harvard magazine in the early days of its greatness, but this was hardly a handicap when that small part of New England could provide as contributors all the great names in American literature. It never had a large circulation, but soon after its founding it became, and continued to be, throughout its existence, a publication of real power and influence because it was read and studied by the leading men of the country. Poets, historians, scholars, said what they had to say in the *North American,* which thus made "the best that has been said and thought" available to those who affected the thinking of their fellows.

A roster of *North American* contributors would include almost every good American writer from Bryant, Longfellow, Emerson, and Irving through Mark Twain; historians such as Parkman, Motley, and Prescott; critics from E. P. Whipple almost to the present; such novelists as Henry James and William Dean Howells; public men from John Adams himself, who wrote for the *North American* in 1817, to Theodore Roosevelt and Charles G. Dawes. Editors of the *North American* included William Tudor, the first editor, who was assisted by Edward Tyrell Channing and Richard Henry Dana; Jared Sparks, Edward Everett, James Russell Lowell, Charles Eliot Norton, Henry Adams (1870–1877), Henry Cabot Lodge, and Colonel George Harvey.

A major purpose of William Tudor, and one that prevailed in many minds at the time, was to free the United States of literary dependence on England. During its best years, or until about 1878 when the magazine moved to New York and tried for a brightness of a kind it never quite attained, the *North American* did perhaps more than any other magazine of its time

PAINTED BY E. LANDSEER   ENGRAVED BY L. SARTAIN

Return from Hawking

Engraved expressly for Grahams Magazine

Graham's was notable for its pioneer use of fine illustrations. This Sartain engraving, after Landseer's "Return from Hawking," appeared in April, 1842.

to implement what Emerson described in 1837 as our "Intellectual Declaration of Independence."

Neither *The Knickerbocker* in New York nor *Graham's* in Philadelphia was started with such lofty aims or written with such high intents. Both were meant primarily to be readable, and they were. They were addressed not to the intelligentsia but to the entire literate public. They were bright, alert, diversified, and *Graham's* in particular pointed the direction that general popular magazines were to take.

The Knickerbocker, as its name indicates, was peculiarly of New York, and a list of its leading contributors emphasizes that it was essentially a New York magazine. As the *North American* was doing for New England and the *Atlantic* was to do later, it brought to an appreciative public the best writers of what is now generally called the Knickerbocker school. There were occasional contributors from New England, but Irving, Cooper, Paulding, Halleck, Sands, Verplanck, were its characteristic writers. Charles Fenno Hoffman was the first editor of the *Knickerbocker* when it was founded in 1833. Its most famous and its best editor was the genial Lewis Gaylord Clark. Through his Philadelphia brother, Willis Gaylord Clark, such Philadelphia writers as Richard Rush, William Dunlap, and William E. Burton were brought into the *Knickerbocker* fold. The most prominent of the New England contributors were Hawthorne, Whittier, Holmes, and Longfellow. One Clark innovation marked the extension of the magazines' field of interest. In 1846 *The Knickerbocker* ran serially Francis Parkman's *The Oregon Trail*. Clark published other western writers and western copy, western humor, a series of H. R. Schoolcraft on the Lake Superior region, and stories of the West, including some by the incredible Ned Buntline.[1]

[1] Ned Buntline, whose real name was Edward Zane Carroll Judson, hunted and trapped in the Far West, was a founder of the Know-Nothing party, the leader of the Astor Place riots against the British actor Macready in 1849, and impresario for Buffalo Bill. One of the inventors of the dime novel, he wrote some 400 of them.

Graham's Magazine was in oblique fashion an offshoot of *The Saturday Evening Post*. Samuel C. Atkinson and Charles Alexander in 1826 began to publish from the *Post* offices a monthly magazine called the *Casket*. Some of the stories in its early issues were merely reprinted from the *Post*. In 1839 George R. Graham of the *Post* bought the *Casket*, combined it with Burton's *Gentleman's Magazine*, which he bought the same year, and issued the first *Graham's Magazine* in 1840, when he also became part owner of the *Post*.

Graham hired good editors. At various times his staff included Edgar Allan Poe, Rufus Wilmot Griswold, and Bayard Taylor in addition to those already mentioned. He made it his practice to pay contributors well and in this way obtained some of the best works of Longfellow, Lowell, Poe, Bryant, Cooper, R. H. Dana, J. K. Paulding, and other "name" writers. Where magazine contributions had been anonymous in the earlier magazines, and the ultra-conservative periodicals like the *North American* were not printing authors' names until late in the nineteenth century, Graham in his magazine inaugurated today's practice of advertising the names of famous writers on the front cover.

Graham made another important departure in magazine publication by stressing the use of illustrations. By employing John Sartain [2] to work exclusively for *Graham's* he made pictorial illustration a distinctive feature of American magazines. Magazines had carried a few illustrations before this time, but often these were merely reprints from plates already used in other publications. A Sartain mezzotint and a fashion plate—published in competition with those already being issued by *Godey's Lady's Book*—appeared in every issue of *Graham's*

---

[2] London-born John Sartain was one of the best-known painters and engravers of his time. After the failure of Graham in 1848, he purchased the *Union Magazine* and established *Sartain's Union Magazine of Literature and Art* in Philadelphia. It ran only until 1852, but published notable writing, including Thoreau's *Ktaadn* and Poe's "The Bells," and his important critical writing, "The Poetic Principle."

and other engravers brought their work to *Graham's*. It was these illustrations which were in large part responsible for the popularity and wide circulation which *Graham's* achieved.

Still another reason for the success of *Graham's* was the appeal of its astute publisher to women readers. The fashion plates and other illustrations of domestic scenes were part of this appeal. So were the sentimental love stories which *Graham's* ran. It published material from the pens of well-known women writers of the time: Mrs. Seba Smith, Mrs. Frances Osgood, Mrs. Ann Stephens, and others. There was, of course, the poetry of Mrs. Lydia Huntley Sigourney; the sentimental poetry of the omnipresent Mrs. Sigourney appeared in almost every magazine of the mid-nineteenth century. These features, though some of them disgusted Poe, brought *Graham's* its feminine audience. Its short stories, particularly those of Poe, its criticism by Griswold and Poe, its essays by Nathaniel Parker Willis, Bayard Taylor, and similar writers, its verse by the established poets of the day, gave the magazine substance and quality. By 1842, Graham could claim a circulation of 40,000, no mean circulation when the population of the entire country was only 17,000,000, when facilities for shipping magazines were inadequate, and when the price of a magazine was a much larger part of a subscriber's income than it is today.

The January, 1842, issue of *Graham's Lady's and Gentleman's Magazine*, as its title read in that year, was a typical *Graham's*, handsomely printed and illustrated. Its contents were varied, interesting, and highly readable. The hand-colored fashion plate with which each issue began was followed by a beautiful Sartain engraving, "The Shepherd's Love," as the illustration for a story by R. H. Dana. There were also, in order, "Goblet of Life" by Longfellow, a sonnet by Thomas Noon Talfourd, and "Highland Beauty," a story in camp by "Oliver Oldfellow," with an engraving of the Scottish beauty herself by E. T. Parris. There were pages more of poetry by Park Benjamin, Lowell, Louis Fitzgerald Tasistro, George

Morris, Lydia H. Sigourney, and "Lines Written on a Portrait of William Henry Harrison" by Mrs. Amelia B. Welby. Stories and prose sketches appeared in profusion: "The Snow Storm," by Jeremy Short, Esq.; "Dreams of Land and Sea" by Dr. Reynell Coats; "The False Ladye" by "The Author of 'The Britishers,' 'Cromwell,' Etc."; a nautical story, "Harry Cavendish," by "The Author of 'Cruising in the Last War,' 'The Reefer of '76,' Etc., Etc."; and "Cousin Agatha" by Mrs. Emma C. Embury.

The most entertaining feature article in this issue was "An Appendix of Autographs" by Poe. In it Poe analyzed the signatures, reproduced in facsimile, of Charles Sprague, Cornelius Mathews, Horace Greeley, Charles Fenno Hoffman, Prosper M. Wetmore, Epes Sargent, Oliver Wendell Holmes, Ralph Waldo Emerson, and a dozen others. From the handwriting of each he deduced—quite a feat even for Poe—a sentence or two descriptive of the man's character and a sharp critical estimate of his writing. Under the reproduction of Emerson's signature, Poe's dislike of the New England writers was, of course, notorious, he wrote:

> Mr. Ralph Waldo Emerson belongs to a class of gentleman with whom we have no patience whatever—the mystics for mysticism's sake. . . . His present rôle seems to be out-Carlyling Carlyle. . . . His MS is bad, sprawling, illegible, irregular —although sufficiently bold. The latter trait may be, and no doubt is, only a portion of his general affectation.

The serial which started in this January issue was "The Daughters of Dr. Byles, A Sketch of Reality" by Miss Leslie. Ann S. Stephens contributed a short story, "The Two Dukes." Preceding five pages of well-written book reviews, evidently by Poe, who was literary editor, came another *Graham's* monthly feature, an inset of sheet music. This one was a ballad, "Thy Name Was Once a Magic Spell." It was presented as written by the Hon. Mrs. Norton and "as sung by Mr. Dempster."

In June, 1842, *Graham's* cover listed George R. Graham and Rufus W. Griswold as editors and the following, divided by sex, as "principal contributors": William Cullen Bryant, James Fenimore Cooper, R. H. Dana, Henry Wadsworth Longfellow, Charles Fenno Hoffman, Theodore S. Fay, J. H. Moncure, Mrs. Emma C. Embury, Mrs. Seba Smith, Mrs. "Mary Clavers," Mrs. E. F. Ellet, Mrs. Ann S. Stephens, Mrs. Frances Osgood. Though Lowell was not listed among the principal contributors, his poems appeared often during the year. Any magazine could well be proud of such a list of authors.

Graham's Magazine came to its end not through its own fault but because Graham invested heavily in newspaper ventures and in other speculations and lost control of the magazine in 1848. Before its demise, under other hands, in 1852, it had suffered from another cause. American magazines and, consequently, American letters all suffered by the policy of *Harper's Magazine* of reprinting English writing. As no international copyright laws were in force until 1891, it could do this with impunity, printing for an eager American audience the most popular English work almost as soon as it appeared in England.

A recurrent advertisement in *The Saturday Evening Post* at this time—similar advertisements had run in the *Post* before 1848 and were to run for many more years—was this one:

To the Ladies of the United States. It being now conceded that

GODEY'S LADY'S BOOK

Stands at the Head of American Magazines, it becomes the duty of the publisher to show what amount of reading, and how many embellishments she will receive for $3. . . . The coloring of our Fashion Plates—we say nothing of the Flowers and Cottages, costs us over

$2,000 in One Year.

To omit this is certainly a savings, but is it just to subscribers? Is it honorable? We cannot practice such a deception! . . .

The advertisement continued for another four inches of small type. Chatty, entertaining, persuasive, it extolled the beauty, the elegance, the virtue, the wonder of one of the most famous of all American magazines. It was signed, as were all such advertisements, by L. A. Godey himself.

In the opinion of Fred L. Pattee, a pioneer historian of American literature, the era of the magazine can be said to have begun with *Godey's Lady's Book* which, founded in 1830, three years before *The Knickerbocker* and ten before *Graham's*, ran almost to the end of the nineteenth century. *Godey's*, like the fat and happy little man who owned it and like Mrs. Sarah Josepha Hale, the stalwart feminist from Boston, who edited it from 1837 to 1877, was marvelous. Far removed from the academic and often arid *North American* of the 1830's and 1840's, but lacking the brilliance and charm of *Graham's* or the alertness and readableness of *The Knickerbocker*, the popular *Godey's Lady's Book* under the militant Sarah Josepha Hale [3] had more real influence on American life than any of these basically superior magazines.

Though *Godey's* was directed entirely to women, *Graham's* and many lesser magazines imitated many of its features. *Godey's* became an American institution in the nineteenth century. It affected the manners, morals, tastes, fashions in clothes, homes, and diet of generations of American readers. It did much to form the American woman's idea of what she was like, how she should act, and how she should insist that she be treated. *Godey's* had no interest in political matters or in intellectual subjects. It published nothing of either. It published Emerson, Longfellow, Hawthorne, Simms, and some of Poe's critical writing, but their contributions were not the most important *Godey's*

---

[3] In softer poetic mood she wrote an American classic:

> "Mary had a little lamb;
> Its fleece was white as snow;
> And everywhere that Mary went
> The lamb was sure to go."

features. T. S. Arthur [4] was a more characteristic *Godey's* writer than Hawthorne. More characteristic than even Arthur were the admired women writers of the day! Mrs. Sigourney, Miss Leslie, Mrs. Stephens, Mrs. Seba Smith, Harriet Beecher Stowe, and hordes of other women writers whose names no one would recognize today.

Fashions first, then moral stories, elegant tales of the chaste and the pure which were meant to instruct as well as to entertain, sentimental, didactic, and moral verse were the Hale-Godey staples. Much of the verse and more of the fiction reads like drivel now, but they must have been adored in their day, for Godey claimed a circulation of 25,000 in 1839—which might well mean 100,000 readers—and his magazine reached a circulation of 100,000 before the Civil War.

Besides fashions, shown in black-and-white line drawings and engravings as well as in the justly famous hand-colored plates, fiction, and feminine verse, *Godey's* published recipes, embroidery patterns and instructions, beauty and health hints, and elaborate illustrations—"embellishments," as both *Graham's* and *Godey's* called them. Its appeal was both practical and aesthetic. Small wonder that Louis Godey could claim in the *Post* advertisement that his magazine stood at the head of American magazines at the time. In popular acceptance and influence it did.

In 1848, T. S. Arthur, "Grace Greenwood" (Sarah Jane Lippincott), William Gilmore Simms, and Longfellow were prominent in *Godey's* along with the usual run of "female scribblers," as Hawthorne called them. "Hints on Equestrianism for the Fair Sex" ran as an illustrated feature through several issues. Every issue contained—a feature developed by the *Ladies' Home Journal* a half century later—complete plans and

[4] T. S. Arthur was a very popular magazine writer of the mid-century. He wrote in most of the Philadelphia magazines, including *The Saturday Evening Post* and *Graham's* as well as *Godey's*. Of his almost 100 moral tales and tracts only one is now generally remembered: "Ten Nights in a Barroom and What I Saw There" (1854).

illustrations for a model cottage, together with prices of materials needed in its construction. Only one advertisement seems to have been run during the year. This was a full-page advertisement for *The Saturday Evening Post*, run perhaps as an exchange for the *Godey's* advertisement which the *Post* carried.[5]

Mrs. Hale's influence was apparent through all of *Godey's*. It was her tastes and her ideas of what was or was not proper material to be spread before the eyes of American womanhood that determined the magazine's contents. A strong editor, she made her magazine a distinct force in American life, just as she and Godey made it a remarkable publishing success. Mrs. Hale campaigned for the recognition of women writers. Before her time women had either used masculine pseudonyms or initials or had hidden coyly behind anonymity. She had them boldly sign their names. She insisted on the simple and familiar as against the foreign and extravagant fiction. She introduced Harriet Beecher Stowe, who was still an unknown writer. She advocated educational opportunities and physical exercise for women. She argued in *Godey's* for national recognition of Thanksgiving Day until Lincoln proclaimed it on October 20, 1864.

Godey's Lady's Book lasted until almost the end of the nineteenth century, vanishing finally in 1898. Mrs. Hale gave up its editorship in 1877, two years before her death, and Louis A. Godey died in 1878. By 1883, when the *Ladies' Home Journal* was founded, the magazine had deteriorated. Its illustrations were crude, its makeup ugly, the quality of its paper bad. It featured "Gothic Country Houses," incredible monstrosities,

---

[5] The *Post* was described as "Always in Advance! Truly a Mammoth Sheet!" A portion of the advertisement headed "Our Contributors" read: "Our original contributors are the AUTHORS OF AMERICA. We always hold ourselves ready to purchase articles offered to us at a price proportionate to their merits. But authors whose writings are of a ridiculously exaggerated and immoral character may save themselves and us the trouble of sending them for examination. The Post is a family paper—and no article not calculated to enter the family circle can be admitted to its columns."

Godey's Lady's Book, famous for its hand-colored fashion plates and the rest of its ornate "embellishments," deeply influenced feminine taste, dress, and manners.

THE SATURDAY EVENING POST.

A MAMMOTH PAPER.

DEVOTED TO MORALITY, PURE LITERATURE, FOREIGN AND DOMESTIC NEWS,
AGRICULTURE, SCIENCE, ART AND AMUSEMENT.

*This Paper now contains from one-fourth to one-half more than the generality of Two Dollar
City Weeklies.*

J. Bayard Taylor, Grace Greenwood, T. S. Arthur, &c., are regular correspondents to the Post. We expect to publish,
in a few months, a thrilling novelette by Mr. Arthur, called "The Child Stealer"—also a novelette by R. Phipps, Esq.,
called "Henry Benson; or, the Events of Twenty Four Hours."
Nearly every week, one or more portraits, or pictures, are laid before the readers of the Post.

TERMS.—The terms to single subscribers are $2 per annum, in advance—$3 if not paid in advance. For $5 in
advance, one copy will be sent three years.
TERMS TO CLUBS.—In order to accommodate the large number who wish to take a first class paper, but mistak-
ingly think they cannot afford it, we continue the following low terms for Clubs—to be sent in the city to one address,
and in the country to one post office.

Four copies,	- - - - - - - - - -	-	$5 00 per annum.
Eight "	(and one to agent or the getter-up of the club,)	- - -	10 00 "
Thirteen "	(and one to agent or the getter up of the club,)	- - -	15 00 "
Twenty "	(and one to agent or the getter-up of the club.)	- - -	20 00 "

ONE COPY of the Saturday Evening Post and ONE of either Godey's Lady's Book or Graham's Magazine, for
FOUR DOLLARS.
The money for clubs must be always sent in advance. Subscriptions may be sent at our risk. When the sum is
large, a draft should be procured, if possible—the cost of which may be deducted from the amount. Address

DEACON & PETERSON, 66 *South Third street, Philadelphia.*

Editors copying the above, or who will give a fair notice of the paper, with a list of our terms, in their editorial
columns, shall be entitled to an exchange. Such as are already entitled to an exchange for the current year, shall receive
our thanks.

N. B.—Any person desirous of receiving a copy of the POST as a sample, can be accommodated by notifying the
publishers by letter, *post-paid.*

OPINIONS OF THE PRESS.

THE SATURDAY POST.—We have to congratulate our friends Edmund Deacon & Henry Peterson, upon the elegant
appearance of their enlarged paper, which is now the very pearl of the literary weeklies. The literary reputation of the
Saturday Post is widely known, and its circulation has been steadily increasing. It has our sincerest good wishes for its
success *for we think it has done much toward correcting the taste of the newspaper-reading public.*—Phil. North American.

THE SATURDAY EVENING POST is now the best paper of the kind that comes under our observation—Franklin Dem.
The original and selected articles of the Post are *generally better than those in any other paper.* If any of our readers
wish the best general weekly in the country, we say subscribe for the Post.—Syracuse Democrat.
The Post may justly be called the handsomest, best and cheapest paper in the United States.—Niagara Iris.
The Post always ranked among the best family newspapers of the country, and now that it is decidedly the largest
and most handsome, will soon take the lead of its cotemporaries.—Reading Gazette.

This advertisement for *The Saturday Evening Post,* "the very pearl of
literary weeklies," ran, with minor variations, in *Godey's Lady's Book*
and other magazines in the 1840's.

instead of cottages, and there were several pages of small advertisements in the back of each issue; but despite these changes it was still functioning distinctively as *Godey's*.

Godey's, with *Graham's*, *Sartain's*, and *Peterson's*, maintained Philadelphia as the center of successful popular-magazine publishing. In the face of this competition from Philadelphia there was doubt in 1850 whether another popular magazine, *Harper's*, could be successfully established in New York. *Harper's Monthly*, founded in 1850, and *The Atlantic Monthly*, founded in 1857, both of them still current, were important and powerful magazines in the second half of the nineteenth century, but those which have just been discussed were the magazines which exerted the most marked influence in the 1830's and the 1840's. Other magazines which were distinctive and effective during the early nineteenth century include *The Southern Literary Messenger*, *The Dial*, *The United States Magazine and Democratic Review*, and *The Youth's Companion*. *The Southern Literary Messenger*, founded in 1834, is important both because Poe was its editor from 1835 to 1837, and because of the literature, most of it by Southern authors, which first appeared in its pages. *The Dial*, 1840–1844, edited by Margaret Fuller, Thoreau, and Emerson, will always be fascinating to the student of American letters for its association with Concord and transcendentalism. *The United States Magazine and Democratic Review*, a favorite magazine of Andrew Jackson's, published many of Hawthorne's early tales. *The Youth's Companion*,[6] founded in 1827, delighted millions of avid youthful readers for more than a hundred years before it disappeared in 1929.

[6] Founded in Boston by Nathaniel Willis, father of N. P. Willis, *The Youth's Companion* was first intended to amuse and instruct children. Under Daniel Sharp Ford, who purchased it in 1857 and ran it until his death in 1899, it was made a magazine for adults as well. Harriet Beecher Stowe, Gladstone, Kipling, Tennyson, Whittier, Hardy, William Henry Huxley, James Bryce, Jules Verne, Jack London, Hamlin Garland and T. B. Aldrich all wrote for the *Companion* which at one time had the largest circulation (about half a million) of any American magazine.

The newspapers of the 1830's and 1840's were filled with bitter political disputes. They gave the news, but in news columns as well as in editorials they spent much of their energy and space in acrimonious party attack, shrill dispute, and violent abuse. Even the better newspapers, though in 1842 Charles Dickens exempted them from his bitter condemnation of what he saw as America's "licentious press," [7] were continuously and rancorously involved in party controversy. Dickens seems not to have looked at magazines while he was here for six months of that year, except the *Lowell Offering,* published by girl employees of the Lowell, Massachusetts, textile factories, and this he saw as a social phenomenon rather than as a magazine. Had he looked, he might have had more hope for American democracy and American culture.

The North American Review performed well the function for which it was intended. It provided a vehicle for the expression of critical literary thought and its dissemination to the comparatively restricted audience which could appreciate the ideas expressed. It provided magazine publication for poetry, fiction, travel, history, biography, economics, political science, and other scholarly writing. It compared favorably with the English quarterlies and reviews of the time.

The Knickerbocker and the Philadelphia magazines reached far wider audiences with less erudite materials and more popular writers, though often they brought to the general public the same great literary figures who appeared in the *North American* before a more select group of readers.[8] This was part of the

[7] Though he praised some things American, Dickens in his *American Notes* (1842) attacked slavery, using a profusion of newspaper accounts of cruelty and maltreatment to prove his point, criticized American manners, emphasized the lack of cleanliness and sanitation he found here, and saw the position of letters as hopeless because of American preoccupation with trade. Dickens, who had suffered great financial loss through pirating of his work, was incensed by the lack of adequate international copyright laws.

[8] It is of interest to note that many *North American* writers, a number of them the founders of *The Atlantic Monthly* and its chief contributors during its first greatness, were, before that, contributors to the popular magazines. Bryant, Poe, Hawthorne, and Emerson all appeared in the early *Saturday*

distinct service which these magazines rendered. It was certainly a part of the educational force which they exerted.

There were general magazines now for the classes and the masses. Magazines were beginning to cover the field. Though by modern standards they were small, the circulations, particularly of *Godey's, Graham's* and *The Saturday Evening Post,* were large for the time, and circulation is a primary index of a periodical's strength. The contents of a magazine may give it great potential influence on the lives of the individual and the group, but with only a limited audience its actual persuasiveness may be nil.

Literary matter predominated in the magazines of the 1840's and 1850's. This was the period of the greatest development of a native American literature, and American magazines aided greatly in its growth. It is not improbable that the prose writings of Emerson and the verses of Longfellow have had as much to do with forming American character and ethical concepts as the more technical psychological and sociological articles in twentieth-century magazines.

These magazines also brought information, intelligent discussion, and entertainment into the home. They provided in verse and in stories what Dickens said in his *American Notes:* "The stern utilitarian joys of trade" in the United States made impossible "cheerful recreation and wholesome fancies" to a people who needed them in almost direct proportion to their immersion in the more practical problems of building a nation. The criticism of Dickens and of other travelers from Europe and its older civilization are in themselves enough to show just how vital was the service of the magazines in spreading awareness of manners, morals, taste, and a mild "culture" throughout the States. The superior illustrations in *Graham's* not only

---

Evening Post. Emerson, Holmes, Longfellow, Lowell, and Bryant were all published in *Graham's* and, most of them, in *Godey's.* Poe, of course, died before the *Atlantic* was founded. It is doubtful that, given his literary sentiments and his animosities, he would ever have been an *Atlantic* contributor.

aided in the success of that impressive magazine, but also made Americans conscious of better art than they had been accustomed to see in newspapers, other magazines, or even in most books of the time. They foreshadowed the increased use of illustrations in magazines that reached full development in the late nineteenth century and appeared anew in the pictorial magazines founded in the mid-1930's.

Godey's early campaigns for education for women, for child welfare, and for national recognition of Thanksgiving made people aware of the importance of the subjects and brought eventual results. Such campaigns were a portent of magazine crusades, such as those carried on by *Harper's Weekly*, by Edward Bok in the later *Ladies' Home Journal* of the 1890's and the early 1900's, and by the muckrakers in *McClure's Magazine*, which brought about important social reforms in American life.

Chapter 5

EMERGENCE OF THE MAGAZINE JOURNALIST

Horace Greeley and Henry David Thoreau met in 1843 when Thoreau spent a year on Staten Island as tutor to the sons of Ralph Waldo Emerson's brother, William Emerson. Greeley, acting virtually as the younger man's literary agent, helped Thoreau to place his manuscripts with *Graham's, Putnam's,* the *Union Magazine,* and other periodicals. After Thoreau had returned to his beloved Concord the powerful editor of the *The New-York Tribune* wrote him shrewdly:

> This is the best kind of advertisement for you. Though you may write with an angel's pen yet your work will have no mercantile value unless you are known as an author. Emerson would be twice as well known if he had written for the magazines a little just to let common people know of his existence.[1]

Horace Greeley, one of the great journalistic figures of the nineteenth century, knew what he was talking about when he urged Thoreau to write for the magazines. He himself had been a magazine editor and publisher before he established the *Tribune.* In 1834, with Park Benjamin, Rufus Wilmot Griswold, and Henry J. Raymond, later editor of the *New York Times,* as his assistants, he had established the *New-Yorker,* "a weekly journal of literature, politics, statistics, and general intelligence." It was the *New-Yorker* which first gave Greeley his wide reputation. Strongly attached to the magazine, Greeley

---

[1] Emerson had written more for the magazines than Greeley realized. He was editing *The Dial* at this time and was to help found the *Atlantic* in 1857, but Greeley evidently was talking of magazines with a wide general circulation.

continued to edit it even while he edited the Whig papers, the *Jeffersonian* and the *Log Cabin,* for Thurlow Weed and William H. Seward. In 1841, the *New-Yorker* became the weekly edition of the *Tribune.*

For such writers as Lowell, Hawthorne, Cooper, Irving, and those others now recognized as classic American authors, the magazines provided just the service which Greeley indicated they would render for Thoreau. They offered an attractive vehicle for their work, extended and added to their reputations, and provided financial means of subsistence. Magazines were also beginning to develop a class of writers who were facile and deft, and who possessed a light touch and a sense of the dramatic and the timely that fitted the particular needs of periodical publication and matched the writing skills of the men and women themselves.

Poe invented the term "magazinist"—"magazine writer" would be a modern equivalent—to describe one of them. As Professor Pattee has pointed out, Poe himself was eminently a "magazinist." He traveled from city to city, Richmond, New York, Philadelphia, as his work for this or that magazine took him to one and then another. Almost everything he wrote, short stories, verse, critical articles, was written for the magazines. It was for magazines that he, with Hawthorne, developed the peculiarly American form of short fiction characterized by its conciseness, plot, and single action, a form essentially different from the earlier simple tale and later known as the short story. Rufus Wilmot Griswold, anthologist and critic, developed his distinctive editorial and literary talents for the magazines with which he was connected—the *New-Yorker, The Saturday Evening Post, Graham's,* and the others.

The writer whom Poe described as the very type of the magazinist was the exciting and romantic Nathaniel Parker Willis, a great and glamorous journalistic and literary figure in the last century. Willis was hailed as a leading American poet while still a Yale undergraduate. By the time he was twenty-three he had established in Boston his own magazine, the *American Monthly Magazine*. Before long, already known as a fluent and graceful writer of prose as well as verse, he was in New York helping Samuel Woodworth, author of "The Old Oaken Bucket," to edit the *New York Mirror*. The *Mirror* daringly sent Willis abroad as its foreign correspondent. The letters which Willis sent back to the *Mirror* during his five years of travel were compiled into *Pencillings by the Way* (1844) and made him one of the best-known American men of letters abroad. When, elegant, assured, and famous, he returned to the United States in 1840, he commanded the highest prices paid by *Godey's* and the other magazines. *Graham's* paid Willis eleven dollars a page and Poe only four or five dollars. Willis in his best years is said to have had a magazine income of several thousand dollars, while his many books of verse, short stories, and travel sketches, almost all of them compilations of his magazine work, brought him additional sums. Willis, a prolific and successful magazine writer, forerunner of such other magazine correspondents as Richard Harding Davis, though his only war reporting was from Washington during the Civil War for the *Home Journal*,[2] was greatly admired in his generation both by the literati and the public. Oliver Wendell Holmes in a much-quoted passage recalled the twenty-five-year-old Willis: "young . . . and already famous . . . he was tall; his hair, of light brown color, waved in luxuriant abundance. . . . He was something between a remembrance of Count D'Orsay and an anticipation of Oscar Wilde." When Willis was in England, only the intervention of seconds prevented a duel with Captain Marryat, the nautical novelist, following a dispute caused by Willis' alleged indiscretions in some of his published magazine reports. Later he was involved in the divorce trial of the Shakespearean actor Edwin Forrest.

[2] The *Home Journal*, which Willis and George Pope Morris founded in 1846 as an elegant magazine which would be an arbiter of culture in the United States, became *Town and Country* and is still a luxury-class magazine. In 1946 it celebrated its centennial with a 350-page issue.

Bayard Taylor, an equally brilliant figure in the magazine world of the last century, got his start when in 1844 *The Saturday Evening Post* and the *United States Gazette* advanced him money for travel letters he was to send back for publication. Taylor, who was then only nineteen, but who, like Willis, had early shown his ability as a writer, spent two years abroad. After travel in England, Scotland, Germany, France, he returned to the United States and in 1846 published his *Views A-Foot*. He became a staff member of the *New York Tribune* and, in 1849, was sent by Greeley to cover the California Gold Rush; *Eldorado* resulted in 1850. Taylor soon became the most famous American world traveler of his day, and most of the accounts of his travels in Europe, including Russia, and in Syria, Turkey, China, and Africa saw magazine publication before they were put into book form. Later Taylor, who was a facile poet as well as a writer of travel sketches and of fiction, held a number of diplomatic posts. He was minister to Germany when, still in his early fifties, he died in 1878.

Poe, Griswold, Willis, and Taylor are only examples of the best known among the host of characteristic writers developed by the advancing and developing magazines of the middle years of the last century. The competent, adequate to mediocre, magazine writers of our day are their professional descendants. The magazines were a natural outlet too for the major American writers of this period. *Godey's* and *Graham's*, as already noted, published the works of many of them. After *The Atlantic Monthly* was founded in 1857, they had still another periodical vehicle for their literary productions.

The *Atlantic* paid Thoreau $198 for his "Chesuncook," thirty-three pages at the rate of six dollars a page. It was the most money Thoreau had ever earned by publication of his writing in a magazine. Until the publication of *The Scarlet Letter* in 1850, what little income Hawthorne received outside his salary from the various political jobs obtained for him by his Bowdoin classmate Franklin Pierce came from the magazines and the Christmas annuals. His *Legends of the Province House*, for example, was first published in *The United States Magazine and Democratic Review*. This magazine, edited by the colorful John L. O'Sullivan, who had founded it in 1837, also published writings of Poe, Whitman, Bryant, Epes Sargent, and Paulding. Many of Hawthorne's other short tales appeared in the *Token*, the gift book which S. G. Goodrich published in Boston.

The close connection between the magazines and the best writers of this time is shown by the number of these writers who, at one period or another in their careers, were magazine editors as well as contributors. Poe's magazine alliances have been described. In 1836 the shy Hawthorne emerged from his seclusion in Salem to edit the *American Magazine of Useful and Entertaining Knowledge*. Thoreau and Margaret Fuller were, with Emerson, *Dial* editors. One of James Russell Lowell's first literary ventures was to found and edit the short-lived *Pioneer*. A few years later Lowell was a contributing editor of the *National Anti-Slavery Standard*. He was the first editor of *The Atlantic Monthly* and then the editor of *The North American Review*.

The magazines published the works of other, less notable, writers. Even the *Atlantic* was not solely the province of the Concord and Cambridge writers of the New England group. It printed Bayard Taylor as well as Longfellow, Holmes, Emerson, and the others. The magazines had their T. S. Arthurs and their Fanny Ferns, and Lydia Sigourney, the almost indecently prolific poetess, was a more popular and better-known magazine writer than Emerson. The articulate magazine journalist, able to turn a ready pen from subject to subject and to write competently about most of them, was active and admired in this period. It is doubtful that Emerson's essays and poems, Hawthorne's stories, or the longer novels of William Dean Howells, for example, would be accepted by any of the popular magazines today; but N. P. Willis and Bayard Taylor, if they were alive now, with their flair for the timely and their skill in the manufacture of salable copy, probably would turn from the romantic and write articles on economics with an international slant—or international articles with an economic slant—and almost certainly would be feature writers in our best-paying magazines.

· That there were both types of writers in the magazines then, as there are now, was recognized at the time. Boston alone in 1860 had nearly 150 periodicals, about one third of them described by a contemporary writer as "legitimate magazines." In April of that year *The Atlantic Monthly* said proudly:

> Among us . . . the magazine-writer, as he existed in the last
> century [the pamphleteer and the penny-a-liner] has left few, if
> any representatives. He is fading silently away into a forgotten
> antiquity; his works are not on the publishers' counters,—they
> linger only among the dust and cobwebs of old libraries, list-
> lessly thumbed by the exploring reader or occasionally consulted
> by the curious antiquary. His place is occupied by those who in
> the multiplication of books, the diffusion of information, and the
> general alteration of public taste, manners, and habits, though
> revolving in a similar orbit, move on quite another plane,—who
> have found in the pages of the periodicals a theatre of special
> activity, a way to the instruction and entertainment of the
> many; and though much of what is produced may bear . . . a
> character more or less ephemeral, we are sometimes presented
> also with the earlier blossoms and the fresher odors of a rich
> and perennial growth of genius, everywhere known and ac-
> knowledged, in the realms of belles-lettres, philosophy, and sci-
> ence, crowded here as in a nursery, to be soon transplanted to
> other and better abodes.

The language is a trifle elegant for twentieth-century taste, but the points are clear. The many magazines of the mid-nineteenth century were achieving what have been twin magazine objectives from the start: providing information and entertainment for many people. Their contents were vastly superior to those of American magazines a century earlier. Much of the writing was merely the ephemeral work of competent hacks and journalists, but some was the best writing of a splendid period in American literary history.

Chapter 6

MAGAZINES AND THE ABOLITION OF SLAVERY

THE MID-NINETEENTH CENTURY in the United States was a time of ferment. The political liberalism sweeping Europe, largely as a result of the revolutions in America and France, brought their repercussions in American life, and after the 1848 revolutions in Germany, Italy, and France, hordes of immigrants came to swell the rapidly mounting population of this country and to aid in its westward expansion and industrial growth. Three million immigrants entered the United States in the ten years from 1845 to 1855.

New means of transportation, the steamboat, the great canals, the railroads, and new means of communication—the telegraph in 1844, and the steam-driven printing press in 1847 —were speeding the tempo of American life. The development of power machinery in the mills of New England, the invention of the sewing machine in 1844, the opening of new markets in the West by the railroads, and in the Far East by treaty with China in 1844 and Perry's persuasion of Japan a decade later, were emphasizing the change-over from an agrarian to an industrial economy which gathered new impetus between the administrations of Jackson and Lincoln. In 1850 the annual value of the products of American factories was for the first time greater than the value of agricultural products.

Paradoxically, even improvements in agricultural implements and machinery hastened the advance of industrialism. The McCormick reaper, first patented in 1831, freed men from Northern fields to work in the factories—as later it freed men to fight in the Union armies. At the same time that industry was gaining strength and power in the North, the Southern cotton crop was year by year increasing in importance in the world market and in monetary value, reaching $105,000,000 in 1850. The very success of both the factories and the plantations widened the sectional split between the industrial North and the agrarian South. One needed and fought for a high protective tariff; the other fought as bitterly for the low tariff that would favor its position as a seller of raw materials and an importer of manufactured articles. And as the value of cotton rose, the value of the slaves who produced it rose steadily.

New and revolutionary ideas in science, ideas that were to culminate in Sir Charles Lyell's *Principles of Geology* (1830–1833) and in Charles Darwin's *The Origin of Species* (1859) were changing men's social and political, as well as their religious, ideas.[1] In 1847 the American Association for the Advancement of Science was formed in Boston, and in the same year Louis Agassiz left Prussia to begin his scientific work at Harvard.

There were more political ideas seething in the mid-nineteenth century than the Whigs and Democrats dreamed of. Horace Greeley opened the columns of *The New York Tribune* to Karl Marx. Greeley had already avowed his own interest in Fourierism and socialism. Emerson and his fellow transcendentalists, whom Greeley admired, had tried at Brook Farm to put their idealistic socialism into practice in what was merely the most famous of numerous community experiments.

There were other ideas and ideals in swirling circulation. There was agitation for more education. Public school education, through the efforts of such leaders as Horace Mann and Henry Barnard, was already widespread and spreading further. Between 1819 and 1850, fifteen state universities were founded. The cries of Sarah Josepha Hale in *Godey's* and of others who

---

[1] Darwin stated that the two most intelligent reviews of the *Origin of Species* were published in American periodicals; one in *The North American Review*, the other in *The New York Times*.

demanded more education for women were being answered. Mary Lyon's Female Seminary, the first woman's institution of collegiate rank, was opened in South Hadley, Massachusetts, in 1837. Oberlin College was opened in Ohio as a coeducational college in 1833. The University of Iowa admitted women in 1858. There was agitation for temperance, for greater advantages for labor, for religious reform, diet reform, for dozens of other movements, some of them valid, some mere fads. Emerson, shrewd practical thinker as well as mystic and idealist, upon whom most reformers of the time seem to have descended with demands for his support, saw the swirling scene as populated with "madmen and women, men with beards, Dunkers, Muggletonians, Come-outers, Groaners, Agrarians, Seventh-Day Baptists, Quakers, Abolitionists, Unitarians, and Philosophers."

The imperialistic ambitions of the country, stirred by "manifest destiny," helped to bring on the Mexican War, and added California and vast territories—now Arizona, Utah, and New Mexico—to the United States in 1848. Texas had already been annexed in 1845. The discovery of gold in California in 1848 added to the general excitement and posed new problems. In the single year of 1849 some 80,000 immigrants landed in California.

This was hardly the Federalist United States of Joseph Dennie and *The Port Folio*. The "common man" of Jackson's time was becoming literate and articulate. Magazines by the score, most of them short-lived, sprang up to defend the opinions of one group or attack those of another. Frank Luther Mott, using various sources, estimates that there were about a hundred magazines other than newspapers in 1827. The census of 1850 enumerated 214 monthlies, semi-monthlies, and quarterlies, and 1,902 weeklies. Mott further estimates that 2,500 periodicals, not including newspapers, were issued, some for only a short time, others for several years, between 1850 and 1865. The growing urbanization brought about by industrialism was putting more and more people within the reach of magazines.

These new magazines, brought into being as the result of social change, were the implements of more change.

There were still no truly national general magazines. Had there been, it is at least possible that their discussions of vital issues might have aided in the peaceful solution of sectional differences which even in the 1830's and 1840's were threatening the democratic experiment in America. South Carolina threatened secession as early as 1832. Compromise after compromise on the slavery issue was to prove ineffective for more than a few years or months. War seemed imminent when, after the Clay-Webster-Calhoun debates, the Compromise of 1850 was reached. Slavery was the basic issue underlying the political, economic, and sectional dispute; and on this issue the influence of the magazines was strong.

In 1831, a year before the threatened secession of South Carolina, William Lloyd Garrison, using borrowed type on a hand press set up in a mean back room in Boston, issued the first number of *The Liberator.* Like Wendell Phillips, Garrison was a complete and determined abolitionist who had no patience with compromise of any kind, who would not countenance the gradual emancipation by political methods favored by more conservative anti-slavery advocates. He stood radically and unequivocally for the immediate and complete abolition of slavery, no matter what the political result for the country. In the first number of *The Liberator* he wrote: "I am in earnest— I will not equivocate—I will not excuse—I will not retreat a single inch—and *I will be heard.*" Insistent, undaunted even when Georgia advertised a reward for the arrest and conviction of its editor who was mobbed on the streets of Boston, harsh, violent, even abusive, *The Liberator* for thirty-five years fought slavery with every weapon it could find or devise. In January, 1865, Garrison declined a twenty-third term as president of the American Anti-Slavery Society. On December 29, 1865, his great objective having been attained when the Thirteenth Amendment to the Constitution was ratified, Garrison put the final issue of *The Liberator* to bed.

The cause of abolition claimed the services and devoured the energies of great writers of the time. Emerson, Thoreau, Lowell, and Whittier, though more moderate in their views and temperate in their expression than Garrison in *The Liberator,* were as intense in their hatred of slavery. Thoreau is said to have used his Walden cabin as a station in the Underground Railway by which slaves were rushed northward to freedom. Lowell, whose burning interest in abolition was intensified by the abolitionist fervor of the poet Maria White whom he married in 1844, wrote with vehemence and enthusiasm for the cause. His anti-slavery papers, collected now in two volumes, were written mostly for the *Pennsylvania Freeman* and for the *National Anti-Slavery Standard,* of which he was associate editor from 1845 to 1850. The Second Series of Lowell's *Biglow Papers,* supporting the North and attacking slavery, ran in the *Atlantic* during the war. Lowell, a liberal thinker who was against tryanny in any form, saw slavery as the worst tyranny of all. Moral indignation informed his denunciatory attacks on the institution he and his fellows were determined to uproot.

The *Pennsylvania Freeman* was edited in 1838 and 1839 by John Greenleaf Whittier, the gentle Quaker poet who gave so much of his life and of his literary talent to the fight against slavery. The offices of the *Freeman* were burned to the ground by a Philadelphia mob while he was its editor. Like Garrison, who was his friend, he was mobbed when he and George Thompson, an English lecturer, spoke in Concord, New Hampshire. In 1846 his anti-slavery poems were collected and printed as *Voices of Freedom,* and in 1848 he became contributing editor of the *National Era,* which was published as an anti-slavery paper in Washington. In 1852 the *National Era* published serially the one book which is universally acknowledged to have accomplished more for the cause of abolition—and done more to provoke the Civil War—than any other anti-slavery writing. This was Harriet Beecher Stowe's *Uncle Tom's Cabin.*

There were numerous other anti-slavery magazines: the

Anti-Slavery Record, the *Anti-Slavery Examiner,* the *Massachusetts Abolitionist,* the *Emancipator,* and the *Anti-Slavery Reporter.* Despite violence and threats of violence, depredation, and even murder, these magazines carried on their unrelenting warfare against slavery. *The Liberator's* presses were destroyed. In 1835 a mob in South Carolina broke into the United States mails and burned copies of the magazine and effigies of its editor. The press of the *Observer* in Alton, Illinois, was several times smashed by mobs. Attempting to protect a new press sent him by the Ohio Anti-Slavery Society, its determined editor, Elijah Lovejoy, an abolitionist of the uncompromising Garrison type, was shot and killed on the night of November 7, 1837.

Other general magazines took a definite, though less radical, stand against slavery, as did most of the denominational church magazines. The more conservative anti-slavery position of some magazines, whose first consideration was preservation of the Union, was best represented perhaps by *The North American Review.* Though it condemned slavery on humanitarian grounds, it deprecated the dangerous clamor of those who demanded immediate, unplanned abolition without regard to the political consequences. In October, 1848, it said: ". . . If any change takes place, it will be accomplished, not by the declamation and agitation of strangers, but by practical expedients, deliberately considered and spontaneously adopted by the public sentiment and the lawful authority of the States concerned."

Events were moving too fast, however, for the thoughtful approach of the more conservative magazines to check the speed with which the issue was headed for an explosive climax. It was the fiery exhortations of the abolitionist magazines which had the greater effect. These certainly aroused and intensified sectional hatred, incited to violence, worked to bring feelings to fever pitch that precipitated the final conflict—but contributed markedly to incalculable social advance.

Chapter 7

INNOVATION AND EXPANSION IN COVERAGE

THE EDITORS and publishers of early general magazines might look with awe and considerable envy on products of the periodical press today. Successors to Poe, Willis, Taylor, and the other "magazinists" of the 1840's have greatly developed the art of writing articles and stories particularly adapted to magazine publication. Magazine editing as it was developed by such later editors as Henry Mills Alden, Gertrude Battles Lane, Ellery Sedgwick, Edward Bok, S. S. McClure, and George Horace Lorimer, and as practiced today by Henry Luce, Dewitt Wallace, and their contemporaries has become a far more complicated profession than magazine editing as understood and deftly practiced by Joseph Dennie, Charles Brockden Brown, and Sarah Josepha Hale.

The rise of advertising and improvements in printing and in the reproduction of illustrations were partly responsible for this advance. Improved methods of distribution also contributed greatly. Editorial, mechanical, and business skills all combined to make the national magazine into the medium that today functions to bring simultaneously to readers in all parts of the country information and opinion that exert their social force in almost direct ratio to the many millions of people that these magazines reach weekly and monthly. But the best magazines of 1850 could list contributors at least as distinguished and accomplished as those of the best magazines today. As vehicles for the communication of news, ideas, and entertainment those magazines were forceful and effective. The vital magazines of 1850 had form and substantial content. Each was possessed of its own validity and carried its own emphasis. Singly and as a group they exerted their strong force in American thought and American activity. Some of today's "new" ideas in magazine publishing were to have their inception at this time, attain full development before the end of the century, and then practically disappear before their renascence under different conditions and with improved editorial and mechanical techniques in the 1920's and 1930's.

Harper's New Monthly Magazine was founded in 1850 purely as a magazine to present a selection of material first published in other magazines, both American and foreign. Like the modern digest-type magazines, *Harper's* published little or no original material.[1] Its first issue stated that, as the best writers in every nation were then writing for magazine publication, and as no one could possibly read all the magazines, *Harper's* would select and publish a 144-page "monthly compendium of the periodical publications of the day." It promised to "transfer to its pages as rapidly as they may be issued all the continuous tales of DICKENS, BULWER, CROLY, LEVER, WARREN . . ."[2] It also promised, with the success of *Godey's, Graham's* and

[1] An important consideration with Harper & Brothers, the book publishers, in founding the eclectic magazine was that it would serve as an advertising medium for their books. For many years it refused all other advertising. George P. Rowell, founder both of the first American Newspaper Directory and of *Printers' Ink*, writes in his autobiography, *Forty Years An Advertising Agent* (New York: Franklin Publishing Co., 1926): ". . . The writer remembers listening with staring eyes, while Fletcher Harper the younger related that he had that week refused an offer of $18,000 for the use of the last page for a year for an advertisement of the Howe Sewing Machine."

[2] So normal and financially successful was this practice that N. P. Willis wrote in the prospectus to the *Corsair,* a literary weekly which he proposed at first to call *The Pirate,* that its editors intended "to take advantage . . . of the privilege assured us by our piratical law of copyright and, in the name of American authors (for our own benefit) 'convey' to our columns, for the amusement of our readers, the cream and spirit of everything that ventures to light in England, France, and Germany." Quoted by Frank Luther Mott, *A History of American Magazines, 1741–1850* (Cambridge, Mass. Harvard University Press, 1938), pp. 356–357. American writers naturally were resentful of *Harper's* initial policy. Later the magazine began to include original contributions by American authors.

Peterson's evidently in mind, that "a carefully prepared Fashion Plate, and other pictorial illustrations will accompany each number." There was the usual "monthly record of current events." This feature, which was still running in the late 1880's, was edited for some years by Henry J. Raymond, well-known editor of *The New York Times.*

At the end of its first half year of publication *Harper's,* which was immediately successful, could reiterate its purpose, declare its accomplishment, and firmly restate its basic intent:

> It was presented in the belief, that it might be the means of bringing within the reach of the great mass of the American people, an immense amount of useful and entertaining reading matter, to which, on account of the great number and expense of the books and periodicals in which it originally appears, they have hitherto had no access.

It could boast that it had already achieved a monthly issue of 50,000 copies, with circulation increase still unchecked. The publishers hoped for a popular circulation "unequalled by that of any similar periodical ever published in the world." The basic appeal of the early *Harper's* was the same as the present-day appeal of the digest magazines, though selections were not condensed but usually reprinted in full. Editors were already envisioning the kind of mass circulation which did not become a reality until Cyrus Curtis harnessed the force of advertising to magazines.

Harper's in 1850 "transferred" to its pages material on exploration, travel, science, art, on social and domestic life, as well as poetry and fiction. It drew heavily on the English magazines, wholesale from Dickens' *Household Words.* Other magazines whose names reappeared continually were the *Eclectic Review, Sharpes' London Magazine, Howitt's Country Yearbook, Chambers' Edinburgh Journal,* and the *Dublin University Magazine.* It drew on old and new books as well as on the magazines. An 1850 serial was Ik Marvel's (Donald G. Mitchell) best seller, *Reveries of a Bachelor,* "from a new work soon to be issued by Baker & Scribners." The magazine title was "A Bachelor's Reverie." The names of Lord Chesterfield, Harriet Martineau, Southey, Guizot, and Coleridge appeared as authors during the year, and Leigh Hunt, evidently a favorite with *Harper's*, was represented in almost every issue.

American writers might complain bitterly, and publishers like Graham might well protest such competition, but *Harper's* did its job of selection well, and the form proved almost as popular in its time as it is proving in its streamlined counterparts today. By expanding and intensifying the range of periodical materials available, *Harper's* accomplished a distinct service for its readers. After the 1850's it began to publish more American material but always relied heavily on English fiction. It published serially Dickens' *Bleak House* and *Little Dorrit,* Thackeray's *Virginians* and *The Newcomes,* and George Eliot's *Romola.* In January, 1893, at the height of its excellence as a literary magazine under Henry Mills Alden, it began serial publication of Du Maurier's *Trilby,* one of the most popular English novels of modern times. With the *Trilby* text were reproduced Du Maurier's original illustrations. Fine illustrating was by this time a *Harper's* tradition, and part of the magazine's great success was due to the work of its artists. In 1885 and 1886, with Alden as editor, and with George William Curtis in the "Editor's Easy Chair" and William Dean Howells occupying the "Editor's Study"—two famous *Harper's* departments—the monthly was running Oliver Goldsmith's *She Stoops to Conquer* with illustrations by Edwin Abbey. Though most stories and articles were still unsigned even in the 1880's, Brander Matthews, Helen Hunt Jackson, Elizabeth Stuart Phelps, Mary E. Wilkins, James Lane Allen, Thomas Nelson Page, Charles Dudley Warner, and "Charles Egbert Craddock" were prominent American contributors in 1885 and 1886. C. S. Reinhart and later Howard Pyle, A. E. Sterner, and William T. Smedley were, with Edwin Abbey, among *Harper's* best-known artists.

"AH ME! WHEN SHALL I MARRY ME?"

Edwin Abbey's finely executed illustrations for *She Stoops to Conquer* were a leading feature of *Harper's New Monthly Magazine* for a half-dozen issues during 1886.

Harper's published Mark Twain and Thomas Hardy. For many years it brought the best in English letters and some of the most popular American writing to its readers. In the 1880's and 1890's the fiction and verse by present-day standards were thin, but they were the best of their kind at the time. Frederick Lewis Allen, the late editor of *Harper's,* analyzed the defects of the magazines of this period, pointing out that the very excellence of *Harper's* and its competitors in 1891 marked the limitations of these magazines as a social force:

> Fifty years ago a small group of magazines, including the *Century, Harper's,* the four-year-old *Scribner's* and the unillustrated *Atlantic Monthly,* not only led the magazines of the country in literary and artistic quality, but were also among the big sellers. The circulation records of those days are hard to come by, but it is my impression that in 1891 *Harper's* had between 100,000 and 200,000 readers, and that few, if any, periodicals in America had more than that. To us today some of the *Harper's* fiction of 1891 seems naive, some of its verse weakly sentimental, some of its pen-and-ink illustrations too daintily photographic; we wonder at its comparative neglect of the vital social and economic issues of the day, at its preoccupation with the safely remote, the respectably classical, the second-hand literary; and at its careful propriety. We have to remind ourselves that the public for which it was edited was the victim of an attractive but academic and timorous genteelism. . . .[3]

The same limitations that Mr. Allen indicated in *Harper's* of the nineteenth century applied to the other famous magazines which he mentioned. *The Atlantic Monthly* was founded in Boston in 1857 when Moses Dresser Phillips of Phillips, Sampson, & Company invited Emerson, Longfellow, Cabot, Holmes, and Motley to a dinner to discuss Francis H. Underwood's idea for a magazine. E. P. Whipple, the critic whose work appears in almost all the best literary magazines of the second half of the century, was invited to another dinner held the next day. Lowell was made editor and, at his insistence,

[3] Frederick Lewis Allen, "American Magazines, 1741–1941," *Bulletin of The New York Public Library,* June, 1941.

Holmes chief contributor. These founders became, with others of the New England group, the important and regular contributors to the *Atlantic* during its first and best years.

No American magazine has ever had more distinguished original contributors. Though none of their productions were signed, Emerson, Lowell, Charles Eliot Norton, Harriet Beecher Stowe, Parke Godwin, and Whittier all contributed to the 128-page first issue of *The Atlantic Monthly*, published in November, 1857. That famous issue contained the first installment of Oliver Wendell Holmes' *The Autocrat of the Breakfast Table* (Every Man His Own Boswell)—which it is amazing to remember now was bitterly attacked by the evangelical press for its unorthodox remarks. There were several of Emerson's finest poems, including "Days," "The Rommany [sic] Girl," and "Brahma"; several short stories; the first part of a serial, "Akin By Marriage"; a discussion of "The Origin of Didactic Poetry"; a long description of the Manchester Art Exhibition; an article on "British India" and another on the currency; and departments devoted to "Literary Notes" and "Music." Surprisingly, the lead article in this issue was an appreciative essay on Douglas Jerrold, the great "Q" of *Punch*, who had died during the year. Although Holmes was a humorist and Lowell paraded a punning humor of a kind, it is difficult to associate the dignified *Atlantic* with the satirical wit and epigrammatic humor of the English comic weekly.

Whittier's "Skipper Ireson's Ride," which, on Lowell's advice, he wrote in New England dialect, was in the second number of the *Atlantic*. Lowell, always sure of himself, was a sound though arbitrary editor, quite willing to change what he did not like. Sometimes his changes improved a manuscript; sometimes he merely antagonized better writers than he. Thoreau's "Chesuncook," the narrative of his second journey into the Maine woods, was published in June and July, 1858. Without consulting Thoreau, Lowell, who had solicited the manuscript, deleted a passage whose philosophy he disapproved. After writing Lowell a stinging rebuke which was not answered, Thoreau thereupon refused to write again for the *Atlantic* while Lowell remained its editor. Thoreau did not appear again in the *Atlantic* during his lifetime. Though he arranged with James T. Fields, Lowell's successor and a member of the publishing firm of Ticknor & Fields which purchased the magazine in 1859, to publish a part of his *Excursions*, Thoreau died before it appeared. Almost all of his posthumous work, edited from his manuscripts, was published in the *Atlantic*.

The list of *Atlantic* literary triumphs is long; a full list of its early contributors would include almost every revered name of New England in American letters of the nineteenth century. Unlike *Harper's*, which in its first years simply exploited English writers, the *Atlantic* offered the finest American imaginative and critical writers a suitable, periodical vehicle for their work and consequently made great contributions to American literature. In so far as its belletristic product influences the spirit of a country, no American magazine has been more influential than *The Atlantic Monthly*.

One limitation has often been pointed out. The *Atlantic* was meant to be as broad in coverage as its name suggested. In reality, during its first years it confined itself almost entirely to publishing the Boston, Cambridge, and Concord writers. There was some justification for this. Though critics and historians jealous of the literary pretensions of other regions of the country may cavil, and many have cavilled loudly, the fact remains that the best writers of the mid-nineteenth century were concentrated about Boston.

There was another limitation. The *Atlantic* described itself as "a magazine of literature, art, and politics." In actuality, it presented the literary and acknowledged the artistic, but avoided the political and the social. Like *Harper's* of the same period, it suffered from the same restriction that produced its excellence. Neither magazine paid much attention to the Civil War, though the *Atlantic* published Julia Ward Howe's "Battle Hymn of the

Republic" (Fields is said to have affixed the title), and the Second Series of Lowell's *Biglow Papers*. Both magazines stressed the literary and the cultural, largely neglecting other fundamental aspects of American life.

William Dean Howells was the best of the nineteenth-century *Atlantic* editors who succeeded Fields. His was still a literary *Atlantic*, but more a national than a provincial magazine. Thomas Bailey Aldrich, editor from 1881 to 1890, carefully gave the *Atlantic* the same academic, genteel propriety which Richard Watson Gilder guarded so jealously in *The Century*. The next three editors, Horace Scudder, Walter Hines Page, and Bliss Perry, injected more articles on social subjects into the magazine, and the *Atlantic* even indulged in some mild muckraking when the reform movement of the first decade of the twentieth century was in full swing. Yet it was not until 1909, when Ellery Sedgwick, a young editor trained on *The Youth's Companion, Leslie's Monthly* (Sedgwick changed the title from *Frank Leslie's Popular Monthly*), the *American Magazine*, and *McClure's*, bought the magazine, that the *Atlantic* fully recognized the importance of social and political material. Without neglecting the literary, always pre-eminent in the magazine, it broadened its coverage and sharpened its perceptions of the contemporary scene. When Sedgwick bought the magazine for $50,000, it was about to fail. It had a circulation of only 15,000 and was losing $4,000 a year. In his first year as owner and editor Sedgwick showed a profit of $4,000.

Under Sedgwick's direction the influence of *The Atlantic Monthly*, always strong in literature, was reinforced in other directions. The new editor's mail, he later said proudly in *The Happy Profession*, soon bore witness to its expansion and greater strength. Men of national reputation and eminence began to submit articles. Woodrow Wilson, while President, sent the *Atlantic* an unsolicited article. Later Al Smith, still later Wendell Willkie, appeared in its pages. Ellery Sedgwick used these illustrations to show that such men deliberately chose

The Atlantic Monthly as an effective medium for dissemination of their ideas. Every editor likes to believe that his magazine is, for one reason or another, pre-eminent in influence with the public. With more justification than some, Ellery Sedgwick could say: "To inoculate the few who influence the many is the *Atlantic's* perpetual formula." Edward Weeks, Jr., editor of the *Atlantic* since 1938, has successfully applied his inherited formula.

It was another magazine, also founded in 1857, which became a strong political and social force and accomplished much toward the advance of the American magazine. *Harper's Weekly,* through its development of illustrations into vivid pictorial journalism and through its news coverage and comments as well as its feature articles, can easily be seen as the precursor of today's weekly pictorial and news magazines. *Harper's Weekly,* "a journal of civilization," as the line under the logotype read, was founded largely as a vehicle to carry the kind of political writing eschewed by the literary *Harper's Monthly.* From its first number in 1857 to its last in 1916, it was a bright, alert, well-illustrated weekly, offering fiction, both short stories and serials, essays, editorials, news, advertising, poetry, and humor. It began to run full-page pictures in its first year. These full-page pictures that always told a story became one of the best and most characteristic *Harper's Weekly* features.

There had been illustrated magazines before this time. The first of them, *Gleason's Pictorial,* was founded in 1851. Under the guidance of Henry Carter, the English-born engraver and publisher who later changed his name to Frank Leslie, it was a successful weekly for most of the 1850's. *Frank Leslie's Illustrated Newspaper,* founded a year before *Harper's Weekly,* was a sensational sheet. Leslie distributed the wood blocks among a force of engravers, then assembled the parts so as to hit the streets quickly with his eight-page tabloid of murders, fires, railroad disasters, lynchings, morgue scenes. By 1868 he was running a two-page spread of such cultural occasions as the grand dress rehearsal at Pike's New Opera House at 23rd Street and Eighth Avenue—which Jim Fisk bought and over which he and Jay Gould had their resplendent offices—in order to give variety to his enticing displays of home accidents, charred bodies, gun fights, and spectacular street accidents.

Undoubtedly *Leslie's Illustrated Newspaper* suggested the pictorial idea to the Harpers, and some of Leslie's artists, notably the young Thomas Nast, joined the new magazine, but well before 1868 *Harper's Weekly* had brought pictorial journalism to a kind of perfection never achieved by Leslie's newspaper. Its aim was not sensationalism but accurate graphic reporting, and that is what it provided. The Civil War was its great opportunity. Just as today's magazines sent their corps of correspondents and photographers to cover World Wars I and II, *Harper's Weekly* sent a staff of writers and artists to the Civil War battle fronts. William Waud, Theodore Davis, Thomas Nast, A. W. Warren, and Andrew McCallum sent back pencil or pen-and-ink drawings of battle and camp scenes which were published as half-page, full-page, and sometimes double-page engravings. The magazine so admirably succeeded in its reporting of the war that its files for the period are well known as a vivid pictorial and authentic news source for Civil War history. Besides engravings, *Harper's Weekly* by 1863 was publishing reproductions of Brady photographs, though these were usually portraits of the various Union generals and naval commanders.

The accomplishments of *Harper's Weekly* during the war were recognized at the time. Fletcher Harper, working editor of the *Weekly* as he was of *Harper's Monthly*, went to Washington during the war to defend the magazine against Secretary of War Stanton's accusation that it had given aid and comfort to the enemy by publishing pictures of Union fortifications, and to fight the Secretary's order for the magazine's suspension. Harper obtained both a revocation of the order and Stanton's thanks for the services his paper was performing. Lincoln later was reported to have said that Thomas Nast, through his cartoons and drawings in *Harper's Weekly*, had been the country's most effective recruiting sergeant.

The most spectacular magazine success of the mid-century showed, in other directions, ways in which the mass magazine was to develop. *The New York Ledger,* which Robert Bonner began to publish in 1855, was sensational in its day on several counts. Five years after its founding it had attained the then unheard of circulation of 400,000—at a time when the population of the entire country was only 31,000,000. It paid tremendous sums to "name" contributors. It made its publisher a millionaire. And, though Bonner would admit no advertising to the columns of the *Ledger,* he made uninhibited use of advertising to sell his magazine. Bonner, like those who publish the magazines of large circulation today, aimed at mass readership. What he gave his readers in a well-printed eight-page magazine was the work of the best-known magazine fiction writers of the day, the work of the most popular poets, and special features written by all the literate figures in public life whom he could persuade to write for him.

In 1859 the masthead of the *Ledger* listed among "regular contributors": George D. Prentice, John G. Saxe, Col. W. B. Dunlap, Fanny Fern, Mrs. Sigourney, Mrs. Southworth, Alice Cary, Augusta Moore, Sylvanus Cobb, Jr., and Emerson Bennett. Bonner ran one after another that year and for many years afterward the melodramatic serials of Sylvanus Cobb, Jr., and all the stories and essays of the sprightly Fanny Fern." The Hidden Hand" by Emma D. Southworth, "The Little Foxes" by the omnipresent T. S. Arthur, "Raphael; or The Fugitives of Paris" by Dr. Henry W. Wadsworth, and similar fiction were continued all through 1859.

But Bonner, a shrewd magazine publisher who had begun his career as a Hartford printer, also began to publish in 1859 "The Mount Vernon Papers" by Edward Everett, Harvard president and professor, *North American* editor, statesman and writer. For the series Everett, who was also president of the

Ladies' Mount Vernon Society, received $10,000 which he con-
tributed to the fund for the preservation of Washington's home.
Later, in 1870, Bonner was featuring weekly articles by the
popular and admired preacher Henry Ward Beecher and autobiographical writing by Horace Greeley. Along with the inevitable Cobb thrillers and the "Fern Leaves" was highly reputable
biographical writing by James Parton, and with the mawkish
verse of women poets Bonner ran serious articles by "twelve
distinguished Senators of the United States." By paying liber-
ally for them Bonner was able to obtain poems from Longfellow
and Bryant, prose from Harriet Beecher Stowe, work from
leading college presidents and scholars.

According to Bonner himself, as he is quoted by George
Rowell, again and again he would gather all the money he could
obtain and spend it in advertising his magazine. Before he returned to his office, it seemed, all his money had come back and
more with it. What Bonner did was to publish a page or two
of *Gun Maker of Moscow* by Sylvanus Cobb, Jr., or some similar *Ledger* story in the pages of a newspaper, then break it off
with "Continued in *The New York Ledger*!" The idea was new
then. Or he would buy whole newspaper pages and fill them
with display advertising after this fashion:

```
THE NEW YORK LEDGER
THE NEW YORK LEDGER
THE NEW YORK LEDGER
    WILL BE FOR SALE
    WILL BE FOR SALE
    WILL BE FOR SALE
TO-MORROW MORNING
TO-MORROW MORNING
TO-MORROW MORNING
  THROUGHOUT THE
  THROUGHOUT THE
  THROUGHOUT THE
    UNITED STATES
    UNITED STATES
    UNITED STATES
  AND NEW JERSEY
  AND NEW JERSEY
  AND NEW JERSEY
```

Bonner is said to have paid as high as $27,000 for one week's advertising of his magazine, and up to $150,000 in a year. These were large figures eighty and ninety years ago. Bonner could claim with some accuracy in an editorial in one issue of the *Ledger:* "More money is spent upon the *Ledger* to make it a good paper than is spent upon any other paper in the world. . . . It has the largest number of great and distinguished writers. . . . The principal Bishops, Doctors of Divinity, and Clergymen write for it. . . . Distinguished public men, including Foreign Ministers, Members of the Cabinet and Senators in Congress write for the Ledger. . . ."

Bonner reveled in the success of his magazine and bought famous race horses with part of his profits. He did not believe in stake racing but enjoyed a match race with some other horse fancier like Commodore Vanderbilt on a country road. Bonner liked to talk brightly and briskly to his readers and in one editorial, with the mixture of effrontery, complacency, and trust that were part of his charm, he quoted the Commodore. People were continually stopping him on the street, Bonner said, to express their approval of the newest *Ledger.* He was reminded of Vanderbilt's retort to those who had exclaimed that they liked a new ocean steamer. "Well," said the Commodore, "you'd be confounded fools if you didn't!" [4]

Robert Bonner's conception of a profitable magazine was very modern. The body of the *Ledger* was staff-written by popular writers whose work was produced exclusively for the *Ledger.* He gathered in special articles from writers whose

---

[4] Robert Bonner always kept his readers informed and advised. He did not call a spade by prettier names. "We employ no traveling agents," he wrote in 1859. "If any party pretends to act as such, you can put him down as a swindler." He suggested in another editorial that people stop bothering him. "We are," he wrote, "constantly receiving letters from parties whom we highly esteem and would be glad to oblige, but . . . we are so loaded with labors that every moment of our time has to carry double . . . our friends . . . will see how impossible it is for us to act upon our friendly impulses and answer their letters. Don't expect it of us; and don't send us any manuscripts."

names would add luster to the magazine. His uninhibited and successful use of advertising was in advance of his time. If it seems an anomaly that he would print none himself, it must be remembered that many other editors of the time also refused it. The wily Bonner may have felt that its absence gave his *Ledger* a certain *cachet* and respectability in the eyes of those who viewed the prolific outpourings of Sylvanus Cobb, Jr., Fanny Fern, and their fellows with something less than complete critical approval.

Chapter 8

MAGAZINES AS A WEAPON AGAINST
POLITICAL CORRUPTION

IF, UNDER the determined leadership of crusading editors, magazines were made a dynamic force for social betterment in the opening years of the twentieth century, it was the rival illustrated weeklies founded just before the Civil War, *Leslie's* and *Harper's Weekly*, which first demonstrated the effectiveness of the American magazine as an instrument of civic and social reform.

In 1858 *Leslie's* began a bitter campaign against "swill milk" in New York City. Cows in dairies supplying New York's milk were being fed distillery mash and refuse. The diet stimulated the milk production of the animals, but they developed sores, their tails rotted off, and the milk was filled with disease germs. *Leslie's* described the situation in vivid editorials, ran pictures of filthy conditions in the dairies and of the diseased and dying cows. "For the midnight assassin," Leslie wrote, "we have the rope and the gallows; for the robber, the penitentiary; but for those who murder our children by the thousands we have neither reprobation nor punishment."

But both distilleries and dairies were protected by the politicians in power. An investigation by the board of health found no alarming conditions, and so reported. *Leslie's* pressed the fight. It had milk carts followed, and addresses where deliveries were made were published in the magazine, together with a warning that the buyers were feeding poisoned milk to their children. Another investigation showed that dairies and distilleries were blameless, whereupon the attack in *Leslie's* grew more virulent. The chairman of the exonerating committee *Leslie's* described as "a barefaced, shameless rascal." Another alderman was described as his superior "in all that constitutes the scurrilous blackguard and mouthy poltroon."

Leslie's printed cartoons now as well as pictures. It attacked the entire city administration which was responsible for the milk scandal. The report of the committee of the New York Academy of Medicine, which the mayor was forced to appoint, found the abuses as bad as the magazine had pictured them. An attempt was made to indict Frank Leslie for criminal libel, but the action was thrown out by the grand jury. The exposé in *Leslie's* put an end to the sale of milk from herds fed with waste from the distilleries. The New York State legislature was acknowledging a magazine-accomplished fact when it acted to forbid the traffic in 1861.

Harper's Weekly, under the idealistic leadership of George William Curtis [1] and with the devastating cartoons of Thomas Nast as the principal weapon, entered on the far more formidable task of overthrowing Tammany and smashing the notorious Tweed Ring. J. Henry Harper in *The House of Harper* (New York: 1912), tells in full a story of magazine courage which other magazine and social historians have noted and approved.

In 1870 the Tweed Ring, composed of William Marcy Tweed, Peter Barr Sweeny, Richard B. Connolly, and A. Oakey

---

[1] George William Curtis, like Charles A. Dana, famous editor of the *New York Sun,* was a product of Brook Farm, the transcendentalist community near Boston which Emerson had helped found and where Hawthorne lived for a year before his marriage. Like George Ripley, the community's president, he later joined the staff of Horace Greeley's *New York Tribune.* Curtis traveled in the Far East as a *Tribune* correspondent, wrote amusing travel books, several sentimental novels, and then became a strong reform editor, writing both in *Harper's Weekly* and in the "Editor's Easy Chair" in *Harper's Monthly.* Unlike Dana he remained an idealist, fighting first against slavery, then for women's rights, civil service reform, and industrial harmony. It is hard to reconcile *Harper's Weekly's* brutal ridicule of Horace Greeley during the presidential campaign of 1872 with Curtis' character and principles.

Hall, completely controlled not only the New York City administration but the Tammany governor of New York and a working majority of the state legislature.[2] Elated by their success in Manhattan, they were gleefully preparing extension of their very remunerative activities on a national scale. "Next year we shall be in Washington," Hall is reported to have asserted confidently. When the investigation into its intricate and widespread activities was completed, it was proved that the Tweed Ring had robbed the city of $200,000,000 by tax-dodging, blackmail, and extortion, by floating vast issues of fraudulent bonds, by selling favors and franchises, and by a multitude of other assorted swindles. Yet so deeply intrenched was it that when *Harper's Weekly*, joined later by *The New York Times,* began its exposure Tweed could coolly ask, "What are you going to do about it?"

For one thing, records of the city's expenditures were conveniently missing.

The opening attack in *Harper's Weekly* was mild by comparison with what followed. Editorially on October 29, 1870, it said:

> Tammany Hall, which absolutely controls the city by the most notoriously criminal means, and which, under popular forms, has annihilated popular government, justly excites the apprehension of all good citizens. Unless its power can be broken the most disastrous results and the most desperate civil convulsions are sure to come. Tammany Hall governs by terrorism and corruption. It relies upon cheating at the polls. And no free people can long tolerate such a system, when its character is exposed, as that of Tammany now is.

Later editorials described Tammany as "the rule of corruption by money and fear," and as a "plague spot in the center of the American system." *Harper's Weekly* pointed to its control of

[2] The Ring members were known by names reminiscent of those popularized by the comic strips of a later date. Tweed was known as "the Boss," Sweeny as "the Brains," Connolly as "Slippery Dick," and Hall as "O.K. Haul." It was Nast who invented the last alias.

A GROUP OF VULTURES WAITING FOR THE STORM TO "BLOW OVER."—"LET US *PREY*."

"Let Us Prey" was one of the most devastating Nast cartoons which *Harper's Weekly* loosed in its successful fight to demolish the Tweed Ring in New York City.

the state government and the city courts and to its avowed aim
of conducting its depredations on a national scale.

The editorial language of *Harper's Weekly* was strong and
grew stronger, but Nast's caricatures were ruthlessly destruc-
tive. Nast, the German-born cartoonist and illustrator, who
through his work in the magazines helped develop American
public opinion for more than a quarter of a century, had begun
his attack on Tammany in *Harper's Weekly* in 1869. Among
the most devastating of his later cartoons in the war on the
Ring were "Tweedledee and Sweedledum," which showed
Tweed and Sweeny dispensing funds to greedy henchmen and
setting aside their own generous take; "The Boss," which
showed the city flattened under a gigantic thumb; "The Only
Thing They Respect or Fear," which showed the four Ring
members cowering under four nooses dangling from a gibbet;
"Let Us Prey," which showed the four perched as waiting vultures on a mountainside while lightning flashed about them;
and "The Tammany Tiger Loose," in which Tweed, cast as
Nero looked happily on while a tiger in a Roman arena tore
into the prone figure of the republic.[3]

It was the cartoons that woke the Ring. "Let's stop them
damned pictures," J. Henry Harper reports Tweed as saying.
"I don't care so much what the papers write about me—my con-
stituents can't read; but, damn it, they can see pictures!"
Alarmed now, Tweed and his fellow statesmen tried threats, in-
timidation, and physical violence. All Harper books used as
texts in New York City schools were thrown out and texts published by the New York Printing Company, a Tammany-owned
business, were substituted. Tweed threatened to horsewhip
Nast, but did not when they met. Mayor Hall forbade the sale
of *Harper's Weekly* on the newsstands.

[3] Use of a tiger's head as the symbol for Tammany stemmed from the
picture on Americus No. 6, engine of the volunteer fire company Tweed had
helped organize as a young man. Nast himself invented and used in cartoons
the elephant as a symbol of the Republican party, and the donkey as the
Democrats' symbol.

By a clever trick the missing city records were obtained. Samuel Tilden infiltrated the office of the comptroller, placing there as an employee one of his adherents, William Copeland, who carefully transcribed the damning accounts. Another investigator, Matthew O'Rourke, a county bookkeeper, gathered in further proof of enormous frauds. The records were turned over to the *Times* for publication. Begging and pleading, Comptroller Connolly called on George Jones, proprietor of the newspaper. He offered Jones $5,000,000 not to publish the records. Jones refused. The records, when they appeared in July, 1871, told an almost incredible story. The Ring had employed devices of every kind in its gouging of the people. One of its happiest ventures, the records showed, was a courthouse being built in 1870. One plasterer on this job, according to the city's accounts, had received $2,870,464.06. During one month he had been paid $50,000 a day.

The Nast cartoons continued. " 'Twas Him" showed a group of the looters each pointing to one of the others when asked "Who Stole the People's Money?" "Shadows of Coming Events" prophesied the rioting that such misrule would cause. On July 12, 1871, the rioting broke out when Tammany-inspired ruffians, vowing vengeance on everything they disliked, especially on Nast, who was marching with the Seventh Regiment, and on *Harper's Weekly*, attacked marchers and onlookers in an Orangemen's parade. One hundred people were killed or wounded.

As the Ring had, in desperation, attempted to bribe Jones, it also approached Nast. An officer of the bank in which the Ring kept its funds offered him $200,000 to study art abroad. According to Albert Bigelow Paine, biographer of the cartoonist, Nast considered the matter a few moments, then asked if the Ring could not do better. The offer was immediately raised to half a million in gold if he would drop his attack on the Ring and leave the country. Nast said that, instead, he would remain where he was and bend his further efforts to placing the Ring members behind bars. The emissary left with the warning that he might first put himself in a coffin.

Though the Tweed-controlled papers, especially the *New York World*, continued to support the Ring, other newspapers and magazines which had dared not take the lead joined in the attack. The *Tribune* was first. Charles Nordhoff, managing editor of the *Evening Post,* which William Cullen Bryant owned and published, lost his job as the result of his onslaughts on the Ring. Charles A. Dana's *Sun* printed one or two damaging indictments but did little more. Among the magazines which allied themselves with *Harper's Weekly, The Nation,* edited by the militant E. L. Godkin, came out strongly for its distinctive solution to the problem. It advocated hanging. On September 2, 1871, *The Nation* said:

> . . . In our opinion Hall, Connolly, Tweed, Barnard, and all the class to which they belong . . . fear no penalty for their misdeeds except a violent death. They are indifferent to public opinion and have matters so arranged that the prison pen has no terrors for them, and a natural death they calculate upon. But the prospect of a violent death, which would suddenly stop their champagne, knock the satin sofas from under them, shut out the velvet carpets from their view, cause their fast horses to vanish into thin air, and launch them into the cold unknown would terrify them exceedingly; and such a death, we repeat, a large and growing body of respectable citizens think they ought to die—first and foremost in order to stop their thieving and rid the community of them, and secondly, to prevent an unwholesome influence on public and private morals of the spectacle of the peaceful close of their career in the enjoyment of their stealings.

Tammany was defeated in the elections of 1871, and the Ring was smashed. William Marcy Tweed was arrested, freed on a million-dollar bond supplied by his friend and Erie associate, Jay Gould. He served a short prison term, was rearrested, and escaped. He fled to Spain disguised as a seaman. Spanish officials identified him from a Nast cartoon, and Tweed died in

New York's Ludlow Street jail in 1878. Other members of the Ring fled into exile or died in jail, though Sweeny returned from France, made restitution to the city of $400,000 of what he had stolen, and was allowed to go free.

The circulation of *Harper's Weekly*, 160,000 in 1872, trebled as a result of the magazine's bold and successful fight against the Ring. Though it centered in a struggle against corrupt municipal administration, the drama received nationwide attention because of the fundamental issues of government involved. The whole country had an opportunity of watching a magazine match its force against a powerful enemy of the people and saw it prove its strength.

Chapter 9

EMERGENCE OF THE NATIONAL MAGAZINE

THE NEED for adequate communication of facts and ideas to all parts of the country at the same time was a lesson taught forcibly by the Civil War and emphasized by the sectional animosities and misunderstandings that persisted in the postwar years. Congress in the 1870's fully realized that the circulation of news, information, and intelligent discussion by reliable means was vitally necessary for the maintenance and strengthening of national unity.

The magazine could now be distributed nationally. Machinery for speedier distribution had been built up to meet war necessities. It was available now for the distribution of magazines as well as all other commodities. The magazine was a vehicle which could present simultaneously identical facts, uniformly treated, in every locality. Men and women, North, South, East, and West, could read and judge the same materials, instead of forming their beliefs and reaching their decisions on the basis of varied accounts published in different sections and often distorted by regional prejudice. Such at least, was the ideal possibility.

Realizing that in the magazine, which had already proved its effect on public opinion, the United States had a solid instrument for developing and reinforcing national sentiment, Congress passed legislation which established favorable mailing privileges for the periodical press. In a House debate on the subject Representative H. D. Money, who incidentally was a newspaper publisher, voiced the considerations that prompted the measure:

Mr. Speaker, the object of the government in establishing a postal service was for the dissemination of useful knowledge for the public good and to promote communication between its citizens in the several sections of the country. . . . The Post-Office Department, looked at in that light, may be considered as a great educator of people in all parts of the country. . . . That highest class of literature in which are ranked all monthly, bi-monthly, and quarterly publications, is excluded from the privileged rate, although they are in their very nature the highest educators that reach the people in that way. . . . Take all the monthlies of the country and I say if you examine the character of those monthlies you will find more than two-thirds of the monthlies of the country are not the mere vehicles of literature to the people, but are instructors in the highest sense of the term. (Congressional *Record,* January 23, 1879)

The postal act of March 3, 1879, which gave second-class mailing privileges to magazines "originated and published for the dissemination of information of a public character, or devoted to literature, the sciences, arts, or some special industry," was recognition of the stature which magazines were achieving in the years of accelerated industrial and economic growth in America that began with the Civil War and continued through the remainder of the nineteenth century. Of these years, Edward Atkinson, the economist, wrote in 1891 : "There has never been in the history of civilization a period, or a place, or a section of the earth in which science and invention have worked such progress or have created such opportunity for material welfare as in these United States in the period which has elapsed since the end of the Civil War." [1]

East and West coasts had been joined by rail when in 1869 tracks laid from the east by the Union Pacific were joined at Promontory Point near Ogden, Utah, to those laid from the west by the Central Pacific. Chicago was growing almost incredibly as the principal rail center of the Middle West. Pitts-

---

[1] From Arthur M. Schlesinger, *Political and Social Growth of the American People,* 3rd ed. (Copyright, 1941 by The Macmillan Company and used with their permission.) P. 42.

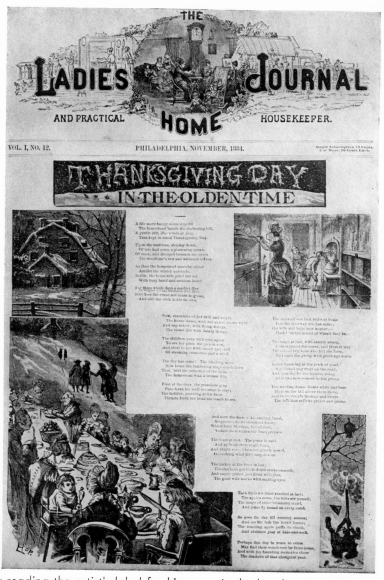

By reading the artist's label for his scene in the heading into the magazine's title, the public of 1883 changed Cyrus Curtis' *Ladies' Journal* into the *Ladies' Home Journal*.

burgh was rapidly becoming the great steel and iron center that it is today. Other cities were developing as manufacturing and distribution, given tremendous impetus by the war, were intensified to meet the demands of a population that grew from 31,000,000 in 1860 to 50,000,000 in 1880, to 76,000,000 in 1900. And it was a population increasingly urban and industrialized.

Less than 62,000 patents had been granted before 1865. The number during the remainder of the nineteenth century reached nearly 638,000. The value of manufactures in the United States trebled from 1860, when it was less than two billions of dollars, to 1880 when it was over five billions. By 1890 it had reached nine billions and the United States ranked as the first manufacturing nation in the world, its output exceeding that of Great Britain and Germany combined.

American engineering and production methods were speeding the vast and fundamental changes sweeping over the nation. Steel, oil, the application of steam to machinery, brought material progress, but in its wake new social and economic problems. This was the period of the Robber Barons and the Gilded Age, of new social patterns, of political corruption and economic conflict, as well as a period of material advance for the middle class that was growing in power. It was this class, made literate through public school education, that formed a new and wider audience of readers not reached by the rather staid monthly and quarterly magazines.

To reach this audience a whole new group of magazines sprang up: *McCall's*, 1870; *Popular Science*, 1872; *Woman's Home Companion*, 1873; *Leslie's Monthly*, 1876; *Farm Journal*, 1877; *Good Housekeeping*, 1885; *Cosmopolitan*, 1886; *Collier's*, 1888; *National Geographic*, 1888; *Capper's Farmer*, 1889; *Vogue*, 1892; *Outdoor Life*, 1898. All these (*Leslie's* is the present *American*) are still published.

From 1860 to 1900 the number of monthly magazines alone rose from 280 to over 1,800. "Never before," says Schlesinger, "had they [the magazines] reached so high a plane of general excellence, or represented so well the diversified interests of the public." Mott gives some 700 periodicals of all kinds for 1865; over 1,200 for 1870; more than 2,400 for 1880; and some 3,300 by 1885.

Improvements in printing, the roller press, the halftone engraving, the use of the linotype machine which Ottmar Mergenthaler perfected in 1885, and the increased use of advertising made lower magazine prices possible, thus insuring vastly larger circulations. *McClure's Magazine* appeared in May, 1893, at fifteen cents a copy, *Cosmopolitan* in July, at twelve and a half cents, and *Munsey's* in September, at ten cents. By 1898 there were some 750,000 regular magazine-reading families in the United States. By 1900 there were at least fifty well-known national magazines, a number of them with circulations of over a hundred thousand. There was one magazine with a circulation of a million. This was the *Ladies' Home Journal,* founded by Cyrus Curtis only seventeen years before.

The *Journal's* circulation accomplishment marked more than the unprecedented achievement of one magazine. It marked the beginning of new concepts in the publication and distribution of national magazines, with circulations running into the millions, that were to be characteristic of successful magazine publishing in the twentieth century. The change was largely brought about by one man, Cyrus H. K. Curtis, who "developed the magical possibilities of national advertising, and demonstrated more clearly than anyone else that you could lose millions of dollars on your circulation by selling at a low price yet make more millions out of your advertising, and build up such a mammoth enterprise you could pay unprecedented prices to contributors and thus command the market for writers and illustrators." [2] Curtis was the first to apply the intensive use of promotion to obtain a large circulation, and the first to weld the editorial force of magazines to the growing force of advertising.

[2] Frederick Lewis Allen, "American Magazines, 1741–1941," *Bulletin of the New York Public Library,* June, 1941.

Chapter 10

EDWARD BOK AND THE AMERICAN HOME

Cyrus H. K. Curtis, born in Portland, Maine, in 1850, evinced an early interest in magazines when as a thirteen-year-old schoolboy he commenced publication of *Young America*. Setting type himself and using an aged hand press which he purchased for two dollars and a half, he brought out his two-cent weekly for more than a year, selling advertising space in his magazine and doing job printing on the side. His schooling finished, Curtis became a dry-goods clerk in Portland and then went to Boston where in 1872, after several years' work as an advertising solicitor for obscure papers, he and another young man founded *The People's Ledger*. Curtis moved to Philadelphia and in 1879 began publication of *The Tribune and Farmer*, a four-page weekly with a subscription rate of fifty cents a year.

The *Ladies' Home Journal* originated from a department of *The Tribune and Farmer* which was devoted to subjects of interest to women. Noting the popularity of this department, which was written by his wife, the former Louisa Knapp, he decided to publish it as a separate monthly supplement to his magazine. The first issue of the *Ladies' Journal*, the magazine's original title, consisting of eight pages of domestic articles, appeared in December, 1883. It contained an illustrated serial, articles on flower culture, fashion notes, advice on the care of children, and articles on cooking, needlework, and handicrafts —substantially the same material which, expanded and improved, characterizes the *Ladies' Home Journal* today.

The supplement, under the editorship of Mrs. Curtis, was immediately successful. While it took five years for *The Trib-*

une and Farmer to reach a circulation of 48,000, the *Ladies'
Home Journal,* as the new magazine came to be called, had
25,000 subscribers by the end of its first year.[1] Curtis thereupon
relinquished his interest in *The Tribune and Farmer* and devoted
all his attention to the new magazine.

At this point Curtis put into action some of the methods by
which his success and the success of mass magazines in general
were attained. Seeking well-known contributors for the *Journal,* he got Louisa M. Alcott, though it was hard for a comparatively unknown publisher to obtain writers already tied to
other magazines. His success with Miss Alcott attracted other
popular authors. He advertised the new magazine extensively;
F. Wayland Ayer of N. W. Ayer & Sons extended him liberal
credit for this purpose and obtained other credit for him. Curtis
allowed club rates for women banding together to subscribe to
the magazine. Within six months the circulation of the *Ladies'
Home Journal* reached 50,000. In another six months it reached
100,000, equaling and even surpassing the circulation of many
of the well-known established magazines of the period. Curtis
doubled the size of his magazine, raised his advertising rates,
and circulation climbed to 700,000. In 1889 he raised the subscription price again, this time to one dollar a year, deliberately
losing thousands of subscribers in order to stabilize circulation
and consolidate his gains. He continued to pour money into
advertising, spending more than half a million dollars in the
first five years of the *Journal's* existence.

In 1889 Curtis hired as editor of the *Journal* Edward Bok,
an employee of Charles Scribner's Sons in New York, whose
syndicated literary letter he had seen and admired in the *Philadelphia Times.* Bok, who had been brought to this country
from Holland as a child, was young, ambitious, didactic, and

[1] The logotype of the first *Journal* had carried a fireside scene labeled
"home" between the words "Ladies'" and "Journal." Thus the public began
to call the new monthly the *"Ladies' Home Journal"* and the title was
adopted.

self-assured. For the next thirty years the *Ladies' Home Journal* was Edward Bok, backed in every one of his varied and often daring ventures for the magazine by his shrewd employer. *Godey's Lady's Book,* though it continued to be published in Philadelphia until 1892, had declined after the death of Sarah Josepha Hale in 1879. *Peterson's Magazine,* also in Philadelphia, was still going strong, but the *Ladies' Home Journal* was beginning to supplant both these earlier women's magazines when Edward Bok—with fanfare and wide publicity which spotlighted him as the youngest and highest-paid magazine editor of the time, and which made the most of the loud astonishment that a man should become the guiding light of a woman's magazine—took over its editorial direction.

The same sixteen-page issue of January, 1889, which announced the rise in price from fifty cents to one dollar a year, carried a signed announcement by Cyrus Curtis offering a prize of $500 to the person sending in the largest number of subscriptions by July 1. There were second and third prizes of $400 and $300. There was also a plenitude of advertisements for organs, watches, corsets—many kinds of them—hair curlers, self-wringing mops, jewelry, ornamental hairpins, linen, books, dolls, tools, and many other products, mostly for household use. It was "Rubifoam for the Teeth" in one dentifrice advertisement. Another advertisement read:

1,000 Gentlemen Want You

to take an interest in their well-fare and comfort. You cannot commence better than by urging them to shampoo regularly with Packer's Tar Soap, a remarkable remedy for, and preventive of, Dandruff and Baldness.

A half-page advertisement in the March, 1889, issue, its lead lines in large type, read:

Braided Wire Bustles Have Come to Stay
For Women Understand that they Cannot Afford
to Let Them Go

If a woman has too large hips, the Bustle relieves them of their protuberance; if she have no hips at all apparently, the Bustle supplies the lack; if she have too large an abdomen, the Bustle gives her symmetry, if she be too tall and thin, the Bustle helps her, if she be too short and broad, the Bustle helps her none the less. Of course, there are women so divinely moulded, so exquisitely symmetrical, that they do not need it and may not wear it; but there is only one in a thousand so perfectly proportioned, and the other nine hundred and ninety-nine will still avail themselves of its usefulness.

Edward Bok made his first appearance in the *Ladies' Home Journal* in the issue of September, 1889, with his syndicated column "Literary Leaves." Part of this gossip read:

It is estimated by reliable judges that one out of every thirty novels printed in this country pays the author for his trouble. This will not be encouraging to those who are writing novels, but the statistics are authoritative. . . .

The family of General Grant have thus far received $90,000 from the sale of the General's "Memoirs."

Mark Twain's new book will be out in December. It is called "A Yankee at the Court of King Arthur," and is said to be a satire on the English nobility.

Boston will again be the residence of Mr. W. D. Howells. His brief stay in New York, it is said, did not please him.

Robert Louis Stevenson will not return to America for fully six months yet, unless he changes his mind, which is not an infrequent thing with him. At present the novelist is in Samoa.

Jean Ingelow's health is so precarious as to prevent her from doing any literary work of moment.

The widow of E. P. Roe has come to New York to reside.

A Bok article on "Forgotten Graves of Famous Authors" appeared in October; one on "Gladstone's Love for Reading and Bismarck's Literary Tastes," in December. Bok's accession was announced and his name appeared in the *Journal* masthead as editor in the issue of January, 1890; Mrs. Louisa

Knapp Curtis, pleading that domestic duties no longer permitted her to give full services to the magazine, was to remain on the staff. A characteristic Bok innovation came in this number. Bok, undeterred by modesty or tradition, believed both in making himself as editor well known, in contrast to the anonymity of most magazine editors at the time, and in establishing the closest possible relationship between the editor and his readers. "The method of editorial expression in the magazines of 1889," he wrote years later, "was distinctly vague and prohibitively impersonal. The public knew the name of scarcely a single editor of a magazine; there was no personality that stood out in the mind. . . . He felt that the time had come . . . for the editor of some magazine to project his personality through the printed page." [2]

To stimulate reader response Bok, immediately on assuming the *Journal* editorship, turned to what is now called the "survey technique," offering a series of prizes for the best answers to questions he put to his readers. What in the magazine did they like least? Why? What did they like best? Why? What new features would they like to see started? Thousands of answers were returned, and the editor acted on the reader advice thus obtained. Bok had, he says, "divined the fact that in thousands of cases the American mother was not the confidante of her daughter, and reasoned if any inviting human personality could be created on the printed page that would supply this lamentable lack of family life, girls would flock to such a figure." Implementing this belief he wrote under the pseudonym of "Ruth Ashmore" and printed in the January, 1889, issue of the *Ladies' Home Journal* the first of his "Side Talks to Girls." In it he advised girls to "learn to say no. There is in that little word much that will protect you from evil tongues." He circumspectly warned his young readers not to give their photographs to every Tom, Dick, and Harry. In February, "Ruth Ashmore"

[2] Edward Bok, *The Americanization of Edward Bok* (New York: Charles Scribner's Sons, 1923), p. 162.

wrote about "The Girl Who Hints," the wearing of jewelry, neatness in dress, and when dancing is wrong. "It's all very well to say that there is no harm in dancing. There isn't. But there is harm in having about you, a sweet, pure girl, kept as much as possible from the wickedness of the world, the arm of a man who may be a profligate, and not possess the first instinct of a gentleman."

Letters asking advice and describing problems of the feminine heart began to pour in. "Ruth Ashmore" became a woman writer to whom Bok turned over what rapidly became one of the most popular features of the *Journal*, and he went on to develop other features that would cause readers to write in to the editor. Determined to make his magazine an agency for service to American women, he urged his readers to make it a clearing house for information of all kinds. He used many devices to stimulate personal contact between the magazine and its audience. To many, the twenty-six-year-old Bok seemed brash. There was jeering as well as praise. He encouraged both, for both meant attention to him and his magazine.

Bok was derided for some of his novel undertakings. As late as 1916 Algernon Tassin [3] wrote that it seemed Bok's intention to place the two hemispheres on a family basis by introducing everybody in the world to everybody else. No sooner had "Unknown Wives of Well-Known Men" run its course than along came "Unknown Husbands" or "Famous Daughters of Famous Men." But Tassin also pointed out that the editors of the new popular magazines and of some of the conservative older magazines were quick to imitate Bok, seeking to emerge from their traditional editorial anonymity into places in the limelight.

By 1893 the *Ladies' Home Journal* was a magazine of thirty-four pages with a differently illustrated cover each month, new features, many illustrations. It was running William Dean

---

[3] See his *The Magazine in America* (New York: Dodd, Mead & Co., 1916), p. 354. *Cf.* John E. Drewry, *Some Magazines and Their Makers* (Boston: The Stratford Co., 1924).

Howells' *The Coast of Bohemia* as a serial and Mamie Dickens' *My Father As I Knew Him,* in addition to all the domestic departments and other literary offerings of the Laura Jean Libbey type. Ella Wheeler Wilcox was in almost every 1893 issue. Mrs. Lyman Abbott was contributing "Just Among Ourselves," and "Clever Daughters of Clever Men" was appearing month after month. Pages of sheet music were another new feature. In April, 1893, there were six pages of the "Magnolia Blossom Waltzes" by Reginald de Koven. "The Manhattan Beach March" by John Philip Sousa was in the Christmas issue; so was "A Pioneer Christmas" by Hamlin Garland. "Name" writers were usual in the *Journal* by this time. Bok in his "At Home With the Editor" columns was writing on such subjects as women in business. He was against it:

> The atmosphere of commercial life has never been conducive to the best interests of women engaged in it. The number of women in business who lose their gentleness and womanliness is far greater than those who retain what, after all, are woman's best and chief qualities. To be in an office where there are only men has never yet done a single girl any good; and it has done harm to thousands. . . . I know whereof I speak, and I deal not in generalities.

Many of Bok's readers were office workers by this time, but even they must have approved Bok's stand. It was characteristic of the 1890's to place women on a pedestal. Women themselves did all they could to encourage the flattery. In the same 1893 issue "Ruth Ashmore" wrote "My Sweetheart and I." Despite the saccharinity with which it was written, her advice was practical and probably palatable. The gist of it was—hang on to him.

Five years later, with the magazine marking its fifteenth year of publication, the *Ladies' Home Journal* was forty-eight pages instead of the original eight. It was printed on "slick" paper, profusely illustrated. Its circulation, 440,000 when Bok assumed the editorship, was now 850,000. In an editorial Bok wrote proudly, "Wherever the mail goes, the *Journal* goes. . . .

The *Journal* crosses every sea and ocean." It was being circulated to fifty-nine of the sixty-five civilized nations of the globe. In the same editorial Bok wrote:

> The fact must never be forgotten that no magazine published in the United States could give what it is giving to the reader each month if it were not for the revenue which the advertiser brings the magazine. It is the growth of advertising in this country which, more than any other single element, has brought the American magazine to its present enviable position in points of literary, illustrative, and mechanical excellence. The American advertiser has made the superior American magazine of today possible.

Bok could honestly describe the American magazine as having achieved literary and illustrative excellence. His contributors included Kipling, Howells, Mark Twain, Conan Doyle, Sarah Orne Jewett, John Kendrick Bangs, Kate Douglas Wiggin, Joel Chandler Harris, Jerome K. Jerome, Eugene Field, James Whitcomb Riley, and others of the best writers of the day. He had published work by Grover Cleveland and Benjamin Harrison, and was later to publish William Howard Taft and both Theodore and Franklin D. Roosevelt.

As illustrators the *Journal* had Edwin Abbey, Howard Pyle, Charles Dana Gibson, Will Low, W. T. Smedley, and W. L. Taylor. In the late 1890's it was running full pages of photographs which made good picture stories even by present-day standards. Typical picture stories showed the home and life of Mary Anderson, then living in England; Lew Wallace, the author of *Ben Hur*, writing at his home in Indiana; Joe Jefferson, the actor who achieved his greatest fame in the role of Rip Van Winkle, playing the amateur painter at his home in Buzzard's Bay. Bok could claim to be one of those editors who realized a picture can sometimes tell more than pages of print.[4]

---

[4] Bok's ideas on the use of pictures in magazines were decidedly modern. In the November, 1898, editorial which he headed briskly "Fifteen Years of Mistakes," he wrote: "After the editorial part, the picture side of a magazine naturally always receives the most thought. The *Journal's* pictorial aim is

At the same time the *Journal* stressed in every issue the domestic concerns of particular interest to its women readers, and Bok published all the true-life story material he could obtain. Another series was "Clever Daughters of Clever Men." He got Mrs. Henry Ward Beecher to write "Mr. Beecher As I Knew Him," and had Dwight L. Moody conduct "Mr. Moody's Bible Class" in the *Journal*. He published one entire issue written by "Famous Daughters of Famous Men." In it were contributions by the daughters of Dickens, Hawthorne, Harrison, Greeley, Thackeray, Howells, Gladstone, and Jefferson Davis.

By 1898 Curtis and the energetic, confident, crusading Bok had built a magazine with a large and loyal audience which felt itself closely connected to the editor and his paper. The *Ladies' Home Journal* had become known as "the monthly Bible of the American home." "And," said Mark Sullivan in *Our Times,* "there was a measure of allegorical truth in what was sometimes jeeringly spoken."

Edward Bok was determined not only to make the *Ladies' Home Journal* a magazine which provided intimate and personal service to its readers, but also to bring about changes for the better in American home life. He intended to improve standards in everything that pertained to the home, and he went about realizing his intentions in a direct and practical manner. At the same time that he was advising women about affairs of the heart, telling them how to dress, how to conduct themselves, how to feed their families, even how to bring up their children, he strove to effect changes in home architecture and in home decoration. He employed physicians and nurses to write on health long before this practice was adopted by the

---

to give its readers not only good pictures, so far as their art value is concerned, but interesting pictures from the standpoint of composition. The modern tendency is to illustrate almost everything. . . . But the danger has been to overdo illustrating—to push it into disrepute. Pictures are valuable only where they illustrate something or tell something. . . . A picture must tell something, it must, if possible, tell a story apart from what it seeks to illustrate."

newspapers. Their duties included both the writing of material for publication and the answering of letters from readers provoked by their articles. He employed other experts, experts on cooking, nursing, beauty care, household management.

In 1895 he set out to wean American taste away from the ornate in home construction and furnishing and to direct it toward the simpler, more attractive, and more practical. He began publication of plans for a series of houses that could be built for from $1,500 to $5,000. Complete scale plans and specifications, together with estimates from builders, were offered at five dollars a set. *Ladies' Home Journal* houses began to go up in all parts of the country. Building promoters built whole suburban communities according to *Journal* plans. Bok, who believed always in the concrete and visual, published pictures of the completed houses, offering prizes for the best interior pictures of homes built on *Journal* specifications. The Victorian parlors were left out of these plans. Two windows were placed in the maids' rooms. Kitchens were made more compact, and built-in cupboards were substituted for pantries. Cupolas, balconies, gingerbread decorations, were discarded. Other practical and aesthetic improvements were made. Architects, among them Stanford White, acknowledged leader of the profession, opposed Bok's plans at first, but later White said: "I firmly believe that Edward Bok has more completely influenced American domestic architecture for the better than any man in this generation." Bok quoted the admission proudly in his autobiography.

The *Ladies' Home Journal* then turned its attention inside the house. It ran pictures of home interiors in every issue, labeling this living room, dining room, bedroom, as either good or bad. A photographic series run all through 1898 was the "Inside of One Hundred Homes." A similar series, "Outside of One Hundred Homes," ran in 1899. Bok printed pictures of furniture. Captions read, "This chair is ugly" or "This table is beautiful." These comparisons of the ugly and the aesthetically pleasing covered tables, beds, curtains, carpets, and other household furniture. The very pictures on the wall were changed by *Journal* teachings. Bok published pictures by Abbey, Pyle, Gibson, and others, and the *Journal* conducted art exhibitions of 250 originals in full color. Those which readers chose as their ten favorites were then sold in portfolios for use in their homes. Two hundred thousand pictures were thus introduced into American homes. "For certain elevations in the taste of houses and housefurnishings," said Mark Sullivan, "he is more to be thanked than any other one man."

Bok went on to exert the continually growing influence of the *Ladies' Home Journal* far beyond the domestic sphere, though he started in its immediate neighborhood. He began a campaign to clean up and beautify American communities. He showed "how much can be done with little" through pictures of back yards before and after planting of flowers and shrubbery. In a department called "Beautiful America" he printed pictures of localities cluttered with disfiguring billboards and advertising; then pictures of the same places with the objectionable signs removed. Bok succeeded in getting rid of a huge billboard erected at Niagara Falls and, by the mere threat of publication, prevented erection of another sign, described as "the largest advertisement in the world," on the rim of the Grand Canyon. Lynn, Massachusetts; Trenton, New Jersey; and Memphis, Tennessee, were featured in that order as "dirty cities," and the *Journal* published photographs to uphold the accuracy of its choice. Municipal authorities threatened suit, and local newspapers were virulent in their abuse of Bok and his magazine, but the cities were cleaned up, and other cities, fearing like publicity, swept and scoured.

In 1892 the *Ladies' Home Journal* announced that it would no longer accept advertisements for patent medicines. It was the first magazine to refuse advertising of this type, though within the next two years seven other newspapers and periodicals did likewise. In 1904 and 1905 Bok attacked the entire

patent-medicine industry with every weapon at his command.
In a series of exposures he attacked the evils of the industry
from all angles. Bok tells the story graphically in his autobiography:

> The Editor got the Women's Christian Temperance Union
> into action against the periodicals for publishing advertisements
> of medicines containing as high as forty per cent alcohol. He
> showed that the most confidential letters written by women
> with private ailments were opened by young clerks of both
> sexes, laughed at and gossiped over, and that afterward their
> names and addresses, which they had been told were held in the
> strictest confidence, were sold to other lines of business for five
> cents each. He held the religious press up to the scorn of church
> members for accepting advertisements which the publishers
> knew and which he proved to be not only fraudulent, but actually
> harmful. He called the United States Post Office authorities to
> account for accepting and distributing obscene circular matter.[5]

Bok reprinted in the *Journal* a patent-medicine advertisement which urged ailing women to write for advice to a woman
represented as working in her laboratory to lessen their suffering. Next to the advertisement Bok ran a photograph of this
woman's gravestone which showed that she had died some
twenty years before. Bok likewise reproduced the American and
English labels for a medicine used for quieting fretful infants.
They were identical except that the English label, acceding to
the provisions of the English Pharmacy Act, read: "This preparation, containing, among other valuable ingredients, a small
amount of morphine, is, in accordance with the Pharmacy Act,
hereby labelled 'poison.'" The American manufacturers of the
remedy thereafter cooperated by publishing their formula.

The *Journal* then published a list of twenty-two patent medicines and told what each contained. An expert's mistake back-
fired in the case of one and The Curtis Publishing Company lost
a suit brought by its manufacturer, but Bok and the *Journal*
kept on arousing public opinion against a vicious social abuse.

[5] Bok, *The Americanization of Edward Bok,* pp. 340–41.

He hired Mark Sullivan, recently graduated from Harvard Law School, who unearthed and published in the *Journal* more damning evidence of abuses wrought by patent-medicine companies. The *Journal* had kept up the fight singlehandedly for two years when *Collier's Weekly* joined in. Other periodicals and various groups broke into the conflict. An exhibition of adulterated canned and bottled foods was shown at the St. Louis Exposition in 1904. In 1905 President Theodore Roosevelt recommended to Congress passage of an act regulating interstate commerce in misbranded and adulterated foods, drinks, and drugs. Despite the bitter organized opposition of Bok's antagonists, the Food and Drug Act was passed in 1906.

Chapter 11

FURTHER ACCOMPLISHMENTS OF THE WOMEN'S MAGAZINES

Edward Bok was not always successful in the many crusades which his energy and reformer's zeal led him to undertake in the *Ladies' Home Journal*. Ironically he failed where the object of his attack was a matter of purely feminine concern, and succeeded where it was of national importance.

Bok preached dignity and modesty in women's dress. In 1909 and 1910 he undertook to demolish Paris as the dictator of women's fashions, a state of affairs in dressmaking which he believed unpatriotic, economically unsound, and sometimes basically fraudulent. The *Journal* employed experts to design frocks and hats, inaugurated contests, and in every issue banged away with the slogan "American Fashions for American Women." Bok had designers visit the Metropolitan Museum of Art in New York. The designs they worked out were judged by a board of women experts in New York, then published in the *Journal*. It was proved that many Paris models which would have been rejected by European women of taste were concocted for the "barbaric" American trade. It was also proved that Paris labels made in this country were attached to goods of American manufacture. The *Journal's* campaign failed completely. Thanks to the free advertising, more Paris models were sold than previously, and the trade in spurious labels increased.

Bok was likewise defeated when, on humanitarian grounds, he urged women not to wear the aigrettes then considered fashionable millinery adornments. The *Journal* printed photographs of the killing of the mother birds to obtain the plumes, and pictured the bird's starving young. The articles and pictures drew the attention of women who had not before realized the need of aigrettes for their hats. Sales of the feathers more than quadrupled before the *Ladies' Home Journal* dropped the campaign.

In a more important and more spectacular undertaking, Bok and the *Journal* accomplished a great social and physical gain for the American people. Lyman Abbott, successor to Henry Ward Beecher both as minister of the Plymouth Congregational Church in Brooklyn and as editor of *The Outlook*, a magazine which had started as *The Christian Union,* convinced Bok that he should take up the fight against venereal disease. More cautious friends advised against such a radical and dangerous attempt. Cyrus Curtis told Bok to go ahead if he thought he was right. Bok published an editorial on venereal disease in 1906. Immediately the protests began to arrive at the *Journal* offices. Thousands of subscriptions were stopped. Advertisers notified Curtis that they would cancel their advertising. Outraged *Journal* readers refused to admit the offending magazine to their homes, and some of the editor's own friends tore the wicked pages from the *Journal* before allowing it to be seen by their families. Despite losing about 75,000 subscribers, the *Journal* persisted. Finally such writers and public figures as Jane Addams, Cardinal Gibbons, Henry Van Dyke, President Eliot of Harvard, and the Bishop of London came to the aid of the indomitable Bok. They risked public indignation and wrote *Journal* articles supporting the magazine's position.

The *Journal* published article after article. A full-page editorial declared that seventy of every one hundred special surgical operations on women were directly or indirectly necessitated by venereal disease; and that sixty of every one hundred babies blinded soon after birth lost their sight from the same cause. Piously shocked men added their protests to those of the horrified women. The subject was not one to be talked of. If talked of at all, it was a subject for males only. But Bok insisted "that the time had come when women should learn the truth, and that, so far as it lay in his power, he intended to see that they did know."

Though completely open discussion of venereal disease did not become common for perhaps another twenty-five years, the *Ladies' Home Journal* made the facts known, made a forbidden topic a possible subject of open and sensible discussion in the press, in books, in schools and colleges.

It was in 1935, fifteen years after the resignation of Edward Bok and following a succession of short-term incumbents, that Bruce and Beatrice Blackmar Gould, both Iowa-born, were made co-editors of the *Ladies' Home Journal*. Under their continuing editorship the *Journal* was restored to the pre-eminence among women's magazines which it had held under Bok. The *Ladies' Home Journal* in 1956 has the largest circulation of any women's magazine and one of the largest newsstand circulations of any general American magazine. More than five million women buy the magazine every month.

It was the Goulds' belief when they took over the *Journal* editorship "that the working intelligence of the average American woman was far greater than generally believed." It was the new editors' aim "to bring our readers not only the most accurate and honest information possible in the traditional areas; health, nutrition, education and the moral guidance of children; community, social, and cultural activities . . . but also to widen the boundaries of her traditional areas of interest."

Because the *Ladies' Home Journal* does not consider itself merely a woman's service magazine, it carries articles on politics, foreign affairs, medicine, education, and social welfare. In 1947 it established a forceful "Public Affairs Department." The well-known "How America Lives" series, articles on the lives and homes of "typical" American families, was started in February, 1940, and planned to run for a year. The series is still running, though the title is now "How Young America

Lives." Typical of the magazine's contents are the *Journal*'s more intimate offerings: "Tell Me Doctor," "Dr. Spock's Talks to Mother," "Can This Marriage Be Saved?" and other departments of peculiarly feminine appeal.

Perhaps the most outstanding feature of the modern *Ladies' Home Journal* is its consistent performance in publishing best-seller fiction. At a time when fiction has disappeared from many magazines and been relegated to a subordinate position in others, when its quality in many of the larger magazines is very poor, the *Ladies' Home Journal* year after year publishes novels that later attain wide popularity in book form. It does as well with its biographies and autobiographies of prominent women—entertainers or royalty, aristocracy at the very least, seeming the preferred subjects. One reason is that the *Journal* can afford to buy such manuscripts. Another has to be shrewd editorial selection.

Examination of the parts cannot fully explain the *Journal*'s pre-eminence among women's magazines. It seems more sophisticated and more intimate, at once more feminine and feminist than its peers. It is persuasive. It stimulates pleasurably by describing and picturing fashions and household decor that are ordinarily beyond the means of most of its readers. Calling itself "The Magazine Women Believe In," and coyly, insistently, complacently warning the world that it must "Never Underestimate the Power of a Woman," the magazine itself probably cannot define its achievement or fully describe its operation. A statement of editorial philosophy released a few years ago reads in part: "Primarily it is what goes into the editorial pages of a magazine that makes the magazine live and breathe and sing . . . A magazine like ours is . . . a moral force. It must have integrity and respect for American principles as well as entertainment and utility value. No formula will help us, no balancing of pictures or text, long articles or short, reprints or new. There is no possibility of laying down a pattern and then following through."

All magazines of this type, conceived and operated as money-making businesses, were built on the idea of service to women and to the home. These women's magazines were the first to achieve the vast circulations characteristic of the mass magazine. Through their crusades and campaigns they gave women, who had not yet attained political franchise, an opportunity to express their opinions and the gratification of seeing their opinions acted upon. Paradoxically, though they were first directed to women as housewives and homemakers, their development accompanied the emergence of women from the confines of the domestic sphere into the world of jobs, community activities, and politics; in fact, the magazines were largely instrumental in forwarding it. Bok, as reactionary in some directions as he was modern in others, protested against the entrance of women into what he considered masculine affairs, but his magazine and other women's periodicals did more perhaps to make it possible and even inevitable than any other single factor. They applied a social force and achieved a fundamental social change on which some of them at least had not counted.

Collier's, as has been indicated, fought valiantly beside the *Journal* in the battle for pure food and drug legislation. Dr. H. W. Wiley, chief chemist of the United States Department of Agriculture, was so vigorous a proponent of this legislation that the measures were for a time known as the "Wiley Laws." Shortly afterward Dr. Wiley became the head of the famed Good Housekeeping Bureau.

Good Housekeeping had been founded in Holyoke, Massachusetts, in 1885 by Clark W. Bryan, who described it as "conducted in the interests of the higher life of the household," designed "to produce or perpetuate perfection, or as near unto perfection, as may be obtained in the household." In 1901, a year after the magazine was purchased by the Phelps Publishing Company, the Good Housekeeping Institute was inaugurated as an editorial department which could provide detailed and accurate information on home economics subjects. It developed laboratories and kitchens for the testing of household appliances, textiles, home cleansing agents, and similar consumer products. In its more than fifty years of activity the Good Housekeeping Institute has become justly one of the most famous operations of its kind in the world.

In 1912, shortly after *Good Housekeeping* had been moved to New York as the property of Hearst Magazines, Inc., the Good Housekeeping Bureau was instituted with Dr. Wiley as its director. Almost immediately it began the investigation of food and drug products, of pharmaceuticals and cosmetics, which, on a much larger scale, it carries on today. Both the Good Housekeeping Institute and the Good Housekeeping Bureau have accomplished much in raising standards and improving products for the home, as well as in providing their readers with home information and ideas in the best traditions of the women's service magazine. Fashions, beauty advice, and baby and child care were added at various times to *Good Housekeeping* as editorial departments backed by Institute or Bureau findings or by work in specially devised clinics and centers for study of the problems. A building forum, devoted to home and community planning, was established in 1945.

The *Woman's Home Companion* was founded ten years before *Ladies' Home Journal,* beginning life in Cleveland as the *Home Companion,* changing its name to the *Ladies' Home Companion* in 1866, and adopting its present title in 1897. Developing in much the same manner as *Good Housekeeping* and the *Ladies' Home Journal*—that is, as a service magazine for women—it was long edited (1911–1940) by the well-known Gertrude Battles Lane. It was she who, decrying "the cat in the cracker barrel," crusaded in her magazine for packaged groceries, created the *Companion*'s Better Babies Bureau, and in 1935 set up a reader-editor service through which readers were asked periodically for editorial service. During her long editorship the circulation of this Crowell-Collier magazine rose from 727,000 to more than 3,500,000.

The *Companion* now divides its monthly offering into articles, public affairs, fiction, help for love and marriage, features, home service center, fashions, beauty and grooming, teens, children, homemaking, and workshop. This run-down of the table of contents largely describes the attempt at editorial coverage of all the women's magazines today. Any difference there is lies in the phrasing of titles, the selection of diversified subjects for a given isue, and in the physical presentation of the material. From 1953 through 1955 the following were among the names appearing either as writers or as subjects of articles in *Woman's Home Companion*: Jack Benny, Pearl Buck, Queen Elizabeth, Mrs. Norman Vincent Peale, Thomas Costain, Marlene Dietrich, Mamie Eisenhower, Daphne du Maurier, the Duchess of Windsor, Joan Crawford, Arnold Toynbee, Alfred H. Kinsey, and Lloyd Douglas. They typify the writers and the types of people written about not only in the *Companion* but in all the mass women's magazines.

McCall's Magazine assumed that name in 1897. In the 1870's and 1880's it had been *The Queen,* and in the early 1890's, *The Queen of Fashion,* indicating that *McCall's* was originally a fashion journal. It still emphasizes fashions but also includes all the service departments characteristic of its sister magazines: beauty, children, home, food, feature articles. It does more. In May, 1954, *McCall's* announced major changes in editorial policy. Prompted perhaps by the success of the so-called "shelter magazines" like *Better Homes and Gardens,* it announced that it would no longer look upon itself simply as a woman's service magazine, but that it would devote itself to the American woman and her family, becoming a publication for the entire household. Advertisements at the time stated that the new *McCall's* melody would be "togetherness." In appearance and content *McCall's* still looks very much a woman's magazine.

Usually there is an article on sex, another on marriage, and the life story of a motion picture or television actress or of some woman in public life. Often there is a complete novel. Always there are fashions, recipes, housekeeping hints. The names that appear and reappear are much the same as those that appear in the other women's magazines. Eleanor Roosevelt, once a *Ladies' Home Journal* regular, now writes monthly in *McCall's*. Other writers include Alfred H. Kinsey, Mary Pickford, Dr. Norman Vincent Peale, Taylor Caldwell, Edward R. Murrow, Anthony J. Drexel Biddle, Audrey Hepburn, the Duchess of Windsor.

McCall's circulation, now over four and a half million, holds third place among all United States magazines; the standing reads *Life, Ladies' Home Journal, McCall's.* Twelve million readers are claimed for the publication.[1] The McCall Corporation, which dropped *Bluebook* in 1956, publishes *Redbook* and conducts a gigantic contract printing business. Among other magazines, it prints the large domestic editions of *The Reader's Digest, U. S. News,* and *Nation's Business.*

Through their general contents, but especially through the campaigns and crusades they have sponsored, these women's magazines of large circulation have influenced the homes and communities of the nation, and influenced them generally for the better. In February, 1949, for example, *McCall's* ran the first of four full-length articles and five smaller items on its "Yardville Plan." This was a plan by which city dwellers in congested urban areas would bring themselves some of the pleasure and recreation of the suburbs and open country by merging their two-by-four back yards into communal open spaces of grass, trees, and flowers. It was a plan for civic improvement which took hold immediately. Some 355 cities in the United States wrote in asking for plans and suggestions. Civic groups adopted the project wholeheartedly. Inquiries came from Hawaii and Puerto Rico, from eleven cities in Canada, and from two in England. Children took up the plan and pushed it. Minneapolis, Schenectady, Detroit, Chicago,

[1] Advertisement in *Printers' Ink,* July 15, 1955.

Atlanta, Seattle, Washington, Jacksonville, Indianapolis, Denver, Wilmington, and Fresno were among the American cities participating in this plan for better city living, sponsored and promoted by *McCall's*.

Similarly, the articles and fiction in these magazines have affected the minds and imagination of millions of individual readers. Fiction has always served purposes other than diversion, and the women's magazines, since their inception and publication on a large scale to huge circulations, have published fiction of many kinds, some of it excellent.

It would be hard for any literate individual to decide which of his beliefs, opinions, sentiments, and ideas, and even how much of his general knowledge, have been formed or affected by the fiction he has read. If the analysis were possible, many individuals would find that fiction has provided much of their basic knowledge of people and some of their ethics and has generally affected their approach to human relationships. Very likely, the proportion would be higher among the educated, the imaginative, and the sensitive than among the ignorant and uninterested.

Undoubtedly much of the fiction in the women's magazines, like much mass-magazine fiction in general, has made a specious sentimental appeal, provided an illusory never-never land of incredible slickness and glamour, inhabited only by impossibly beautiful girls and incredibly handsome men. Much other women's-magazine fiction has been the noteworthy work of writers ranking high among the novelists and short story writers of the day. Both *McCall's* and the *Ladies' Home Journal* feature a complete novel in one issue. The *Woman's Home Companion* under Gertrude Battles Lane developed and printed the work of such popular women writers as Dorothy Canfield Fisher, Zona Gale, Willa Cather, and Edna Ferber. Edith Wharton, Mrs. Humphrey Ward, and Kate Douglas Wiggin appeared in the *Ladies' Home Journal*. Well-known names are a characteristic of the fiction of women's magazines. At various times they have included Anne Douglas Sedgwick, Corra Harris, Grace Richmond, Hamlin Garland, Ernest Thompson Seton, Mary Johnston, S. Weir Mitchell, Sarah Orne Jewett, Joseph Lincoln, Bret Harte, Zane Grey, Booth Tarkington, William Dean Howells, Robert Hichens, J. P. Marquand, Franz Werfel, Lord Dunsany, Mignon G. Eberhart, and I. A. R. Wylie. The list could be made unnecessarily long by the addition of many other famous names.

In all the women's magazines autobiographical and biographical materials, usually of the inspirational type, have capitalized on the perennial human interest in other people. The thoughts and ideas of famous people—presidents and ex-presidents, actors, singers, social workers, churchmen, and generals—have been published in articles which they have signed and sometimes written.

The basic subject of most of the editorials is sex in domesticated guise—how to get, train, and keep a husband; why this marriage failed and this one succeeded; how to bring up your children; what to ask the doctor; and all the rest. The basic approach is that of flattery. The great success of women's magazines in this country seems to have been due in large part to the acumen of publishers and editors in realizing that they can more profitably address women as women rather than women as people. Men like Edward Bok were shrewd enough to realize that the mass of women applaud rather than resent the distinction, and his successors have wisely followed the same policy.

Women's magazines are likewise a valuable advertising medium. Editorial and advertising pages naturally complement each other. Love is the subject of a romantic short story; the accessories of love are for sale in the advertising pages. A glamorous heroine walks the stage of a short story, and her counterpart—dressed in trade-marked girdle, shoes, brassiere, stockings, dress, suit, coat, and cosmetics—parades through the advertising. The beautifully furnished home interior shown in color photography in an article is matched by the beautifully furnished home interior in an equally colorful advertisement.

A distinct group of women's magazines have intensively and extensively influenced, and even directed, American women in one of their deepest interests. These are the fashion magazines, typified by *Harper's Bazaar* and *Vogue,* the élite among such periodicals.

Harper's Bazar was founded in 1867 after Fletcher Harper had seen and admired a German fashion magazine called *Der Bazar.* Already the publisher of two very successful magazines, a weekly and a monthly, he resolved to produce an equally good magazine which be "a respository of fashion, pleasure, and instruction" for American women. The new magazine, promptly dubbed "the ladies' *Harper's Weekly,*" which first appeared in November, 1867, was immediately successful under the editorship of Mary L. Booth. A sixteen-page weekly, it used cuts shipped from *Der Bazar* in Berlin to bring American women news of the latest continental fashions almost as soon as European women knew of them.

Always profusely illustrated with half- and full-page engravings and many smaller ones, *Harper's Bazar,* in the last century, carried editorials, serial fiction, columns of "Sayings and Doings" and "Personals," but was seriously dedicated to women's fashions. Gowns and bonnets, jackets, ornate slippers, cloaks, and directions for embroidery work filled its columns. Patterns for the gowns and coats illustrated in its pages were offered for sale for twenty-five cents. In April, 1878, for example, the *Bazar* featured cut paper patterns of an elegant French Coat, Pleated Over-Skirt, and Demi-trained Skirt, and also a new and useful set of Lady's Princesse Lingerie, consisting of Princesse Petticoat, Princesse Chemise, Combination Chemise (with Drawers), and Long Sacque Night-Dress. After the turn of the century the magazine declined. It climbed back into popularity and influence when it was purchased by Hearst

Magazines, Inc., in 1913. The spelling of the key word in its title was changed from *Bazar* to *Bazaar* in 1929.

Vogue, established in 1892, absorbed *Vanity Fair* in 1936. "A weekly show of political, social, literary, and financial wares," *Vanity Fair,* which had been founded in 1868, was a sophisticated review edited for a time by Frank Harris and for a much longer time by Frank Crowninshield, who had been an assistant editor of *Munsey's Magazine* and art editor of the *Century.* Published by Condé Nast, *Vogue,* whose masthead reads *"Vogue,* incorporating *Vanity Fair,"* has retained some of the *Vanity Fair* flavor and sophistication, carrying articles on the arts and social graces; but it is pre-eminently a fashion magazine. Its lead position as such is credited to Edna Woolman Chase, who joined its staff in the 1890's, became the magazine's editor in 1914, and did not give up day-to-day editing until 1952. "For almost sixty years," she said in her autobiography, which was published in 1954, "my job has been the true love and focus of my life." [2]

Both *Vogue* and *Harper's Bazaar* are heavy, many-paged periodicals, opulent in appearance, colorful, luxurious. Throughout, they are sacred to fashion. Advertisements and editorial contents alike depict, with all the allure that handsome models handsomely posed can give their pages, the newest, most exquisite, and usually most expensive in women's fashions. Some attention is given to people and ideas, usually the wealthy and the social life of the wealthy, women in their roles as dowagers, matrons, debutantes or subdebutantes, but the emphasis is all on clothes and beauty modes. Advertisements in these magazines are for gowns, cosmetics, lingerie, fabrics, jewelry, de-

---

[2] Edna Woolman Chase and Ilka Chase, *Always In Vogue* (New York: Doubleday, 1954). A reviewer of the book wrote in the *Saturday Review,* October 30, 1954: "Mrs. Chase's judgment, taste, uncompromising standards of perfection were the real heart of *Vogue's* success. She stood up to advertisers with the courage of a small, ferocious lion, flatly refused to give editorial mention to any merchandise she thought in bad taste . . ."

odorants, yarns, fashionable resorts, and the more decorative household items. Often it is difficult at first glance to distinguish a page of advertising from an editoral page, so much skill is exercised in color, composition, and sensuous appeal of the advertising.

The influence of *Harper's Bazaar* and *Vogue* is as strong as women's desire to know what is *de rigueur* in the newest fashions and to do something about it. The consequent influence of these magazines in the market place is powerful. Women decide after carefully scruitinizing their pages—for fashion magazines are studied and intensively considered, not merely read—what they will buy and where they will buy it. Even those women who cannot afford clothes and beauty preparations designed obviously for the well-to-do which they see in these magazines are affected in their choice of cheaper substitutes. The fashion magazines and the fashion departments of the women's general magazines vitally influence the clothes, activities, and the thoughts about clothes and social activities of American women.

Other fashion magazines, launched from time to time, have been specifically planned to exercise such an influence over special groups in the female population. *Glamour,* another Condé Nast publication, is directed to the attention of the career girl. *Mademoiselle* and *Charm,* both published by Street and Smith, are intended for the college girl, and as much for the girl who plans on marriage as for the one intending a career in business or in one of the professions.

A column firm in support of the American matriarchy, the women's magazines are a vital force in intelligent public communications. As advertising media they perform an equally important function through stimulating consumption of the goods produced under a luxury economy.

Chapter 12

SOCIAL CONSCIOUSNESS OF MAGAZINES:
THE MUCKRAKERS

Public reaction against the machinations of the Robber
Barons in the period after the Civil War, touched off by such
magazine articles as Charles Francis Adams' exposé of political and financial manipulation in "Chapters of Erie" and by
his castigation of the Tweed Ring in *The North American Review* in the 1870's, and by the *Harper's Weekly* campaign
against political criminality in New York, mounted strongly
in the 1880's. People learned of the ruthless methods by which
a small group of capitalists obtained control of great natural
resources, whole railway systems, and great industries, and
then manipulated these so as to amass large fortunes for themselves rather than for the public good. What started as indignation and resentment toward some of the most flagrantly
unjust monopolies became suspicion of all trusts and "interests."
Corporate business was soon under attack from many quarters.

Edward Bellamy of Chicopee, Massachusetts, editor and
founder of the *Springfield Daily News,* published his immensely
popular *Looking Backward* in 1888. His predictions in this
romance of a new social and economic order stimulated the
growth of the proletarian movement. The Sherman Anti-
Trust Act was passed in 1890. Henry D. Lloyd's *Wealth
Against the Commonwealth* was published in 1894. A year before that Samuel Sidney McClure had founded his famous
magazine. The name of *McClure's Magazine* is almost synonymous with "muckraking." McClure and his editors made it the
chief periodical weapon in the spectacular fight for business,

social, and political reform in American life which took place between 1900 and 1910.

Irish immigrant and graduate of Knox College, S. S. McClure had founded the first newspaper syndicate in the United States. With John S. Phillips, another Knox graduate, he had bought novels from such writers as Kipling, Howells, Hardy, Stevenson, and Frank Stockton, and then peddled them to newspapers for simultaneous publication across the country. Short, blond with blue eyes and a wire voice, a human dynamo as William Allen White described him, McClure was already a successful businessman when he founded his magazine and installed John S. Phillips as managing editor. It was to be an extension of his other profitable publishing activities. From traveling this country and Europe in search of authors and ideas, McClure knew that a large audience existed in the Middle West, especially in the country districts and small villages, for a magazine that would tell them something of world affairs, of matters beyond the confines of their own communities, and he decide to exploit that market.

McClure's Magazine began to bring these readers the fiction McClure syndicated, the work of Hardy, Stevenson, and Kipling and of George W. Cable, F. Marion Crawford, Joel Chandler Harris, and other American writers. Between 1902 and 1906 it also brought them, and a much larger audience than even the energetic and enthusiastic McClure had visualized, Ida M. Tarbell's *History of the Standard Oil Company,* Ray Stannard Baker's *The Railroads On Trial,* Lincoln Steffens' *The Shame of the Cities* and *Enemies of the Public,* and Burton J. Hendrick's *The Story of Life Insurance.* These were not the kind of articles McClure had first intended. They were even better, and McClure was quick to recognize their value both as prestige and circulation builders for his magazine and as social documents.

Ten years after *McClure's Magazine* was founded its influence was such that William Allen White accounted S. S. Mc-

Clure among the ten most important men in the United States.[1]

It was in Paris that McClure found Ida Tarbell studying and writing. She had already produced biographies of Napoleon and Lincoln for his magazine. McClure hired her for the staff of the monthly. He assigned to her the writing of a series of articles on the operations of the Standard Oil Company, intending to use the most famous of the trusts as an example of the achievements of business in production and efficient distribution. Ida Tarbell worked in cooperation with Standard Oil executives who gave her assistance and full access to the records of the company. Her investigation was long and thorough, her report objective and complete. Ida Tarbell, a scholar and idealist, spent five years in preparing and writing fifteen *McClure's* articles on the Standard Oil Company, articles which it has been estimated cost the magazine about $4,000 each. The articles showed that Standard Oil was magnificently organized, that it functioned superbly, but that the methods by which the corporation had been built included bribery, fraud, violence, the corruption of public officials and railroads, and the wrecking of competitors by fair means and foul. What had started out to be a study of a great business became, by virtue of the facts uncovered, an exposé of big business as sometimes practiced.

The History of the Standard Oil Company, clear, truthful, and vividly written, not only provided *McClure's* with material that was exactly in keeping with the anti-trust sentiments of the public, but also fixed the pattern for the other exposés which *McClure's* published in rapid succession. Ida Tarbell was soon joined on the magazine by two other muckrakers, who became, with her and McClure, the leaders in the magazine exposure of criminality and corruption in American business and government.

[1] When McClure died, March 21, 1949, at the age of 92, the press paid little attention. The magazines, except *Publishers' Weekly,* which gave him a one-paragraph obituary, paid no attention at all.

Lincoln Steffens was the second of the muckrakers. Hired by McClure as an editor, Steffens was sent to the Middle West to gather material. His first story was an interview with the prosecuting attorney of St. Louis, who had been gathering evidences of graft and had come to the conclusion that business was corrupting city officials, that for the sake of good business citizens were glad to support bad city governments. Steffens began the investigations that resulted in another series of *McClure's* exposés. In *The Shame of the Cities* and *The Struggle for Self Government,* Steffens, who talked frankly with financiers, philanthropists, and ward heelers, with all those against whom he had gathered damning evidence, showed that American cities, whatever the form of their government on paper, were actually ruled by political bosses supported by reputable businessmen who needed the accommodations they could obtain from corrupt politicians.

Ray Stannard Baker, a Chicago newspaperman, was the third of the trio of crusading muckrakers. He was invited to join the magazine by John Phillips, who had been impressed by his stories in *The Century* and *The Youth's Companion.* Baker became associate editor of *McClure's* and manager of the McClure syndicate. Like Tarbell and Steffens, Baker was given a free hand in the preparation and writing of his exposure articles. He was assigned the management of American railroads and labor-capital relations as his special province, and the facts he uncovered were as damning as those found by the others in their investigations. Baker's articles in *McClure's* described labor racketeering, abuses both by organized labor and by associations of employers. He found all the conditions familiar today, unions preventing non-union men from getting jobs, employers boycotting workers, and all the rest of it, rife in the first decade of the twentieth century. He found, too, that whichever group, capital or labor, was in control, worked according to pattern with machine politicians and with the criminal element.

McClure's Magazine

VOL. XX   *NOVEMBER, 1902*   NO. 1

THE HISTORY OF THE STANDARD OIL COMPANY

BY IDA M. TARBELL.
Author of "The Life of Lincoln"

CHAPTER I—THE BIRTH OF AN INDUSTRY

ONE of the busiest corners of the globe at the opening of the year 1872 was a strip of Northwestern Pennsylvania, not over fifty miles long, known the world over as the Oil Regions. Twelve years before, this strip of land had been but little better than a wilderness its only inhabitants the lumbermen, who every season cut great swaths of primeval pine and hemlock from its hills, and in the spring floated them down the Allegheny River to Pittsburg. The great tides of Western emigration had shunned the spot for years as too rugged and unfriendly for settlement, and yet in twelve years this region avoided by men had been transformed into a bustling trade center, where towns elbowed each other for place, into which the three great trunk railroads had built branches, and every foot of whose soil was fought for by capitalists. It was the discovery and development of a new raw prod-

GEORGE H. BISSELL

The man to whom more than any other is due the credit of what is called the "discovery" of oil; for it was he who first took steps to find its value and to organize a company to produce it. It was he, too, who suggested the means of getting oil which proved practical. After the oil company which he organized obtained oil in the Drake well, he aided in establishing the needed industries and institutions in the new country.

uct, petroleum, which had made this change from wilderness to market-place. This product in twelve years had not only peopled a waste place of the earth, it had revolutionized the world's methods of illumination and added millions upon millions of dollars to the wealth of the United States.

Petroleum as a curiosity was no new thing. For more than two hundred years it had been described in the journals of Western explorers. For decades it had been dipped up from the surface of springs, soaked up by blankets from running streams, found in quantities when salt wells were bored, bottled and sold as a cure-all—"Seneca Oil" or "Rock Oil," it was called. One man had even distilled it in a crude way and sold it as an illuminant. Scientists had described it, and travelers from the West often carried bottles to their scientific friends in the East. It was such a bottleful, brought as a gift

3

One of the most famous magazine exposés of the muckraking period, Ida M. Tarbell's *History of the Standard Oil Company* began in *McClure's Magazine* in November, 1902.

The December Special Number

THE SATURDAY EVENING POST

An Illustrated Weekly Magazine
Founded A? D¹ 1728 by Benj.Franklin

Volume 173, No. 25   Philadelphia, December 22, 1900   Five Cents the Copy

The Plight of the Democracy
and the Remedy
By
Ex-President
Grover Cleveland

The Curtis Publishing Company Philadelphia

Public men before and after Grover Cleveland have used the pages of nationally circulated magazines as an effective means of broadcasting their political ideas.

His investigations of American railroads provided *McClure's* with more startling articles.

These *McClure's* muckrakers were capable and honest investigators, of great journalistic ability, who had the gift of making dramatic and damning the material they uncovered and wrote into their brilliant exposés. Strictly truthful in their reporting, they were indignant and outraged at what they saw, and so skillful in arranging and proportioning their facts as to make flagrant abuses manifest. A reformer's zeal motivated and fired their work.

McClure, who knew the value of establishing a reputation for honesty and fearlessness for his magazine, published their sensational articles with gratifying results. *McClure's Magazine* thrived. Instead of being deterred by the attacks on business, advertisers were attracted to a medium which was achieving great circulation and great attention. Appearance in its advertising pages must have seemed almost a guarantee of the honesty of their business. While *McClure's* was running *The World of Graft,* Josiah Flynt's exposures of the league existing among criminals, the police, and politicians, the June, 1901, issue carried 104 pages of advertising. In more *McClure's* articles, which in book form were entitled *The Powers That Prey,* Flynt reported on the underworld's contribution to politics and business.

The *McClure's* exposures of graft and corruption in city government, of fraud and dishonesty in business and finance, of the vicious practices of corporations and labor unions alike, led not only to popular disapproval of the conditions, but also to reform, to legislative action, and to improvement in politics and the conduct of business. The magazine's influence on public opinion was enormous. Its circulation skyrocketed. Copies were difficult to obtain at the newsstands, which sold out their supplies quickly. Leaders in American public life responded enthusiastically. Theodore Roosevelt sent for the *McClure's* writers and discussed with them the conditions they described.

Carl Schurz, German-born liberal thinker, statesman, and journalist, invited Baker to come to Wisconsin for a discussion of fundamental labor-capital questions.

The general public, stirred to indignation and aroused to anxiety for the future, devoured the long, serious dissertations, which is really what many of the *McClure's* articles were, and demanded more of the same. Ray Stannard Baker, writing of the popular reception of the exposure articles in his *American Chronicle,* expressed his belief that the articles took such a hold on the public mind because the magazine reporters had looked squarely at the facts and stated them as they were. Their accounts verified suspicions of corruption and privilege which had previously been heard only in the oratory of politicians. At the time, the disclosures of the muckraking reporters had the additional force of being new, of being news. The *McClure's* crusade for better government and for the destruction of the worst practices of business continued. McClure, who like other editors knew the value of names and personalities in the pages of his magazine, had William Allen White do a series of sketches of political leaders—Cleveland, Bryan, Theodore Roosevelt, and others. When Senator Thomas Platt, "Boss Platt" of New York, who was largely responsible for making Theodore Roosevelt governor of New York and then for shunting him into the vice presidency when he proved difficult to manage, threatened a libel suit after the story about him appeared, the editors of *McClure's* let it be known that they had unpublished material about him still more damning, and Boss Platt reconsidered.

President Roosevelt, progressive, announced foe of boss rule, and "trust buster," took prompt action upon many of the evils exposed by the muckrakers. In another series of political articles which he wrote at this time for *The Saturday Evening Post,* William Allen White praised Roosevelt for launching anti-trust suits against monopolies, and described him as an attorney for the people who was leading the fight against the domination of the country by financiers. In a *Post* article, pub-

lished in Ocober, 1902, for the crusading fervor of *McClure's*
had infected other magazines, White wrote: "There are well
known bands or gangs of nomadic financial marauders strolling
over the American stock markets with no more moral sense
than pirates. They are drunk with the power that crass wealth
gives them over American civilization. . . . New laws are required to bring these brutes to the halter."

State governments as well as the federal government were
forced to take action on facts published by *McClure's* and the
other muckraking magazines. For *McClure's* Burton J. Hendrick wrote *The Story of Life Insurance.* In July, 1904, in
Everybody's Magazine, Thomas W. Lawson, a Boston financier
who knew the unsavory story from the inside, began publication of *Frenzied Finance.* In this series of articles, Lawson
condemned the investment syndicates used by some of the
larger insurance companies, the huge profits made by top insurance executives and the means by which they made them, the
expensive sales methods used to sell insurance, and the heavy
loss, through lapses, to policyholders.

As a result of these two exposés the New York legislature
instituted the Armstrong Investigation in 1905. Charles Evans
Hughes, acting as counsel for the legislative committee, proved
the truth of many of the accusations brought by Hendrick,
Lawson, and Louis D. Brandeis. The result was an over-
hauling of the entire life insurance business for the greater protection of the policyholder. New York passed stringent new
laws governing the activities of the insurance companies, and
other states quickly followed. The investigation proved that a
number of the large companies had been deliberately influencing
insurance legislation through lobbying and methods involving
virtual bribery of legislators, and that wealthy executives had
drawn exorbitant salaries and swollen these by manipulating
profits earned through investment of company funds. Through
this investigation Charles Evans Hughes acquired a national
reputation.

McClure's Magazine, originator of muckraking and the leader in exposing evils and urging reform movements, was at this time the leading magazine in the country in terms of the social and economic force exerted and successfully applied to the structure of American life. Tarbell, Steffens, Baker, and their peers were firm believers in the democratic system of government, in free American industrial and business enterprise. They desired not to change the system but to see that the system functioned cleanly and fairly. They demanded destruction of evils and abuses, not fundamental change. Reform writers in the other magazines held like convictions and expressed them in forceful writing.

The Cosmopolitan, which had been founded in 1886, was a family monthly of the same general type as *McClure's* and *Munsey's.* Its contributors included Mark Twain, Henry James, and Conan Doyle. In December, 1900, it was a magazine of 107 editorial pages and almost as many filled with advertising. The issue carried fiction by Grant Allen, H. G. Wells, and Kipling; articles on "Life in Warsaw" and on "The Country Fair"; and a feature on feminine beauty (with pictures of Maxine Elliott, Sarah Bernhardt, Mary Anderson, Julia Marlowe) by Harry Thurston Peck, the Columbia professor whose penchant for feminine pulchritude led later to his tragic death.

The Cosmopolitan joined in the muckraking with "The Treason of the Senate" by David Graham Phillips. Phillips, seated in the press gallery of the Senate, came to believe that these representatives of the people were not representatives of the people at all, but of the special interests, which had placed them in the Senate seats. This was the thesis of his *Cosmopolitan* story. It is said to have been Phillips' writing which caused Theodore Roosevelt, a phrasemaker as well as a politician, to dub the investigations and reports of the magazine writers with the term "muckraking." Though he was in sympathy with the ideals of the reformers and was himself a leader of the reform movement, he complained that the muckrakers were beginning to see only the bad and none of the good in the activities they scrutinized and reported.

David Graham Phillips went on with his muckraking in *The Cost* (1904) and *The Deluge* (1905), both dealing with undercover financial manipulations in Wall Street through which the few profited and the many suffered. In *The Light-Fingered Gentry* (1906) he used material disclosed in the Armstrong Insurance Investigation. Charles Edward Russell was another muckraking journalist, who, in *The Greatest Trust in the World,* exposed the conspiracy between the meat packers and the railroads to keep meat prices high to the consumer while meat producers were kept poor and in debt.

Upton Sinclair was commissioned by a socialist magazine to go to Chicago to write a novel about the deplorable conditions under which packing-house employees worked. The result was *The Jungle,* which disclosed not only economic and social injustices and the same evidences of political corruption which Tarbell and Baker had found in other industries, but also the foul conditions under which meat products were produced. Sinclair's novel created a great stir. As Lloyd Morris points out in *Postscript to Yesterday,* a few pages of gruesome detail in *The Jungle* accomplished more in arousing public indignation than some of the factual and carefully documented reports of the other muckrakers.

In 1906 a split between S. S. McClure and his managing editor, John S. Phillips, resulted in the most famous group of all the muckraking writers leaving *McClure's Magazine.* Phillips, Ida Tarbell, Lincoln Steffens, Ray Stannard Baker, and Albert Boyden purchased *Frank Leslie's Popular Monthly,* changed its name to the *American Magazine,* and began to publish, edit, and write it as a magazine of progressive democracy. With them as associate editors went William Allen White and Finley Peter Dunne. White, a milder, more easygoing reformer, advised the others to go more slowly, to be less the "thin red line of heroes" with do-or-die determination written in their grim faces. Possibly as a result of his advice, probably through the wish to make their magazine a financial success, certainly because Finley Peter Dunne was on the staff, the *American* tempered the severity of its muckraking with material dealing with the homely affairs of average people.

Finley Peter Dunne, another Chicagoan, worked first as a newspaperman in that city, becoming editor of the *Evening Journal*. In 1900 he went to New York as editor of the *Morning Telegraph* for William C. Whitney, who practically adopted him. When he became associate editor and part owner of the *American,* Dunne took over a department of the magazine called "In the Interpreter's House," and in it continued the kind of humor for which his Mr. Dooley stories had made him famous. Dunne had invented Mr. Dooley, the Irish saloon-keeper, in the early 1890's, some years before he left Chicago, and Mr. Dooley, who first appeared in the *Chicago Times-Herald,* had made his creator famous as a humorist and social satirist. Using Irish dialect and conversations between the skeptical Mr. Dooley and his friend Hennessey, Finley Peter Dunne not only convulsed a generation of readers who appreciated the shrewd humor of the stories, but also was able to express his hatred of social injustice, of stupidity, pomposity, and the pretensions of politicians in a way that was as effective as it was readable. *Mr. Dooley in War and Peace, Mr. Dooley in the Hearts of His Countrymen, What Dooley Says, Mr. Dooley's Philosophy, Mr. Dooley Says,* were characteristic volumes in the long series that ended in 1919 with *Mr. Dooley on Making a Will.* Mr. Dooley, who became one of the most popular characters in the United States of his day, was informed by the same spirit which moved the muckrakers of the magazines.

The touch of Finley Peter Dunne lightened the *American Magazine.* The partial metamorphosis of another of the magazine's owners and editors further softened the sternness of its continued muckraking activities. Soon after the group had taken over the *American* Ray Stannard Baker, as "David Grayson," began to write for the magazine the long series of narrative essays, cheerful, humorous, filled with platitudes and homely philosophy, which, published as *Adventures in Contentment, Adventures in Friendship, Adventures in Solitude, Adventures in Understanding,* etc., attained great popularity. Baker's literary career was one of surprising contrasts. Originally, like Dunne, a Chicago newspaperman, he became one of the most incisive of the muckrakers. With his "David Grayson" writings he turned sentimental essayist. Meeting Wooddrow Wilson first in 1910 when Wilson was governor of New Jersey, he served as press director at the Versailles Conference, and after Wilson's death was made editor of his posthumous papers. As such he became Wilson's biographer, winning the Pulitzer Price in 1940 for the eight volumes, 1927–39, of *Woodrow Wilson: Life and Letters.*

Other magazines performed notable public service during this muckraking period. *The Outlook,* of which Theodore Roosevelt became an associate editor in 1909, campaigned, under Lyman Abbott, against the vicious admixture of politics and business. *World's Work,* founded in 1900 by Walter Hines Page, who became ambassador to England during World War I, was devoted primarily to discussing American participation in international affairs, but it campaigned against those senators who opposed railroad reform. *The Century* attacked slum conditions and turned its efforts to arousing public interest in improved sanitation. *Collier's Weekly,* in a campaign that was synchronized with Edward Bok's efforts in the *Ladies' Home Journal,* published *The Great American Fraud,* attacks on the "poison trust" by Samuel Hopkins Adams, a former *McClure's* writer.

Collier's was founded in 1888 by Peter Fenelon Collier to promote the subscription book business he started two years after coming to this country to study for the priesthood. The magazine's original title, *Once A Week,* was changed in 1896 to *Collier's Weekly,* and Robert Collier became its strong publisher. Collier immediately set about transforming the magazine into "the national weekly" and adopted this subtitle. Like the publishers of other mass magazines, he tried to obtain big-name writers and artists to build up *Collier's*. One of the first serials he published was Henry James' *The Turn of the Screw*. He hired Frederick Remington to do his highly colored paintings of Southwestern scenes and Maxfield Parrish for his delicately colored fantasies. He got Charles Dana Gibson from *Life* by paying $1,000 a drawing. He paid Richard Harding Davis $1,000 a week to cover the Russo-Japanese War.

On the advice of Finley Peter Dunne, Robert Collier hired as editor Norman Hapgood, a scholarly writer who had forsaken law for literature. Hapgood became one of the leaders among the magazine editors who were crusading for social reforms. When Mark Sullivan, working in New York, ostensibly as an independent lawyer but actually as an investigator and writer for Edward Bok in his crusade against the patent-medicine industry, produced an article too long for the *Ladies' Home Journal* to use, Bok took it to Robert Collier and Norman Hapgood. *Collier's* bought and published Sullivan's "The Patent Medicine Conspiracy Against the Freedom of the Press," and in 1906 hired him as a staff writer. Led by Robert Collier and featuring Hapgood's forceful editorials and Mark Sullivan's political articles, *Collier's* fought for the income tax, the direct election of senators, votes for women, railroad rate legislation, pure food laws, the abolition of slums, workmen's compensation laws, and the limitation of the hours of women in industry.

Theodore Roosevelt singled out *Collier's* for special praise when, as an editor of the *Outlook*, he wrote on "Applied Ethics in Journalism." The newspapers, Roosevelt wrote in the *Outlook* in April, 1911, continued to print objectionable advertisements of a kind that the better magazines, both weekly and monthly, had thrown out. *Collier's* had not only refused such advertising but had also publicized the false claims to medicinal properties of a patent breakfast food and had ably defended itself in suits brought against it as a result of its attacks. "We are bound," wrote the ex-President, who had been so strongly supported by the magazines in his reform activities, "to pay a tribute of deserved respect to a paper like *Collier's* when in a matter so vital to the public well being it wages so fearless, aggressive, and efficient a fight for honesty and decency."

By 1908 the muckraking movement had spent its force. Its best writers were turning to material of a different kind, leaving the work they had started and performed well to be carried on by lesser talents. Many of those who followed lacked the skill of the original McClure group, and often presented their materials with more regard for its sensationalism than its accuracy. Writers who wished merely to exploit the popular revolt against the plutocracy wrought some damage with indiscriminate adverse criticism of business and government which did not much slacken until the start of World War I. But they could not undo the good which had been accomplished.

McClure's Magazine, Everybody's, The Cosmopolitan, and the others, but especially *McClure's*, let light into situations which had long needed light and air. They instilled a sense of responsibility into the wide public which read them, for the muckrakers made clear their belief that, in the last analysis, the complacent public which allowed and even supported the abuses by business and political bosses was to blame for the appalling conditions they exposed.

These magazines, and again the major credit must be assigned *McClure's*, accomplished one other definite change. Magazines wrested from the daily newspapers the influencing of public opinion by the direct discussion of public affairs, and they have retained the pre-eminence in actuality and in the public view since that time. What had been the chief muckraking magazines degenerated into purveyors of light fiction, but the precedent had been established. All the important general weeklies and monthlies began to give more coverage and more thorough discussion to public matters and thus to exert a greater influence on the minds of their readers. "Did you see what *Time* (or *The Saturday Evening Post,* or *Collier's,* or *Life* or any of a dozen other magazines) said about this or that?" or "I read last night in *The Atlantic*—" are typical of remarks that can be overheard in casual or serious discussion daily wherever people meet and talk in this country.

The group which had spearheaded the muckraking on *McClure's* ran the *American Magazine* until 1911 when it was purchased from John S. Phillips by Joseph Palmer Knapp and made one of the Crowell publications. Ida Tarbell, Lincoln Steffens, Ray Stannard Baker, and the others moved with the magazine to the Crowell Company, but soon left, and the *American Magazine* began to specialize in inspirational biographies of well-known men. With S. S. McClure these writers had wrought important changes in the complexion of American business and government and greatly expanded the public usefulness of the magazine in the United States.

Chapter 13

MAGAZINE REFLECTION OF A NATION: *THE SATURDAY EVENING POST*

A<small>MERICA'S</small> oldest magazine, though it printed the articles of William Allen White and backed the reforms of Theodore Roosevelt's administration, did not join in the hue and cry of the muckrakers. *The Saturday Evening Post* was a proponent of business, which both its publisher and editor regarded as one of the most characteristic expressions of American energy. It was less concerned with emphasizing the mistakes of business than with publicizing and romanticizing its leading figures and advertising its dramatic accomplishments. It found most things good in a good, materialistic American world.

In 1848 *The Saturday Evening Post,* one of the most important weeklies of the time, was a four-page periodical printed on large royal sheets. It ran serials, news, poetry, "selected" articles, financial news, and fashion notes. The first page of the issue for January 8, 1848, carried a "Romance of Reality"; "Notes of the Dead Sea," clipped from the *Living Age*; two poems "written for *The Saturday Evening Post*"; and one, by Martin Tupper, clipped from the *Literary World*. The inside pages had a department called "Postscript," but unlike "Postscripts" in the *Post* of today it contained shipping news. Editorials dealt with "Peace Prospects" (the Mexican War was not yet officially over), "The Origin of Railroads," "Temperance," "Eye-Glasses," and "Leap Year."

In a two-column box on page three the proprietors of *The Saturday Evening Post* returned their thanks to the "friends of morality and pure literature" for their liberal support during

1847. They did better than that. They announced a "great increase of circulation" and made a new and liberal offer:

> The Post Office of any town in the Union, from which we shall receive the greatest number of subscribers between the 1st of November, 1847, and the 1st of November, 1848 . . . shall be entitled to a continuance of the whole number of subscriptions *gratuitously* for one year after the expiration date for which their subscriptions shall have been paid.

A footnote in four-point type with a pointing-finger cut added further inducement: "Editors copying the above will be entitled to an exchange." On page three appeared, "Fun and Frolic," a "Tale of the Mexican War," and a biography of John C. Calhoun, plus the perennial essay on the "Employment of Leisure Hours." Advertisements were scattered through all but the front page. A filler at the bottom of the page informed the world that "the Pittsfield *Eagle* says that the negro girl, who was put into a mesmeric sleep in that town, has awakened after a nap of forty hours." The 1840's were much interested in mesmerism.

The *Post* was a strong and thriving weekly in 1848. Charles Dickens had been a contributor the year before. Bayard Taylor, Grace Greenwood, T. S. Arthur, Ned Buntline, and Nathaniel Hawthorne were 1848 writers. A January editorial congratulated *Blackwoods* for *not* comparing Emerson, who was then traveling in England, with Carlyle. Henry Clay and Mrs. Myra Clark Gaines, according to a February account, were the lion and lioness of Washington. On March 4, a two-column editorial under the great seal of the United States and a draped flag told of the death of John Quincy Adams in the House of Congress. A feature throughout the year was "Our Portrait Gallery," which displayed engravings of eminent English and American statesmen and writers.

The 1858 *Saturday Evening Post* was a strong and vital paper. Even today it reads with a certain freshness, but by 1865 the *Post* was beginning a long period of decline. Eight pages, of smaller size, still on newsprint, it boasted a more florid logotype, more "literary" content, more advertisements, more dignity, and a pervading dullness. Pages two and three of the April 22, 1865, issue were bordered in heavy black. The lead news story, "Assassination of the President," was sub-headed "Probable Murder of Mr. Seward," and stated that "J. Wilkes Booth, the alleged murderer of the President, has thus far succeeded in eluding pursuit." Like *The Atlantic Monthly,* the *Post* had paid little attention to the Civil War.

This was a poor magazine which grew yet worse. By 1874 it was solidly subliterate serials. The entire front page of one issue, and half the second page, was *Davy Crockett on the Track; or, The Cave of the Counterfeiters* by Frank Carroll. Where Crockett stopped, Chapter XLVI of *Claudia's Triumph* by Clementine Montagu began. The issue's only illustration was a four-column engraving of the fabulous Crockett winning an incredible rifle match. The rest of the magazine was more of the same. Perhaps the best serial, certainly the best known, which the *Post* ran in this period was *East Lynne; or, The Elopement* by Mrs. Henry Wood, which began in February, 1874. By 1889 the magazine had doubled its number of pages to sixteen, but in content it was much what it had been in the previous decade.

In January and February of 1895 the *Post* switched over to twenty-four pages of smaller size but returned two months later to the sixteen-page format. The issue of August 21, 1897, was delayed. A notice stated:

> The sudden death of Mr. A. E. Smyth, late publisher of the *Post,* and the legal formalities consequent on the settlement of his estate constitute the cause of, and our apology for, the delay in issue of the paper. We ask your indulgence for a few days, as we expect to be regularly on time commencing with the issue of the 28th.

The simple fact was that the *Post* had no more money. An appeal was made to Cyrus H. K. Curtis who bought the magazine for a thousand dollars. The next week's issue was thrown together so as to save the title rights by continuous publication, and the imprint of The Curtis Publishing Company, which had been established in 1890, was placed on it. Most of the 2,000 subscribers objected to the new material in the issue. They had been used to reprints clipped and pasted up by a reporter on the *Philadelphia Times* who earned ten dollars a week by editing the *Post* in his spare time. They canceled their subscriptions. So Curtis started with an established magazine title and a tradition, but practically no subscribers and no advertising.

It was the nearly unanimous opinion of other publishers and of the editors of the time that this time Cyrus Curtis had made a bad mistake. The weekly magazine, they said, was a dying form. *Printers' Ink,* journal of the trade, prophesied early failure for the venture.

Well into the next year Curtis kept the magazine much as it had been. He decided to obtain as its editor John Brisben Walker, a former managing editor of *Cosmopolitan,* but hired as a stop-gap incumbent George Horace Lorimer, a young reporter on the *Boston Post,* who had applied for the job. Before Curtis could keep an appointment with Walker, then abroad in the diplomatic service, Lorimer had published four issues of the *Post,* and Curtis realized that he already had the editor he wanted.[1]

It would be hard for millions of Americans today to recognize the American scene without the modern *Saturday Evening Post* a part of it. It has been a solid reality in the minds of almost three generations of readers. But the modern *Post* did not originate as did the sun, the moon, and the stars; nor did it spring full-blown from the brow of Jupiter. It sprang from certain conceptions in the minds of Curtis and Lorimer. *Harper's Weekly, Frank Leslie's* and *Collier's* were the established

[1] See John Tebbel, *George Horace Lorimer and The Saturday Evening Post* (Garden City, N. Y.: Doubleday & Co., 1947). This is an excellent story of Lorimer and *The Saturday Evening Post* as it operated under his editorial direction.

weeklies in 1899. Each was sold at ten cents. Each was concerned almost wholly with the news, news pictures, and politics in competition with the newspapers. The *Post* halved their price and made no attempt to compete with these magazines or with the newspapers as a spot-news medium.

The basic conception of *The Saturday Evening Post* in 1899, when Lorimer took on his active editorship, was that Americans would read and like a certain type of story, certain types of articles, a kind of soothingly competent reporting that it can almost be said to have originated, a certain type of humor, and a distinctive editorial approach. It would make its primary appeal to the intelligent businessman. To do this, it eschewed both the sensational and the intellectual. (If it had employed sensational tactics, it is conceivable that one of two things might have happened: either it would not have outlasted its infancy, or its present circulation would be even larger than it is.) Obviously, it has not emphasized the cultural. There are not twelve to fifteen million intellectuals in the United States of today.

In the *Post* of 1899 the businessman and his family were given action stories, romances, stories of business; the life stories of successful men of action; articles on economic and political subjects so dramatized that they were at once informing and entertaining; comment on current events; and a modicum of the serious and sentimental poetry countenanced by businessmen of this period. The issue of September 30, the "Fall Fiction Number," was the first recognizable modern *Saturday Evening Post*. Of the same general dimension as the magazine is today, it wore its first color cover, and carried its first full-page advertisement in color. Every article and every story was illustrated. The issue ran to thirty-two pages and contained thirty-two columns of paid advertising. The cover, under what was to be the familiar *Post* logotype for more than thirty years, showed action aboard a pirate ship. The lead story was "The Sergeant's Private Madhouse" by Stephen

Crane; a story by Cyrus Townsend Brady followed. There were "Blaine's Life Tragedy" by John H. Ingalls, and "Under the Eaves" by Bret Harte. The life of Portus B. Weare, a pioneer trader, was dramatized in a "Men of Action" series. Julian Ralph wrote on "The Making of a Journalist." There were also a poem by Bliss Carman, a current events department, "Publick Occurrences," and book reviews. In his editorial, "A Retrospect and a Prospect," Lorimer wrote:

> With this issue, The Saturday Evening Post is permanently enlarged from sixteen to twenty-four pages, with monthly special numbers of thirty-two pages. As soon as the necessary machinery can be installed—and work upon it is being pushed with all possible speed—The Saturday Evening Post will contain thirty-two pages every week. . . .
>
> There is nothing worthy or permanent in life that is not clean, and in its plans and purposes the new Saturday Evening Post preaches and practices the gospel of cleanliness. It appeals to the great mass of intelligent people who make homes and love them, who choose good lives and live them, who seek friends and cherish them, who select the best recreations and enjoy them.

Lorimer had definite editorial ideas, and definite plans for realizing them. His ambitious master plan was to interpret America to itself. To accomplish this he started quickly to forge his weapons.

To revitalize the ancient weekly he deliberately sought, as Bok had done for the *Ladies' Home Journal,* contributors who were already well-known writers. In 1899 and 1900 he had Stephen Crane, Robert W. Chambers, Rupert Hughes, Jerome K. Jerome, Bret Harte, Joseph Lincoln, and Richard Harding Davis. In 1901 and 1902 came Emerson Hough, Owen Wister, and William Allen White. In addition to these professional writers, he had public men as contributors in those early days: Senator Albert J. Beveridge was one, Speaker Tom Reed and Champ Clark were among the others. In *Post* pages, Beveridge predicted, two years before it occurred, where and how the Russo-Japanese war would break out and its results.

Lorimer introduced business fiction into *The Saturday Evening Post*. Years before in Portland, Cyrus Curtis had read and been impressed by Richard B. Kimball's stories about business. "I want business stories like Kimball's," he said when he bought the *Post*. Lorimer wrote and serialized two books of his own, *Letters of a Self-Made Merchant to His Son*, which presented shrewd business advice in colloquial language, and *Old Gorgon Graham*, a similar tale. Harold Frederic's *The Market Place*, a business tale, as its title indicates, was the *Post*'s first serial of the new type under Lorimer. Soon came Frank Norris' great novel, *The Pit*.

Lorimer had another idea, that of a magazine written chiefly by a group of contributors who were identified with the magazine and would give it its peculiar tone and slant. Members of the group changed from time to time, and one group has replaced another, but this scheme of editorial production was characteristic of the *Post* all during Lorimer's long editorship and is, in part, characteristic of the *Post* today.

In 1905, six years after his first novel, *The Gentleman from Indiana*, was published, Booth Tarkington appeared in the *Post*. Almost all his best work during a long and productive literary career was published in the magazine. "Mr. Rumbin's Blessed Misfortunes" appeared in the issue of May 19, 1945, exactly one year before Tarkington's death. James Branch Cabell, Wallace Irwin, George Barr McCutcheon, Jack London, Zona Gale, Harry Leon Wilson, and Ring Lardner were others who contributed notable novels and short stories to Lorimer's early *Post*.

By 1900, because of writers of this stature, Lorimer's editorial direction, and the determined efforts of Cyrus Curtis to see through a venture that at one time showed a deficit of $1,250,000 the reborn weekly had a circulation of half a million. It reached 700,000 in the spring of 1904; 1,000,000 in 1908. By this time the list of *Post* contributors read like a roster of the popular writers of the time whose books are still read. Joseph Conrad, O. Henry, Stewart Edward White, Corra Harris, Robert Chambers, Jack London, Montague Glass, Owen Johnson, Gouverneur Morris, George Pattullo, and Melville Davisson are merely the best-known names among a famous list. By 1909 the *Post* had assumed the pattern and the character that still identify it.

The Saturday Evening Post became, as Lorimer had promised it would, "the largest weekly magazine in the world." Its circulation rose from less than 2,000 in 1899 to more than 3,000,000 at Lorimer's retirement in January, 1937. For years it was virtually without a competitor as the largest weekly and, if such can be said to have existed at all, the most typical of American magazines. The historian Arthur M. Schlesinger in 1941 described it as "the dinosaur among the periodicals." It was seen and read everywhere. People came to know it as they knew their own names. Its influence was pervasive and immeasurable, spreading simultaneously in many directions. The magazine was continually improved. Its influence mounted continually. But the fundamental Curtis-Lorimer attitudes and ideas on which it was based did not change appreciably for many years.

The *Post* operated from the first to reinforce the conservatism, the middle-class sanity, of the economically and morally controlling class in the American community. To do this, it avoided the esoteric, the sensational, and, usually, the adversely critical. It stressed American nationalism, American business, material success, the economic viewpoint; assumed accepted morals and mores without question and built from there. It provided information on every subject of conceivable interest to its readers, information obtained and capably presented by unexcelled reporters. It printed inspirational biographies and the best entertainment fiction of its kind, broadening the horizons of its readers' experience and at the same time providing the factual reports and sensible interpretations which enabled them to form their judgments on subjects of national concern.

The contents of the whole magazine were written for, often by, and editorially directed to, the intelligent, middle-of-the-road, but neither overly intellectual nor overly imaginative American. The *Post* upheld, as it still upholds, free enterprise and competition, the right of the individual to work for a profit. It saw, and sees, monopolistic control, whether by business, labor, or government, as dangerous and undemocratic. As a weekly magazine of this kind, informative, entertaining, clear, and direct, its influence permeated the population, from its leaders down through the mass of their literate followers. The *Post* became both a powerful and continuing social force and almost a sign and symbol of the country itself. As Curtis and Lorimer intended, the *Post,* with an accuracy that many have tried to describe and analyze, reflected the United States to itself—its brilliance and its mediocrity, its materialism and its ideals, its energy, confusion, complacency, its weaknesses, and its strength.

One of the most intelligent estimates and analyses of *The Saturday Evening Post* as it was thirty years ago, and as it had been even then for almost twenty years, was made by Leon Whipple in 1928. Whipple described the *Post* as a five-sided enterprise. It was at once, he said, a giant, money-making business; a miracle of technical publishing; a purveyor of entertaining fiction and articles; a supersalesman through advertising and thus a main cog in the mass distribution of the products of American industry; and "an engine for propaganda in favor of American nationalism and the present economic system." Whipple, adopting rather than inventing his figure wrote:

> This is a magic mirror; it not only reflects, it creates us. What the SatEvePost is we are. Its advertising helps standard-ize our physical life; its text stencils patterns on our minds. It is a main factor in raising the luxury-level by teaching us

new wants. . . . But it does more than whet our thing-hunger;
by blunt or subtle devices it molds our ideas on crime, prohibition, Russia, oil, preparedness, immigration, the World Court.
Finally it does queer things to our psychology by printing tales
that deceive us with a surface realism but are too often a tissue
of illusions. This bulky nickel's worth of print and pictures is a
kind of social and emotional common denominator of American
life.

Who reads the Post? Who looks in the mirror? Everybody
—high-brow, low-brow, and mezzanine; the hard-boiled business man and the soft-boiled leisure woman; the intelligenzia,
often as a secret vice. . . . You read it—and I. . . . In 1926 it
was figured that if from our population of 105,710,620 you sub-
tracted the children under fourteen, illiterates, foreign language
readers, the criminal, insane and paupers, the residual possible
market for publications in English was 60,872,577 . . .
20,674,346 families. More than one in ten of these took the
Post.[2]

Whipple pointed out what he considered the limitations of
the *Post* as well as its virtues. He noted its conservatism, its
tendency to support the *status quo,* its ardent nationalism, but
he also pointed out: "The Post may neglect new forces, but the
forces it understands are very old and very human." Of the
cumulative force of the magazine he was describing, Whipple
could make no real estimate. He could only exclaim. Other
assayers have experienced the same difficulty. A spot-check
analysis of just one year of the *Post* during the period about
which Whipple wrote may explain their failure to grasp all that
the *Post* represents and accomplishes.

In 1924 *The Saturday Evening Post* contained 21 serials,
11 novelettes, 339 short stories, and 413 articles. The articles,
among other subjects, dealt with the American merchant marine, the agricultural situation, taxes and tax reduction, immigration, Prohibition, the presidential campaign, war and preparedness, foreign policy, the narcotic trade, the tariff, aviation,

[2] Leon Whipple, "SatEvePost, Mirror of These States," *Survey,* March 1,
1928.

and conservation. In addition to sixteen general articles on foreign countries, there were eleven dealing exclusively with Great Britain, seven with Russia, five with Germany, three with Italy, three with Mexico, two with India, two with Turkey, and individual articles about Arabia, Poland, South America, South Africa, China, Canada, Norway, and Holland. Other 1924 articles treated of animals, antiques, auctions, automobiles, building and real estate, general business, crime and law, education, finance, health, food, labor, mining, entertainment, music, the outdoors, patents and inventions, radio, railroads, ships and salvage, travel, and subjects of especial interest to women.

Leading article writers during the year were Kenneth Roberts, Isaac Marcosson, Cosmo Hamilton, Philip Gibbs, Meade Minnigerode, Garet Garrett, Roger Babson, David Lawrence, Samuel G. Blythe, Richard Washburn Child, Henry H. Curran, and Albert W. Atwood.[3] Public men who wrote for the 1924 *Post* included Herbert Hoover, who was then Secretary of Commerce; Joseph Cannon, colorful Speaker of the House; Hubert Work, Secretary of the Interior; Senator George W. Norris; and Brigadier General William (Billy) Mitchell, the famed military air pioneer, who was condemned for beliefs and statements which were vindicated by the events of World War II. *Post* fiction writers during this typical year of the mid-1920's included Ben Ames Williams, I. A. R. Wylie, Roland Pertwee, J. P. Marquand, Earl Derr Biggers, Harry Leon Wilson, Joseph Hergesheimer, and P. G. Wodehouse.

Scores of widely read books resulted from fiction and articles first published in the 1924 *Post*. A few of them were:

Bill the Conqueror by P. G. Wodehouse
Professor, How Could You? by Harry Leon Wilson
The Black Cargo by J. P. Marquand

[3] Atwood said at this time: "The evidences which come to me of the extent to which my articles are read, and the quarters in which they are read, often oppress and frighten me with a sense of the responsibility under which a writer for the *Post* labors." Quoted by Whipple, *op. cit.*

A South Sea Bubble by Roland Pertwee
Manhandled by Arthur Stringer
Unwritten History by Cosmo Hamilton
The Danger of Europe by Philip Gibbs
After Lenin—What? by Isaac Marcosson
The Fabulous Forties by Meade Minnigerode
The Diary of a Dude Wrangler by Struthers Burt
Racial Realities by Lothrop Stoddard
The Roar of the Crowd by James J. Corbett
Letters from Theodore Roosevelt by Anna Roosevelt Cowles
Balisand by Joseph Hergesheimer
The Rational Hind by Ben Ames Williams

Fifty-seven illustrators and eighteen cover artists saw their work appear in the *Post* in 1924, and in a *Vanity Fair* article on American illustrators, Frank Crowninshield wrote: *"Vanity Fair* here takes the opportunity of pointing out that *The Saturday Evening Post* has done more for American illustration than any other periodical in the history of our country—with the possible exception of *Punch,* in England, more than any periodical in any country. It has brought a discriminating art to the attention of millions of weekly readers—good art—art removed from sentimentality and fraud."

George Horace Lorimer was undeniably a prejudiced witness, but there was truth in his own description of the magazine. "In every number," he wrote, "stories unite with the *Post*'s editorials and articles to portray American life—its ideals, its struggles, its defeats, and its successes, in a way that has made it recognized as the dominant and representative American publication not only at home but in every country abroad."

During the first score of years Lorimer, intent on moulding his magazine, refrained from strong expression of editorial opinion. In 1919, after it became apparent that World War I, instead of solving world problems, had only intensified those that existed and added new ones, Lorimer began in his *Post* editorials to attack some of the problems in positive fashion. He began the fight for restricted immigration. Lorimer argued that further immigration had to be limited in volume and that the possibilities and desirabilities of different races had to be analyzed. Risking the displeasure of the industrial class among his advertisers who demanded an unlimited labor supply, he maintained that arguments for unrestricted immigration always went back to some selfish reason, never to the greatest good of the country. Henry H. Curran and Kenneth Roberts presented the subject in a series of *Post* articles. According to W. W. Husband, then Commissioner General of Immigration, the articles by Roberts were responsible for the passage of the restrictive Immigration Act of 1924. Curran became Commissioner of Immigration at the Port of New York.

Lorimer struck at cancellation of World War I debts, pointed out the weaknesses of the Treaty of Paris, which he said "carries the seed of future wars in its text," supported honest overtures for disarmament, and condemned excessive taxation and unrestrained government spending. He wrote and published editorials which required of the reader a serious and intelligent concern in his government and society at large. He warned against bureaucracy: "The simple and amply proven fact is that government ownership does not make men, and rarely makes money. It makes weaklings, dependents, grafters, bureaucrats, autocrats, and deficits. It is the first lession in Socialism. . . ." Editorially the *Post* argued throughout the 1920's for the kind of nationalism it had always supported.

If the *Post* mirrored the United States to itself during the 1920's some explanation may be found in the mere names of some of its contributors. It reflected the words and ideas, the life stories, the thoughts and actions of Americans of all kinds, presidents, prize fighters, coaches, statesmen, poets, detective story writers, teachers, humorists, new writers, old writers— Jack Dempsey, Scott Fitzgerald, Will Rogers, Emerson Hough, Calvin Coolidge, Katharine Brush, Sophie Kerr, Guy Gilpatric, Dr. A. S. W. Rosenbach, Bugs Baer, Alexander Woollcott, General J. G. Harbord, Alonzo Stagg, Al Smith, Sinclair Lewis,

Roy Chapman Andrews, Mark Sullivan, Bernard Baruch, Irving Thalberg, Helen Wills. Like the *Post* the full list would be as diversified and as many-faceted as American life.

The influence of *The Saturday Evening Post* of this period was probably the strongest of any weekly magazine, but it was a permeating and stabilizing influence, not a force making for social or economic change. When the United States was enjoying Coolidge prosperity, it was this prosperity and national self-satisfaction that the *Post* mirrored. Liberal movements were afoot. Social, economic, and literary changes, changes in morals and mores, had begun or were imminent. They were not reflected in *The Saturday Evening Post*.

George Horace Lorimer resigned as an editor of *The Saturday Evening Post* and president of The Curtis Publishing Company in 1936, and died in 1937. *Post* editorship went to Lorimer-trained Wesley Winans Stout, who put out a magazine hardly distinguishable from Lorimer's. Fiction predominated; articles were prolix but thin. America for Americans, big business, isolationism, the Republican Party were *Post* policy and one no longer in accord with prevailing public opinion. The *Post* had begun to lose circulation, advertising revenue, and its long-established hold on popular favor. Stout resigned in 1942 and was succeeded by Ben Hibbs, Kansas newspaperman who had been for a year editor of the Curtis-owned *Country Gentleman*.

The new editor stated his principles immediately. "I believe firmly in the American system—freedom of living—freedom of enterprise. Above all, I believe it is the patriotic duty of the *Post* to help keep alive in the minds of the people that free enterprise literally has made America—that it is the only system under which we can prosper and enjoy the fruits of democracy."

This was familiar *Saturday Evening Post* doctrine. In its essential economic Americanism the magazine would be unchanged. But the new editor had other plans and ideas, and from them a new and more liberal *Post* resulted. "The problems that confront the American people," he said also, on taking over the office that had been Lorimer's for thirty-nine years, "are staggering. It is our responsibility to weigh, analyze, and explain these problems. America's life will be affected by what happens in Brazil, in Turkey, in Hong Kong, in Russia. To the greatest degree in its history the *Post* will report and interpret these happenings." Other changes would be made in the magazine. Entertaining new short features would be introduced. There would be more stories of American business, more appeal made to women readers, more material of interest to young readers. There would be physical changes in the magazine.

The Lorimer *Post* was primarily a magazine of fiction. The Hibbs *Post* became primarily a magazine of feature articles— shorter, sharper articles. The long-familiar script logotype of the magazine was dropped and replaced by POST in large block capitals with the words "The Saturday Evening" in letters less than one-fifth the size.[4] Layout and style of illustrations were changed throughout the magazine. More vivid titling was adopted and teasing subtitles were introduced. More cartoons and short humorous bits enlivened "the back of the book." A greater variety of subjects in shorter form took the place of fewer subjects and more extensive treatment.

An ordinary issue of *The Saturday Evening Post* now contains eight articles, four short stories, and two serial installments. In a year's time the *Post* uses about four hundred articles and two hundred short stories. The "typical" *Post* has a humorous and sentimental cover painting in full color by Norman Rockwell or by one of a group of *Post* artists who paint

---

[4] Many magazines followed suit, dropping or diminishing words in their titles to emphasize a key monosyllable easily spoken and heard at the newsstand. *Time, Life, Fortune* held this advantage from the beginning.

in the Rockwell manner. It carries part of a serial narrative by Clarence Buddington Kelland, Erle Stanley Gardner, or their literary equivalents. These are the recognizable and long-standard *Post* pieces.

More characteristic of the newer *Post* are the highly promotable biographies and autobiographies of entertainers, politicians, military or naval heroes, and other public figures. Usually these are strongly featured in cover publicity and by editorial position and display and carried in six to eight installments. They began in 1952 with "I Was the Witness," in which Whittaker Chambers told in prose-poetry the story of his confessed Communist activities and his part in the trial of Alger Hiss. Then came a series of autobiographies in which popular actors and entertainers, a *Post* editor doing the actual writing, told their life stories in *Post* pages. Bing Crosby's "Call Me Lucky" was followed by Bob Hope's "This Is On Me." The life of Groucho Marx by his son was succeeded by the autobiography of Ethel Merman, "That's the Kind of Dame I Am," then by Arthur Godfrey's "This Is My Story." The life stories of other movie actors followed.

During this same period the *Post* published in weekly installments biographies or autobiographies of Winston Churchill, Alben Barkley, Charles A. Lindbergh, General William F. Dean, and "Murder on His Conscience," the life in prison of Nathan Leopold. These major pieces were offered in the *Post* against a background of articles on diversified subjects: national and international affairs, politics, invention, medicine and health, race relations, light short stories, and the *Post*'s long-continued series of articles on the "Cities of America" which runs now as "Cities of the World."

In 1955 *The Saturday Evening Post* underwent further physical changes. With the issue of October 1 it began use of a different body type, changed its title displays, adopted different layouts for both small and large features, widened the vertical space between columns, and made greater use of white space throughout the publication.[5] The *Post,* which used photographic illustrations for articles, art work for fiction, had already introduced more new editorial features. Chief of these was a two-page spread in each issue, bleed color photograph and sentimental-rhetorical text describing "The Face of America." All of these changes serve to make the magazine look more like its competitors, which depend heavily on illustration and layout for their allure.

Despite these changes of 1942 and 1955, *The Saturday Evening Post* remains basically what it always has been since its publication under Curtis management began in 1897. It is a text magazine, a magazine to be read. Today it is less biased politically and socially than it was under George Horace Lorimer and serves wider interests. It still balances entertainment and information, maintains its conservative approach to the American family, keeps its articles alert and brightly written, but, as the mass magazine must, generally avoids controversy. Three-quarters of the editorial material in *The Saturday Evening Post* is written and signed by writers who are not in the employ of the magazine.[6] This makes for variety and diversity of subject matter and style not possible in entirely staff-written magazines, where the anonymous articles are sometimes monotonously uniform in treatment. The *Post* likes to think that it remains, too, about the only mass magazine which will publish in full text the serious, often dull, sometimes disputable, ideas of generals, politicians, and other public figures who wish to get their message

---

[5] The new *Post* body type is 10¼-point Baskerville for the opening pages of a piece. The magazine had been using 10-point Century Schoolbook.

[6] The character of the writers in many cases, and for almost all of the major nonfiction pieces has changed. They are not professional writers but "personalities." It was a change Lorimer recognized during his editorship. He wrote Kenneth Roberts in 1935: "It does seem these days as though the way to get an opportunity to write is to do something spectacular that has nothing to do with any training for writing. If you swim the Channel or your husband figures in a spectacular kidnapping, the newspapers open their arms to you." Quoted by Tebbel, *op. cit.* Names of many of the major *Post* pieces are signed by celebrities "as told to" a professional staff journalist.

before a large and presumably influential audience. The *Post* publishes such pieces as deliberate editorial policy. This upholds the magazine's tradition of serving as platform for public men; it also gives it first call on what may be important manuscripts. Such pieces, *Post* editors feel, lend substance to the magazine but at the same time act to limit *Post* circulation. Conceivably circulation could be increased if material of this kind were omitted and more Marilyn Monroe features were substituted.

Underneath its surface changes *The Saturday Evening Post,* with its circulation of more than four and a half million copies weekly, has retained its long recognized identity, its middle-of-the-road respectability, and even the affection in which it has been held by several generations of readers. This quality in the magazine and reader attitude toward it cannot be defined easily nor are they satistically provable, yet their existence is generally acknowledged. Some of it is legacy from the years when *The Saturday Evening Post* stood virtually alone as a weekly text magazine. The *Post* is always recognizable, and it has been around for a long time. Its performance is consistent. It will never shock; it will seldom surprise.[7] What it does, it does well. Its standards do not vary. Its taste does not change. Most of the mass circulation magazines are stridently overpromoted. Often it seems that as many words are written and broadcast in praise of them as the magazines themselves contain. There seems some modestly stated truth in the contention, reiterated in advertising for *The Saturday Evening Post,* that it is "big, believed, beloved."

---

[7] Sometimes it does surprise. At risk of losing circulation and of offending important advertisers, the *Post* came out editorially in support of Eisenhower two months before he was nominated for President by the Republican convention of 1952.

Chapter 14

THE FARM MAGAZINES

In 1938 *Scribner's Magazine* ran a series of eight articles entitled "Magazines That Sell." Rather caustic articles with more than a touch of the exposé about them, they analyzed some of the more spectacular modern magazines in an attempt to discover the reasons for their popular and commercial success. The last article in the series discussed a group of magazines, many of them founded in the pre-Civil War period, which have exerted and still exert a powerful social and economic force on one vital department of American life. "Farm Magazines," in the issue of October, 1938, was different in tone from preceding articles in this series. Harland Manchester, its author, found much to praise in farm magazines.[1]

The first agricultural paper in the United States, as Mr. Manchester pointed out, was founded by Luther Tucker. Success with the *Rochester Daily Advertiser,* a newspaper which he had established in 1826, led Tucker to bring out the *Genesee Farmer* in 1831. It was the *Genesee Farmer* which became the *Country Gentleman.*[2] The first issue of *Country Gentleman,*

[1] The other articles in the *Scribner's* series were "Geography, Inc." by Ishbel Ross; "The Love Pulps" by Thomas H. Uzzell; "One Every Minute; The Picture Magazines" by Jackson Edwards; "High Hat; The Luxury Magazines" by Henry F. Pringle; "Romantic Business; Fortune Magazine" by William A. Lydgate; "True Stories; The Confession Magazines" by Harland Manchester; and "Sex, Esq." by Henry F. Pringle.

[2] The *Genesee Farmer* was merged in 1839 with *The Cultivator,* which had been established at Albany in 1834 by the New York Agricultural Society. The *Country Gentleman* began as a weekly edition of *The Cultivator.* By 1858, it reached a circulation of a quarter of a million. In 1866, the offspring having outstripped the parent magazine in popularity and circulation, they were merged, becoming *The Cultivator & Country Gentleman.* Luther Tucker also established the *Horticulturist* in 1846 and edited it until 1852.

"A journal for the farm, the garden, and the fireside," appeared in 1853. It was "devoted to improvement in agriculture, horticulture, and rural taste; to elevation in mental, moral, and social character, and the spread of useful knowledge and current news." Luther Tucker explained the title and purpose of *Country* Gentleman in the first editorial column:

> Wherever the honest, earnest feeling of the heart finds utterance—wherever the deed of generous sympathy is performed—wherever the life is ruled by the principles of honor and religion, do we find the gentleman. . . .
>
> Country life is particularly adapted to inspire character of this sort, and the *Country Gentleman* is therefore in truest exponent of those characteristics which should prevail in the American. There is then a propriety in styling a paper for country circulation, and devoted to the interests and pursuits of farmers, the *Country Gentleman*.
>
> In answer to a very natural inquiry as to some one individual to whom the term, as we use it, would properly apply, we have placed a portrait of Washington in our vignette. The independence and magnanimity of his character, the energy and decision of his actions, the excellence and simplicity of his whole life; his love of rural pursuits, and his devotion to his country, make him a fit type of the American country gentleman.

In the very first issue Tucker made *Country Gentleman* a practical agricultural paper. There was a sensible article on the professional education of farmers and other informative articles on subjects of basic interest to the farmer: "Farm Economy," "Farm Profits," "The Culture of the Hop," "What Shall We Do for Fodder This Winter?" In addition to departments headed "The Grazier," "Horticultural Department," and "The Fireside," there were a "Record of the Times," which gave domestic, foreign, Congressional, and California news, and a "Farm Products Market," giving Albany and New York prices on cattle, wood, flour, grain, hogs, and whisky. Illustrations in this issue showed Trump, a prize Hereford bull belonging to

The Country Gentleman.

A Journal for the Farm, the Garden, and the Fireside.

VOL. I.   ALBANY, N. Y., JANUARY 6, 1853.   No. I.

Our Title and Purpose.

THE term GENTLEMAN, like most expressive ones, has been from time immemorial subject to animadversion and misconstruction. It has been made to apply to persons of widely different conditions of life, of radically opposite characters, and diverse pursuits. In its best and proper signification, the word is defined to mean a man of cultivated mind, of refined manners, of genuine kindness of heart, and consequent purity of life. The fashionable acceptation of the term, that obtains in cities and watering places, and its meaning as applied to residents in the country, are essentially different. In the first case, it stands for men of means and leisure, in distinction from those of business; in the latter, it properly embraces all those whose characters recommend them to the respect and confidence of their fellows. In cities it stands more for outward show; in the country, for the possession of sterling virtues. Still the true gentleman is the same in essence, in all situations, in all circumstances, and to all men. The coxcomb and dandy are beings of another order, while the real gentleman is, in all ages, the type of genuine humanity. Politeness, which is considered the evidence of gentlemanliness, though often judged of by formal rules of etiquette, exists in opposition to them, and even in spite of them. Wherever the honest, earnest feeling of the heart finds utterance—wherever the deed of generous sympathy is performed—wherever the life is ruled by the principles of honor and religion, do we find the gentleman. His acts are unconsciously polite, his bearing has on it the stamp of nature's nobility, and his whole character is imbued with those qualities of mind and heart, which endear and dignify man.

Country life is peculiarly adapted to inspire character of this sort, and the COUNTRY GENTLEMAN is therefore the truest exponent of those characteristics which should predominate in the American. There is, then, a propriety in styling a paper for country circulation, and devoted to the interests and pursuits of farmers, THE COUNTRY GENTLEMAN.

In answer to a very natural inquiry, as to some one individual to whom the term, as we use it, would properly apply, we have placed a portrait of WASHINGTON in our vignette. The independence and magnanimity of his character, the energy and decision of his actions, the excellence and simplicity of his whole life, his love of rural pursuits, and his devotion to his country, make him a fit type of the American country gentleman. In his public career, in his social relations, in his efforts for the highest individual and common good, he stands as a model for all time. Placed by Providence and his own superior wisdom, at the head of our nation, before it was rent by political faction and private interest, there has never been a time when the entire population of the United States have not been ready to rally with his name for a watch-word. We place his likeness, then, with confidence at the head of our sheet, and write his name as Father of his Country, and the true representative of a gentleman, without fear of contradiction. Let no one object to our title, who is not prepared to falsify the claim of WASHINGTON to the name of Country Gentleman, or willing to allow that he is not emulous of a similar character, and does not respect his virtues.

It is a fixed fact, that the progress of our rural population demands a journal, independent in its character, and safe and reliable in its teachings, an advocate and representative of the great agricultural interests of the country. Improvement begets a desire for farther advancement, and so fast as high culture takes the place of low culture on our farms, so rapidly will a taste for literature, for home embellishment, and true refinement, succeed to the surprising apathy on these subjects which has so long prevailed. It is a truth worthy of remark, that the highest forms of eloquence, the purest diction, the most beautiful works of art, the sweetest music, have always been appreciated by the masses of the people. We hold it an axiom, that the love of the really beautiful, admiration of noble and manly qualities, and respect for genuine virtue and excellence, are instinctive in the heart. The sickly taste for light and rapid reading, is not natural. It has been formed as the taste for sweetmeats is in children,—by feeding sugar plums when they cried for food. But allowing that there are a large class of readers, whose vitiated appetite must be pandered to by a literature as degraded, we deny that our farmers or their families form, to any considerable extent, this class.

We propose, then, to make THE COUNTRY GENTLEMAN the repository of such Agricultural and Horticultural matter, such thoughts and principles, such information and current news, as in our judgment will most safely and surely promote the best interests of all country residents. Our readers must bear in mind that our subscribers are scattered over a great part of the Union, and that what may seem of little moment to one, may be of the most vital importance to another. We have so arranged the matter under topics, that one can turn, without inconvenience, to the several departments, and this system will be carefully pursued.

The general arrangement and typographical execution of THE COUNTRY GENTLEMAN, have been studied with a view to combine uniformity and good taste; and it is our intention to make its external appearance a true index to its contents.

With this exposition of our purpose, we invite the attention of every one into whose hands this sheet may fall, to a careful perusal of its entire contents, with the request that if they find it adapted to their wants, they will become permanent subscribers, and use their influence and exertions in its behalf.

Farm Economy.

"I am not rich enough to be economical," said a young friend of ours, when we strongly recommended to him the profits of a certain improvement. "The want of means compels me to work constantly to a disadvantage, and I cannot enjoy the privileges and profits of my richer neighbors." This is a difficulty in which many intelligent farmers have found themselves placed, and from which they would most gladly be extricated. Innumerable instances are occurring in their daily practice, where they could secure golden results, had they only the lever of capital placed in their hands; but as they are now situated, they seem to themselves like the man who is digging the earth with his unassisted hands, or the one who is compelled to carry water in an egg-shell, while their more fortunate neighbors are turning up the deep soil with the most perfect instruments, or sending streams of refreshment and fertility through easy channels over their entire farms. Now, we are not about to plan a "royal road" of escape from this difficulty; it must be met and conquered. If the attack is rightly made, the conquest will be comparatively easy; if wrongly, it will be the discouraging and formidable task of a life time.

The eager inquiry is now made, What is the easiest mode of conquest? We answer, the first and great leading means, is a large fund of thorough and practical knowledge. The man who, by a close observation of results in his own practice and in the experience of others, in connection with the immense amount of useful suggestions, (to say nothing of distinct practical directions) contained in the best publications of the day, possesses, even with a very short purse, a vast advantage over the short-sighted, ignorant, and unobservant capitalist. He will turn to advantage, even with his very limited means, a thousand resources which others would allow to sleep unemployed forever.

We once had occasion to observe the contrast in the condition of two young farmers, one of whom had a four-hundred acre farm "left" to him; the other had but fifty acres, which he had paid for in part, by previously laboring on a farm for some years by the month in summer, and teaching a district school in winter. The one had the capital of money which his own hands had never earned; the other possessed the more valuable capital of knowledge and indomitable perseverance. The young heir was more interested in

---

The first issue of the *Country Gentleman*, January 6, 1853, carried a picture of George Washington in its vignette as the very type of the country gentleman.

Mr. Allen Ayrult of Geneseo, New York, and dwarf or pompon chrysanthemums in full blossom.

During the next year *Country Gentleman* advocated the first test plots for corn and announced the seedling grape which was developed by E. W. Bull of Concord, Massachusetts, and was to become known as the "Concord." In 1857 Luther Tucker visited the Middle West and, in a *Country Gentleman* article, pointed out that "one of the advantages the prairie farmer possesses over his eastern brethren is the peculiar adaptation of his land to the use of labor-saving machinery."

It was largely through Tucker's interest in the Middle West, where he appointed correspondents, that *Country Gentleman* became the first truly national farm magazine, reaching just the next year a phenomenal 250,000 circulation. As Mott has reported, the files of *Country Gentleman* during these years mirror the development of the western ranges, the improvement of farm stock, the coming of ensilage and silos, and the growth of the Grange and the Farmers' Alliance.

Country Gentleman did more than record. It interpreted and often led the changing developments in American agriculture. As far back as the 1850's it declared that a milking machine was the most needed improvement in dairying. It urged farmers to prepare for the readjustments that would inevitably follow the close of the Civil War. In 1884 it described the economic advantages of what is now called "baby beef." It recognized, well in advance of the fact, the effect that refrigeration would have on markets for agricultural products. It prophesied with remarkable accuracy: "Florida is to become, at no distant day, the winter garden of the Northern cities."

By the 1890's magazine advertising had become a primary means of distributing farm goods and equipment. To be effective this advertising required a large circulation, which *Country Gentleman* in Albany did not have the facilities to achieve. Competition in the 1880's and the 1890's from an increasing number of regional farm papers resulted in a decline in *Country*

Gentleman's circulation and forced it into editorial coverage more regional in nature than that which had characterized the magazine earlier. In 1911 Gilbert Tucker sold the weekly to Cyrus H. K. Curtis.

The first number of *Country Gentleman* issued from Philadelphia over the imprint of The Curtis Publishing Company appeared in July, 1911. The magazine, made a weekly for nationwide circulation, concentrated on farm and country life. Power farming, road building, and taxation and freight problems were stressed, but attention also was paid to the rural woman's interests, and popular fiction of the outdoor type was published. Circulation began to rise almost immediately. It reached 300,-000 in 1916, and about half a million in the next five years. Circulation was 800,000 in September, 1925, and twice that by 1930, the largest circulation ever achieved to that time by a farm magazine.

Many of the objectives at which Luther Tucker had aimed in the early *Country Gentleman* were reached. By the time that Curtis took over the magazine there were agricultural colleges, agricultural experiment stations, new services, inventions, and agencies to help the farmer. The farmer needed less instruction from magazines on how to do things, now that he had available the professional aid of institutions which magazines had helped to build. Recognizing this, its editors provided a rural magazine of different type with broader aims and interests.

In 1925 the change was made from weekly to monthly publication. Full-color covers, superior makeup on good white stock, illustrations in color, and contents of a quality equal to that provided metropolitan audiences by the general weeklies and monthlies made it a modern farm magazine for a rural America modernized by the automobile, the radio, and power equipment. Fiction was made important in the *Country Gentleman* of the 1920's, when such popular writers as Ben Ames Williams, Joseph C. Lincoln, Zane Grey, Courtney Riley Cooper, and others appeared in its pages.

Country Gentleman began in the 1920's to stress the value of scientific research to agriculture. In five years' time it ran 300 articles on grass breeding. Largely through *Country Gentleman*'s efforts, Congress in 1935 passed the Jones-Bankhead Act, under which twelve regular grass-breeding stations were set up in the United States. Soil conservation and erosion prevention were emphasized in a series of articles by Hugh H. Bennett and by other authorities who contributed to *Country Gentleman* for a five-year period. The soil conservation programs inaugurated by the federal government in the 1930's resulted. Bennett, who was made director of the Soil Conservation Service, said: *"Country Gentleman* may have pride in its consistent editorial 'fight' for practical, workable soil conservation." Lespedeza, a nitrogen-fixing legume, was discovered by J. Sidney Cates of *Country Gentleman*'s staff. Grown now on millions of acres throughout the country, it serves both to rebuild worn soil and to provide a useful silage and roughage crop. Other agricultural ideas initiated or backed by *Country Gentleman* have produced action with far-reaching social and economic consequences. American farmers first learned about hybrid corn from *Country Gentleman* in 1924.

Country Gentleman first publicized in its pages how plant hormones could be used to retard blooming of fruit trees until late spring frost had passed, to speed root growth in transplanted cuttings, and to kill weeds. In 1937 it described how phenothiazine could destroy livestock parasites. The use of this new drug now saves farmers millions of dollars a year.

Country Gentleman was credited by *Scribner's* with having discovered Paul de Kruif, for many years now a regular contributor to *The Reader's Digest* and author of most of its spectacular pieces on medical discoveries, as a writer on health and medical subjects. In 1936 it published portions of his *Microbe Hunters,* and subsequently many of his crusading medical articles. For a dozen years *Country Gentleman* focused attention upon tuberculosis, infantile paralysis, malaria, and other diseases in campaigns for the improvement of public health. It even dared discussion of syphilis. Thus, said Harland Manchester, "the home magazine *Country Gentleman* pioneered in smashing the great taboo." [3]

Luther Tucker had a department called "The Fireside" in the first issue of *Country Gentleman,* and he consistently ran material of interest to the entire family. The farm magazines as a group have devoted intelligently used space to the farm home as well as to the field. They have acted as a definite force in the betterment of farm living as well as in the advance of farming.

In February, 1954, *Country Gentleman,* in financial difficulties and severely pressed by competition, cut its page size. In January, 1955, the name of the magazine was changed to *Better Farming.* Advertising losses continued. In June of the same year The Curtis Publishing Company announced sale of the magazine to the competitor which had outstripped it in both circulation and advertising revenue.[4] *Country Gentleman* was merged with *Farm Journal.*

The September, 1955, issue of *Farm Journal,* the first after the merger, was a magazine of 226 pages, *Time*-sized, modern in appearance, illustrated in full color, replete with advertising, and heavy with a varied editorial offering. It bore little resemblance to the eight small pages of newsprint first issued from Philadelphia in March, 1877. Now the largest and most important national farm magazine with a circulation exceeding 3,400,000 and copies going monthly to half the farm families in the United States, *Farm Journal* had been founded by Wilmer Atkinson as a paper for farmers in the agricultural area about

---

[3] A half dozen or more magazines claim credit for this. The story of Paul de Kruif and *Country Gentleman* was told in a small book by Ben Hibbs, since 1942 editor of *The Saturday Evening Post,* but then associate editor of *Country Gentleman. Two Men On a Job* was issued by The Curtis Publishing Company in 1938.

[4] The purchaser discarded the name *Better Farming* and referred in his announcements and advertising to the merging of *Country Gentleman* with *Farm Journal.*

Philadelphia. Atkinson's approach was terse, direct, and homey. He stated his principles in his first editorial.

> There will be 25,000 copies of the first issue of *The Farm Journal* printed and mailed to farmers and other rural residents within a day's ride of Philadelphia. . . . The publisher will insert advertisements of an unobjectionable character, at 40 cents a line. No lottery swindles, cheap jewelry announcements, quack medical advertisements, nor Wall Street speculator's cards, can find admittance at any price. . . . The publisher does not intend to fill much space with puffs of *The Farm Journal* leaving it for the intelligence of the reader to discern merit, if any exist. Enough said; send along the 25 cents [for a year's subscription].

Wilmer Atkinson, who tells the full story of the founding and the early years of his magazine in a charming autobiography, posthumously published in 1920, wrote a pithy prose and wanted his contributors to do the same.[5]

"After the manuscript is prepared," he told them in his magazine, "strike out the bottom and the top and condense the middle." Direct, economical reporting has characterized *Farm Journal* from the beginning. Atkinson prided himself that:

> *Farm Journal* says a thing and stops after it has said it. It prints no long-winded tiresome essays, and it knows what to leave out as well as what to put in.
>
> It is cheerful and hopeful and wants everybody to have a good time.
>
> It is full of snap and ginger, and hits the nail squarely on the head. . . .
>
> It thinks the humans on the farm are the best stock on it.

Direct, economical reporting and a friendly attitude toward "our folks," as Atkinson called his readers, has characterized *Farm Journal* from the beginning. Early, Atkinson gave practical proof of the responsibility he felt toward the farm families

---

[5] Wilmer Atkinson, *An Autobiography* (Philadelphia, Pa.: Wilmer Atkinson Co., 1920).

he wrote to. In 1880 he guaranteed to make good any loss readers sustained by "trusting advertisers who proved to be deliberate swindlers. Rogues shall not ply their trade at the expense of our readers." His action made *Farm Journal* the first magazine to guarantee its readers repayment of money lost because of fraudulent advertising in its pages.

That same guarantee, somewhat preciously worded, appears in every issue of the *Farm Journal* still: "To prove our faith by works, we will make good to actual subscribers any loss sustained by trusting advertisers who prove to be deliberate swindlers. Just as we cannot guarantee a pig's tail to curl in any particular directions, so we shall not attempt to adjust disputes between subscribers and honorable business men, nor pay the debts of honest bankrupts."

Wilmer Atkinson published and edited *Farm Journal* for forty years, making it an agricultural magazine of national prominence and importance. He had been joined in 1883 by a young nephew, Charles F. Jenkins, who became the magazine's business manager. Arthur H. Jenkins, a brother, took over the editorship in 1921, after his uncle's death. He did not retire from active participation in the business until 1955.

Atkinson's *Farm Journal* flourished. Its circulation grew far beyond the bounds the founding editor had first set for himself. It exerted a strong influence on the agricultural community through the simple and basic magazine function of keeping its readers informed. A noteworthy accomplishment was recognized when in 1926 the then Secretary of Agriculture gave the magazine a large share of the credit for effort that resulted in the establishment of the Rural Free Delivery postal system.

As *Farm Journal* had flourished, it declined. It lost circulation and influence. Financially, it was near failure. Just as the magazine, a victim of the great depression, was about to be sold at public auction in 1935, it was purchased by Graham Patterson, publisher of the *Christian Herald*. Wheeler McMillen, who had been editor of *Country Home* was made editor-in-chief in 1939. The development of the modern *Farm Journal* began at this time. The change of owner, publisher, and editor was followed by a refurbishing and revitalizing of *Farm Journal*. The format was changed (it has since changed again) to resemble that of *Time*. Stress was placed on the speedy publication of agricultural news. Strongly anti-New Deal during the administrations of Franklin D. Roosevelt, it criticized, as well as reported fully, actions and trends in Washington which affected the farmer and farm life. Printing was shifted to high-speed presses in Chicago. Another important move was made in 1939. *Farm Journal,* with a circulation then of 1,400,000 absorbed *The Farmer's Wife,* published in St. Paul, whose circulation was about 1,200,000. The first issue of the merged magazines appeared in May, 1939, and proudly announced a circulation of more than 2,400,000, "the largest circulation in farm magazine history." The title *Farm Journal and The Farmer's Wife* was used from 1939 to 1945. "The Farmer's Wife" was retained as a separate section of *Farm Journal,* a magazine within a magazine, starting, behind its own full-color cover, about midway in each issue. Firm business and editorial concepts lay behind these changes made to establish *Farm Journal* as "the news magazine of agriculture."

During World War I a shortage of men for farm labor coupled with a world-wide demand for food forced an increase in farm efficiency. The first changes took place in farm practice, in horticulture, and in animal husbandry. The tractor and the tools that it pulled, the automobile, and the farm truck marked the beginning of farm mechanization. Broad social changes reached the farm with the advent of better roads brought by the automobile. At the same time, the teaching of vocational agriculture in rural schools, the development of the Agricultural Extension Service of the Department of Agriculture, and the establishment of 4H clubs all augmented the drive toward better education and created a demand for channels of rural information. This the farm magazines supplied, keeping pace with the rather slow evolution taking place on the farm.

The rate of rural change was speeded by several factors. Beginning in the 1930's the influence of the federal government on agriculture increased rapidly. Adjustment to swift-changing farm programs and legislation put a premium on the farmer's keeping well and quickly informed. Fast, current, accurate information became a requisite for the advantageous marketing of his products. *Farm Journal* established a full-time editor in Washington. In 1944 it began to build a staff of field editors to obtain maximum coverage nationally of farm news. Increasingly *Farm Journal* was planned and edited to translate available speed of printing and transmission into terms of editorial function.

The need for this was reinforced, in the opinion of *Farm Journal* editors, by the fact that agricultural research since World War II has shifted from agricultural methods to farm products. Insect and disease control by chemical means opened up entirely new growing methods. New insecticides, herbicides, and antibiotics were made available for general use and farm application. The agricultural process was speeded and improved. *Farm Journal* kept pace, emphasizing its practice of getting usable, profitable information quickly to the farm. Brief, fast-paced articles, their contents immediately applicable, kept the farmer informed. The last pages of an issue of *Farm Journal,* which is printed on the same presses as *Time,* go to the printer's just four days before the magazine is received by the subscriber.

At the same time the magazine manages to keep something of the warm, homey touch that had been Wilmer Atkinson's. The language is direct, the approach colloquial. The editorial ideal is that *Farm Journal* reach the farm family in the guise of a well-informed and friendly neighbor. The tone of the magazine is particularly apparent in *The Farmer's Wife,* which still functions as a complete woman's service magazine. The increasing urbanization of the farm family is recognized through slick paper, smart text, and modern illustrations. Fashion, food, home decoration are treated as glamorously as in any of the other women's magazines. There is no condescension. In fact there is flattery in recognition of a real difference in its readers. The farm woman may be as well dressed, as well informed, and have many of the same family interests and problems as the city women, but she occupies a more central position in her household. As one *Farm Journal* editor commented, she may also "hold a flashlight while her husband acts as midwife at the delivery of a stubborn calf." The farm woman is the cultural and moral leader of her family and a partner in her husband's enterprise; there is usually one checking account for the business of the farm and for household expenses.

The editorial offering in any issue of *Farm Journal* is diversified. There is a certain amount of "corn" in the humor, in the glib, vernacular titles, often in the text; there are "Slick Tricks," "Up in Polly's Room" (letters from teen-age girls and editor replies), a "Children's Corner," a joke page headed "Passed by the Non-Sensor," "Rambling with the Editors." More to the point is the practical advice on gardening, hog raising, diet, apple storing, dairying, and scores of other farm subjects—something on every page. Most typical of *Farm Journal* and what it conceives as its function are the up-to-date and practical articles headed "Last-Minute Report," "Business of Farming," and its "Farmcast." The last is a yellow page near the front of the magazine covered with one- or two-sentence items written and printed in telegraphic style. It deals, staccato, with spot price and marketing information and sharp bits of agricultural advice.

Farm Journal, published nationally in three section editions, East Central, Western, and Southern, calls itself on its contents page "The Most Influential Farm Magazine." Since its absorption of *Country Gentleman,* chief contender for the title, there can be little doubt that it is. It achieved the position and its present pre-eminence among national farm publications in large part because it recognized and used twentieth century trends in magazine publishing and magazine reading. It made thorough news coverage in its field, fast reporting, and factual information its business, instead of leisurely and discursive essays. Through his demonstrated preferences for news briefs, digests, and digests of digests—no words at all if a picture will do—the modern reader had already shown where his tastes lay. He wants to down his reading at a gulp. He wants facts. Suffering from what someone has called decline of attention, or the inability to concentrate for more than a few minutes, the modern reader, urban or bucolic, has little time or inclination to ruminate. *Farm Journal* gives the farmer and the farm family the facts. It talks to them in the kind of language it believes they know and like. It gives them the kind of entertainment they relish.

Country Gentlemen, for the 102 years of its existence, was an important and influential national farm magazine. *Farm Journal* has been leaving its firm imprint on farm life since 1877. But, they do not constitute isolated instances of magazine influence on the farmer, the farmer's family, and on agricultural advance in this country. Since the founding of the *Genesee Farmer* in 1831, hundreds of agricultural magazines and farm papers, many of them still extant and still influential and effective, have been printed and circulated. Each has made, or is making, 'ts specific contribution, nationally or in an important farming section, to the improvement of agriculture and the betterment of rural life.

The *American Agriculturist,* founded in 1842 and national in scope from the beginning, was one of the country's earliest and most powerful farm periodicals. As early as the 1860's it was stressing the scientific as well as the practical approach to farm problems. Orange Judd, an agricultural chemist, was perhaps its most famous editor; men of the stature of Asa Gray, the botanist, were among its contributors in the last century. The magazine combatted frauds, encouraged experimental farming, conducted crop contests. The *American Agriculturist,* which at one time had a very large circulation, absorbed a score of competitive farm papers in its long history, and itself went through changes both in name and in place of publication, but is still published, now in Ithaca, New York. It had a circulation in 1955 of over 221,000.

Other famous and long-lived agricultural papers are still published and circulated to loyal audiences. The *Rural New Yorker,* first established in Rochester in 1849, is now published in New York and had a circulation in 1955 of nearly 400,000. The *New England Homestead,* founded in Springfield, Massachusetts, in 1855, is still published there one hundred years later. *Farm and Home,* nationally circulated to a large audience between 1880 and 1925, was a monthly offshoot of the *New England Homestead,* which at one period owned and published the *American Agriculturist.* The *Southern Agriculturist,* one of the oldest of the regional farm magazines, was consolidated in 1950 with *Farm and Ranch.* The combined periodical circulation from Nashville, Tennessee, went to over 1,300,000 subscribers. The *Southern Planter,* published in Richmond, dates back to 1841. Today's *Prairie Farmer* was founded in Chicago in 1840 as the *Union Agriculturist,* changing its name in 1843. The *Ohio Farmer* was founded in 1848 and is still published.

One hundred years ago there were about twenty-six agricultural periodicals being published in the United States. Today there are 76 national farm magazines, 64 sectional farm magazines, and over 125 state farm papers.

The great majority of those listed as "national farm magazines," so described because they circulate nationally, are devoted exclusively to covering specific agricultural interests, such as fruit growing, dairy farming, livestock, bee culture, and poultry raising. They are in reality trade and professional journals. The leaders among the farm magazines of general agricultural coverage and wide appeal are *Farm Journal, Successful Farming, The Progressive Farmer,* and *Capper's Farmer.* A fifth member of this important group of general farm magazines of large circulation, *Farm and Fireside,* established in 1877, became *Country Home* in 1929 and ceased publication ten years later, though its 1938 circulation was 1,648,000.

Successful Farming and *Capper's Farmer* are primarily directed to specific agricultural sections of the Middle West. *Successful Farming,* which in size and general format is more nearly akin to *Farm Journal* and *Time* than to the larger-sized farm magazines, is written basically for what it describes as the "heart states," those between Oklahoma and Canada and between the western border of Nebraska and the eastern boundaries of Ohio and Michigan. *Capper's Farmer,* published in Kansas, concentrates its efforts also on the rich farm country of the Middle West but includes more of the southwestern states. Practical farm facts and advice are a mainstay of both *Successful Farming* and *Capper's Farmer,* but both cover national affairs in special departments and in general articles, devote generous amounts of space to the farm home, and keep their readers informed through editorial and advertising pages of the latest developments in agriculture and in agricultural implements. *The Progressive Farmer* is published for the agricultural South.

A typical 1955 issue of *Successful Farming,* "The Magazine of Farm Business and Farm Homes," contained 170 pages. About half the editorial space was devoted to management and business, articles on herds, flock, crops, farm building and machinery, and about half to "successful homemaking," with articles on home decoration, menus, furnishings, sewing, sandwich and salad making, and how-to-do-it tips. The "Farm Outlook" (market forecasts) was followed by "What's New in Farming," and "The Farmer's Washington." Instead of separating items about the farm from those of interest primarily to the farm household, the two were interspersed; an article on social security was followed by pictures showing how to add to home storage space, and that by a colorfully illustrated piece on cornstalk silage; variety, vitality, practicality. *Successful Farming* has some 1,300,000 subscribers.

Capper's Farmer, "The Business Farm Magazine for Mid-America," founded in 1889, features a page of briefs entitled "Foresight—what to expect—what to do—tomorrow, next week, and in the months ahead." It is presented as economic advice by a six-man panel of experts. Washington news of interest to the Midwestern farmer has its own department. The table of contents lists articles under livestock, foods, dairy, poultry, home equipment, farm management, country living, crops, home decoration, farm policy, and machinery and equipment. Like *Country Gentleman, Capper's Farmer* went to smaller page size in 1952. At the same time it began to appear on good quality paper instead of a near-newsprint, with greater use of color on glossy stock. The magazine's circulation exceeds 1,360,000.

The Progresive Farmer, which circulates from Birmingham, Alabama, to about one and a quarter million homes throughout the South, is published in five editions, one for Virginia and the Carolinas, a second for Georgia, Alabama, and Florida; a third for Mississippi, Arkansas, and Louisiana; and the other two for Kentucky-Tennessee and Texas-Oklahoma. Unlike the other farm magazines, it has retained the large page size (approximately that of *The Saturday Evening Post*). Issues run usually over 150 pages and are heavy with editorial content and advertising. The editorial matter is divided into four main parts: "For Everybody This Month," "For Progressive Farmers," "For Progressive Homemakers," "For Progressive Youngfolk." This alignment on the editorial page typically describes the attempt made by all the farm magazines today— material of general appeal, vocational material directed to the farmer, material for the housewife, and material that will encourage youth readership. Like the other farm magazines, *Progressive Farmer* runs a page of Washington briefs and a forecast, this one entitled "What's Ahead—and What To Do About It."

Originally the farm magazines were founded in the nineteenth century to give farmers practical, rule-of-thumb advice about their jobs. They were a means of sharing, through periodical communication, the successful farm experiences of one farmer with his interested fellows. From this, the farm magazines progressed to explanations of scientific agricultural procedures as these were discovered in the laboratory and tested in the field. Their reiterated approval of the newer methods was largely influential in overcoming the natural reluctance of the farmer to try and then adopt the newer, more efficient, and more productive methods advocated.

The farm magazines enlarged their activities. Besides disseminating practical farm knowledge and explaining the new scientific methods, they led in the fight for rural improvements and for the establishment of government agricultural agencies and schools of agriculture. Then, through their articles and their advertising, they brought the farmer news and facts about the farm implements and labor-saving devices, as these were developed and perfected, which have improved farming and made farm life more comfortable.

To these basic functions the national farm magazines, the regional farm magazines, and, to a lesser extent, the state farm papers of comparatively local circulation have added increasingly the social and economically important function of informing the entire rural community about national and international affairs. Through the medium of the farm magazines the farmer and the farm family are now brought significant news and thoughtful comment as fully, as accurately, as quickly—and as attractively—as the general magazines bring them to a largely urban audience.

There are a million less farms in the United States than there were in 1910 and 10 million fewer people on farms.[6] The number of farms and of people engaged in farming will probably dwindle further as mechanization and agricultural chemistry continue to increase farm productivity. Farm incomes, bolstered by government subsidies, remain high. Standards of living on the farm, educational advantages, opportunities for recreation at least equal those of city and town dwellers. For some of this the farm magazines can justly claim a share of the credit. All of the important farm magazines recognize the changes that have taken place on the farm, and the most successful of them have made corresponding changes in their traditional approach to the farmer and his family. Because of this, the farm magazines have retained and strengthened their usefulness in informing and moulding an important segment of public opinion.

[6] 6,361,502 farms in 1910; 5,382,162 in 1950. Farm population was 32,077,000 in 1910; 22,158,000 in 1955. "Farm Population," *Census-AMS* (P27), No. 21, August 11, 1955.

Chapter 15

LIBERALISM AND ICONOCLASM
IN THE MAGAZINES

W<small>HEN</small> *McClure's,* the *American,* and the other muckraking magazines ceased to be organs of reform and liberal thought, while the mass weeklies, like *The Saturday Evening Post* and *Collier's* after the days of Norman Hapgood, stayed conservative or neutral in their discussion of business, social questions, and public affairs, another group of magazines—in some respects far more radical than the more powerful muckraking monthlies —upheld the liberal tradition in the twentieth century.

The Nation was founded in 1865 by E. L. Godkin, a twenty-five-year-old Irish immigrant. Designed as a liberal weekly, it has consistently remained what it was intended to be: a magazine which would discuss current affairs, uphold what it considered truly democratic principles, and work for the elevation of labor as a class and for the improvement of the Negro's lot. Godkin edited *The Nation* until 1881 when he merged it with the *New York Evening Post.* Under Godkin, *The Nation* fought for social improvement, for greater good for all, not only for the economically fortunate few.

Henry and Charles Francis Adams, Henry James, Sr., Henry James, Jr., William James, Francis Parkman, and other scholars and writers were all contributors to Godkin's *Nation,* which struck at political corruption and advocated both tariff and civil service reforms. Under later editors, particularly under Paul Elmer More, classicist and humanist, author of the many volumes of *Shelburne Essays,* it continued its liberal attitude and interpretation of events, but stressed literary criticism. Its literary standards have always been high. Carl, Irita, and Mark Van Doren were all *Nation* literary editors during the editorship of Oswald Garrison Villard, who ran the magazine from 1918 to 1933. Villard retained the magazine's liberal viewpoint, opposed ratification of the Versailles Treaty, adopted a sympathetic atitude toward Soviet Russia, and had *The Nation* pay especial attention to foreign affairs.

Leading liberals either have been on the editorial staff of *The Nation* or have appeared frequently as contributors. Heywood Broun, H. L. Mencken, Norman Thomas, Max Lerner, George Seldes, have all been on its editorial board. Its contributors have been and are a mixture of professors, intellectuals, and journalists; Allen Tate, Dorothy Thompson, John Haynes Holmes, Raymond Clapper, Stuart Chase, Louis Adamic, and Reinhold Niebuhr have been some of them. Heywood Broun, consistent opponent of social injustice, ran a page in *The Nation,* variously entitled "It Seems to Heywood Broun" and "Broun's Page," for many years in the 1920's and the 1930's.

The Nation has long been prolabor, a foe of all racial discrimination, collectivist in its leanings, and critical of the free enterprise system. It retained, perhaps intensified, its general characteristics after Freda Kirchwey, who was long associated with the magazine, became its editor and publisher, in 1933. The new editor believed in collective security as the only defense against the rising tide of fascism in Europe, and *The Nation* advocated it editorially. It advocated lifting the embargo on arms to help the Loyalist government during the Spanish Civil War, and favored collective action to check Japanese aggression against China. During World War II, it criticized the American entente with Vichy France and the appeasement of Franco in Spain. *The Nation* after the war advocated world government and the sharing of atomic information.

Always subsidized but long in financial difficulty and unable to raise sufficient funds through continued campaigns, *The Nation* was in still other difficulties by 1951. A former *Nation* art critic accused the magazine of closely following the Communist line in its comments on American foreign policy. *The Nation,* a foe of censorship and shrill in protest at the banning of any of its issues when they contained unpopular opinions, refused the critic a hearing in its pages. When the accusations were published in the *New Leader,* Freda Kirchwey promptly sued both writer and magazine.

In protest Reinhold Niebuhr resigned from *The Nation*'s editorial staff. A political writer who had once been the magazine's managing editor also resigned. People who thought of themselves as liberals were shocked at what seemed illiberal intolerance. Granville Hicks, writing in the *Commentary,* said: "One looks back with regret to the time when *The Nation* spoke for all liberals. . . . *The Nation* has preserved what was weakest and blindest in the old liberalism and has carried over attitudes that once were irresponsible but now are dangerous." [1]

There were other signs of unrest at *The Nation.* Its longtime literary editor left in 1953. In September, 1955, Freda Kirchwey relinquished her dual position as editor and publisher. Editorship of *The Nation* went to Carey McWilliams, who had been editorial director. In assuming the office of publisher to which he brought needed new capital, George G. Kirstein reiterated *Nation* policy in the issue of September 17, 1955. "This magazine has been and will continue to be frankly partisan. Our hearts and our columns are on the side of the worker, of the minority group, of the underprivileged generally. We side with the intellectual and political non-conformist in his clear constitutional right to refuse to conform."

Far younger than *The Nation,* for it was founded in 1914, less austere but roughly resembling it physically and in general intent, *The New Republic* is a companion liberal magazine as sharply critical of the social and political scene and until recently more radical and outspoken than its fellow. *The New Republic* also has been the friend of labor, the foe of fascism or anything

[1] Quoted in *Time,* April 19, 1951.

it sees as fascistic in tendency, the enemy of economic privilege, and a strong proponent and defender of civil liberties. It is now consistently liberal but definitely anti-Communist.

Herbert Croly was the founding liberal editor of *The New Republic*. He called it "a journal of opinion," and the magazine still uses this phrase to describe itself. *The New Republic* was intended to be antidogmatic. Croly and his associates, as he wrote later, wanted to arouse in readers "little insurrections in the realm of their opinions." The magazine was to "prick and even goad public opinion into being more vigilant and hospitable, into considering its convictions more carefully." Under Herbert Croly and then Bruce Bliven, such writers as Walter Lippmann, Edmund Wilson, Malcolm Cowley, Robert Morss Lovett, Stark Young, and John Dewey made *The New Republic* a sharp-spoken and distinguished weekly. Consistently critical in its attack, it has been more discursive than *The Nation,* and though sometimes shrill, often more tolerant, and at least as sharply perceptive. Social philosophy and prophecy, science, education, morals, economics, and politics have been its chief concerns, as they have been the concerns of *The Nation*. Both magazines, in subject matter if not in viewpoint, more nearly resemble such English periodicals as the current *Spectator* and *The New Statesman and Nation* than their American contemporaries. Both *The Nation* and *The New Republic* stress literary, theatrical, and musical criticism. Both magazines, in the English fashion, devote considerable space to letters from readers. These letters are regular features, designed to encourage further expression of opinion on subjects of social and political interest. They are not filler material, as they often appear to be in some of the larger magazines which have adopted the ancient device.

With the issue of December 16, 1946, *The New Republic* changed its page size, going into a smaller-sized page. It changed its format generally, and changed its editor. In this issue Henry Wallace, ex-Secretary of Commerce and ex-Vice-

President, was announced as editor, Michael Straight as publisher, and Bruce Bliven was moved up to be editorial director. During his year and a half as *New Republic* editor, before he resigned to head a third party in the presidential election of 1948, Wallace's extreme liberalism was reflected in the magazine. A weekly page carried his opinions on national and international affairs.

These changes were designed to make *The New Republic* look more like a news weekly. Cartoons, caricatures, graphs, and simplified charts appeared as illustrations for articles bearing catchy titles and subtitles. New departments—"Farm," "Labor," "Washington Wire," and the like—made their appearance; and the masthead, showing the influence of the Luce publications, paraded a long list of "senior editors," "associate editors," and "researchers." With Bruce Bliven remaining as editorial director and Michael Straight, son of the magazine's founding family, as editor, the appearance of *The New Republic* changed again, returning to something more nearly akin to its earlier conservative format, but the attempt to popularize the magazine was still evident.

In March, 1953, *The New Republic* suffered a severe blow. Financial support derived from a trust fund set up from the Whitney fortune was withdrawn. Michael Straight and the magazine's new publisher, Gilbert Harrison, were faced with a difficult situation. Publication was continued despite a formidable weekly deficit which they had somehow to make up. The magazine still tried, as it said in various editorials during this time while it was appealing desperately for funds, to be nonconformist, original, challenging, militant, and controversial. *The New Republic* was saved when in the spring of 1954 the publisher's wife fell heir to a few millions of McCormick reaper money. There is some irony in the fact that both *The New Republic* and *The Nation* depend for their existence on funds from capitalistic system private enterprise, a system they accept but do not publicly admire.

On November 22, 1954, *The New Republic* published an impressive 40th anniversary issue of 126 pages. Its glossy cover listed the names of forty-one eminent contributors of the past, among them Shaw, Wells, Yeats, Santayana, Joyce, D. H. Lawrence, Hemingway, Dreiser, Faulkner, T. S. Eliot. Their original contributions were reprinted in the issue and Bruce Bliven reviewed the magazine's forty years. *The New Republic,* he said, had consistently represented minority, unpopular opinion. It had been, he admitted, left of center in the 1930's. "Most of the ideas of the New Deal," he claimed, "first saw the light in its pages."

A visitor from the world of the popular magazine (and *The New Republic* has certainly never been loud in its praises of that world), Henry Luce, was the guest speaker at an anniversary dinner in Washington. "Forty years after its formation," Michael Straight said on the occasion, "the place remains for a liberal journal of opinion. So does our ambition to fill that place."

Both *The Nation* and *The New Republic* have been outspoken in their adverse criticism of political and social activities and tendencies. *The Nation,* touched with the formal academic manner, has been on the whole more restrained; *The New Republic* the more aggressive in its support of minority groups, minority opinion, and advanced thought generally. Neither magazine, until *The New Republic* in its most recent phases, has made any attempt to be popular or to entertain. Both of them have served as useful gadflies, and as antidotes to the complacency, the materialism, and the intrenched conservatism of some of the larger, more widely circulated magazines.

The influence of these liberal weeklies has been circumscribed by several factors. They have always had comparatively slight circulations, standing now at about 30,000 for each of them. Serious and unrelentingly earnest in their efforts, they have not attracted a large enough audience to circulate their ideas widely. Directed largely to the intelligentsia, they have mainly reached readers already sympathetic to the liberal views they express, and have failed to reach a wider audience whose interest might be aroused and which might be converted to the application of greater mental effort in the consideration of problems beyond their immediate personal sphere. Neither *The New Republic* nor *The Nation* attracts much advertising. Published on a heavy-grade newsprint, sparsely illustrated, they lack the physical attractiveness of the mass magazines. Because of all these limitations, they have remained periodicals for the elect and select.

All such magazines, of course, have a stronger effect than their limited circulations indicate. A very high proportion of their readers are intellectuals, educated people, many of them university and college teachers who disseminate in their classrooms and in their professional associations the ideas obtained from the magazines they read. There is still the limitation that their ideas are spread mostly among the young whose idealism has not been subdued by much actual experience. Neither directly nor indirectly does this magazine liberalism touch forcefully on men and women engaged in practical business or industry, as the liberalism of the profitable and widely circulated muckraking magazines very definitely did.

Another insurgent magazine became one of the social and literary phenomena, as well as a social and literary force, of the 1920's. This was *The American Mercury*. The movement (if so formal a word can describe anything as difficult to classify as the vigorous and untrammeled reform efforts and the startling effects which this magazine obtained issue after issue) had started, long before the *Mercury*'s founding in 1924, in another magazine which was turned widely from its original course.

The Smart Set was founded in 1890 by William D'Alton Mann as a journal for New York "society." At first it was written and read mostly by members of this self-consciously exclusive group. Arthur Griscom and Charles Hanson Towne, when they become its editors, transformed *The Smart Set* into a witty literary journal, a kind of dilettante's delight, which they had no hesitation in describing on the front cover as "A Magazine of Cleverness." Nor were they casting pearls before swine. *The Smart Set* was edited, on its own declaration, "to provide lively entertainment for minds that are not primitive." Despite this pose of snobbish discrimination, despite a certain preciosity, *The Smart Set* published notable work. It accepted O. Henry's first short story. It began, after its purchase in 1900 by John Adams Thayer, to publish such writers as Gertrude Atherton, James Branch Cabell, Richard Le Gallienne, and other writers of the more aesthetic persuasion.

In October, 1902, its cover—the familiar *Smart Set* cover with a gentleman in tails bowing to a curtsying lady in evening costume, a cupid with drawn bow in the lower right-hand corner, a masked satyr in the upper left, and the red logotype lettered in flowing capitals—opened on prose and verse by Hildegarde Hawthorne, Arthur Symons, Bliss Carman, Ridgley Torrence, Madison Cawein, Ella Wheeler Wilcox, Arthur Macy, and a score of lesser-known writers. James Branch Cabell was already represented with a romantic story in the genteel mode of the day, its author barely recognizable as the more daring romanticist he was to become in the 1920's. The issue was all fiction and verse. There were no articles. The love stories were of a most sentimental kind, and the jokes, of which they were many scattered as filler, were of such appalling insipidity that it is hard for a modern reader to visualize the kind of man or woman who could ever have found them amusing. There was already, at both the front and back of the issue, a plenitude of advertising for more plebeian articles than those touched on in the editorial pages.

The editor of *The Smart Set* from 1912 to 1914 was Willard Huntington Wright, aesthete and sophisticate, who was later to achieve a different fame as a writer of detective fiction. His *Canary Murder Case*, written under the pseudonym of S. S. Van Dine, and run in *Scribner's Magazine* in 1927, broke all publishing records for the sale of detective fiction. He had set the pattern for a series of Van Dine thrillers with *The Benson Murder Case* the year before. Wright was the first American editor to print James Joyce, George Moore, D. H. Lawrence, and other writers of advanced literary and moral ideas whose work was not acceptable to the mass magazines.

The change in *The Smart Set* in ten years' time was marked. Contributors to the issue of May, 1913, included John Hall Wheelock, Louis Untermeyer, Owen Hatteras, Sara Teasdale, Wright and—certainly a sport in this galley—Irvin Cobb. Most significant, George Jean Nathan and H. L. Mencken, besides conducting, respectively, the departments of theatrical and literary criticism, were each represented by an article. Mencken, who wrote on "Good Old Baltimore," a subject on which he has touched several times since, opened his lead book review with this line: "Morality, like culture, belongs to what the psychiatrists call the circular insanities, at least in these states." This reads like a portent of the later Mencken.

There was a further portent in an advertisement in the issue of June, 1913. The advertisement stressed the first of a series of satirical sketches called "The American" by H. L. Mencken. "These articles," ran the blurb, "are to deal with all phases of the native male product of this country—his religion, his ideas of beauty, his politics, his habits, and his social life. The essays will represent the most solid work that Mr. Mencken has ever done. The fact that they deal with the American dispassionately and satirically will make them at once unique and interesting."

The 1913 *Smart Set* was a much stronger, more advanced, more daring magazine than it had been a decade earlier. One lead story, "Daughters of Joy" by Barry Benefield, described the funeral of a New York prostitute, dead of tuberculosis, at her place of business, with her employer and business associates acting as mourners. Editorially the magazine pointed out: "Sex itself is not indecent. It is the innuendoes that make it so." Another editorial deplored the low state into which humor had fallen: "Puritanism and conventionalism have limited our joke-sters thematically, and our funny men find their best jokes un-salable. The average American is unable to laugh at himself; he is unable to appreciate sarcasm and cynicism if the ridicule touches any of his pet beliefs." In these editorials it is easy to perceive the hand of Mencken, to read what were to become the familiar Mencken themes. In 1914, Nathan and Mencken be-came coeditors of *The Smart Set*. World War I hindered them a little, but after its close the new editors went to work with a will on their vigorous campaign to change the prejudices of Americans, to demolish their conceptions of themselves, to rout puritanism and the genteel, to champion realism and naturalism in writing, to shock everyone out of his complacency, to smash every idol within reach, and to tremble all the others off their pedestals by the reverberations of their raucous derision.

What Mencken began in *The Smart Set* he continued from 1924 to 1933 in *The American Mercury*. The new magazine was edited during its first year by both Nathan and Mencken, but after that by Mencken alone. He boomed Theodore Dreiser and Sinclair Lewis; published Eugene O'Neill, Thomas Beer, Lewis Mumford, and F. Scott Fitzgerald. Strident, racy, irrev-erent, Mencken, by sheer force, was making a place for the newer kinds of writing, throwing out the dainty and delicate, yammering for more realism and stronger naturalism, for litera-ture of the actual, not literature of the ideal. He published Sher-wood Anderson, Joseph Hergesheimer, Carl Van Vechten, the naturalists, the aesthetes, the realists, the "new" writers. Mean-while, in "Americana," a department of clippings selected from newspapers to show the appalling stupidity of the American mass mind, Mencken was berating the American public, and the public loved it. *The American Mercury* struck out in every direction. Irony, satire, burlesque, and outright bludgeoning were its weapons.

The American Mercury of the 1920's was not, any more than *The Smart Set* had been, a muckraking magazine after the pattern of *McClure's*. Neither did it resemble the liberal *Nation* and *New Republic*. It was out, not to reform government or business or social conditions, but to unmake the character of the individual American, to upset the pattern of his conventionalized ethics and his ways of looking at things. It had no positive philosophy to offer. It did not wish to remake the individual in any other mould, except posibly that of a milder Mencken; it intended to disturb, to shock, to arouse, to make people question. Like most magazines which take a discernible stand on any issue, it preferred its own prejudices to those of anybody else. It wanted people to be unconventional, but not so unconventional as not to recognize how daring they were. It was all loud and boisterous, vital and amusing.

It was also effective. The newer naturalism in literature, partly as a result of the *Mercury's* insistence, was recognized as worthy of critical consideration as well as reading. The loud boisterousness of Mencken and his magazine offended the fastidious and displeased many academic critics, but Mencken won. Stuart Sherman, Illinois professor, conservative critic in the style of Matthew Arnold, whose biography he wrote, humanist after Irving Babbitt and Paul Elmer More, kept up a long running fight with Mencken. Sherman defended puritanism and the literary values of the student and the scholar, defended the ethical standards and moral codes which *The American Mercury* seemed to be trying to demolish. Mencken won the battle when Sherman, after he became the editor of the book section of the *New York Herald Tribune,* modified his literary opinions and changed to a liberal viewpoint nearer Mencken's. Mencken had already overcome easier opponents.

The American Mercury became the college undergraduate's bible of cynicism and wickedness in the 1920's. The young intelligentsia of an excited decade, who felt that all their standards of value had been upset by World War I, scarcely knew what to think on artistic, literary, aesthetic, and moral questions—especially on moral questions—until the next issue of the

Mercury came out. Not to know and admire the magazine was to prove oneself an uncouth barbarian, a member in good standing of the "booboisie" which Mencken attacked with such contempt and savagery. The beauty of the *Mercury* was that, looking as sedate in its green cover as *Harper's* or the *Atlantic,* looking like a scholarly monthly thick and rich with advertising, it yet attacked everything. And everything, believed its audience of the 1920's who looked on the *Mercury* as a religion rather than a magazine, needed to be attacked.

In 1927, when *The American Mercury* was at the height of its spectacular career and its influence on at least a part of the literate population was amazing, the November number carried an article on genetics; a study of Tom Heflin; a sketch entitled "A German Grandfather" by Ruth Suckow; a gruesome description of the brutal treatment of convicts on a Texas chain gang, written by Ernest Booth, then an inmate of a California prison where he was serving a life sentence for robbery; and "Days of Wickedness," a story by Herbert Asbury of the gangs in New York's infamous Fourth Ward. In "Clinical Notes" George Jean Nathan commented caustically on the debasing of fine liquors by American drinking habits, and concluded that the American people, acting in this instance as boorishly as they usually acted, deserved the visitation upon them of the Eighteenth Amendment. The issue contained a curious piece entitled "Body's Breviary" by Joseph Warren Beach, critic, literary historian, and university teacher, and a sharply written article on the rise, through dubious means, of the tabloid press in New York. Nathan, of course, reviewed the current plays, and Mencken the new books. Discussing *The Natural History of Revolutions* by Lyford P. Edwards, Mencken concluded that there were (in 1927) many signs of a possible revolution in the United States. He noted a widespread sense of oppression, not coordinated, not voiced, but real. "The peaceable citizen feels a heavier weight of government every day; the army of professional regulators and oppressors grows at a dizzy pace."

One of the advertisements—there were nearly one hundred pages of advertisements in this issue—near the back of the magazine was for Mencken's *Prejudices: Sixth Series.*

Mencken's *American Mercury* created a magnificent stir in its day. It did more than that. It permanently affected American fiction and American literary criticism. It changed the attitude toward the conventions and affected the tastes of an entire generation. *The American Mercury* was one of the loudest voices whose noise combined to make the Roaring Twenties roar.

Magazine liberalism and iconoclasm have both declined in the years since World War II. The reasons in both instances are apparent. Most of the old idols have been smashed, and the clay feet of newer ones have not yet been identified. Approval of communism, possible and often applauded among intellectuals in the 1930's and even during the war years, is now dangerous and forbidden. Domestic liberal reforms need not be pushed as fiercely. Most of the immediate social gains have been gained, and newer causes either have not been invented or have not been formulated distinctly enough for journalistic clamor. The economically overprivileged class has been abolished through confiscatory income taxes, and a new one has taken its place; the have-nots of the 1920's and the 1930's are the have-its of the 1950's and the immediately foreseeable future, and the newer tyrants are not yet assailable. The cynicism fashionable a generation ago has been scourged out of the temple in the upsurge of religious emotion reflected in swollen church attendance and in the worship of such newer prophets as Dr. Norman Vincent Peale and Billy Graham.

Chapter 16

MAGAZINES AS NATIONAL NEWSPAPERS

Eᴀʀʟʏ in the twentieth century *The Independent,* at the time a powerful weekly, could say editorially: "Modern American magazines have to a large extent fallen heir to the power formerly exerted by pulpit, by crowds, parliamentary debates and daily newspapers in the molding of public opinion, the development of new issues, and dissemination of information bearing on current questions." [1]

Colonel George Harvey,[2] later ambassador to Great Britain, long editor of *The North American Review* and *Harper's Weekly,* and when he spoke, president of Harper & Brothers, also emphasized the mounting importance of the new mass magazines in influencing public opinion. Addressing the Sphinx Club in New York, on March 8, 1910, he said that the chief appeal of the low-priced magazines "is to interest in public affairs, and their *motif* is timeless." He continued:

[1] October 1, 1908. *The Independent* editorial writer expanded his argument by specific illustrations: "The magazine represents intellectual activity in its terminal buds. Its function is to work over old plots into new stories; to rewrite biography and history in accordance with the taste of the time, to resurrect forgotten truths, to make sound information palatable, to convert abstract science into applied science, to throw a searchlight into dark corners of the earth and some spots of our civilization, to start new movements and to guide old ones, to wake up people who are asleep by sounding the burglar alarm, to twist around the heads of those who are looking backward over their shoulders; in short, to inspire, to instruct, to interest."

[2] Colonel Harvey also enjoyed the title "President-Maker." It was his hotel suite at the Blackstone Hotel in Chicago which became the famous "smoke-filled room" of the Republican Convention of 1920. A conference of party leaders there resulted in the nomination of Warren G. Harding for President.

How admirably they have performed their functions and
how accurately they have gauged the public's requirements and
inclinations may be judged from their obvious popularity.

The alert new periodicals have been called national newspapers, and to this extent the term is warranted: They do deal
largely with vital topics of immediate interest, they do take sides,
they do aim to guide as well as interpret public opinion, and
their field is the whole country. They are public journals. . . .
As such they have done much good and no little harm, but that
the good they have done greatly outweighs the harm seems to
be evidenced by the apparent fact that their power is increasing.

Colonel Harvey could scarcely have foreseen the extent to
which the power of the mass magazines would reach. Four
years later, in 1914, the average circulation for one issue of the
54 magazines then checked by the Audit Bureau of Circulation
was less than 18,000,000 copies. Now the per issue circulation of the 268 magazines checked by A. B. C. is over
166,000,000.

One of the powerful magazines performing the functions
which both the *Independent* editorial and Colonel George
Harvey described is no longer in existence. Others had not yet
been established.

The *Literary Digest,* founded in 1890, became an influential
weekly journal of current events, reaching a circulation of
almost two million in the 1920's. Never "literary" and scarcely
a "digest," the magazine was written almost entirely with the
scissors. Every week its editors pasted up, side by side, clippings from the country's newspapers and magazines on current
questions. They did not digest, rewrite, or interpret. They
simply presented news and editorial comment, including cartoons. Where the interpretations of political events, world happenings, and developments in art, literature, science, and religion
differed, they presented both sides of the question and showed
the source making the original comments. Regular features of
the *Digest* during the days of its greatest success were Topics
of the Day, Foreign Comment, Science and Invention, Letters

and Art, Religion and Social Service, Current Poetry, Personal Glimpses, Investments and Finance, Current Events, Spice of Life, Radio, and the Lexicographer's Easy Chair.

The virtues of the *Literary Digest* were its careful winnowing of the newspaper and periodical press, and its presentation of information in such a way that the reader could make up his own mind on the basis of all the published facts. It provided the data from which public opinion could be formed, but did not attempt to hand out that opinion ready-made. Such an editorial policy sometimes made for dull reading and always required more active and intelligent participation than some readers could or would give, but, as an accurate and unbiased vehicle of current information, the *Literary Digest* maintained a high standard. Recognition of its complete and unprejudiced reporting caused its wide adoption throughout the American public school system, particularly in the high schools, for classes in English, public speaking, debating, civics, and history. This, added to its general acceptance by the magazine-reading public, made it one of the potent magazines, of the strictly informational type, in the first quarter of the twentieth century.

During the 1920's the *Literary Digest* originated the device of straw polls for measuring public opinion on important questions. It is popularly supposed that the magazine's ultimate failure was caused by its mistake in prophesying, on the basis of a reader poll, the outcome of the presidential election of 1936. This was undoubtedly a contributing factor, but only a factor. If the failure of such polls necessitates collapse of the sponsoring publications and organizations, the ground should have been littered with wrecks of magazines, newspapers, and professional oracles after the debacle of election forecasting in 1948, when the polls were virtually unanimous in picking the losing candidate as the certain victor in the presidential election. There are probably technical and less technical explanations for their loud and concerted failure. Discussion of these would be impertinent here. It is pertinent to note that the *Digest,* by its consistent and successful use of the poll technique and the accuracy of many of its earlier survey results, demonstrated the usefulness of sampling public opinion. Opinion polls, with improved sampling and interviewing techniques, are now widely used to gauge public reaction to important social and economic questions, and their results are useful where a greater margin of error can be tolerated than in the forecasting of closely contested elections. In 1938 the waning *Literary Digest* was purchased by the publisher of a much younger competitor which is now the best-known weekly news magazine in the United States.

The man who bought the *Literary Digest* was by 1938 one of the most powerful magazine publishers and editors in the United States. His influence on magazines and, through his magazines, on contemporary American civilization is comparable to that of Curtis, Lorimer, Bok, and McClure a few years earlier. Henry Luce, born in China where his father was a missionary, first went to school in England, then prepared at Hotchkiss for Yale, from which he was graduated in 1920. At Hotchkiss, Henry Luce met Briton Hadden, and it was while they were still preparatory school students that they first had the idea for an informative weekly news magazine. The idea developed further while they were together as undergraduates at Yale, where, significantly, Luce made a tabloid of the Yale *Daily News,* which he edited.

In 1923 Luce and Hadden founded *Time.* The two young men had very definite ideas about the kind of magazine they wished to publish and very definite purposes in mind. Both were dissatisfied with existing journalism. They found that the newspapers were diffuse and disorderly in their presentation of the news, and that most of the magazines gave what they considered inadequate coverage to world events. Their earnest purpose, didactic from the start, was to shape and circulate a magazine which would do what they felt both newspapers and magazines failed to do. In the prospectus for the "weekly newsmagazine," a descriptive phrase which they coined and

Time continues to use, Luce and Hadden stated flatly: "People in America are, for the most part, poorly informed." Americans, they said, were uninformed because "no publication has adapted itself to the time which busy men are able to spend on simply keeping informed." This deplorable condition they intended to correct.

Their proposed magazine would organize the week's news in a pattern of departments, give the news in narrative form, and describe the people who made the news. *Time* would select the facts, tell what the facts meant, and state or strongly suggest what the reader should think or feel about them. The new magazine was to be "curt, clear, complete," so written and arranged that each issue would be an orderly and coherent account of the preceding week's news.

Its determined founders had difficulty in obtaining financial backing for their venture. It was five years before *Time* was soundly established. By 1928, with Hadden as editor and Luce as business manager, it had attained a circulation of 200,000. Long since, *Time* "the weekly newsmagazine," has been firmly fixed in the American scene. Its circulation is over 1,860,000.

Unlike the *Literary Digest,* the powerful predecessor and at one time strong competitor which eventually it absorbed, *Time* did not limit itself to clippings and quotations. It could not and fulfill its self-imposed mission of instructing the populace. It presented each news story crisply and smartly in what it is charitable understatement to describe as *Time*'s distinctive style, a style which has since been happily modified. It spoke from the beginning with complete assurance, *ex cathedra* authority, and metallic certainty. Hadden and Luce had introduced a new kind of magazine.

They put new practices to work in publishing it. One was the use of library research to make each news story not an isolated occurrence but part of a continuous historical stream of events. Another was the technique of writing and editing by which reporters, writers, researchers, and editors pooled their knowledge and skills to produce the copy published anonymously in each *Time* issue. In its early years *Time* proudly used the phrase "group journalism" to describe this operation. It has since gone on record as regretting invention and use of the term. "Its Editor and Managing Editor, like those of any other publication, are and always have been responsible editors. Every other *Time* staff member is responsible for whatever he or she contributes (or omits to contribute) to the week's work."[3]

The pattern of departments the editors adopted has varied little since the beginning. Currently it is: Art, Books, Business, Cinema, Education, Foreign News, Hemisphere, Letters, Medicine, Milestones, Miscellany, Music, National Affairs, People, Press, Radio and Television, Religion, Science, Sports, Theater, United Nations. *Time* coverage is wide. People, *Time*'s founders had said in their 1923 prospectus, subscribing readily to the hero theory of history, make the news; so *Time* would tell about these pepole. With very few exceptions, there has always been a picture of a man or a woman on the cover of each *Time* issue. Inside the magazine, a featured cover story tells about the person's life, thoughts, ideas, and accomplishment— and always, as with every subject, how *Time* views them.[4]

The first issue of *Time*, March 3, 1923, was written, edited, and published in New York by a small group of young men, most of them but a few years out of college. A large central office staff of writers, editors, and research assistants puts out the magazine now. Besides using the facilities of the standard news-gathering services, *Time* has its own bureaus in thirteen United States and Canadian cities, a large Washington force, and fifteen bureaus in important news centers abroad. All of these and field correspondents report to the editors in New

[3] *The Story of an Experiment* (New York: Time, Inc., 1948).

[4] It is of passing interest that Whittaker Chambers, then a senior editor of *Time*, wrote the cover stories on Marian Anderson, Arnold Toynbee, Rebecca West, and Reinhold Niebuhr.

TIME

The Weekly News-Magazine

VOL. 1. NO. 1   MARCH 3, 1923

The first *Time* cover, in black and white, pictured Uncle Joe Cannon, Speaker of the House, who was retiring at the age of eighty-six after serving twenty-three terms in Congress.

York. Unlike most newspapermen and magazine article writers, *Time* reporters do not write directly for publication. They gather facts and opinions for transmittal to the New York editorial group who write, shape, and polish the material for publication in the issues which appear every Thursday. Besides the domestic, there are four international editions of *Time,* all in English. *Time Pacific* is printed in Tokyo and Honolulu; *Time Atlantic* in Paris. They are identical in content with the domestic edition. *Time Canadian* and *Time Latin American* carry additional pages of editorial material on the areas in which they circulate, and, of course, different advertising. In 1923 the brash idea of two idealistic and intensely ambitious recent Yale undergraduates, *Time* is now one of the most influential of all American magazines.[5] It is circulated and read in 188 countries, islands, and territories; distributed, as the *Time* organization points out, "in every continent on the globe except Antarctica."

Time is prepared for and directed to a hypothetical man who is assumed to have no other source of information on current events. *Time*'s purpose is to provide him with all the important news of the week, background enough to make the news intelligible, and enough comment to direct his opinion. Its intent is to enlighten by presenting information as complete as possible, and by interpreting the information provided. Each issue is prepared much as a newspaper is prepared and sent to press. Everything in each issue is checked and approved by one man on *Time*'s staff, its managing editor. Henry Luce himself approved the *Time* jargon, the inverted sentences, slick epithets, the air of brassy omniscience which *Time* intentionally displayed in its earlier years. He is still, as *Time*'s editor-in-chief, its directing force. The magazine not only reflects his belief that the world needs information, but also presents the news accord-

[5] Briton Hadden's chief ambition was to make a million dollars by the time he was 30. When he died in 1929 at the age of 31, his *Time* stock was worth over $1,100,000.

ing to definite Luce concepts; facts are aligned, joined, related, explained, and built toward an opinion ready-made for the peruser of *Time*.

Time's first editorial employee—he became its managing editor, later its chief foreign correspondent—once described the ideal *Time* story. "The basis of good *Time* writing is narrative, and the basis of good narrative is to tell events, 1) in the order in which they occur; 2) in the form in which an observer might have seen them—so that readers can imagine themselves on the scene. A *Time* story must be completely organized from beginning to end; it must go from nowhere to somewhere and sit down when it arrives." [6]

This calm and pleasantly worded description of an intense performance omits one important ingredient, the editorializing which is an essential part of most *Time* stories. Far from hiding the attempt, *Time* boasts of it. From the beginning it said it would give both sides of a story but clearly indicate which side it believed to have the strongest position. Its editors have reiterated their conviction that it is the duty of the press to evaluate as well as to report. *Time* has never claimed to be objective. In fact, it derides objectivity as impossible, which probably it is. The very selection of facts to report implies the action of some interpreting and, per se, prejudiced mind. *Time* goes further. It puts its selected facts into selected concepts. Inevitably there is distortion in its effort to make the isolated news event part of a significant body of coherent thought—or a coherent body of significant thought.[7] This does, though, make it easy for *Time*'s mythical one-man reader to feel that he has both got all the news and placed it in context and perspective.

Before Hadden's death Luce had conceived the idea of another magazine. This magazine, like *Time,* would educate its readers. Again the Luce purpose was didactic. *Fortune* was

---

[6] *The Story of an Experiment, op. cit.*
[7] Because they describe a mystical ideal, the phrases seem readily interchangeable.

conceived in 1928 as a magazine which would describe American business. A *Time* editor provided the inspiration when he discovered "the vast, lurid, and exciting bibliography of balance sheets." Like Curtis and Lorimer, in this instance at least, Luce felt that business was the basic expression of the American spirit. He proposed to establish a magazine which would "reflect industrial life as faithfully in ink and paper and word as the finest skyscraper reflects it in stone, steel, and architecture."

The first issue of *Fortune,* an expensive, beautifully dressed monthly, went to 30,000 subscribers in January, 1930. Started shortly after the 1929 stock market crash, by 1933, in the middle of the depression, *Fortune* was earning money. The magazine, physically magnificent, handsomely printed and illustrated on quality stock, was addressed not to the masses but to business owners and executives. Business alone was the subject of articles during the first years. As government became increasingly important in business and to the business community in the 1930's, *Fortune* branched out into governmental and social subjects. The pages of a current issue of *Fortune* may include the biography of an eminent industrialist, an article concerned primarily with economics, or a complete description of the organization and operation of one great business house—an oil company, a baking company, an advertising agency. There is an opening Business Roundup. Departments deal with Labor and Technology.

Like *Time, Fortune* is staff-written. Articles, with few exceptions, are anonymous. They are the product of thorough and extensive research. A staff of women researchers does an exhaustive job of file research. Staff writers or their assistants interview anyone and everyone who can give them the facts they need to know in order to present a full and accurate picture. *Fortune* articles, in their length and thoroughness, and in the completeness of the research done in preparing them have been compared to the full-bodied studies done by the muckrakers for

McClure's. They are hardly comparable otherwise. Once there was more than a touch of iconoclasm about many *Fortune* articles. There is none now. *Fortune's* purpose is not to expose but to explain. Though facts are given as they are found, the effect of the articles in *Fortune* is to make glamorous the industry or business described. Luce originally wanted to find and describe "the technological significance of industry." Actually, *Fortune,* though it took a stand for the Wagner Labor Relations Act when it was under attack by business generally, and has never modified its conclusion to suit the prejudices of overconservative businessmen, presents, handsome issue by handsome issue, the romance of American business as it is.

In two magazines, *Time* and *Fortune,* Henry Luce had undertaken and practiced the education of the American public. In 1936 he purchased a name made deservedly famous as that of the best of American humor magazines [8] and borrowed the pictorial weekly idea originated by Frank Leslie and practiced so successfully by *Harper's Weekly* until it ceased publication in 1916. Despite gloomy prophecies by trade observers who based their predictions largely on the comparative failure of *The New York Times' Mid-Week Pictorial,* Henry Luce combined title and old idea to produce one of today's most important weekly magazines.

[8] *Life,* founded in 1883, was a magazine devoted to delicate social satire, a little more subtle than its contemporaries *Puck* and *Judge.* Charles Dana Gibson created his "Gibson girl" for the earlier *Life.* All three magazines have now ceased publication in anything like their original form. Most of the college humor magazines which imitated them have also disappeared. *The New Yorker,* satirical, sophisticated, an institution in its own right since its 1925 founding, is the sole important survivor of the type.

Luce paid $85,000 for the old *Life.* According to Margaret Case Harriman in a two-installment *New Yorker* "profile" of Clare Boothe Luce, entitled "The Candor Kid," the idea had been forwarded three years earlier. Henry Luce married Clare Boothe, playwright and later Congresswoman, presently Ambassador to Italy, in 1935. When he told her of his purchase of *Life,* she brought out a memorandum she had written in 1933, when she was managing editor of *Vanity Fair.* The memorandum suggested that Condé Nast purchase *Life* for $20,000, at which price it was said to be purchasable in 1933, and turn it into a picture magazine.

Success of the venture was astounding from the start. There were 230,000 subscribers even before the new magazine, which had had dry runs as *Dummy* and *Rehearsal*, had a name. The first print order was for 466,000 copies. A month later it was for 533,000; four months later for 1,080,000. *Life*'s total circulation now is 5,552,276.[9] It claims a total readership of 26,-350,000 for each issue.[10]

In purple rhetoric *Life* announced its purpose in its original prospectus:

> To see life; to see the world; to eyewitness great events; to watch the faces of the poor and the gestures of the proud; to see strange things—machines, armies, multitudes, shadows in the jungle and on the moon; to see man's work—his paintings, towers, and discoveries; to see things thousands of miles away, things hidden behind walls and within rooms, things dangerous to come to; the women men love and many children; to see and take pleasure in seeing; to see and be amazed; to see and be instructed.

The educational intent of *Life* has been basic from the beginning. The magazine was formulated to instruct as well as to attract, entertain, and amuse. As evident was *Life*'s early journalistic formula: lavish use of sex pictures and of gruesome pictures displaying slaughter, executions, strewn corpses; deliberate appeal, through publicizing their activities in glamorous photographs, to the "smart set," the sporting group, the college and preparatory school crowd, and every group susceptible to the flattery—as what group or individual is not?—of attention and favorable display in a national magazine.

Life covers the news pictorially. It shows in photographs the dramatic and spectacular events that will strike the reader with greatest force. Its picturing of sex, glamour, violence, crime, and disaster is effective. These are subjects of intense and lasting interest to everyone, from the vulgar to the fastidi-

[9] A. B. C. Publisher's Statement for the second six months of 1955.
[10] *Study of Four Media*. Conducted for *Life* by Alfred Politz Research, Inc., New York, 1953.

ous. It shows public figures in action, gangsters and prime ministers, actors and presidents. People, places, and events are spread before the reader in their authentic actuality. *Life's* picture reporting made World War II more vivid than any words could have made it. Timely, informative, entertaining journalism is a part of *Life's* function.

Life has other functions and performs them superbly. By pictures, diagrams, and charts, it explains scientific and medical facts, facts about the world's food supply, facts about color, about electronics. World affairs, industry, labor problems are explained in pictures, charts, and text. *Life* stories are designed to increase its readers' knowledge of what is happening in the world, why things are happening, and what they mean. One of *Life's* most important contributions to the adult education of Americans has been its full-color reproductions which have acquainted millions with classical and modern masterpieces of painting. It has not only reproduced the work of Titian, El Greco, Grant Wood, Van Gogh, and scores of other painters from the Italian Renaissance to the contemporary American, but has also commissioned modern artists for particular work and published their interpretations of what they saw. During World War II it took over the contracts of a group of artists whom the War Department had commissioned, sent them to paint and draw scenes at the battle fronts, and later published their work.

Besides recording contemporary history, *Life* has devoted whole issues to such historical periods as the Renaissance and the Middle Ages. Almost completely a pictorial magazine when it was established, *Life* has increasingly admitted more and more text to its pages. It publishes feature articles now in almost every issue, some of them staff written, some of them notable contributions by outside authorities on the subjects of which they write. In signed articles historians have written of history, statesmen of world affairs, and critics of the arts they patronize. The intellectual level of many of these contributions is high. Most of the editorial text, however, as in all Luce magazines, is anonymous. *Life* performs its stated function of balancing the attractive and entertaining with the educational and informative in still another way—by publishing condensations or abstracts from books, some merely journalistic successes of the day, others thoughtful literary productions.

Life has changed as it has grown older. Glamour girls predominate on its covers, but there is less cheesecake in the editorial, more homey Americana. In both pictures and text there is less news; there are more essays. It has published noteworthy issues: its tenth anniversary issue, November 25, 1946, surveyed a decade that had seen a major war and much social change. It reprinted historical events it had depicted and had Mark Sullivan do an *Our Times* of 1936–1946. It spoke proudly of controversies the magazine had stirred up, particularly when after printing pictures of actual childbirth in "The Birth of a Baby," April 11, 1938, the magazine was banned in various cities, and its publishers were arrested.

January 2, 1950, *Life* printed its mid-century issue, making it a pictorial history of "American Life and Times, 1900–1950." A Gibson Girl cover, pages of vital statistics, Prohibition, the Hall-Mills murder case, early magazine advertisements; all came in for attention. There were pictures of Ford, Edison, Burroughs, and Firestone, of Lindbergh and Grover Whalen, of Red Grange, Clara Bow, Jack Dempsey, Gilda Gray, Herbert Hoover, each allied to his own specialty. *Life* goes in for nostalgia often, as well as for entertainment and easy education.

Life has always its more pretentious projects—Winston Churchill's war memoirs, the autobiography of the Duke of Windsor, its successive outlines of history from the beginning to the end of time, "MacArthur's Rendezvous with History," its impressive series on "The World We Live In." It ran its special series on America's arts and sciences, closed its series on great religions by a thick special Christmas issue in 1955 which told the story of Christianity. But *Life* has its other points and pleasures. August 11, 1941, it printed a picture of Rita Hayworth in attractive *deshabille*. It reprinted the same picture in its tenth anniversary issue, saying, "When they first saw it, *Life's* editors thought it the best girl picture ever taken. They have never changed their mind." The picture was printed for the third time some years later in the *Life* department called "What's In a Picture." This time the text divulged more of *Life's* philosophy: "Pretty girls are as much a part of today's life as the irrational bloodiness of war, the unrealities of some contemporary art, and the devious channels of international politics."

All of these things, sentiment and sensation, cuddly things and stark things, war, archeology, religion, physics, and fashions, *Life* covers. It can make drama of them all—insanity, storms, jail riots or Kant—and it does.

Millions of people, those who receive the magazine through subscription or buy it on the newsstands, and those who see it after it has been passed along by the first reader, read each single issue of *Life*. Other millions read *Fortune* and *Time*. This huge audience not only demonstrates the success of the three magazines established and published by Henry Luce, and designed to his editorial concepts, but serves also to demonstrate the widespread force in the mid–twentieth century of magazines of these kinds. Obviously Henry Luce was correct in his original belief that the busy twentieth-century American hungered for adequate, easily assimilated news of his increasingly complex world. Everybody who ever decided or guessed that pictures attract more people, and attract people more readily, was also correct.

Time and *Life,* in a primary sense, are complementary. One gives the news crisply in words and briskly explains it. The other gives the news in pictures, dramatizes it. Together they give the impression of confidence, speed, and alertness. Together they make what is, in effect, a national tabloid weekly newspaper. Together they show the magazine taking over what had been almost solely the central function of the newspaper—dissemination of the news, of the week if not the day, as it happens throughout the world.

It is hardly surprising that the *Time-Life* concept of instructing its readers should provoke severe criticism from those who believe in the right of the individual to look over the facts, weigh the opinions, and make up his mind for himself. The Luce publications have often been adversely criticized for the very concept of their journalistic responsibility in which they take most published pride.

Oversimplification of complex subjects is one point on which they are attacked. An Emersonian disregard for consistency is another. Marked shifts in editorial position is still another. In the opinion of one sharply spoken observer, *Time-Life* thought jumps from Jeffersonian materialism to Neo-Toryism by way of Niebuhrism or sometimes Roman Catholic humanism. "What it amounts to is a complete lack of any kind of principle at all." [11]

Others have pointed out ambiguities in the thought apparent behind *Time* or *Life* stories or editorials, shifting viewpoints, changes in position. *Life* upheld General Douglas MacArthur as commander in the Far East early in the Korean War. It cooled toward MacArthur after his recall by President Truman. Later, with marked approval, it ran his life story by General Courtney Whitney. It wavered in its attitude toward American foreign policy much as American public opinion—which it helped form—wavered. "Luce's theory of history and human destiny is simply too superficial . . . Luce and his school seem to be trapped by the very American blandness which is his real enemy—immaturity, provincialism, and love of surrogate excitement." [12]

[11] Anthony West, "The Mind and Muscle in Luce's Empire," *Saturday Night* (Toronto, Canada), March 20, 1954.

[12] John P. Mallan, "Luce's Hot-and-Cold War," *New Republic,* September 28, 1953. A further Mallan comment: ". . . they accept their own righteousness before the Lord too comfortably to be successful apostles."

Even the superficial reader cannot help being impressed by the studied omniscience of both *Time* and *Life*. An opening editorial in *Life,* more homey and colloquial in tone than it would have been a few years earlier, cheerfully recognized public awareness of this. "Each issue of *Life*," it admitted, "contains a lot of pretty positive statements, and we have been asked, not always jokingly, 'Do you guys ever admit you just don't know something?' "[13]

Few readers of *Time* or *Life* care one way or the other. Why should they? The magazines are modern, bright, and alert. They are infallibly informative and too vital to be indifferent. They are diverting. They give pleasure; they instill confidence. They make life both more exciting and more intelligible. That is a major accomplishment, and if the intelligibility they offer is an illusion, it is at least a comfortable one to have.

Time, Inc. publishes two magazines which do not fall into the general category of a text or illustrated news weekly. In 1932 it purchased *Architectural Forum*, which had been founded as *The Bricklayer* in 1892. As usual, there was no understatement of intentions. The magazine was to be published to "bring together, around the central art and science of architecture, all the influences which will build the new America." *Architectural Forum* is a handsome professional journal. In 1951 Time, Inc. began publication of a companion magazine, *House & Home*. It is addressed to building professionals concerned with light construction.

The latest Luce venture is more of a piece with *Time* and *Life*. After long struggle and more than a year of trade rumor *Sports Illustrated* made its first appearance with the issue of August 12, 1954. Again the prospectus was colorful. The goal of the new magazine was "to cover all sports; to turn to the world of sports the talents of the best writers and the best photographers; to find in every sport not only the enduring

[13] *Life,* February 9, 1953.

essentials of human achievement, but the exuberance, color, and quiet pleasure of sports; above all to be authoritative."

Certainly during its first year of publication *Sports Illustrated* competed successfully with its program. It covered 95 sports. It talked pleasantly and expertly of matters of import at Wimbledon, Forest Hills, Churchill Downs, Belmont Park, Yankee Stadium, Indianapolis, Saratoga, and all the other hallowed spots. In text and sharp pictures it gave over 600,000 readers the dope on fights, football, tennis, soccer, chess, baseball, track, golf, swimming, and all the other 86 diversions. Nobel and Pulitzer prize winning authors wrote for it—William Faulkner, John Steinbeck, J. P. Marquand—as well as writers more closely connected with sports, like Paul Gallico, Herman Hickman, and Red Smith.

Other magazines have been established on the general *Time-Life* pattern and function in much the same way. The vigorously promoted and very successful *Look,* a pictorial magazine in the *Life* manner, appeared for the first time in January, 1937, just two months after *Life* began publication. Though it has since moved to New York, it was founded in Des Moines, Iowa, by Gardner Cowles, who is still its president and editor, and John Cowles, the venture growing out of their newspaper experience with the Des Moines *Register and Tribune.*

"*Look* gives you a thousand eyes to see round the world," the first issue stated. It promised to bring "current events, science, sports, beauty, education, all in interesting pictures, to both the Colonel's Lady and Mrs. O'Grady (and their respective husbands and children) to make them better informed on what's happening in the world."

In practice *Look,* with a biweekly circulation of over four million, brings them mostly to the O'Gradys. It differs from *Life,* which in format it resembles, without *Life*'s smartness of appearance and crispness of presentation, basically in that it does not report the news. Instead it relies on feature articles, combining text and pictures to form dramatic, full-length pieces which are mostly about people. Today's events and people are Look's primary subject.

Started as a monthly, Look changed to biweekly publication after the first four issues. The early Look went in for a sensationalism which has since moderated in the magazine's effort to attain family appeal. Like Life, Look covers national and international affairs, but the approach is more popular, and the published product is different. "Life is an example of glittering objective reporting," Associate Editor Fleur Cowles is reported to have said. "Ours is—we hope—the warmest form of subjective reporting." [14] To give its audience this kind of reporting (and some marked variations) Look uses such contributors as Adlai Stevenson, Monsignor Fulton Sheen, Ernest Hemingway, Robert Sherwood, Earl Warren, John Gunther, and even Bertrand Russell. Big names appear frequently as by-lines.

Look splurges on stories of the lives and loves of entertainers. Its covers exploit the mass public's adoration of film and television personalities. It gets Julian Huxley to write a lead piece on "All About Love." It never neglects sex in its pictures, but balances this with "Norman Vincent Peale Answers Your Questions." The magazine is full of Sunday newspaper-type features, yet Look runs earnest articles on health and education, on human relations, religion, safety, civic responsibility. The magazine is conscious of its function, and the function and responsibility of magazines in general. A 1954 promotion piece opened with this statement: "Any general magazine which draws to its pages millions of people across the country, issue after issue, is . . . a powerful social force. And, as such, it has certain obligations and responsibilities, not only to its readers but to the nation at large. One of these responsibilities is to encourage better citizenship—to quicken people's latent desire for improved standards of health, education, safety, government, and tolerance."

[14] "Cowles Empire—A Magazine Phenomenon," Business Week, October 8, 1949.

The success of *Look*—its circulation went from 1,900,000 in 1946 to 4,076,869 in 1955—led to other Cowles magazine ventures. *Quick,* condensations strangled to capsule size, was started in 1949. Though it attained a circulation of 1,300,000, it was dropped as unprofitable in 1953.[15] The much more ambitious *Flair,* a class magazine of fashion, art, literature, travel, entertainment, and decor, all in very elaborate dress, lasted eleven months after its debut in February, 1949.

Newsweek, founded in 1933, ten years later than *Time,* is similar to it in editorial coverage but differs fundamentally in journalistic practice. It insists upon its objective presentation of the news. It tries to present clearly the events of the day and the people prominent in those events.

Instead of anonymity enforced by the *Time* concept of group journalism, it emphasizes signed opinion in departments conducted by specialists, in addition to its unsigned news columns and brief paragraphs. "The Periscope," a page of forecast and prophecy, and "Washington Trends," tersely informative statements of significant movements in the nation's capital, precede the editorial body of the weekly which, like *Time,* is divided into a score of categories running from The Americas, Books, Business, Education, and International Affairs to Theater, Transition, and United Nations. As "Signed Opinion," it carries the writing of columnists on "Business Tides," sports, "Perspective," "Washington Tides," and sometimes other subjects. *Newsweek* is published in European and Pacific editions and circulates in South America.

An unbiased, clear, and honest account of happenings in government, science, international affairs, and in all the significant movements of the day is the attempt made by *Newsweek,* whose slogan reads: "A well-informed public is America's greatest security." Less colorful than *Time,* it performs much the same

[15] The title was quickly purchased by Walter Annenberg, publisher of the *Philadelphia Inquirer,* the *Daily Racing Form,* the New York *Morning Telegraph, TV Guide,* and *Seventeen. Quick* was republished for nine months, abandoned again in 1954.

service in not too different a way, despite the obvious differences in their approach and reporting. Like other magazines, whose basic purpose is to inform, it must also entertain. As one of its editors explained, "We can't be more substantial than our audience will let us be. We print pictures of Marilyn Monroe along with articles trying to explain why Albert Einstein was the great man of our time; anatomical studies along with intellectual exercise." [16]

U.S. News, founded in Washington the same year that *Newsweek* first appeared in New York, confined itself largely to national affairs until it combined in 1947 with *World Report,* which was started the year before, and began publication as *U.S. News–World Report.* It still stresses affairs of national interest, though it has widened the scope of its news coverage. Feature articles on economic and political subjects, signed editorials, its telegraphic "Newsgrams," and succinct reporting of business trends make it distinct from either *Time* or *Newsweek,* both in its emphasis on economic subjects and in its featuring of forecasts.

Edited by David Lawrence, who writes the back-page editorial for each issue, *U.S. News & World Report* is noticeably lively in its editorial presentation. "The March of the News," "Tomorrow" ("Newsgrams"), "Washington Whispers," and "People of the Week" precede fast-moving articles on economic, political, and international subjects. "Special Reports" follows on education or an industry or a city or kindred subjects. "Business of the World," like "Tomorrow," is in telegraphic paragraphs.

Another magazine, founded in 1949, calls itself "A Fortnightly of Facts and Ideas." *The Reporter,* originated and edited by Max Ascoli, an Italian-born antifascist and political scientist, stated its basic editorial position in its first issue:

[16] Kenneth Crawford, Manager, *Newsweek* Washington Bureau, before the Editor-Educator Conference, Washington, D. C., May 11, 1955. His is an old editor's plaint.

"America as a nation is inseparably tied to the freedom and well-being of other nations." Staffed by ex-newspapermen and using name article writers, *The Reporter* claims to give the whole picture of the news, bringing its readers in penetrating, factual reporting of national and international affairs the kind of information to which, ordinarily, only specialists have access. A friendly contemporary (*Newsweek,* April 18, 1949) could see no close line drawn in the new magazine's pages between "facts and ideas" and "news and opinions"; yet *The Reporter* shows a nice diversity in its editorial coverage, and its articles read pleasantly and sensibly. Modest in format, old-fashioned in appearance through its profuse use of pen and ink illustrations and ornaments between pieces, the magazine has won several awards in journalism, including a Benjamin Franklin Magazine Award in 1954 for a short story and another in 1955 for an article.

Pathfinder was founded in 1894 as a news sheet originating in Washington. In 1943 it was purchased by *Farm Journal.* It was transformed into a biweekly news magazine resembling those already described but aimed editorially at the small town. In 1953 the descriptive phrase "The Town Journal" was added to the magazine's title. The name "Pathfinder" has now been dropped and *Town Journal* is published monthly from Philadelphia as "the family magazine of home-town America." Its already expanded circulation was increased to nearly 2,000,000 when *Farm Journal* purchased *Country Gentleman* in 1955 and began to fill the unexpired subscriptions of subscribers whose addresses showed that they lived in rural population centers rather than on farms with the news magazine of the small town.

The primary importance of *Town Journal* editorially is that it attempts to expand the news coverage of the town with articles and comment ordinarily superior to those in the daily press of such centers. Commercially, it enables Farm Journal, Inc. to offer advertisers a "countryside unit" through purchase of space in both *Farm Journal* and *Town Journal.*

The editorial offering of *Town Journal* is comparatively thin : light feature articles on popular subjects with a profusion of photographic illustrations, many in color, a telegraphic "Newsfront" of tips "Straight from Washington," home and garden hints—everything in friendly, home-town style. In "Talking It Over," the publisher chatted with his readers, September, 1955 : ". . . every month we'll be talking about many subjects that concern you—your health ; travel and recreation ; your community ; personalities in the news you'd like to know better— in short, a broad selection of the things that you as an intelligent, informed person want to know about. . . . Here is the best . . . for dad, for mother, and for the teen-age boys and girls."

In a world where the flux of history has increased rapidly and even terribly, where the need for timely knowledge across the United States and outside of it seems insistent and imperative, the news and pictorial magazines do well—for themselves and their readers. In part they owe their success to the modern reader's nervous impatience, his desire to gulp the news— arranged, predigested—as he runs. In larger part, they have succeeded because of the skill with which they perform their adopted function.

Chapter 17

THE GREATEST COMMON DENOMINATOR:
THE READER'S DIGEST

The desire of the modern reader for brief, preselected, easily comprehensible reading must account in part for the spectacular success of the only other major magazine idea originated and developed thus far in this century. The original *Harper's,* the *Literary Digest,* and other eclectic periodicals had profitably clipped, pasted, and reprinted. In 1922 a new ingredient was added, the skillful digesting or condensing of material already published in other periodicals in a pocket-sized magazine. The result was *The Reader's Digest.*

In 1920 when the idea was suggested to many of them, no established publisher would seriously consider it. In February, 1922, the man who had conceived the idea and experimented with the form he was to perfect, published the first issue of *The Reader's Digest.* The first issue was 5,000 copies. It was edited and distributed from a basement room in New York's Greenwich Village. DeWitt Wallace, founder, editor, and with his wife, Lila Acheson Wallace, still co-owner of the magazine, did not expect to reach a wide audience. He felt that serious material digested from serious publications would not command the attention of a great mass of readers. The operation soon outgrew the basement room, however. It was moved to a room over a garage and an adjacent pony shed in Pleasantville, New York.

Today *The Reader's Digest* goes to one of every four families in the United States.[1] Its domestic edition has a circulation of

[1] "Candor at Chappaqua," *Tide,* November 30, 1954.

over 10 million copies every month. Printed in thirty other editions in twelve languages, it has a world circulation of well over 18 million copies monthly. Though the *Digest* itself makes no such claim, *The Times* [London] describes it as a multi-national magazine with a world-wide circulation reaching some 90 million families every month.[2]

It is usual, it is hardly avoidable, to speak of *The Reader's Digest* in superlatives. It has by the far the largest circulation of any American magazine. It is, or has been one of the most profitable magazines in the country. It is a phenomenon. It is unique. Legions of faithful readers look upon it almost as Holy Writ. The *Digest*'s success has called forth awed admiration, inarticulate dismay, rhetorical wonder, envy, scorn, bitter derision, and unsuccessful imitation. The magazine is probably what one of its executives called it: "The greatest common denominator in communications we have." [3]

DeWitt Wallace, son of a Presbyterian minister, attended a small Midwestern college, Macalester College, of which his father was president, and then the University of California.[4] He worked for a Minnesota publisher of farm magazines and books, then became a salesman for a firm of calendar printers in St. Paul, then a publicity man for Westinghouse. It was while working for the farm publications company that he first got his idea for a little magazine which would reprint articles, in condensed form, from other magazines. While hospitalized after being wounded in World War I, he practiced digesting magazine articles. With his wife, also the offspring of a

[2] R. J. J. Pollock, "The Multi-National Magazine," *The Times* [London], Printing Supplement, July, 1955.

[3] Attributed to A. L. Cole. *Tide, op. cit.*

[4] DeWitt Wallace is the son of a minister. Henry Luce is the son of a missionary. The father of George Horace Lorimer was a famed Baptist evangelist. Joseph Palmer Knapp's mother was the daughter of a Methodist evangelist and the composer of hymn music. The evangelical strain is strong in the heredity of some of the most influential editors and publishers of our time. Observers have noted the evangelical strain very apparent in some of their magazines. Though differently manifested, it is evident in both the Luce publications and in *The Reader's Digest.*

Presbyterian minister, he issued the first number of *The Reader's Digest.*

It was then a monthly periodical, pocket-sized, thin, unillustrated. It offered, clearly printed on poor paper stock, deftly cut-down versions of articles previously published in other magazines. A magazine now of over 200 pages in most issues, it is still a monthly, still pocket-sized, but is well printed on better stock, illustrated, and contains at least as much original as digested and reprinted material.

In the early years of the *Digest*'s existence, other editors were glad to give DeWitt Wallace permission to reprint, without charge, articles from their publications. They had already used the material. Its reproduction, with credit in the *Digest,* looked like good, free publicity. As the *Digest* grew in circulation and importance, and it grew rapidly, Wallace began to pay an annual fee to other magazines for the right to digest and reprint articles he selected. Though there are a few such blanket contracts still in force, a different arrangement prevails now. The *Digest* pays both the magazine from which it extracts material and the author for specific articles used.

In 1933 (11 years after its founding), *The Reader's Digest* began to produce a limited number of original articles. It instituted special departments, "My Most Unforgettable Character," "Drama in Everyday Life," "Life in These United States." By this time a number of well-known magazines on which Wallace drew had ceased publication. The *Digest,* to keep itself supplied with sufficient good copy, was almost forced into some original production. By this time Wallace also had devised another method of keeping his magazine supplied with the kind of folksy, humorous, inspirational, sometimes journalistically provocative material to which his audience had become accustomed. *Digest* originals, articles assigned to staff or free-lance writers, were also prepared in more extended form and placed for first publication in other magazines. After initial publication, they were reprinted in digest form in *The*

Reader's Digest, with credit given the cooperating outside publication. Some of the best material appearing in the *Digest* has been developed in this fashion. A study of the *Digest's* content from 1939 through 1943 showed that 42 per cent of the articles appearing during that period were straight reprints. The remaining 58 per cent were originals, some appearing for the first time in *Digest* pages, some prepared cooperatively with other magazines. Similar percentages were found in 1944 and 1945.[5] Thus, well over half the articles in *The Reader's Digest* are now prepared directly for the magazine.

DeWitt Wallace once said the intent of *The Reader's Digest* was to print "articles of lasting interest which will appeal to a large audience, articles that come within the range of interests, experience, and conversation of the average person. The over-all emphasis . . . has been a more or less conscious effort to promote a Better America, with capital letters, with a fuller life for all, and with a place for the United States of increasing influence and respect in world affairs."

In practice, *The Reader's Digest* has presented digested material with unfailing mass appeal. Stories of human kindness, of successful community experiments, of new inventions and devices, popularized medical articles, biographical sketches of entertaining characters, and anecdotes of simple human goodness triumphing over inimical forces are its stock in trade.

Articles on the art of living, on health, and medical topics are *Digest* staples. Issue after issue has described, sometimes almost rhapsodically, new and quick cures for new and old diseases. Homey success stories, stories showing how ambition, thrift, and kindness paid high rewards, sometimes material as well as spiritual, but always spiritual, usually to lovable little people in small towns or in the country, are unfailing in the *Digest.* There is inspirational material in most American mass magazines. The proportion in *The Reader's Digest* is high. There

[5] Study made by George W. Bennett described by John Bainbridge in *Little Wonder and How It Grew* (New York, 1946).

is emphasis on sex in *The Reader's Digest,* not the blatant cheesecake of some of the picture magazines, but sex in simple and soothing guise. Articles on married life, on childbirth and child-rearing, on what men think of women and women think of men, on the mating of animals, and the like, appear and reappear in *Digest* pages.

The *Digest* specializes in striking titles followed by entertaining but often superficial accounts of diverse subjects. It disliked the New Deal and the Fair Deal and has consistently attacked the extravagance and overexpansion of bureaucratic government. Aware of the widespread human liking for accumulating unusual facts, it specializes in providing odd bits of factual information. Complicated analyses of facts, figures, and theories it avoids. These are not easily adapted to the condensed form in easy words, nor are they within "the range of interests, experience, and conversation of the average person" at whom the *Digest* is directed.

Human interest anecdotes abound in such departments as "Life in These United States" and "The Most Unforgettable Character I've Met." These departments, and others which appear occasionally, supply a considerable part of the sentimental humor characterizing *The Reader's Digest.* The jokes, strewn profusely throughout each issue as an integral part of the editorial offering rather than as filler, are sharper. They often contain the play of real wit and often are surprisingly risqué.

Such, in large part, is *The Reader's Digest.* In addition to the familiar domestic edition, it is published in two Australian and two Canadian (one English and one French) editions. It appears in three German editions, three French, excluding the Canadian, and in Spanish, Danish, Finnish, Italian, Norwegian, and Portuguese, as well as in Braille for the blind and on talking records. If world-wide circulation and diffusion of its subject matter are measures of the influence of a magazine, no magazine exerts a wider influence than *The Reader's Digest,* and few editors are more influential than DeWitt Wallace.

That influence operates less in the political and economic spheres than in the social. Its message is to the individual. Its strongest influence is on the reader's personal life. The *Digest* operates to make the individual feel more secure, more successful in his human contacts, better satisfied with his lot in life. It assures him month by month that he is a member in good standing of a country-wide or world-wide group of people much like himself. They are decent, good people. He likes them, and they like him. The *Digest,* and this is the magazine's artistic and editorial triumph, makes the world seem understandable and warmer.

Despite scientific advance, socialism acknowledged or merely practiced, a near-Utopia of material prosperity, television and even larger food freezers, the human spirit has not ceased to want hope and comfort. The optimism, the moral precepts, the gentle parables of *The Reader's Digest* supply to millions some of the same sustenance they once imbibed from prayer meeting and Sunday school. The magazine gives simplicity to a world gone frighteningly complex, offers spiritual help and moral guidance to many who have few other sources from which to obtain them. This is a fundamental part of its hold on its readers and a fundamental part of the magazine's accomplishment.

We have lost little of our taste for miracles, and *Reader's Digest* is continually announcing miracles, miracles of science, education, medicine, personality, and human accomplishment. It offers that satisfaction, too.

An earlier generation took a lively interest in patent medicine. It read the advertisements for a thousand nostrums and cure-alls with avidity, and generally was most convinced when the claims forwarded were most incredible. Men and women tried each new pill or liquid as it came along, in no way deterred because the last one tried had failed to work the wonders expected. The recurring medical articles in the *Digest,* many excellent of their kind, are hardly comparable to the ads for now discredited patent medicines. What are comparable are the psychological needs to which both the articles and the patent-medicine advertisements appeal. Understandably, most people wish to make their bodies last as long as possible and to have them perform as efficiently as they can be made to perform. The diseases to which the flesh is heir, the most common and the most obscure, and the ways in which they can be avoided or cured, are of perennial interest to everyone. It is not an interest which the *Digest* slights.

Toward the end of the nineteenth century the new magazines drew on an audience untouched by the literary monthlies. *The Reader's Digest* has drawn largely on an audience whose wants were not fully satisfied by the popular weeklies and monthlies founded or resuscitated in the 1880's and the 1890's. There are readers of the *Digest* who read no other magazines. In this way, it has vastly widened the total magazine-reading population. Its digested articles and condensed versions of current books bring to the attention of millions subject matter which, if published only in its original form and vehicle, these millions would never see at all.

From its garage room and pony shed, *Reader's Digest* burgeoned during the 1930's into all the available office space in Pleasantville. Stores, lofts, offices, and garages bulged with *Digest* workers and activities. Between 1933 and 1937 its circulation, during bitter depression years, went from less than 500,000 to almost two and a half million. In 1939 the magazine was moved into a $1,500,000 towered Georgian headquarters which sprawls over spacious and pleasantly landscaped grounds at Chappaqua,[6] a few miles north of Pleasantville. There, though the post office address of Pleasantville has been retained, the *Digest* is edited and published now with a base force of about 1,500 employed in its offices.

[6] Horace Greeley, ridiculed as "the woodcutter of Chappaqua" in the uneven Presidential contest of 1872 and no mean journalist himself, would be amazed at circulation figures achieved by the *Digest* and the physical evidences of journalistic success in his town today.

During World War II, when all mass magazines registered large circulation gains, *Digest* circulation rose from under four million to more than nine million. For many years *Digest* profits were high. The income from its vast circulation and sale was sufficient for expenditures that would seem extravagant to the editors and publishers of less successful periodicals. This halcyon situation ended abruptly in 1954 when, reportedly, the astonished *Digest* found itself faced with a deficit of about one million dollars for the year.

Paper, printing, and other production costs, together with increased postal rates, had mounted greatly during the years, and *The Reader's Digest* was still selling at its original 1922 price of twenty-five cents a copy or a year's subscription for $3. For thirty-three years, though it took advertising in its foreign editions, the *Digest* had thrived without the advertising revenue on which all the other large-circulation magazines depend for the bulk of their profit. A decision had to be reached on whether to accept advertising or to raise the newsstand and subscription price of the magazine. DeWitt Wallace took the question to his readers and awaited their answer before reaching a decision.

A New York research agency was retained to find out through personal interviews whether *Digest* readers preferred to pay an increased price for their copies or to have the *Digest* print advertising. Eighty-one per cent of the respondents, forming a cross section of the magazine's readers, declared in favor of advertising. Late in 1954 *Reader's Digest* announced that it would accept 32 pages of advertising for the first time in its April, 1955, issue. It would accept no liquor, tobacco, or medical remedy advertising. Its editorial policy would remain unchanged.

The *Digest* had many times attacked the abuses of advertising in its columns. Motivated by a crusading zeal that is often a concomitant of its kind of idealism, it had never hesitated to attack what it disapproved. Its anticigarette articles had provoked a furor, actually affected the manufacture and sale of cigarettes in this country. It had forthrightly printed exposés of government inefficiency, of labor abuses, of fraudulent dealings with the public. Its exposés of the bilking of the public by unscrupulous garages, watch repairers, radio experts, and purveyors of eyeglasses were well known. It had brought other abuses of public trust to public attention.

On the other hand, the *Digest* had often singled out branded devices and products for praise in such a fashion that its manufacturers profited hugely. It brought a preparation for waterproofing cellars to favorable notice. It praised a comparatively unknown adhesive. It lauded a rug cleaner. An enthusiastic report on a meat tenderizer resulted in its manufacturer's expanding from one to six factories but finding himself still unable to keep up with the demand caused by the magazine's article. Many advertisers built entire testimonial campaigns around *Reader's Digest* consumer articles which expressed or seemed to express approval of given brands of dentifrices, cigarettes, paper filters, and the like. Some of them quoted praise out of context or in other ways misrepresented facts and opinions. The advertising fraternity was well aware of all of this.

With this record, what would be the result of the *Digest*'s announcement that it would accept advertising? Also, would the publishers of other magazines continue to extend the *Digest* reprint permission now that it was to become a competitor as an advertising medium?

Answers were soon known. Requests for space—at $31,000 for a full-color page, the largest price of any magazine—poured in. There were over one hundred in a matter of hours. Within two weeks after the *Digest* announced its decision to take advertising, orders were received for 1,107 pages, more than three times the number that could be accepted for the entire first year. Before any issue of the *Digest* containing advertising had appeared, $11 million had been placed. The *Digest* found itself in the difficult, if pleasant, position of having to decide which advertisers it would admit to its pages.

The April, 1955, issue, when it appeared, contained 216 pages instead of the previous 168. Full-color advertisements on glossy stock made it a thicker and more colorful book. The list of advertisers read like a bluebook of American industry: American Telephone & Telegraph, Eastman Kodak, Union Carbide and Carbon, Ford, Procter & Gamble, General Electric, General Mills, Borden, Chrysler, Goodyear, and the others. Advertisers and media buyers in advertising agencies had no hesitation. The astronomical *Digest* circulation provided a market potential for products of all kinds. The unusual faith that *Digest* devotees seem to have in their magazine, a faith attested to by a subscription renewal rate of about 80 per cent, might easily extend to the new advertising pages.

No magazine withdrew from the *Digest* its permission to condense and reprint selected pieces. Many welcomed the *Digest*'s move as an aid in achieving magazine solidarity against the competing media of television and radio. The business community and its periodical peers were merely affirming their belief in the influence of the *Digest* that had been discernible for a long time. In April, 1956, the *Digest* began to accept additional advertising up to 20 per cent of the total pages in an issue.

Digest influence is pervasive, seems ubiquitous. The magazine is read, admired, and quoted by people of almost every age and profession, by high school students and teachers, clergymen, public officials, housewives, mechanics, and circus performers. Its first foreign edition was in Spanish. It was published solely because Latin American readers asked for it. Editions published in Iceland, in Italy, and in Egypt came into being at the direct request of officials in those countries. In 1935 the *Digest* published what is probably the most successful magazine article ever printed in this country: "—And Sudden Death" by J. C. Furnas. Its realistic description of bloody highway maimings and fatalities at a time when automobile accidents were killing thirteen people for every 10,000 cars in use shocked the American public. The *Digest* article has been more widely reprinted than any magazine article before or since. About five million copies have been distributed.

Other *Digest* articles have had an almost equally wide dissemination. *Digest* pieces have provoked social reforms, legislative changes, and wrought emotional and spiritual changes in the lives of countless individuals. Readers in their letters to the editors have insisted that *Digest* pieces have saved their health, their marriage, or even their lives. A young Venezuelan, who seemed doomed to spend his life in a wheel chair, read "Where What's Left Works Wonders," scraped up passage to New York, and learned to walk again at Dr. Howard Rusk's rehabilitation clinic. A young mother read a *Digest* excerpt describing an antidote. She made up a batch, administered it promptly after her small son ate some poisonous food, credited the *Digest* with saving his life. *Digest* pieces are quoted in conversation, recommended from the pulpit, read to traffic offenders from the judicial bench; and its jokes are repeated with relish in dimly lit bars.

The influence of the magazine's domestic and foreign editions has been augmented by corollary publications issued from Chappaqua. Half a million copies of the *Digest*'s school edition circulate in the country's high schools every month. Articles which might embarrass parents or teachers are omitted from this edition. *Digest* pieces, further digested and simplified, are published in a series of "Reader's Digest Reading Skill Builders" designed for use in the elementary grades. For use at the junior high school level the *Digest* publishes a series of anthologies entitled "Successful Living." These are promoted as study aids that will produce high ideals at the same time that they stimulate the mind. The saccharinity is undiluted in these paper-bound collections of *Digest* pieces intended to teach "honesty, courage, kindness, courtesy, reverence, cooperation, appreciation, responsibility, and respect for law."

The Reader's Digest now runs the largest book club in the world. Current popular books, both novels and nonfiction, are cut down, four or five titles to the *Digest* volume and issued quarterly. Titles are well selected. The condensation is done with the usual *Digest* expertness. The volumes, bound pleasantly in matching format, are always readable. Testimonial advertising quotes authors of the books which have been condensed as delighted with the results. Even the redoubtable H. L. Mencken said, in commenting on the digest technique as applied in the magazine, "I have yet to encounter an article that was seriously damaged by the condensation. And I can recall dozens that were palpably improved." Much depends here, of course, on the article or book selected for digesting. Obviously there are subjects and treatments, short or booklength, which do not lend themselves kindly to condensation. The *Digest*'s accomplishment remains.

As a writer in *Time* said: "No one can measure the influence the *Digest* has had on its readers, but it has certainly been considerable. It has also had a marked influence on other U. S. magazines—and through them on U. S. education. . . . Wallace has lured many people to read about serious topics and, in this sense, has helped raise the reading level of America. He may even succeed in getting Americans to read books—in abridged form." [7]

How is it all done? There are numerous partial answers. The *Digest*'s editorial purposes are clear. The magazine is expertly edited. Its large staff of senior and roving editors scour the field for ideas. These editors are well paid. Writers are very well paid for anything the *Digest* accepts. *Reader's Digest* editorial costs are high.

The digesting itself is done with meticulous care. A reading and cutting staff examines all the other magazines of any importance for its purposes, about 300 of them. The staff recommends articles for *Digest* use, and makes the original cutting.

---

[7] "The Common Touch," *Time*, December 10, 1951. The same article commented that the *Digest*'s articles in its international editions "have probably done more than all the government propagandists combined to allay the fear, prejudices, and misconceptions of the United States in other lands."

Beyond the storied Khyber Pass lies a high wild land of extraordinary people. Geographically close to Russia, the Afghans look to America for friendship

Afghanistan:

Domain of the Fierce and the Free

By James A. Michener *Author of "Tales of the South Pacific," "The Bridges at Toko-Ri," "Sayonara," etc.*

ONE DAY last spring I stepped into the shop of Mr. K. A. Gai, Wholesale Grocer and Wine Merchant, in Peshawar at the eastern end of the Khyber Pass. There I was handed a message for the truck driver waiting outside: *"Sir: In obedience to your order I herewith beg to send the following to Afghanistan: Mr. Michener. Please sign and state the number of empties returned."*

Thus I started one of the finest trips of my life, for Afghanistan is a profoundly exciting part of the world.

Here in this high wild land the traveler finds a way of life at least 5000 years old and a people who are used to seeing strangers. Their country has perpetually been the meeting place of nations. Alexander the Great, Genghis Khan and Tamerlane passed through Afghanistan to conquer vast dominions, and in later years fiery

161

Originally unillustrated, *Reader's Digest* now uses art work in color on front and back covers and colored line drawings, often in lighter vein, on editorial pages. Advertising adds more color to the magazine.

An editor goes over the cut article. The managing editor goes over it. One of the executive editors goes over it. If the condensed article has survived the scrutiny and editing of all of these, DeWitt Wallace, expertness sharpened by the experience of over thirty years of condensing and digesting, goes over it himself. He may restore portions of the original text deleted along the line or make further cuts. This excising of selected and adapted material is a continual process.

The selection of a subject for original *Digest* treatment and its assignment to a writer for preparation are done with the same care. The idea may originate with Wallace, with one of the top staff editors, with a roving editor, or reach the magazine as a suggestion from an outside writer. There is no direct chain of command. If the idea is adopted and the article is written, it gets the same scrutiny and editing to which an already published and adapted piece is subjected. It may emerge, like some famous *Digest* pieces, with little resemblance to the original article.

Beyond all this, there is something else underlying the success of *The Reader's Digest* less easy to define. There is a kind of mysticism and magic at Chappaqua. No one has yet proved that these are bad things, and at the *Digest* they are allied to great journalistic skill and shrewdness. DeWitt Wallace's editorial associates are men long experienced and skilled in magazine editing and publishing. Several were editors of magazines from which, in the early days of the *Digest,* Wallace sought permission to extract articles. One of the *Digest*'s two executive editors was the editor of the highly literate *North American Review*; the other was editor of the once powerful and influential *American Mercury.* The magazine's managing editor was editor of *Scribner's,* which before its unhappy demise was one of the best of the literary monthlies. A leading senior editor was editor of the *American Magazine.* Other members of the governing editorial group have backgrounds attesting magazine experience and competence. These men are where they are because they share or reflect Wallace's beliefs. They like the kind of thing he likes.

DeWitt Wallace likes inspirational pieces. He likes writing that proffers hope, that tells of courage, that exemplifies kindness, that shows simple human goodness triumphant. The *Digest*'s editor and his staff can make stories of this kind read so simply that reading is almost as painless as watching television. There is no pain in the act of reading, no pain in what you read. There is a better, simpler, happier world in *The Reader's Digest,* and it does not go away. It returns once a month forever. The reader is reassured. Life is better than it was before the new *Digest* came in the mail. There are miracles still, and there always will be—and in between the miracles are the earthy jokes, the best humor, probably, in any modern mass magazine.

Heroes and heroines in *Digest* pieces are people like the reader. Villains are the big things, the government, criminals, cigarettes, those who try to mislead or defraud, things the reader already detests or knows he should. Every line justifies him in what he wants to believe and feel. The *Digest* is an anodyne, a palliative, and a stimulant. It is easy, it is comforting, it is exciting—and "Did you hear this one?"

Digest editors select articles from other periodicals for digesting because they like them. They assign original subjects which appeal to them. They state that they do this, and there can be little doubt that what they say is true. A more cynical approach could not, consistently, produce the product, ensphered in its own sincerity, that the *Digest* is. The *Digest* is edited with unmistakable individual sincerity by men who dislike the abuses of power whether by big government or by big labor, who dislike seeing people pushed around, who have a crusading spirit about some things, who believe in faith, hope, charity, and the ability of man to rise above adverse circumstances. As one of them said, they concentrate on the human in the animal, rather than on the animal in the human. They believe that goodness is a good thing, and say so.

If there is a secret underlying the whole, the secret is simply DeWitt Wallace. He had an idea. He has carried it out. It is his idea, his taste, his editorial judgment that govern the whole. He has been described as Everyman—with everyman's hopes and desires, everyman's beliefs and grievances, everyman's sense of humor. In trying to explain their motivation and their magazine accomplishment, the *Digest's* circulation, and its unique hold on its readers, one of the magazine's editors found himself helpless. What he said finally was, "If D. W. likes it, automatically twelve million other people will like it. It's like that."

An editor of one of the best of the other mass magazines tried to analyze. Many magazine editors, he pointed out, started as newspapermen. DeWitt Wallace had been, instead, a press agent for books, then electrical appliances. The ordinary newspaperman, he explained, is always looking for the bugs under the leaves. "Wallace just looks at the leaves, and he thinks they're lovely, and so do his readers."

The Reader's Digest has given rise to a number of imitators. There are numerous other pocket-sized digest magazines with outward physical resemblance to it. The definition of what may properly be called a digest magazine is difficult to fix. The number of these magazines varies almost from month to month as titles disappear from the newsstands and are succeeded by others.

In "What Pocket Magazines Feed On," in *The Saturday Review of Literature,* March 9, 1946, Roger Butterfield analyzed the contents of twenty-one of these periodicals. He found much that the casual observer suspects on slighter evidence. Sex articles were popular with the editors of all twenty-one magazines. The work of regular magazine journalists predominated, followed by that of big-name writers, then by articles under the by-lines of big-name scientists, comedians, politicians, and the like. Scrutiny showed that thirteen of the magazines were liberal in their editorial viewpoint, only four were definitely illiberal; but this is not the most important characteristic of the swarm of pocket-sized digest magazines. Their more salient features show their faithful reflection of their prototype; the amusing stories, the scientific miracles, the ubiquitous success stories, the articles about hobbies and hobbyists and about heroic humble souls. These magazines bristle with novel facts, and, usually, glow with easy optimism.

Just as *Life* has given rise to many imitators, some of which concentrate on the sensationalism to which the pictorial medium readily lends itself and neglect the more substantial features of the periodical they emulate, many of the pocket-sized digest magazines have succeeded only in looking somewhat like *The Reader's Digest* and obviously straining for some of the same effects. They lack the character and consistent pattern the editorial direction of DeWitt Wallace gives *The Reader's Digest*. They lack the quality which its editors and writers give each issue of the *Digest*. Of its kind, and given always the kinds of relatively uncomplicated subject matter which the *Digest* has made its own, the writing in *Reader's Digest* is perfect. Condensation which achieves brevity without destruction of meaning has attained almost the proportions of an art form in the magazine.

The pictorial weekly, the weekly news magazine, and the monthly digest have become magazine types characteristic of our day. They have established themselves firmly alongside the surviving literary monthlies and the older general weekly and monthly magazines, almost all of which have modified their own approach to the hurried and harried twentieth-century reader in line with lessons learned from these newer magazines.

Chapter 18

MAGAZINE SATIRE AND HUMOR:
THE NEW YORKER

IT IS easily understandable that the larger magazines find each
other subjects of fascinating interest. Especially if a magazine
is successful, commercially and in the attention compelled by its
editorial contents, are its competitors given to anxious probing
and peering, and to emerging from their investigations with
puzzled frowns. They seldom completely approve what they
think they have discovered.

The New Republic has written of the Curtis magazines, and
Fortune of the Crowell-Collier group. Writing in the ninetieth-
anniversary issue of the *Atlantic* in 1947, Frederick L. Allen,
late editor of *Harper's,* tried to sum up the peculiar qualities of
all the various types of American magazines which appeared for
the first time after World War I. *The New Yorker* in 1945
had its say, derisively and at great length, about *The Reader's
Digest,* as in 1936 it had passed caustic judgment on *Time,
Fortune, Life,* and Henry Luce.

*Fortune, The Saturday Review of Literature, Advertising
Age, Cosmopolitan,* and the magazine first entitled *'47,* then *'48,*
but never *'49* have all tried to assay and then describe *The New
Yorker.*[1] Usually they have approached their subject with diffi-
dence and even timidity. The disproportion between the maga-

---

[1] "The New Yorker," *Fortune,* August, 1934. Russell Maloney, "Tilley
the Toiler," *The Saturday Review of Literature,* August 30, 1947. Lawrence
M. Hughes, "North American Steppes Yield Gold to Mr. Tilley," *Advertis-
ing Age,* December 1, 1947. Allen Churchill, "Harold Ross, Editor of The
New Yorker," *Cosmopolitan,* May, 1948. Henry F. Pringle, "Ross of The
New Yorker," *'48,* March, April, 1948.

zine's limited circulation which, though not small, is hardly comparable to that of the larger mass magazines, and its undoubted reputation, influence, and high prestige is in itself disturbing. That remarkable prestige is a deterrent to rash judgments. Analysts and critics have squinted respectfully through the haze of legend which already surrounds *The New Yorker,* though it was founded as recently as 1925. They have looked on Harold Ross, the magazine's founder and until his death in 1951 very much its editor, with awe and with incomprehension in which awe has no part, and come away baffled by the contradiction between his appearance, manner, and editorial methods, and the appearance, manner, and reputation of his magazine. Few editors since Edward Bok have received so much publicity. The dramatic contrast between man and magazine, shrill with exclamation points or their equivalent, colors all the articles about them.[2]

Harold Ross, born in Aspen, Colorado, began his journalistic career by leaving his high school course half finished to become a tramp newspaperman in Salt Lake City, Sacramento, San Francisco, New Orleans, and Atlanta. World War I gave him the opportunity he seized. As a private in the railway engineers, he maneuvered himself into the editorship of *Stars and Stripes,* the enlisted man's weekly newspaper of the American Expeditionary Forces, which was published in Paris. With him on *Stars and Stripes* were others who already were, or were to become, literary or journalistic celebrities: Grantland Rice, Alexander Woollcott, John T. Winterich, George Bye, and Franklin P. Adams. When he returned to civilian life, Harold Ross, after his failure in an attempt to carry on *Stars and Stripes* as *The Home Sector,* became editor of the *American Legion*

[2] As might be expected the *Fortune* article, though parts of it are dated now, is the longest, most thorough, and most detailed. It pulled no punches in describing the rages, the naiveté, the uncouthness, and the temperament of "Roughhouse Ross." It printed a gap-toothed photograph, listed his many phobias, noted his prudishness, and made it clear that he was a great editor. Two years later, *The New Yorker's* "profile" of Henry Luce was acid.

Weekly, a position he held for five years. The editorship of *Judge* followed. It was shortly after he left *Judge,* angered by a cut in his editorial budget, that he managed to put into operation his idea of a humorous weekly of and for the New York that fascinated him.[3]

Harold Ross founded *The New Yorker* after discussions with the literati who then frequented the Hotel Algonquin in New York, a group to which he was introduced by F.P.A. and Alexander Woollcott. Raoul Fleischmann put up the money with which to start the magazine, some $560,000 before the venture showed signs of success. Still the chief owner of *The New Yorker,* he has reaped handsome returns on his investment.

Original contributors and advisory board to *The New Yorker* were the Algonquin wits: Woollcott, Robert Benchley, George S. Kaufman, and Dorothy Parker. The first issue of *The New Yorker,* dated February 21, 1925, bore the now famous cover by Rea Irvin of a supercilious mid-nineteenth century dandy considering a butterfly through his upraised monocle. Eustace Tilley, as this exquisite was named by Corey Ford, reappears on the cover of each anniversary issue and is *The New Yorker*'s sign and symbol.

[3] Ross first thought of *The New Yorker* as a humorous magazine modeled after *Punch.* It would carry cartoons and illustrations, but primary emphasis would be on text. Another editor of humorous magazines believed that the future of such weeklies lay in profuse use of cartoons and a playing down of text. Norman Anthony, who had been an editor of both *Life* (the old *Life*) and *Judge,* founded *Ballyhoo* in 1931. Despite the depression, it quickly attained a 2,000,000 circulation. *Ballyhoo* burlesqued advertising: "Keep Kissable with Old Colds," "Avoid Athlete's Brain," "Read a *Fresh* Magazine" (the issue was wrapped in cellophane). *Ballyhoo's* most famous creation was Elmer Zilch, president of the Zilch Corporation, an advertising agency. Elmer was assisted by Langhorne Zilch, Percy Bysshe Zilch, Llewellyn Zilch, and a score more of his relatives, all vice presidents. The magazine disappeared in 1939 after its spectacular short success. An attempt to revive *Ballyhoo* was made in 1948.

The New Yorker did not reach its present position because of dependence on writing, nor did *Ballyhoo* fail because of its extravagant use of cartoons. Quality and appeal determined this, but the contrast in choice between primarily graphic and primarily verbal humor is not without interest.

The New Yorker, wrote Harold Ross in that first issue, would have a serious purpose, but would not be too serious in executing it. It hoped to reflect metropolitan life, to keep up with events and affairs of the day, to be gay, humorous, satirical, but to be more than a jester . It would not deal in scandal for the sake of scandal or in sensation for sensation's sake. It was not out to tap American buying power for its advertisers. *The New Yorker,* nevertheless, has long since become a strong and profitable advertising medium. Half, sometimes more than half, of each issue is advertising. Promoted skillfully as "the most personal of magazines," again as "the national weekly of the leadership market," it carries rich pages of liquor, automobile, perfumery, night club, resort, jewelry, television, fabrics, and department store advertising. *New Yorker* advertising, running from the sedate to the lush, always suggests refined tastes and flatters with the assumption that expense is no handicap to the discriminating. The art and copy for numerous advertisements are done in a style complementary to the cartoons and quips of the editorial.

The early years of *The New Yorker* are those around which the fog of legend is thickest. Ross hired and fired—or, if he did not fire, managed to suggest the wisdom of resigning— rapidly and frequently. The magazine is supposed to have been published in an atmosphere of querulous profanity, spectacular rages, abrupt and arbitrary decisions, quips and cranks and wanton wiles, and a general loud explosiveness. Writers and editors leaped in and leaped out, usually helped both ways.[4] By April, 1925, *The New Yorker* had only 8,000 readers and was losing $8,000 each week. The decision was reluctantly made to abandon what was clearly a practical failure. This

[4] Dale Kramer, in *Ross and The New Yorker* (Garden City, N. Y.: Doubleday & Co., 1951), gives a colorful account of the early years. *The New Yorker,* in a review, found the book conspicuously uninformed if well-intentioned. There is precedent for the attitude. *Reader's Digest* editors were unable to recognize themselves or their magazine in John Bainbridge's "Little Magazine," which *The New Yorker* ran in five installments in 1945.

decision was reversed when Raoul Fleischmann was persuaded to reconsider and to risk more capital.

Many accounts testify, wonderingly, that it was an article by Ellin Mackay—Mrs. Irving Berlin since 1926—which started *The New Yorker* on its way to success. Its author, a post-debutante, wrote on "Why We Go to Cabarets." In her article, which appeared in the Thanksgiving issue for 1925, she explained that debutantes sought refuge in cabarets from the unpleasant kinds of individuals who frequented private debutante parties. The article caused both shocked and amused comment, and placed the name of *The New Yorker* on the front pages of the newspapers.

At various times Robert Benchley, Ogden Nash, Dorothy Parker, Sally Benson, Ralph Ingersoll, Frank Sullivan, Nunnally Johnson, Lewis Mumford, Clarence Day, Robert Simon, Lois Long, H. L. Mencken, Rebecca West, Edmund Wilson, and how many others have written, as outside contributors, staff writers, or both, for the magazine which Ross edited "not for the old lady in Dubuque." Yet the two writers whose names are still most closely identified with *The New Yorker* are James Thurber and E. B. (Elwyn Brooks) White.

E. B. White, a Cornell graduate who had worked in an advertising agency, joined *The New Yorker* in 1926, ran "The Talk of the Town" for eleven years, and contributed signed verse and prose essays to the weekly. In 1929 he married Katharine Sergeant Angell who, first as the literary editor, then as the efficient managing editor of *The New Yorker,* is usually given much of the credit for establishing the high literary standards and the impeccable good taste of the magazine. James Thurber, who was on the staff of the Paris edition of the *Chicago Tribune* when he first heard of *The New Yorker,* started to submit material to it in 1926 after his return to this country. His first twenty efforts were rejected. The twenty-first, written, at the suggestion of his wife, in little more than forty-five minutes, was accepted. Thurber met White, who introduced him to Harold Ross, and Ross immediately hired him for *The New Yorker* staff. Thurber's experience with his humorous drawings matched that with his writing. For two years Ross consistently rejected them. Then his frustrated men, determined women, and strange big dogs became *New Yorker* familiars.

Thurber's *My Life and Hard Times* ran in *The New Yorker* in 1933. Together he and White produced *Is Sex Necessary?* Like White, Thurber is no longer a *New Yorker* editor, but both remain frequent contributors and the two most characteristic *New Yorker* writers. Just as White introduced Thurber to Ross, Thurber later introduced Robert M. Coates, who has been art critic, book critic, short story writer, and prolific general contributor to *The New Yorker*. Wolcott Gibbs, author of the Luce "profile" in 1936, has long wielded one of the weekly's sharpest pens.

It is the severe editing and re-editing of the complete text of each issue that makes *New Yorker* prose what it is, and has produced the famed "*New Yorker* style." Harold Ross edited the full contents of each issue with meticulous attention to detail. Factual accuracy and complete clarity are demanded of every writer in every piece. There may be no recondite references, no unanswered questions in the reader's mind, no learned allusions. Slovenly writing, precious writing, "fine writing" stood no chance of survival. Because all the writing in each issue is still made to conform to these standards, all of it seems sometimes to have been written by one man, the same man who wrote last week's issue and will write the next. Perfection, or *The New Yorker*'s idea of perfection, is alone acceptable. Ross applied a microscope to all copy and wrote his sharp complaints, ironic queries, and firm directions on the galleys. It is in the rewriting, in energetically scouring with steel wool and pumice after applying the putty filler—and not too much of this—that *The New Yorker* surface is applied to its prose.

For twenty-six years the same gimlet-eyed scrutiny bored into the art. *The New Yorker* gives far more space to text than to communication through graphics . Despite this deliberate preponderance of words over pictures, there are many who think of *The New Yorker* as primarily a cartoon vehicle, and look at it first for the amusement which its cartoons afford. Often they never get beyond the cartoons. *The New Yorker* originated the one-line cartoon, and *The New Yorker*'s artists have done at least as much to establish the magazine's reputation as have its writers. Rea Irvin, Gardner Rea, Gluyas Williams, Helen Hokinson, Peter Arno, Whitney Darrow, Jr., and John Held, Jr., R. Taylor, Charles Addams, William Steig, George Price, Steinberg, Kovarsky are names as familiar in *New Yorker* pages as White, Thurber, Liebling, Berger, Maloney, Coates, Gibbs, Perelman, and Ogden Nash. The magazine goes far to insure having the kind of graphic humor it wishes. It may, and often does, supply the artist with the idea for a cartoon. It may change the "gag lines" submitted by the artist, or it may buy the cartoon alone and work up its own captions. However they are developed, the cartoons must measure up to specifications as rigid as those set for *New Yorker* prose. They usually say something and say it clearly.

Its cover cartoons in color are one of *The New Yorker*'s most successful features. Except in its advertising, this is the only place in the magazine where color is used. Unlike the other well-known magazines, almost all of which are using more and more color both in photographs and in artists' illustrations, *The New Yorker* eschews color in its editorial pages. This complete reliance on black and white results in a physical unity and restraint, literally a distinction, when it is compared with most of the other national magazines. It runs no enticing blurbs on its covers. Stories and articles have no by-lines under the titles; authors' names appear at the end. There are no subtitles in display type whipping the reader on. There is not even an itemized table of contents. Regular departments only are listed in a small box on the first page of the weekly calendar of events. The product of all this *Punch*-like restraint, careful selection, and close editing goes each week to a circulation of some 396,000, a circulation which no doubt could be greatly enlarged if *The New Yorker* considered the move profitable. In relation to circulation, its advertising rates are high now.

The New Yorker's distinctiveness is not limited to its chaste format. It is the finest magazine of gentle satire, subtle humor, of shrewd and witty comment on the passing scene which appears in the United States today. Its quiet prose is firm and lucid. It is sane and reasonable, intelligent, urbane, calm, and suave without being fulsome or overly smug. It is also, and basically, informative. "Goings On About Town," at the very front of the magazine, is, as it describes itself, "a conscientious calendar of events of interest" in New York. A section usually of six or seven pages in small type, it is a full, definite, and useful guide to sports, movies, radio programs, plays, concerts, night clubs, hotels, museums, and varied entertainments scheduled for the week. "On and Off the Avenue," farther on in the magazine, is again factual. It is a pleasantly discursive shopper's guide which gives advice and specific information, naming places and things and prices. Like a good newspaper, *The New Yorker* selects its simple, useful facts and reports them accurately. It sections on books, the theater, and the motion pictures are informative as well as critical. "The Race Track" column, which for so long has been signed "Audax Minor," and those departments which treat of the other sports, are likewise given to fact as well as opinion.

Those mentioned are standard *New Yorker* offerings, but it is other long-continued features which are usually considered most characteristic. "The Talk of the Town," the first major editorial piece, with its "Notes and Comment" opening each issue under a cut of Eustace Tilley, supported by an indicative skyscraper and an owl with one eye open and very wise, is the most famous. "The Talk of the Town" seems *The New Yorker* itself. A score of subjects—narrative, anecdote, description, essay, quip—may appear here. Here the tone of *The New*

Rea Irvin's disdainful dandy appeared on the cover of the first *New Yorker*, February 21, 1925. "Eustace Tilley" reappears on the cover of each of its anniversary issues.

Yorker is set. Whimsy, satire, irony, mockery, comment that is aloof and amused, but never vindictive or crude and seldom cruel, are the distilled ingredients. Some of it is just clever gossip. All of it is perfectly formed into a whole of light, firm texture which, like the texture of the entire magazine, is of superior quality.

Almost as characteristic of the essential *New Yorker* are its profiles. *The New Yorker* biographies have influenced—the opinion is neither novel nor original—biographical writing in the other magazines and, indeed, biographical writing of our time. Mrs. E. B. White is credited with having set the pattern for them, and certainly Alva Johnston, who wrote a great number of the early *New Yorker* profiles, established the form. These biographical sketches, some of them brief enough to be run in one issue, others appearing in several installments, are frequently assigned to writers outside the regular *New Yorker* staff. The subject may be an industrial leader, a writer, musician, theatrical character, an editor and his magazine, anyone whom *The New Yorker* considers newsworthy and noteworthy.

Characters as diverse as Nicholas Murray Butler, Jake Ruppert, Sir Joseph Duveen, and W. C. Fields have appeared in the long list of *New Yorker* profiles. Wolcott Gibbs, who thrust and slashed and hammered at Henry Luce in one of them, practically demolished Alexander Woollcott, once a patron saint of the magazine, in another entitled "Big Nemo."

These biographies are far different from the admiring and unctuous success stories of great men which used to be popular in many magazines, a kind of biographical writing which stemmed from the uncritical adulation which Victorian writers thought it proper to accord their eminent subjects. They differ markedly, too, from the kind of debunking biographies popularized by Lytton Strachey and his imitators in the 1920's. *New Yorker* profiles are honest, accurate life stories, told as though their writers had looked squarely at a man or woman, without preconceived estimate, and had put down the facts as they saw them. Often they are astringent and sharply ironic; but the facts, the admirable facts if there are any, as well as the ridiculous facts, especially the ridiculous facts, are there to be read. The reader may not agree with the judgments stated or implied, but he does not doubt the facts.

The reader is not apt to doubt any of the facts in *The New Yorker*. He may cavil at some *New Yorker* opinions and attitudes, or detest some of the arrogance, but *The New Yorker* carries on every page conviction of its own kind of integrity. No concessions are made to the supposed tastes of the masses. No concessions are made to anybody or to anything except *New Yorker* editorial decisions. This is the life of New York, thus the life of our times in epitome, as it looked to Harold Ross and looks to his successors.

Horace Greeley called his weekly magazine of literature, politics, and general intelligence the *New-Yorker,* hyphenating the name of the city as was conventional in the 1830's and 1840's, but the real prototype of today's *New Yorker* among Americans was Joseph Dennie's *Port Folio* in the early nineteenth century. There is a strong family likeness between Oliver Oldschool and Eustace Tilley. Joseph Dennie, wit, dandy, and satirical essayist after Addison, might well have been the subject of a Rea Irvin caricature in 1925. Discounting its political bias, there is a fundamental similarity between *The Port Folio,* the best magazine of its day, sharp, brilliantly written, ironic, boldly addressed only to men of education, taste, and intelligence, and today's civilized weekly, equally witty, fastidious, occasionally as disdainful, as neatly independent, and even more quietly self-assured.

It is often said that *The New Yorker* has developed the short story into a new kind of perfection. Perhaps it has. Certainly, it has offered from the beginning a kind of story superior to the standardized mass magazine product. *New Yorker* stories are unpretentious narratives in monotone and monochrome. Sometimes they have a beginning. Often there is no discernible end. There is no contriving of plot, no straining after obvious dramatic effects, no rhetorical climax. Characters in the stories underact, understate. Here, the stories seem to say, is a bit of life, formless as life itself. They are unperturbed, civilized recitals. No moral is stated, seldom is one implied. The stories are cool. They never shine. At most they glow. They eschew the vulgar with great determination. At their best, *New Yorker* stories can be delightful. At their worst, they show more finish than substance. This is generalization which does not fit "Life with Father," "Pal Joey," "My Sister Eileen," "The Secret Life of Walter Mitty," and other famous *New Yorker* successes and many less well-known *New Yorker* stories.

New Yorker essays are always beautifully finished. The facts, as in the reportorial pieces and even in many of the stories, are accurate; yet the essays sometimes seem pallid, a little bloodless. Irony, when it lacks a real target or motivation stronger than mannered habit, falls short of its proper effect. *New Yorker* humor is sometimes simply not funny. The attitude of censorious superiority, which *The New Yorker* assumes in publicizing the errors of its contemporaries, seems as much informed by a schoolteacherish delight in the discovery of flaws as by wit of any discernible kind. Eustace Tilley can be very squeamish.

Discarding the protective armor of its humor, and lowering its guard a little, *The New Yorker* publishes a certain amount of direct social commentary. Its war reports were noticeable. Its London Letter and the letters from Paris, West Berlin, and other foreign centers, which appear occasionally, are informal but serious in tone. It has written almost soberly about world government and the uneasy peace following World War II. It talks down to these larger subjects indulgently. There is a self-consciousness in some of its writing about them, as though it were a little ashamed to be caught taking them and itself seriously; but it does acknowledge them.

The New Yorker ran a series of articles on Oak Ridge, the warborn town in Tennessee where atom bombs are manufactured. In 1945 and 1946 it carried Rebecca West's almost painfully detailed reports of the treason trials in England, together with her mordant descriptions of William Joyce, John Amery, and Norman Baillie-Stewart, and her analysis of the reasons for their behavior. *The New Yorker* made spectacular play, and undoubtedly carried conviction of grim realities and grim possibilities to many readers, by devoting an entire issue to John Hersey's "Hiroshima" in August, 1946. The magazine is no longer solely, or even principally, concerned with the coffeehouses, or their twentieth-century equivalents, of New York City.

In 1949 and 1950 Harold Ross was gleefully and characteristically busy. Enraged by what he considered an invasion of his privacy, he carried on a one-man, one-magazine crusade against music and commercials blasting out of sixty-five amplifiers concealed in Grand Central Terminal. After persistently castigating Grand Central in *The New Yorker* for its maltreatment of a helpless captive audience, he testified ironically at a Public Service Commission hearing (blandly accepting a description of himself as editor of 'an adult comic book'), and the noise which was bringing the railroad a $93,000-a-year revenue was stopped. As bitterly, Ross ridiculed *Flair,* a lush and pretentious new monthly magazine published by Cowles, deriding it in text and cartoons. Doubtless there were other contributing factors, but *Flair* ceased publication.

The New Yorker was so much the projection of this one mind and temperament, so much the product of one man's intensive editing, that it was often doubted the magazine would survive Harold Ross. *Fortune* said in 1943 that *The New Yorker* might well disintegrate without him. The magazine *'48* said *The New Yorker* would probably disappear if Ross retired. Other opinion and comment were much the same. Harold Ross died December 7, 1951, at the age of 59.

Only one article appeared on the first page of *The New Yorker* of December 15, 1951. It was headed simply, "H. W. Ross." It was not the usual prepared obit, not the usual tribute. No attempt was made to disguise the grief of its writer or to hide the sentiment which, thinly veneered, underlies so much *New Yorker* writing. It was no eulogy either. Ross had lacked formal education. He used two books at *The New Yorker*: a Webster's dictionary and a Fowler's *Modern English Usage*. He had been difficult to understand, but ". . . he wanted the magazine to be good, to be funny, and to be fair." (He had made *The New Yorker* a good magazine, but it was sometimes not funny, and it was often unfair.) "Ross set up a great target and pounded himself to pieces trying to hit it square in the middle."

The ending of the piece was emotional. Ross, it said, had been used to ending his interviews, calm or stormy, with a wave of his hand and, "All right. God bless you." The death notice in the magazine he had created ended: "We cannot convey his manner. But with much love in our heart we say for everybody, 'All right, Ross. God bless you!' " The whole left little doubt that Ross's surviving staff would try to carry on *The New Yorker* in the Ross tradition.

When William Shawn was appointed to the editorship about six weeks later, he said as much. Shawn had joined the *New Yorker* staff in 1933 and become managing editor in 1939. For twelve years he had worked closely with Ross. He thought that any changes reflected in the magazine's pages would simply be those that come normally through changing times and writers.[5]

Basically, *The New Yorker* seems to have changed little since 1951. It looks the same. The writing is as good. Much of it is by the same writers who worked for Ross from the early years of the magazine. Most of the same departments remain. The cartoons, still signed with the familiar *New Yorker*

[5] *Tide*, February, 1952.

names, are as amusing. What is lacking is the Ross ferocity.
Supercilious Eustace Tilley still disdains the world through
his upraised glass, but he seems to have mellowed a bit. Sometimes he sounds more like Oliver Goldsmith than like Horace
Walpole. There is more sentiment and mocking whimsy; more
kindliness, less acerbity. Perhaps Eustace Tilley has simply
got middle-aged and put on a little weight. He has also got very
successful, and that is said to be softening.

The success is marked. *The New Yorker* is a thicker, heavier
magazine. Though it stands 72d in circulation among the 90-
odd magazines reported on by Publishers' Information Bureau,
it ranks 14th in advertising revenue, third in number of advertising pages. In 1954 it gained more pages of advertising than
any other magazine. In that year it served over 1,400 advertisers, published more than 10,000 advertisements. It had published more than 80,000 pages of advertising since its 1925
founding. This record of commercial success is the more remarkable in that the magazine has always been fastidious in its
acceptance of advertising. This policy and the kind of circulation that Ross deliberately set out to reach has attracted the advertising of luxury goods for a class market, particularly advertising from high-priced retail outlets or advertising for
high-priced items by department stores. *The New Yorker* has
found itself in the enviable position of having to turn down
pages of advertising for its Christmas issues in order to maintain the editorial to advertising ratio that insures its second-
class mailing privileges.[6]

[6] "The Talk of the Town," *The New Yorker,* April 16, 1955, was a little
condescending when *The Reader's Digest* began to take advertising. "Well, the
tarnished old *New Yorker,* whose very first issue was loaded with ads (there
must have been at least a hundred dollars' worth) now after all these years
welcomes the *Digest* to the wicked fold, where all is fun and frolic.
    ". . . advertising is the handiest support for the free press, and it's easier
to live with the stuff than without it. However, there is one good rule to go
by. When the advertising manager makes the mistake of showing up in the
editor's office with a suggestion for a piece, he should be rubbed out. That's
all we've learned in thirty years, and it's all you need to know."

The New Yorker audience is composed of people who read, or they would buy instead a different kind of magazine. They will read smartly presented advertising as well as editorial content. They are people of taste, education, and discrimination (or want to be), or they would not like the magazine. That they do like it is attested by the high rate of subscription renewals. Shrewd advertisers of the kind of merchandise that will appeal to such people know this. They know also that *The New Yorker* carries a high carriage-trade prestige.

Besides its regular and critically appreciative readers, there is a class of people, and, fortunately for *The New Yorker*, not a small class, which praises the magazine extravagantly. These men and women, whether or not they understand the more subtle qualities which help to make *The New Yorker* what it is, whether or not they can appreciate the deft wit and artful understatement which characterizes *New Yorker* material at its best, whether, indeed, they often read the magazine, consider it a mark of "sophistication" to admire it uncritically. College undergraduates continually try to imitate the *New Yorker* manner in their themes for English classes. Usually they fail badly in the attempt. Their straining after spare prose produces poverty-stricken prose. They bungle the aloof irony and amused perception, produce instead a bored disdain or a spindly contempt. Occasionally one does almost as well as his model, which shows the same flaws. Seventy per cent of the circulation of *The New Yorker* is reported to be outside the metropolitan area of New York. *The New Yorker* may not be edited for the old lady in Dubuque, but it is to provincial readers that *The New Yorker* seems the essence of the glamour and excitement of the city.

There is little else with which to compare apparent *New Yorker* weaknesses than *New Yorker* strength, or what is best in other very good magazines. Most of what *The New Yorker* does, it does superbly. Some of its weaknesses lie not in the quality of *The New Yorker* or in the skill or clumsiness of its accomplishment, but in the limitations of its medium. Satire, more critical than creative, is a minor art, and it is the art of *The New Yorker*.

It is through satire that *The New Yorker* makes its influence most strongly felt. It influences the opinions of readers capable of having opinions in the first place. It often provides intellectual delight to those capable of intellectual pleasure. The magazine stands for honesty, mental and emotional, for scrupulous exactness, and always for common sense. It loves gossip, not mean gossip but coffeehouse gossip as Joseph Dennie understood it—clever, pleasant conversation. It is no accident that "Shouts and Murmurs," a column of gossip and anecdotes written by Alexander Woollcott, was once a characteristic *New Yorker* department.

Its mockery of stupidity is gentle. Its ridicule is consistently directed against vulgarity, against the fraudulent and false. Its sharpest thrusts are meant to pierce pretense and hyprocrisy, to attack and demolish sham, bombast, and pretentiousness. It seems doubtful that *The New Yorker* has consciously any great social aims, but in a time which continues to offer, and no doubt will offer in ever greater quantity and variety, a wealth of the blatant, the dishonest, and the ridiculous, it is a welcome and powerful corrective. Through its satire and the example of its own cool restraint, through its clear prose, which has had its own influence on contemporary writing, and through its drawings, which have likewise influenced American cartooning and caricature, it looses keen thrusts for sanity, which are often far more effective than the blows of loud critics of our society who prance about belaboring it with pigs' bladders or bludgeons.

Chapter 19

THE GROCERY-DISTRIBUTED MAGAZINES

A FEW YEARS AGO they were nowhere—now they are everywhere. A wholly new category of magazines has sprung into being and prominence. Though two of the leaders were founded earlier, it has been since World War II that the store-distributed magazines, the grocery magazines, made their spectacular debut and established themselves. These periodicals, editorially addressed to the housewife and used by advertisers to appeal to women as purchasers of food, clothing, appliances, and other household goods, have in these years attained a vast combined circulation and rung up huge totals of advertising revenue, though both circulation and advertising fell in the early months of 1956.

These new magazines differ markedly in some important respects from the general and women's service magazines which they imitate and physically resemble. Whatever their corporate organization, they do not function as independent publishing enterprises but as adjuncts to a basic enterprise with universal market, the food business.

These magazines are sold neither through subscription with deliveries by United States mail nor on the newsstands of railroad stations, hotel lobbies, drug stores, or tobacco shops. Each of the store-distributed magazines reaches the grocery or supermarket operator from the wholesaler with his packaged cereal, canned fruit juice, or furniture polish. It becomes one of the multiplicity of items which can be purchased in the supermarket, where it is usually available in a strategically placed rack near the check-out counter. Its cost, five or seven cents, makes it an inconsiderable purchase. Even the few cents spent for the magazine is lost in the total punched out on the cash register. One other point should be made, and made emphatically. In the case of at least two of the largest grocery-store magazines, the copy purchased is well worth the money.

Though standards of editorial selection and mechanical reproduction vary, the store-distributed magazines are attractive. They are thinner and smaller in page size than most of the leaders, but they look like the independent, larger-circulation women's magazines. Cover pictures are pleasant and enticing. In general, the printing, whether by letterpress or gravure, is good. Illustrations are colorful. The contents of the magazine —and they range from thoughtful in the best of the group to flimsy in the least prepossessing—are easy to read, sensible, and realistic in their approach to the interest and problems of the middle- and lower-income-group housewife and her family.

They have been called "primarily 'how to do it' primers," [1] but they are more than that. There are recipes which are generally inexpensive and practical. There are menus which the housewife in ordinary circumstances can use. There are fashion articles with dress patterns given or made available. There are diet discussions, beauty hints, discussions of child care, safety or other problems in which the family is interested. There is movie news. Public affairs, thoughtful biographies, discussions of international problems, subjects which call for educated tastes and appreciations are generally, and properly, left to the established women's magazines; but the store-distributed magazines provide glamour in their mildly romantic, safely domestic fiction, sometimes in an occasional travel article, and always in their illustrations. The names of well-known writers, though seldom attached to their most seriously considered output, appear frequently in two of the grocery magazines.

[1] "Food Store Magazines Hit the Big Time," *Business Week,* February 9, 1952.

The biggest and, in this writer's estimation, the best of the store-distributed magazines is *Woman's Day*. During the economic depression of the 1930's stores of The Great Atlantic & Pacific Tea Company throughout the country began to publish and distribute gratis to their customers a menu leaflet. The A & P leaflet told the housewife how to get the most for her food dollar, then how to use the food purchased to provide her family with appetizing and nourishing meals. The menu was so well accepted that plans were laid in 1937 to enlarge it into a magazine, and a contest was run to select a name for the proposed publication.

The planned magazine was to be, like the menu, a free service to A & P customers. A circulation of 775,000, the same as that of the menu leaflet, was envisioned. The first issue of *Woman's Day* appeared in 1938. It was of 32 pages, six of them given over to recipes and menus. There was one article on "What To Do About Worry" and another which asked, "Is Football Worthwhile?"

Immediate demand sent the circulation of the new magazine up far beyond what had been planned. It was no longer possible to distribute it without charge. After various tests had been run, the price was set at five cents a copy. The magazine sold for five cents until 1951 when, as a result of rising production costs, the price was raised to seven cents. By that time the magazine had grown tremendously in circulation, in size, and in editorial coverage. A year later, 1952, *Woman's Day* could state in its advertising, "More women go out and buy *Woman's Day* than any other magazine in the world." Average sale per issue at that time was given in the magazine's trade advertising as 4,865,000, and the magazine, which is held at a 60–40 editorial-advertising ratio, was carrying more than $6 million annually in advertising. The latest A. B. C. figure for *Woman's Day*, that for the last six months of 1955, was 3,811,320 per issue, and the total advertising revenue of the magazine in 1955 was $9,279,181.

Wholly owned by The Great Atlantic & Pacific Tea Company and distributed only through its stores and supermarkets, *Woman's Day* has made itself one of the large and significant women's magazines. Fiction, reputable feature articles, good writing, and excellent art work, color photography, and reproduction make it a formidable competitor of the standard women's magazines, both for readership and advertising revenue.

The main departments in every issue are Articles and Fiction, the largest; Home Workshop and Decorating; Needlework; Fashion; Food. Under other monthly features come News and Gossip, a section which includes notes on the contributors to each issue; Neighbors, comprised of letters from readers; movie critiques; and miscellaneous discursive, essay-type offerings. In the popular trend, *Woman's Day* has run how-to-do-it material since its first issue. Since 1947 it has run a complete how-to section—its subtitle, "How To Make It—How To Do It—How To Fix It."

The response to the magazine's varied editorial offerings is notable and can serve, to some extent, as a measure of the magazine's influence upon its readers. *Woman's Day* has developed an enviable rapport with the audience it has elected to reach. Readers write in, asking how to repair a roof, how to stop the baby's crying, how to build this or cook that, how to control a child or a husband. They are gratifyingly eager to purchase special items offered in the magazine's editorial pages.

The store-distributed magazines do not have the prestige of the big-name women's periodicals, neither the prestige nor the awesomeness of great reputation. Possibly for this reason, they seem more approachable to many of their readers. There is often the simpler reason that women readers like what they see pictured and described in the magazine's pages and want it.

In 1954 *Woman's Day* ran a series of Audubon bird prints so reproduced that they could be cut out and framed. The

The *pièce de resistance* is hamburger delectably translated and appetizingly displayed, but this *Woman's Day* cover in 1956 combines the allure of food with baseball, a film star, and educational appeal.

magazine received requests for an additional 55,436 sets of the prints, and another 45,000 requests for a series of colored flower prints run in the same year. Patterns for sweaters, plans for lawn furniture, directions for building a skiff, all featured in the magazine, drew hundreds of thousands of requests. A *Woman's Day* piece featured a special fabric for use with a housedress pattern. The manufacturer of the cloth reported sales of a million yards as a result of the *Woman's Day* writeup and its promotion.

Entire communities have been stirred to action by *Woman's Day* features. An October, 1953, article, "Teen-Agers Can Be Skilled—Not Killed," told of the success of a road driving program sponsored by the Junior Chamber of Commerce. Over 30,000 requests for posters on the subject, which the magazine offered, poured in from schools, clubs, and police organizations. Within a few weeks after issue date of the magazine, the Junior Chamber of Commerce received 150 inquiries on how to set up similar programs in other communities.

A comparable article on a schoolchildren's bicycle safety campaign in White Plains, New York, brought a comparable response. Requests for posters offered to stimulate interest in bicycle safety came in from all over the country. Florida used its entire state police force to distribute the posters to all its schools.

Though it is an A & P subsidiary, *Woman's Day* is not editorially directed only to A & P store customers. It is planned and functions as a service magazine for all women, and in content and appearance is most similar to the women's monthly magazines which are not connected with food outlets. Many of its editorial pieces, for example a sound and informative article in February, 1955, "Old Autos Never Die," have not the remotest connection with the sale of food or other supermarket items. The housewife reader is treated as an intelligent, normally curious human being. A thick, full book, to use the trade term,[2] *Woman's Day* is pleasing in appearance, substantial in its editorial offerings. It entertains and informs. It has demonstrated its influence with its readers. It is consistently promoted as a woman's service publication with its own entity as a magazine.

Woman's Day is advertised in magazines, big city newspapers, and the trade press. Its reiterated slogan is that "women go out and buy" or "go out to buy" *Woman's Day*. They have set out with purpose to purchase, and they are in places where purchases can be made of the products advertised in the magazine's pages. The housewife out to shop buys not only foods, but also clothing, drugs, furniture, items for her personal needs and the needs of her family. She patronizes drug, department, and specialty shops as well as the supermarket, and *Woman's Day* has a strong argument in its space selling that the local A & P outlet is usually well located in a shopping center.

All of the grocery-distributed magazines, as already indicated, like many of their independent contemporaries, stress do-it-yourself material. This is a direct aid to advertisers whose materials or tools must be purchased to carry out the do-it-yourself plans and suggestions. It is likewise a comment on the current economic situation. Few middle-class families can any longer afford to have minor, sometimes major, home construction, repair, maintenance, or decoration done by hiring skilled artisans. They must, perforce, do the work themselves. The grocery-distributed magazines perform a useful and necessary service in giving their readers information of this kind.

Oldest of the large-circulation, store-distributed monthly magazines, *Family Circle* was established in 1932. Published in New York by Family Circle, Inc., it is distributed at seven cents a copy through a nation-wide chain of chains. Though the

---

[2] For some reason magazines are always referred to as "books" throughout the periodical publishing industry. It is part of the trade jargon which shows the user to be "in the know."

list is apt to change as grocery chains merge or buy each other
out, or for other reasons, it includes or has included: First
National, Grand Union, Safeway, Bohack, American, Acme,
Dixie Home, Winn & Lovett, Albert Kroger, Weingarten, Butt,
Red Owl, and other grocery store systems. The magazine is
published in twenty sectional editions—in contrast to seven for
Woman's Day. These numerous editions enable it to offer
the advertiser national coverage or any combination of editions
which will provide coverage paralleling the distribution of the
advertiser's product. In 1952 *Family Circle* began to guarantee
a four million circulation. Its total net paid A. B. C. circulation
at the end of 1955 showed a previous six-months' average of
4,060,469.

Though issues seldom run to as many pages as *Woman's
Day, Family Circle* is a full magazine, carrying romantic fiction
with housewife appeal, feature articles on such subjects of
family interest as sports, law, divorce, teen-age problems, gardening, and travel. The magazine's largest department is "All
Around the House." In it offerings are broken down by food,
equipment, decoration, home building, and home furnishing.
Under "Your Children and You" are pieces on child care,
parent-child relationships, party suggestions, and other pertinent material. A typical issue contains, too, stories about
contributors headed "The Personal Touch," movie notices
under "The Reel Dope," Beauty and Health departments, and
a Buyer's Guide giving directions on how and where to obtain
products given mention in the editorial columns.

Family Circle seems to contain fewer articles of general interest than does *Woman's Day*. The entire magazine is more
purely domestic in its approach, with much made of homemade
fun, much figure and complexion advice, and a mild piece which
might well be entitled "How to Enjoy Life" in most issues. All
the editorial is easy to read, easy to take. There is little that will
strain the intellect or titivate the sensibilities. As in *Woman's
Day,* well-known names appear frequently as by-lines. In

April, 1955, Quentin Reynolds became an expert on problems of adolescence with "Help Over the Teen-Age Hurdle." In September, Herman Hickman explained that "Football Is a Ladies' Game." In May, Art Linkletter of radio and television told "Why People Are Funny." Richard Armour, humorous versifier whose lines are chastely printed often on the "Post Scripts" page of *The Saturday Evening Post,* rates a full page illustrated in neon colors when his lines appear in *Family Circle.*

Everywoman's, founded originally in 1939 and distributed by one of the largest wholesale grocers, was later purchased by the Cuneo Press. Its publication as a monthly magazine sold through United States and Canadian supermarkets began in 1951. Price in 1956 raised from five to seven cents a copy, it is distributed by Food Fair, National Tea, Gristede Brothers, and other chains. Here again, the list of distributors is apt to change. Competition among the grocery-distributed magazines is sharp. Chains sometimes switch from one magazine to another. Circulation is enlarged when new stores of a carrying chain are opened; cut if a chain decides to close some of its outlets. *Everywoman's,* which is published in four sectional editions, has a total net paid average circulation of about 1,700,000.

Like its larger counterparts, *Everywoman's* carries romantic fiction, fashion, and beauty departments. It runs feature articles of the Sunday newspaper type. The monthly "Memo" (To: Everywoman; From: The Editor) establishes the kind of intimacy with its readers that the magazine seeks. "Everywoman's Woman" affords audience participation by encouraging readers to send in sketches of some woman whose personality has affected the lives of those nearest to her. The title "Everywoman" appears in many features—"Everywoman Wears Blouses in the Spring," "Everywoman Is Beautiful Thru Pregnancy" were both in the May, 1953, issue. "That Man Is Here," reminiscent of similar offerings in the general women's monthlies, provides whimsical humorous "man talk" as, presumably, the earnest housewife likes to hear it. Often the subject gets around to food and drink.

Largest department in *Everywoman's* is "Food and Equipment." Food, drink, menus, recipes, illustrations of pastries, colorful salads, savory dishes, and decorative servings bulk large in the central portion of the magazine. The full page or double spreads of food advertisers ring changes on the theme with more extravagant illustrations in the advertising pages. The family table is very much the heart of the matter.

Better Living, which made its initial appearance in May, 1951, was founded jointly by the McCall Corporation and a group of capitalists including Nelson Rockefeller, Clendenin Ryan, and Douglas Dillon. It was published in New York by Mass Markets, Inc., and distributed through stores operated by members of the Super Market Institute. Unlike the three store-distributed magazines already mentioned, *Better Living,* which was printed by *McCall's* and offered as a part of a *McCall's– Better Living* advertising package, was a larger magazine when it started than subsequently it became. Selling at five cents a copy, it began with an issue of 100 pages, 42 of them advertising, and a circulation guarantee of 1,500,000. The magazine's circulation rose to over two and a half million in 1954. It began to lose both circulation and advertising in the first quarter of 1956. In April, 1956, it was announced that publication would cease with the May issue.

In general, though it was thinner in number of pages and in scope and depth of editorial content, *Better Living* carried the same type content as the other store-distributed periodicals. Monthly it published one or two pieces of fiction, features which seem of less general magazine appeal than those in its contemporaries, beauty and fashion departments, and a large section on foods. A department called "Let's Shop" told of new items on sale in supermarkets and where to buy clothes and gadgets mentioned in the editorial matter. Markedly throughout the publication the emphasis was on foods and on the supermarket.

Editorial and advertising sections are more frankly complementary in most of the grocery-distributed magazines than in the general women's magazines. Aimed at a specific mass market, these periodicals are rife with advertising for products that the housewife buys or can be persuaded to buy. All of these magazines are strongly promoted for their usefulness as advertising media of this kind.

As indicated, *Woman's Day* carries many features of general interest, editorial pieces which have no direct concern with items sold in A & P stores. Some of the other grocery-distributed magazines waste little editorial space on subjects which do not tie in closely with merchandise for sale in the distributing supermarket.

Often it appears that recipes and menus blown up in the pages of one or another of these periodicals are intended specifically to promote the sale of slow-moving or seasonal grocery items. Many of them call for specialties rather than for staples. Prepared mixes get great play in the culinary concoctions featured, and new items being marketed by canners or processors of frozen foods are not neglected. The impression is unavoidable that the left hand is shrewdly aware of what the right hand is doing—and rather hopes it will soon be shoveling a few million mouthfuls of high-profit-margin food into the great consuming maw.

Woman's Day compares favorably on many counts with the established women's general and service magazines of mass circulation, but none of the store-distributed books can carry the rich diversity of material, the quality of the fiction and articles found in the older magazines. The kind of editorial material which can be proffered is limited. The treatment of that material in some of the grocery-distributed magazines ranges from simple to very superficial. The housewife must be readily attracted when she is buying canned corn or frozen peas. The magazine must offer subject matter that she can skim as she trundles her loaded carrier down the supermarket aisle and her bundles out to the family car.

The grocery-distributed magazine has established itself and is a success by the only criterion it is fair to apply. Individually, these magazines accomplish what they set out to do, whether it is to serve as a well-rounded women's service magazine, which *Woman's Day* is, or merely as one more promotion piece to encourage the sale of supermarket merchandise. The combined monthly circulation of these periodicals indicates that they are well received by an approving public. The many millions of dollars still spent annually for advertising in their pages indicates that interested sections of business believe they perform an economic function.

Chapter 20

MAGAZINE ADVERTISING

ADVERTISING made possible the popular magazines of the 1880's and the 1890's. Almost all of today's leading magazines depend on advertising for the greater part of their revenue. If their income were limited to the prices paid for subscriptions and for single copies bought at newsstands, magazines could not continue publication in anything like the form with which we are familiar, possibly not in any form. As business and entertainment are organized in the United States, it is advertising which pays for the spread of public information through the press, both magazine and newspaper, over the radio, and on television. National advertising began in magazines, and magazines continue to lead other media in the amounts of money collected annually for advertising in them. For this reason alone advertising is an important social and economic force.

Beyond this, national advertising in magazines has directly applied and still applies its own powerful leverage in American life. It played a leading role in originating modern methods of distribution of manufactured goods and has acted as one of the chief means of maintaining that system of distribution. It has helped bring about a virtual revolution in the production methods employed by American industry, mass selling sustaining mass production. Magazine advertising has changed the taste and habits of the population. There is not too much exaggeration in the statement, often made, that magazine advertising has been a primary force in raising the American material standard of living to what it is.

There has been magazine advertising since magazines have existed. Addison's comments in 1710 on the advertising in *The Tatler* were noted earlier. In 1758 Dr. Samuel Johnson wrote: "The trade of advertising is now so near perfection that it is not easy to propose any improvement." In this instance, Dr. Johnson proved his fallibility. Advertising has not yet attained perfection.

The first advertisement in an American periodical is said to have been run in Andrew Bradford's *Weekly Mercury*, a Philadelphia newspaper. In its issue for December 29, 1719, a Phillip Ludwell of Green Spring, Virginia, advertised for a runaway slave. The next year the *Mercury* carried its first product advertisement, one for a patent medicine manufactured by one Frank Knowles. Early magazine advertisements were mostly announcements and notices of various kinds together with the claims of various specifics, listings of books and magazines, and a few outright advertisements for such articles as anthracite ornaments, cheap coffins, India rubber shoes, and patent straw cutters.

In those magazines which carried them at all, the advertisements appeared in columns where notices of the removal of a business from one location to another, marriages, births, deaths, offers of fifty-cent rewards for "indented" apprentices who had run off, notices of public sales, and the claims of compound syrup of sarsaparilla for the cure of scrofula, white swellings, pains in the bones, scaly eruptions, and "all disorders arising from an impure state of the blood" were all run in together. The advertisements were short, an inch or two, three or four at the most; in eye-tearing type. A few were decorated with printer's ornaments or small engravings.

Many of the early magazines completely eschewed advertising. It gained entrance gradually into the stronger periodicals during the second half of the nineteenth century. *The Atlantic Monthly*, which carried none of it during its first three years, began to accept advertising in 1860. *Harper's New Monthly Magazine*, undoubtedly influenced by the company's profitable experience with *Harper's Weekly*, which was a successful advertising medium from the start, began to carry advertising in 1864, but until 1882 the only advertising it published was that for the firm's own books. *Scribner's*, even before this, was a flourishing advertising medium. Its Christmas issue for 1880 carried forty-nine pages of advertisements.

When *Scribner's* became *The Century* in 1881, Roswell Smith began the outright solicitation of advertising. The result was that *The Century* took the lead in advertising volume among the established monthlies and held it until 1890. In that year *Harper's*, making up for lost time and opportunities, overtook and passed *The Century*. By this time Cyrus H. K. Curtis, the first magazine publisher to realize fully the possibilities of advertising, was exploiting it to the full in the *Ladies' Home Journal* and using it to re-establish the moribund *Saturday Evening Post*.

Business was quick to recognize the power of the force intensified and expanded by the popular magazines. In 1892 the astute Chauncey M. Depew, then president of the New York Central and Hudson River Railroad, said: "Every enterprise, every business, and I might add every institution, must be advertised in order to be a success. To talk in any other strain would be madness." [1] In the same year Pennsylvania Railroad spent $230,000 in advertising, and the Union Pacific almost as much.

In 1888 George Eastman invented the portable camera which he named "Kodak." He spent $25,000 in advertising the new device that first year. By 1895 magazine advertising had made "Kodak" and camera almost synonymous. Ivory Soap was being advertised by Procter & Gamble in the magazines of the early 1880's as "99$\frac{44}{100}$% pure." Its advertisement in *The Independent*, November 12, 1885, read: "Did it ever occur to you how much cleaner and nicer it is to wash the Napkins

[1] Quoted in *Printers' Ink, Fifty Years*, p. 26.

$5 Reward.

RAN away, on the 15th of 8th month, from the subscriber, living in Willistown, Chester county, an indented apprentice to the farming business, named WM. HART, aged about 18 years, of a light complexion and hair, of a forward, talkative disposition. Said boy had on and took with him a blue cloth coat, red striped and blue cotton pantaloons, figured waistcoat, fur hat, and sundry other clothing. All persons are forbid harbouring or employing said boy at the peril of the law. ·Whoever takes up said boy and lodges him in jail in Chester, Delaware, or Philadelphia county or city, so that I receive information of him, shall receive the above reward.
aug 23—3t*　　　　　　　MORDECAI THOMAS.

Five Dollars Reward.

RAN away on the 10th of August. from the subscriber, living in Blockley township, Philadelphia county, near Haddingtonville, an apprentice boy, by name JAMES ROBERTS, eighteen years of age, and large of his age, dark complexion, brown hair, grey eyes, and marked J. R. on one arm. Had on striped pantaloons, white roundabout, Marseilles waistcoat, and fur hat. Came back on night of same day, broke open the house, and stole a green cloth coatee, waistcoat, boots, and sundry other articles. Whoever brings back the said boy, or will lodge him in jail, so that I can get him again, shall receive the above reward.
aug 23—3t*　　　　　　WM. CARTER, Farmer.

A Teacher wants a Situation.

A YOUNG man who has had some experience in teaching. and who is well acquainted with the various branches of a polite English education (including Natural Philosophy and Chemistry,) who is also qualified to teach the higher branches of mathematics, desires a situation in a good school, or private family. Satisfactory testimonials of character and qualifications will be given. A few lines addressed to H. Q. W. (post paid) Jefferson College, Canonsburg, Pa., will meet with immediate attention.

P. S. The applicant would have no objections to teach a class of Latin scholars.　　　　　　　　　　　aug 23—3t*

Early advertisements were often simply notices. Runaway apprentices and a jobhunting teacher occupied paid space in *The Saturday Evening Post*, September 6, 1834.

Magazine advertising popularized Pears Soap. Pears ceased advertising and disappeared. Its copy in *McClure's*, June, 1901, quoted Winston Churchill, "English war correspondent."

Towels, Handkerchiefs, Table Linen, etc., by themselves with soap *not* made of putrid fats or questionable grease? Do it with Ivory Soap . . . made of vegetable oil, and use them confident that they are clean and not tainted." The Ivory Soap slogan has been in use well over half a century. It is perhaps one of the best examples of what advertising men call continuity and consistency in advertising. It staggers the imagination to contemplate how many millions of cakes of Ivory Soap that continued repetition of its time-honored slogan has sold.

The same 1885 issue of *The Independent* carried advertisements for Esterbrook's Pens, Royal Baking Powder, Columbia Bicycles, LePage's Glue, R. H. Macy & Co., Connecticut Mutual Life Insurance Company, Massachusetts Mutual, the Travelers, Chicago and North-Western Railway, and Weber Pianos, as well as for a dozen more insurance companies and advertisements for Congress boots (with a patent adjustable lace), corrugated picket fences, a scientific system of protection from lightning, reversible collars and cuffs, curtain grates, cures for deafness, and the Grand Union Hotel at Saratoga Springs.

By 1890 more advertisers had joined Kodak and Ivory Soap and those already mentioned in making their company names and the names of their products more widely known. A few were Rambler Bicycles, Rogers & Brother, Remington Standard Typewriter (and Densmore, Williams, Caligraph and No. 4 Yost), Hires Root Beer, Rubifoam for the Teeth, Ed Pinaud's, Packer's Tar Soap, Scott's Emulsion, Pyle's Pearline, Mellin's Food, Walter Baker Cocoa, W. L. Douglas Shoes, Castoria, Buffalo Lithia Water, and Sapolio. In an 1894 advertisement Mt. Holyoke College, opening for its fifty-eighth year, was advertising board and tuition for $250.

By 1900 the names which magazine advertising was making familiar to everyone included these and many more: Ivory Soap, Sapolio, Royal, Postum, Lea & Perrin's Sauce, Pettijohn's Flaked Breakfast Food, Welch's Grape Juice (for

"Young and Old"), Cream of Wheat, Van Camp's Concentrated Soups, Knox's Gelatine, Hires, 1847 Rogers Bros., Cable Pianos, American Radiator Co., Smith & Wesson ("A Smith & Wesson Revolver is the choice of the Japanese Navy"), Hart, Schaffner & Marx (Varsity Summer Suits at $10, $12, and $14), Wheatena, Johnson's Prepared Wax, Globe-Wernicke, Standard Sanitary Manufacturing Co., Anita Cream, Cascarets, Woodbury's Facial Soap, Cuticura, Boston Garters, President Suspenders, Stein-Bloch Clothes, Lowney's Chocolates, Regal Shoes, Armour & Co., Boston & Maine Railroad (and all the other railroads).

The *pièce de résistance* in the June, 1901, issue of *McClure's Magazine* was an inset full-page advertisement in full color on cardboard, obviously lithographed and beautifully reproduced, for products of the National Biscuit Company. One side of the inset page showed a girl in Dutch costume holding a package of Uneeda Biscuits. The legend, lettered across her wide white skirt, read: "Do You Know You Needa Biscuit?" The reverse of the sheet pictured Ramona sugar wafers appetizingly displayed on delicately colored china, and Athena wafers tumbling out of an upset cookie jar.

This advertising not only made the names of these companies and these products known in households all over the country, but it changed fundamentally the sales methods of manufacturers and the buying habits of consumers. Magazine advertising brought about the sale of goods and products nationally and accustomed purchasers to buy not the articles made and sold locally, but those made and sold on the larger market.

This advertising created new desires in the minds of readers, desires that grew into needs and resulted in purchases. By increasing consumer demands and arousing new ones, the advertisers stimulated the processes of invention. Manufacturers who had previously made their products only on the comparatively small orders, and often to the specifications, of jobbers catering to the retail trade in a few localities, found themselves working for a far larger and very different market. To meet the greatly increased demand from the ultimate consumers of their products in every section of the country reached through magazine advertising, manufacturers were forced into product improvements and into mass production. Mass production for this newly created mass market necessitated improved and more economical methods of manufacture. This resulted in lower prices which, in turn, made the product available to more and more people. Articles once luxuries, obtainable only by the affluent, became available to the average man and woman.

Advertising increased the competition among manufacturers. Only the manufacturer, large or small, making a good product, and succeeding in making that product well and favorably known, could retain his share of the market. Those making inferior merchandise and failing to advertise usually failed. Advertising brought the consumer not only a cheaper, but also an improved article.

The whole process of distribution has had to be enlarged and improved as a result of the huge new markets which advertising has created. Faster, more efficient, and less wasteful methods have had to be instituted to get more and more goods to a continually enlarged market. In all of these and other ways advertising has operated to change the living habits of the American people. It has provided them with those products which science and industry have devised to lessen drudgery in the home and in the office or factory, thus aiding the health and increasing the leisure of the housewife and the worker. It has educated people to demand material and mechanical conveniences unknown to earlier generations, stimulated the production of these conveniences to meet their demands. Magazine advertising has, as its proponents point out, been a causative factor in bringing more and better material things to more people at a lower cost.

As new products have been invented, developed, and perfected, they have been brought to the attention of the public through magazine advertising. The automobile industry, for instance, was quick to capitalize on the selling force of national advertising in magazines, and this advertising was largely responsible for the wide and rapid acceptance of the new vehicle by the American public. Through creating the popular demand that made mass production imperative and economically possible, it helped bring the price (pre-World War II) down to where a car could be purchased by the average family. Other mechanical conveniences—the electric refrigerator, the washing machine, the other household appliances—reached the people who use them largely through the same channel.

The use of advertising of this kind is closely tied to the whole conception of brand merchandise. Magazine advertising on a large scale and the growth of small industries and business organizations to the stature of manufacturers and distributors of nationally known and purchased brands of specific merchandise were coeval. Most consumer advertising in magazines is intended to support the distributor and retailer and to establish and maintain a company or brand name favorably in the public mind.

Trade-marks were originally imposed upon the craft guilds of the Middle Ages as a protection for the public. They were intended as a means of identifying the maker of an article so as to fix responsibility for inferior materials or poor workmanship. The compulsion made the use of good materials and the application of good workmanship a necessity for guild members who took pride in their product, wished to avoid censure and punishment, and likewise wished approval for the articles they made. As a result the trade-mark became a prized asset and, later, a recognized mark of public confidence in a given brand.

It is these trade-marks or brands which are advertised nationally. The purchaser is taught to buy a given make of car, rather than another; to ask for soap or soup of a certain name, rather than for just soap or just soup. Advertising makes this name known; satisfactory use of the advertised product makes that advertising believable. The brand name comes to serve as a guarantee of the good faith and competence of the seller and the reliability of his product.

Advertising of this kind, which names a particular article and fixes responsibility for its manufacture, serves as a guide to the purchaser. It enables the purchaser to identify the article he prefers—and to avoid that brand of a product which he has learned does not meet his requirements. Without the identification made possible by the trade-mark which he has learned to recognize through magazine advertising, the consumer could discover only through repeated trial and error, an expensive process, which make of a given product will meet his needs and which will fail to do so. In this sense, brand advertising is a device for the mutual guidance of maker and buyer.

The consumer, who cannot know the intricacies of an automobile or a washing machine, or the technical specifications which must be met by materials of a stated quality, comes to know an advertised trade-mark, and to look for it or avoid it when he has need to make a new purchase. It is a reliable short cut which the consumer can use in making his purchase decisions; a device, in such a community as ours, of distinct social usefulness.

The owners of trade-marks, which they have established through the manufacture and sale of sound merchandise and through advertising their brands so well that people think of them as almost synonymous with the objects these brand names describe, place a high value on them. As long ago as 1915 it was said that the Royal Baking Powder Company, one of the first national magazine advertisers, considered its trademark worth just $1,600,000 a letter. In 1928 it was estimated that when the Postum Company paid $43,000,000 for Maxwell House Coffee, not less than $30,000,000 of that amount was for goodwill, for the advertised name. In 1935 Adolph Zukor was quoted as valuing the name "Paramount" at $15,000,000.

Actually, advertised brand names, assuming that the public

has had satisfactory experience with the brand advertised, are invaluable. How large a part advertising plays in erecting and upholding their value can be seen from the experience of brands, once well and favorably known through magazine advertising, when they ceased to be advertised. Rubifoam and Sozodont dentifrices, once widely known and sold, disappeared from the market when their advertising ceased. Force and Egg-O-See breakfast foods went the same way. Pears Soap is a classic example. Pears placed its first national magazine advertising in 1901 and continued aggressive advertising for twenty years, spending more than a million dollars annually. The company, considering its brand well established, decided suddenly to cease advertising. Sales dropped $1,500,000 the first year, more the second. An attempt to regain lost ground through the resumption of magazine advertising after several years of falling sales was unsuccessful. Its market completely lost, the company was sold to a competitor.

Some of the effects of modern magazine advertising have been indicated. It has gone hand in hand with "big business" in consumer goods. Without it, it is doubtful that large companies and corporations, large manufacturing in many industries, would have developed or could exist. It seems hardly necessary to point out that this same advertising has had the opposite effect of causing the virtual disappearance of smaller manufacturers and distributors in many lines. Just as magazines, through both their editorial and advertising contents, seem sometimes to have made everyone look and act alike on monotonously uniform Main Streets across the country, national advertising has helped to make successful local enterprise more difficult. It has made for economy and standardization, not for individual craftsmanship, not for art.

The importance of one economic function of advertising has become increasingly apparent since World War II. As C. H. Sandage has pointed out, American industry is now organized

to produce goods and services far in excess of the basic requirements of consumers. To keep capital and the labor force ade-
quately employed, we must consume more than we actually
need. "A luxury or surplus economy," Sandage wrote, "cannot
be built upon the physical needs of society. It is dependent primarily upon the psychological needs and wants of consumers.
If capital, labor, and natural resources are to be combined to
produce non-necessities, . . . the consuming public must be
informed of their existence, educated as to their want-satisfying
qualities, and persuaded to buy them. It is here that advertising plays an important role." [2]

There are many definitions and descriptions of advertising,
each with its own refinements, but analysis of them is beside the
subject here. Fundamentally advertising is information. It
states where an article is for sale and obtainable, what the
article is like, its uses, its quality, and usually its price. The
article is described in terms which will make it appear attractive
and desirable, and which will influence the reader to purchase it.
Like every other tool, magazine advertising can be and has
been misused. Especially in the early days of its modern development, advertising was marred by extravagant and fraudulent claims. Inferior merchandise was described as superior;
injurious products were sold as healthful, and cure-nothings
were described as cure-alls.

Magazines, if only as a means of self-protection, were quick
to recognize the need for control of the force of advertising.
Both the public and the legitimate advertiser had to be protected from the quack and the advertiser who misrepresented
his product. In 1880 *Farm Journal* announced that it would
refund to subscribers any loss sustained "by trusting advertisers
who prove to be deliberate swindlers." The Curtis Publishing
Company in 1892, when the *Ladies' Home Journal* still needed

[2] C. H. Sandage, "The Role of Advertising in Modern Society," *Journalism Quarterly*, Winter, 1951, p. 32.

all the financial support it could obtain, firmly ruled out all patent medicine advertising. This was the real beginning of the move toward establishing standards in advertising.[3]

A second very influential move was made when the Curtis Advertising Code of 1910 was set up and adopted. This code stated that neither the *Ladies' Home Journal* nor *The Saturday Evening Post* would accept advertising meant to deceive or defraud. They would not accept medical or "curative" advertising, advertising which attacked the products of a competitor, advertisements for liquor, advertising from mail-order houses, blind advertising, any advertising of an immoral or suggestive nature, or any advertisements for installment buying. The *Journal,* in addition, would not accept financial, tobacco, or playing-card advertising. The *Post,* though it would accept advertising for reputable bonds, would accept no financial advertising of a highly speculative nature. Cigar or pipe but not cigarette advertising was acceptable for the *Post* of 1910. Parts of this advertising code have been modified as changing social customs have dictated, but its essentials are still rigidly enforced. All advertising must meet stringent standards of responsibility before it can be published today in any of the reputable magazines.

Advertising is a method of selling, of making a product known, of obtaining the widest possible distribution for it. To create the desires that will lead to sales, it uses appeals of many kinds. It appeals to the mind with argument, to taste with artistic display, to fear, to ambition, to envy. It uses every possible device to convince the prospective buyer that he should purchase what the advertiser has for sale. Applied psychology is nowhere more cunningly used than in advertising.

[3] Ralph M. Hower says in *The History of an Advertising Agency, N. W. Ayer & Son at Work, 1869–1939* (Cambridge, Mass.: Harvard University Press, 1939), p. 449: "The main reform [in advertising] waited for the crusading efforts of Edward W. Bok of the Ladies' Home Journal, ably backed by his employer Cyrus H. K. Curtis. This reform began in 1892 with The Curtis Publishing Company's refusal to handle any patent-medicine advertising, and it reached its climax between 1904 and 1906 when the agitation for pure food and drug laws became nation-wide."

Intent calculations and many skills are utilized in forming the presentation that the public finally sees in the pages of its magazines. The advertiser or his agency considers the kind of circulation as well as the extent of the circulation of a given magazine. He wants to know into what income brackets readers fall, where they live, what education they have, what their jobs or professions are. These facts the publisher makes known to him, and the approach of the advertisement is planned on the basis of these and other known factors. They determine, in part, whether the advertisement will inform, coax, wheedle, threaten, or simply announce; whether the display will be violent or delicately restrained. The methods and the emphasis will vary with the nature of the product, the magazine used as a medium, the potential purchasers the advertiser is trying to reach, whether the product is a necessity or a luxury, and whether the advertisement is designed primarily to create immediate sales, to build good will for a brand, or to make the reader receptive to the approach of a salesman.

The contention of those critics who consider advertising unfavorably is not that it is ineffective but that, socially, it is too effective. The prose descriptions and graphic displays of the advertiser have an insidious plausibility which makes expertly presented articles look larger than life and entirely too captivating. Advertising they see as the siren which lures men to their destruction by awakening cupidity and greed, and fastening their attention on the desire for material things. Their objections are based on moral and aesthetic grounds, and certainly there are kinds of advertising, though little of it is magazine advertising, which afford just grounds for complaint.

A point worth noting here was made by a group of Harvard professors who acted as advisory committee for one of the most thorough modern studies of advertising and its effects. Their sharp comment was: "Advertising is sometimes criticized on the ground that as part of the capitalistic system of free enterprise it leads consumers to buy the wrong things and spend too much for them, whereas consumers would be better off if they bought different things and spent their money in different ways. When this criticism implies, as it often does, that someone in authority might better decide what things should be bought and how consumers should spend their money, then the essential clash is between rival ideologies of individualism and authoritarianism; and the basic argument is not really about advertising at all." [4]

The complaint is often made that advertising costs too much. Actually, advertising adds so small an amount to the cost of a product that it makes no appreciable difference in the price paid by the consumer, a price that would be many times higher if advertising did not provide the mass consumption which allows of the economies and efficiencies of mass production. The cost of advertising is said to average out at less than three cents of the consumer dollar. The cost of advertising of one brand of nationally advertised soups has long been estimated by its producer at seventeen hundredths of a cent per can. A manufacturer of nationally advertised biscuits reports his advertising expenditure at less than one tenth of a cent for a ten-cent package. On a passenger car the advertising amounts to about as much as the extra cost of white-wall tires.

Another frequently repeated charge is that advertising only urges people to buy this instead of that brand of the same commodity or to switch brands, with no net gain to consumption. Cigarette and soap manufacturers are among the heaviest and most competitive consumer advertisers. Cigarette consumption rose from 45 billion in 1920 to 387 billion in 1948; consumption of toilet soap per capita, from an index of 1.74 in 1919 to

[4] "A Statement of the Advisory Committee" prefaced to *The Economic Effects of Advertising* by Neil H. Borden (Chicago: Richard D. Irwin, Inc., 1942), p. xviii. Neil Borden is professor of advertising at the Graduate School of Business Administration, Harvard University. The statement of the advisory committee was signed by Theodore H. Brown, Edmund P. Learned, Howard T. Lewis, Malcolm P. McNair, and Harry R. Tosdal.

2.79 in 1937.[5] Advertising, as well as growing addiction to a minor vice and a fever for cleanliness, must assume some of the responsibility for these increases. It must take an equal responsibility for today's congested highways. Advertising, as well as the desire to go somewhere, anywhere, and most of the time, gave the United States to the automobile.

To the basic charge that advertising makes for vulgarization there can be no defense. It does. The whole process of democratization is one of leveling to a classless mean. Advertising, as one of the most vociferously operative agencies in that process, helps do just that. It makes products which were once the possessions of the privileged available to the masses. It stirs desire, dissatisfaction, and material ambition. It invades privacy. Often it violates good taste. The tendency of our society and our time is to do these things. Advertising is in the van of the forces destroying older values and substituting those which it is to be hoped may prove better.

Whether its existence and use in magazines is good or bad, Americans are deeply conditioned to advertising. It is virtually inescapable. We see and hear it everywhere. We would feel somewhat uneasy without it.[6] Because we have little choice, we have learned to take advertising nearly as naturally as we breathe. We react to it almost by reflex. If a product is not advertised, we do not know it; if it ceases to be advertised, we forget it. We are apt to suspect the nonadvertised article when we come on it in a shop. Something must be wrong with it.

Magazine advertising, fortunately for the readers of periodicals, provides certain satisfactions in itself. For familiar, long-advertised products, it seems friendly and reassuring. The Fisk

[5] Otto Kleppner, *Advertising Procedure* (4th ed.; New York: Prentice-Hall, Inc., 1950), p. 678.

[6] "During World War II, men in the armed services overseas received editions of popular magazines without the normal advertising contents. . . . The absence or decrease of advertising was keenly felt by the readers." Darrell Blaine Lucas and Steuart Henderson Britt, *Advertising Psychology and Research* (New York: McGraw-Hill Book Co., Inc., 1950) p. 657.

"Time To Re-tire" boy, the Campbell Soup kids, Aunt Jemima, the fox terrier listening to His Master's Voice were old friends. They have their modern counterparts. De Beer's diamond advertisements and Weyerhaueser Timber paintings are in themselves pleasant things to regard. There is a vicarious satisfaction to be gained from looking at the illustrations and reading the descriptions of luxury items most people could not possibly buy: unique creations in jewelry, costing into the thousands of dollars, in *The New Yorker,* exotic furs in *Vogue.* It is warming to think you might look like the attenuated model in the ravishing Dior frock or the distinguished explorer-sportsman-epicure dining in the smart restaurant pictured in a *Holiday* travel advertisement. If you can't buy "The Best Car in the World," you can at least look at the picture of a Rolls Royce in an English magazine. Few can buy the new Lincoln Continental, but there is pleasure for the many in looking at it in a fold-over advertisement in *The Saturday Evening Post.* Magazine advertising of this kind makes the reader feel a little larger than life, a little better than well. It offers a few moments of escape from pressing anxieties. It demands no thought. It presents dreams of a lovely world, and the reader is grateful. The pages of less splendid advertisements can give the same kind of pleasure as looking at a Sears, Roebuck catalogue on a rainy day in the country or looking at an L. L. Bean catalogue at any time. *Vogue* and *Harper's Bazaar* are read as much for their advertisements as for their editorial content. One suspects that the advertising in many magazines sometimes gives more satisfaction than the articles. Publishers like to think, and their promotion managers often claim, that some of the confidence readers have in an established magazine's editorial content, some of the warmth aroused in the reader by the humor, human interest, and sturdy thinking, is transferred to the advertising pages. The reverse action can and does take place. There has been advertising ever since a man claimed that something he had for sale or to barter was of superior quality, and certainly better than the comparable article which someone else had to sell or barter; but modern magazines have been largely responsible for the growth and development of advertising and for its marked effects on our economic and social life.

In other ways the advertising and commercial side of the national magazine has made its influence felt in the conduct of American business. The advertising agency as it exists and operates today was established and developed largely through the efforts of the publishers of national magazines. These publishers worked with the advertising agencies during their early struggles toward a sound operating basis and, by their encouragement and support, aided in bringing about recognition of the advertising agency as an integral part of the American business structure.

The "agency" method of handling national advertising began a little over one hundred years ago when the first advertising agents were actually employed by the newspaper in which they sold space. Twenty years later, these agents had become brokers who bought and sold space in newspapers and magazines. Publishers had no established rates. Agents bought advertising space in publications at as low a price as possible, then sold it at the highest price obtainable.

In the 1870's publishers again began to employ their own special agents to sell space, and these men operated in competition with the wholesale agents. A step toward more efficient and regular methods was made when, in 1872, N. W. Ayer & Son in Philadelphia established their open contract under which the Ayer advertising agency agreed to buy space to the best of its ability, and then to bill the advertiser at the net rate plus an agreed percentage. George Batten developed a similar idea in New York.

It was in the 1880's, when magazine publishers had begun to stabilize their rates, that advertising agencies, in competing for the business of advertisers, first began to prepare copy for them. The publishers realized that this meant more effective and intelligent use of advertising space. The service agency also had a distinct value for them in the development of new advertisers, and dealing with responsible agencies lessened their own credit risk. As a matter of enlightened self-interest magazine publishers took steps to protect the agency in its efforts to sell advertising.

Standards of advertising agency recognition were discussed by the board of directors of The Curtis Publishing Company in January, 1898. In May, 1901, at a time when 45 per cent of its advertising came directly from advertisers, Curtis adopted and put into immediate effect the first Curtis contract. This contract provided that the advertising agency would maintain, and charge its clients, the full rate for advertising space set by the publisher in *The Saturday Evening Post* and the *Ladies' Home Journal*. In return Curtis would allow the advertising agency a commission of 10 per cent on the cost of the advertising space, plus a discount of 5 per cent for cash payment. It also agreed to accept no advertising, either directly or through any of its agents, at less than the published rates . This contract was far-reaching in its effects. It established the idea among publishers and advertisers that the advertising agency by its presentation of ideas and preparation of copy, art work, and typographic layout, performed a service for the advertiser which ordinarily he could not perform himself and which the publisher was not equipped to perform. It made rate-cutting by either agency or publishers illegal. It recognized the value of the service agency to both periodical and advertiser.

Other publishers followed the Curtis lead, and the position of the advertising agency as a business institution was greatly strengthened. In the conclusion to his thorough study of advertising agencies James W. Young pointed out [7] that the support of publishers hastened the development of the advertising agency. Their recognition standards protected the agency in

[7] *Advertising Agency Compensation* (Chicago: University of Chicago Press, 1933), p. 153.

the development of new advertisers. They encouraged advertising agencies to expand their services and set standards of agency compensation. The standard advertising-agency commission is now 15 per cent plus a 2 per cent cash discount.

Though some magazine publishers operate under contracts made directly with advertising agencies, most magazine recognition of agencies is done now through the various publishers' associations: the Periodical Publishers Association, the Associated Business Papers, the Agricultural Publishers Association, and the American Newspaper Publishers Association. There are now some 1,600 advertising agencies servicing 10,000 or more national advertisers.

What the agency and the advertiser demand of magazines is markets. They are not interested in the possible social or economic significances of their advertising. Like the magazines themselves, they are primarily interested in profits. They select the magazine, or list of magazines, which, all considerations weighed, they believe the most effective medium or media for the sales message they wish to transmit. It follows that advertiser and agency want an audience, circulation, usually the bigger the better; but it must be the kind of circulation which they think parallels the market for their product. It is of small use advertising industrial machinery or hearing aids in *Child Life* or cosmetics in *Business Week*.

Magazine advertising, bought and sold by the page or page fraction, is usually estimated in terms of cost per page per thousand, i.e., the cost of reaching a thousand readers with a page advertisement. This is generally figured on the basis of the black and white page. Space rates for two- and four-color pages, for center spreads, and for back and inside covers are substantially higher than those for black and white and make the cost of reaching a thousand readers through these units correspondingly more expensive. Various discounts sometimes apply to special units and for various advertising schedules, but typical rates for large-circulation magazines of different kinds are:

	Black and white page	Circulation	Cost per page per thousand
Life	$21,775.00	5,552,276	$3.92
The Saturday Evening Post	18,145.00	4,764,879	3.81
Ladies' Home Journal	15,500.00	4,969,930	3.12
The New Yorker	2,600.00	396,309	6.56
Time	9,680.00	1,951,039	4.96
Business Week	2,590.00	272,414	9.51
The Reader's Digest	26,500.00	10,361,531	2.56*

* Page rates and A. B. C. circulation as of December 31, 1955.

"An advertiser," Otto Kleppner wrote in 1950, "can deliver his message any week of the year to the homes of millions of readers of *The Saturday Evening Post* in a full-page advertisement in full colors at a cost of less than one-fourth of a cent per delivered copy. That advertising in the consumer field can be the least expensive salesman of trade-marked products is the common experience of those who use it." [8]

From the viewpoint of the advertiser, magazine advertising is mass selling. It is far-reaching, enabling him to approach customers and potential customers in numbers it would be impossible to reach through the expensive methods of personal selling alone. It has a dignity and restraint of which some other forms of advertising cannot be accused. More to the point, the accumulated experience of thousands of long-term advertisers has proved that frequent and consistent national magazine advertising has accompanied the success of commercial enterprise too often for the circumstance to be accidental.

[8] Kleppner, *op. cit.*, p. 673.

Chapter 21

INFLUENCE ON THE READER AND THE SOCIAL GROUP

THE INDIVIDUAL, if there was ever a time in which he could, can no longer live in a world bounded by the range of his five senses and by what information of people and events outside that small realm he can obtain through rumor. The geographical contraction of the modern world, brought about by speeded transport and viciously improved armament, and the speeded tempo of world activity have emphasized the need for full communication. What is happening in Manchuria, in Germany, in Tibet, at the North Pole, in science, in education, in politics, in industry, is now a matter of vital concern to the man or woman in Brooklyn, in San Francisco, and everywhere else in the United States. Whether he likes it or not, the citizen of Cincinnati is now a citizen of the world. He always was, but he did not always realize it until the magazine, the press, the radio, and television, the forces of communication most important today, told him so. These forces have taught him to be aware of the world, have kept him aware of it, and have made the American probably the most copiously informed citizen of any country.

The daily newspapers tells him, as rapidly as the news can be obtained, transmitted, and printed, of immediate happenings in his own locality and on every continent. Spot news is the essential matter of the newspaper press, and the matter which it handles supremely well. The magazine-like features which large-city newspapers have incorporated have their peculiar entertainment value, serve as circulation builders, and represent the survival of "personal journalism." They often present com-

ment of worth, but are secondary to the newspaper's main purpose and performance. The essence of the daily newspaper's
service is immediacy and transiency. Proverbially, nothing is as
dead as yesterday's newspaper.

Within little more than a quarter-century the radio has become an established feature of American life and a highly important channel of communication. It can and does bring to its
listeners events as they happen and the voices of figures in the
spotlight of public attention. It presents—inextricably confused
with strident advertising—a wealth of musical and dramatic
entertainment. The enrichment radio has brought to American
life and the service it performs are obvious. As obvious are
radio's limitations. The radio program vanishes as it is presented. Discussion must be limited to what can be understood
as it is spoken. Continuity of discussion is limited by the time
allotted to the program. There can be no rereading, no turning
back the page to consider or reconsider a point made or taken.
The social force of the radio, as has been many times demonstrated, is very strong, but it is decidedly limited. Edwin
Muller in "Radio vs. Reading," *The New Republic,* February
19, 1940, concluded on the basis of a two-year study conducted
by the School of Public and International Affairs at Princeton
University, that radio tends to send people to printed sources
for further information on broadcast subjects.

Since the first edition of this book was published in 1949,
television has established itself incontinently in American life,
its amazing public acceptance outdistancing the most optimistic
predictions of its developers and promoters. Experimental operation of transmitting stations and monitors was an actuality in
1939, but public telecasting and the manufacture of receiving
sets for civilian use was not a reality until after World War II.
A few thousand scattered sets were in use in 1946; before the
end of 1948 there were three million. By August, 1952, more
than 18 million sets were picking up signals from 110 stations.
Some 35 million television sets are now in use, serviced by
some 450 telecasting stations throughout the United States.

According to the Bureau of the Census, two out of three American homes are now equipped with television. The likelihood is that set ownership will become virtually universal before long. Color television is already in operation with some 40,000 color receiving sets in use as of this writing. The television industry forecasts that color will go through a five-year period of circulation growth, then achieve approximately national penetration.

Looking at television and listening to it have become a major leisure-time activity of the American family and the chief occupation of some. In an incredibly short time television has become an integral part of the standard mores. Its appeal has proved irresistible, and television has become a formidable competitor of magazines both for the time and attention of the public and for major advertising investment. Television's virtues as a medium of communication are many and obvious. It can bring events in their actuality—Congressional sessions and investigations, meetings of the United Nations bodies, football games, and other public spectacles—directly to the eyes and ears of people at ease in their own homes. Its on-the-spot reporting of events in their actuality and immediacy is matchless. Some of television's achievements are admirable, and the potentialities of the medium are manifold.

Television's flaws and faults are equally apparent. It has become, or been made by advertisers, *the* mass medium, with programing directed to what those responsible for its offerings evidently consider the tastes and intellectual level of the mass audience. It has made entertainment its major objective and conceived of entertainment in terms of endless westerns, crime dramas, soap operas, give-away programs, variety shows, and comedy skits. Much of what is shown on television, whether live or from old film, would be appalling if it were not ridiculous. Perhaps it is appalling anyway.[1]

---

[1] After examining television in *The Great Audience* (New York: The Viking Press, 1950), Gilbert Seldes wrote: "At a moment when every report indicates that television stands a good chance of destroying the habit of reading altogether, the intelligent popular magazine may be the last fortress of those who believe that we cannot survive unless we preserve our capacity to think."

"What have you done with my child?" Lee De Forest, inventor of the audion tube, cried out ten years ago at a time when the National Association of Broadcasters was meeting in Chicago. "He was conceived as a potent instrument for culture, fine music, the uplifting of America's mass intelligence." And De Forest went on:

> You have debased this child, you have sent him out on the streets in rags of ragtime, tatters of jive and boogie-woogie, to collect money from all and sundry for hubba hubba and audio jitterbug. You have made of him a laughing stock of intelligence, surely a stench in the nostrils of the gods of the ionosphere . . . This child of mine, now thirty years in age, has been resolutely kept to the average intelligence of thirteen years. Its national intelligence is maintained moronic, as though you and your sponsors believe the majority of listeners have only moron minds . . .[2]

Perhaps because television fascinates, because it becomes insidious and makes addicts of its adherents, perhaps because it satisfies to numbness the modern American's insistent demand that he be entertained, it has largely taken over the entertainment function once performed for the mass audience by the newsprint story magazines of the nineteenth century with their endless tales by T. S. Arthur, Mrs. Southworth, or Ned Buntline. Television has so far taken over mass entertainment that some editors, generally of news or pictorial magazines, seriously believe popular fiction is no longer a magazine province. They relegate melodrama to television, stress the informative article as the modern magazine staple. *TV Guide,* a magazine which did not exist until 1953, has a newsstand circulation second only to the leader, *Confidential.* Published in sectional editions, it is regarded by the general weeklies as a strong competitor for single-copy circulation.

Television has influenced magazine editorial content in several ways. It has forced magazines to improve in the direction

[2] Quoted in "The Revolt Against Radio," *Fortune,* March, 1947, and in *The Effects of Mass Media* by Joseph T. Klapper (New York: Bureau of Applied Social Research, Columbia University, 1949).

of physical attractiveness, with more pictures and better reproduction, with more generous display. Graphic means have been utilized to make magazine pages pleasanter to look at. Pieces have been shortened and sharpened for greater ease of reading. Some magazines, notably the pictorial weeklies, compete with television "spectaculars" with what are obviously typographic spectaculars of their own. Magazine features vie in attempted glamour and in achieved superficiality with their counterparts in television treatment. Other magazines, and it would seem more wisely, emphasize the difference between the competing media by discussion, authoritative treatment of subjects which do not lend themselves to television screening, and by the greater use of what is clearly print rather than television screen material. Either imitation or accentuation of differences is discernible in periodical after periodical.

That magazine circulations have climbed to new heights during the period of television's expansion and arrival can be taken as proof enough that the appearance and use of the new and powerful medium has far from supplanted the older one. The public seems simply to have added television to newspapers, magazines, and radio, the various media complementing each other. There are even studies which seem to indicate that the people who watch television most are often the same people who spend the most time reading magazines.

The decent and orderly separation of editorial and advertising matter observed in the newspaper and the magazine, blinked at in radio, has been extravagantly abrogated by television. With six or eight commercials, the result of multiple program sponsorship and the uninhibited sale of television spots, inserted in many half-hour programs, the salesman is with the television viewer always. He smirks, cajoles, insinuates, threatens, beseeches, and repeats, repeats, repeats between and in the midst of drama, news, weather, variety, comedy, and crime. The vacuum cleaner salesman has got into the parlor and all the other house-to-house canvassers have burst in too, and they are having a wonderful time. Often the performer takes up the product plea where the professional salesman leaves off. Part of the reason for all this is that the magazine advertiser can purchase and use only white space in a publication; he has no control over the magazine's editorial content or policy. In most cases, the advertiser purchasing television time can use it as he wishes. He plans and produces the "editorial" content as well as the advertising. He and his advertising agency can exploit it as they will.

So expensive is television advertising that only the largest national advertisers of foods, cosmetics, cars, appliances, and a few other products can afford television network advertising. Some 165 advertisers use network television. Television time costs have doubled since 1951 and production costs, always high, increased about 83 per cent.[3] The advertising investment must be large indeed, but the mass audience reached can be counted in the many millions.

The four major forces affecting and controlling national public opinion, the magazine, the newspaper, the radio, and television, first created the public opinion they affect. It is axiomatic that no public opinion exists where no materials, no facts, no ideas have been provided. They serve a hunger they themselves have aroused. The newspaper is local in circulation. Its influence ends at the boundaries of its distribution. The day's newspaper is discarded upon being read, replaced by tomorrow's editions. Except where a definite crusade has been undertaken and is pressed in a journal's pages day after day over a period of weeks or months, the approach of the newspaper is fragmentary. Active human memory being what it is, the strongest effects of television and the radio quickly fade. The magazine suffers from these limitations less than the other major media. Ideally, the national magazine, prepared weeks ahead of issue date, need not compress, limit, or oversimplify in the presentation of a subject.

[3] Robert E. Kintner, President, American Broadcasting Co., in a speech before the annual meeting of the Association of National Advertisers, November 1, 1955.

There is time to deliberate and prepare a full and thoughtful article. The magazine has retained its original characteristics as a *magazine,* a storehouse of varied material. The offerings in every issue—articles, fiction, illustrations, sports, politics, science, economics, fashions, art, music, and all the other subjects covered in the modern magazine—allow reader selection and concentration.

The American public spends an appreciable part of its time reading magazines that have been skillfully enough edited and made physically attractive enough to catch and hold its undivided attention. The magazine is usually retained for further reading, for reading by other members of the purchaser's household long after the newspaper has been discarded and the radio program has faded. Reliance is placed on both the editorial and the advertising contents of the magazine in proportion to the repute which the magazine has established and maintains.

All of these contentions have been substantiated by surveys. A Gallup poll of June 14, 1948, asked how many people recognized a famous magazine cartoon character by sight or by association with the place they met her. Some 30,000,000 people correctly identified character and magazine. Another 25,000,000 recognized, by name or by association with a magazine which frequently carries his work, a famous magazine-cover artist. Other surveys discovered that readers spend an average of two hours and twenty-four minutes in actual reading of copies of a famous weekly. Answers to questionnaires placed in 80,000 copies of one periodical showed that current issues of the magazine were kept by the family in places where it would be picked up and reread, and that 66 per cent keep their copies for a month or longer after the issue is published.

Such studies aid in determining something of the social force of a magazine. Postulating a cause-and-effect relationship, the results obtained by a magazine's definite campaign are concrete evidence of its power. Not as easily determined is the sustained force of magazines in moulding and influencing their readers' attitudes toward people and ideas, in conditioning their reactions, in making them, in part, the people that they are.

Lacking this evidence, perhaps the best proof of the ordinary and continued impact of a strong magazine on its readers is the letters to the editor and similar indications of attentive reading that follow on the appearance of each issue. Here it must be remembered that only a small fraction of those who feel tempted to write the editor do write, and that only a small fraction of those moved to strong agreement or disagreement with some statement in an article even consider placing their comments on paper. Examples of this could be multiplied almost at will from the experiences of any of today's reputable and widely circulated periodicals. It is commonplace for a magazine to receive requests for thousands of reprints of a given article.

"—And Sudden Death" by J. C. Furnas, which appeared in *Reader's Digest* in 1935, was probably one of the most widely circulated magazine articles ever published. A highly dramatic story of fatalities from automobile accidents, and a gruesome warning, it was republished again and again in newspapers and in publications other than the *Digest*. *Reader's Digest* distributed thousands and thousands of reprints to civic societies and other organizations alarmed by the growing number of highway fatalities.

Sixty-eight words in the middle of a 1,750-word *Country Gentleman* article on dogwood trees offered seeds to those requesting them. In less than two weeks 15,000 readers wrote the magazine asking for the seeds; almost 25,000 requested them within a short time, virtually exhausting the supply available for distribution.

Occasionally a magazine article provokes marked and even unexpected results directly traceable to its appearance. Mark Sullivan, while still a student at the Harvard Law School, suggested to William Belmont Parker, an associate editor of *The Atlantic Monthly,* that he do an article on the political corruption in

Pennsylvania. Parker approved the idea, and Sullivan wrote a strong indictment of Pennsylvania politics. He attacked Senator Matthew S. Quay, Republican boss of the state; he described bribery and vote-buying, the parceling out of political favors, the oppression of those who refused to conform to demands of the machine. Pennsylvania, he said, wallowed in corruption. Sullivan went further. He drew unpleasant comparisons between the contributions of Pennsylvania and Massachusetts to literature and public life. Bliss Perry bought his article for forty dollars but suggested that, as Sullivan was young and unknown, it be published anonymously. The article appeared as "The Ills of Pennsylvania" by "A Pennsylvanian" in the *Atlantic,* October, 1901. It created a furor. Outraged Pennsylvanians wrote indignant letters to the magazine. The anonymous author was excoriated. The most forceful reply was written by Samuel Whitaker Pennypacker, a very learned judge in Philadelphia. His able defense of both Pennsylvania and Senator Quay brought him into such favorable notice that he was made Quay's nominee for the governorship of Pennsylvania and was elected.

In 1934, *The Saturday Evening Post* published "Schoolhouse in the Foothills." These articles by Alvin F. Harlow told the story of a young teacher's struggles in her school at "Shady Cove" in the Tennessee mountains. Though no solicitation was made, gifts of money, clothes, books, and other equipment poured into the *Post* from every part of the country for transmission to the teacher. To handle the enormous correspondence which resulted from the articles, the magazine had to employ an assistant for the article writer and a secretary for the schoolteacher. The "Shady Cove" school received everything it needed, and so much more that arrangements were made to direct the continuing flow of gifts to schools in other mountain villages.

It is not always by their expressions of approval that readers demonstrate their reactions to a magazine. When *The Atlantic Monthly* published Harriet Beecher Stowe's "The True Story of Lady Byron" in September, 1869, shocked and horrified subscribers hurriedly canceled their subscriptions, and the magazine was made to feel the sting of popular disapproval. James T. Fields, who succeeded James Russell Lowell as *Atlantic* editor in 1861, may have had this experience in mind when he admitted ruefully: "I could double the merit of the articles in the *Atlantic Monthly* and halve my subscription list at the same time." When Edward Bok dared discussion of sex and venereal disease in the *Ladies' Home Journal* the genteel feminine world of the 1890's declared shrilly for his annihilation, and the *Journal* lost hundreds of indignant subscribers. A few years ago one of the larger magazines published an article which was widely misconstrued. Though the magazine received many letters approving the article, it received thousands from others who believed it inaccurate and unjust. So violent was the attack on the magazine that its editor had to explain and apologize in paid space in large city newspapers the intent of his magazine in purchasing and printing the article.

The significance of these last three illustrations is not that magazine audiences disapproved certain editorial items, but that the influence of magazines is strong enough to cause quick and strong expression of opinion. One newspaper in its bitter attack on a magazine for what it considered a biased and intolerant article inadvertently paid unusual tribute to a competitive medium when it said editorially: "Any magazine that reaches 3,000,000 readers is one that is bound to have far-reaching influence on the thinking of the United States."

The potential influence of material appearing in the modern national magazines is not limited to the readers of the magazine and those influenced by the thinking of magazine readers. The vast audience of these magazines is many times multiplied when the same material is later published in book form and when, as often happens with a novel, the book becomes a motion picture. The modern national magazine exerts its power among the experts discussing economic or scientific questions, and affects the adolescent sighing and bubbling bubble gum in a darkened movie house while she lives vicariously the life of her Hollywood heroine.

The magazine pours its stream of facts and ideas into the great well of information and suggestion to which other sources, radio, television, newspapers, speeches, books, also contribute. Given the great number of American magazines, their large circulations, the number and diversity of subjects which they cover, and the important fact that magazines are periodical—that they come out each week or each month, each time with new diversions and new facts, or at least rearrangements of old ones— their contribution to this pool of knowledge and sentiment for the forming of public and private opinion is immeasurable.

According to the Magazine Advertising Bureau, American magazines are read by nearly seven out of every ten adults of fifteen years of age or older. Eight out of ten families in this country read magazines regularly. *Life* alone claims a total readership for each issue published of over 26,000,000. Others of the most widely distributed magazines claimed proportionately high readership figures, figures running well into the millions. Magazine penetration is deep. Magazine pressure on the American mind is continuous and unrelenting.

These readers are directly subject to magazine influence. The same magazine material, or the sustained editorial attitude of some one magazine or a group of them, may reach others through a lecture, a sermon, a serious discussion, or a newspaper account of something a magazine has published. Whether or not they are acknowledged as the source, magazines have certainly provided the material of countless sermons, books, and lectures.

It is probable that in the Presidential election of 1928 many citizens voted for or against Al Smith because of what he said and the way he said it in *The Atlantic Monthly*. Many whose attitude toward the New Deal, and later toward Russia, was determined by what they read in *The Saturday Evening Post* might not have acknowledged, perhaps had ceased to be aware of, the source of their disapproval; just as others, consciously or unconsciously, had their opinions of Prohibition changed when *Collier's* articles showed that it was not working successfully. The hostess who is complimented on the appearance of her dinner table is not apt to credit the illustration in an advertisement in one of the women's magazines as the inspiration she carefully followed. Thousands of young women today are wearing "Gibson Girl" costumes. Many of them were born almost a quarter of a century after Charles Dana Gibson influenced the dress, manners, and appearance of an earlier generation of American young women by his famous drawings in the old *Life* and then in *Collier's*.

Most individuals find it difficult to isolate the original bases of their opinions, tastes, prejudices, and beliefs. Often they can distinguish no single source. They stem from conversations, from odds and ends remembered of their formal education, from their experience with people and things, sometimes from simple imitativeness. More often than they realize, their conceptions, sometimes their misconceptions, had their ultimate origin in a magazine.

Society lives by ideas and the communication of ideas. It is itself the result of ideas and discussion of ideas, and must depend for its continued sustenance and growth on the circulation of facts, opinions about facts, beliefs developed from these opinions, and decisions reached on the basis of considered judgments. There is today no scarcity of the raw material on which social decisions must be reached and social action taken.

There is a great glut of communication. The individual and the social group are assailed, and sometimes almost overwhelmed, by facts and fiction, by fantasies labeled fantasy, and by other fantasies labeled fact. Truths, partial truths, distortions, mistaken convictions, and deliberate falsehoods confront us everywhere in print and in broadcast speech. The fulsome mouthings of omniscient radio and television commentators, the eternal knowingness of political columnists, freshly agog every day over new and horrendous revelations that they have just divulged and delirious over new alarms that they have originated or helped manufacture, are part of our daily diet. The smirkings of gossip columnists, as they ladle out juicy rumors of marital discord among the glamorous great of the entertainment and sporting world, and post advance notices of obstetrical events among the same group, are as familiar as the syndicated advice of tipsters on romantic love, etiquette, health, and "life." Daily a flood of expertly prepared publicity is released on behalf of corporations, government departments, labor organizations, or anyone willing to pay generously for the purchase of public approval and affection.

With all of this there is the unceasing clamor of pressure groups of every kind, all intent, for purely selfish reasons, on influencing private and public opinion favorably, and the vociferous outcries of injured minorities—all minorities, seemingly, being injured, and all of them shrilly articulate. So many groups are continually engaged in lobbying, jockeying for advantage, strenuously engaged in putting both their best feet forward in print and on the radio, that the reading public must sometimes be inclined to distrust most of what it reads and hears.

The reputable magazines, "class" or "mass," are comparatively free of the worst material of this type. A glance at the contents of a representative group will bear out the truth of this assertion. Though it would be absurd to attribute to all of them ethical impulses which many of them do not share, or claim for them ethical practices which some of them do not perform, magazine standards of editorial responsibility are fairly high. Magazine traditions, professional pride, and the interest in matters of public concern which the magazines have shown since 1741 account in part for this circumstance. There are practical as well as idealistic reasons.

The reputation, hence the acceptance and circulation, of a magazine can be seriously damaged by publication of irresponsible material. One seriously mistaken article, or an article which is merely sensational, can do almost irreparable damage to a magazine's standing. Again, the national magazines, as business enterprises, are directed at people with the money to buy the products which they advertise. These people are apt to be those with enough taste and education to discriminate between reputable and disreputable editorial content, as well as between superior and inferior merchandise. The demands of their audiences operate to keep magazine editorial content at a certain level of intelligence and public usefulness.

The magazines are comparatively free of special pleading, if only for the reason that special pleading will inevitably offend groups of readers whom the magazines wish to retain, readers whom they must retain if they are to keep their circulations at the figures guaranteed to advertisers. The weakness here is that, for the same reason, magazines of wide circulation must be circumspect in their treatment of some controversial issues. Some magazines are so circumspect as to omit treatment of some serious social and political issues altogether, a policy which vitiates their force as instruments of social persuasion. Allied to this avoidance are the superficiality, oversimplification, and glibness which weaken the substance of material of social import communicated in some widely circulated magazines.

The distinctness of individual magazines helps to prevent their publishing some of the kinds of material, running from the vicious to the useless, which are printed or aired today. The magazine which is all things to all men has not yet been developed and will not be. A magazine has to establish its identity in order to be recognized and received. The most successful large magazines—and "successful" is used here to mean financially profitable and widely known, read, and respected—have made themselves as nearly as possible synonymous with specific kinds of editorial attempt and performance. The words or phrases "picture," "news," "business," "women's interest," "literature," "geography," "farm," "fashion," "general weekly," will almost automatically bring to mind the names of specific magazines. These terms serve not only to describe particular magazines, but also to indicate lines of direction through what might be otherwise the trackless morass of public communication in the United States in the mid-twentieth century.

The character of a magazine limits its audience, and thus, to some extent, the spread of its influence, its educational force, its persuasion to belief, and possibly to individual or social action. A reader, on the basis of his experience with the periodical, knows that he will find certain writers, at least writers of certain recognizable types, in one magazine; and that the magazine will consistently display attitudes which he approves or disapproves. He may read or avoid a particular magazine for this reason. He can, if he wishes, read one magazine as an antidote to another. The diversity of magazines enables him to strike a balance between facts as stated and opinions as offered in one magazine, and treatment of the same subject in another magazine. Despite its partisanships—and most of the stronger magazines are partisan politically and socially—one periodical will often present authorities and arguments on several sides of controversial issues.

Magazines are in competition with each other and with the other media of public communication. This competition provides another safeguard against magazine publication of ill-considered material. Magazines do not willingly invite the adverse criticism which is sure to follow its publication. That same competition, of course, is one insurance the public has that the magazines will try to cover every subject of public concern and will offer various interpretations of such subjects. As an integral part of the free press of a free society, magazines share this privilege and responsibility.

Except in arithmetic texts and tables of scientific formulas, little unbiased writing has ever been published. Everything is written by someone, someone with beliefs, emotions, prejudices, and ignorance of his own. Usually a writer has the desire, and

sometimes the skill, to sway his readers to his views, but acceptance of what any writer says in any magazine, as in any newspaper or any book, must depend finally on the education and
critical intelligence of the reader. Honest and careful magazine
editing can screen out obvious inaccuracies and distortions, but
the last and final editing the reader must do for himself. For a
long time the better magazines have been providing him with
the information and helping to develop in him the critical equipment which will enable him to do this.

In recent years much has been written—little has actually
been discovered—about how, how much, and in what ways the
mass media of communications affect their vast audience. Research in what has come to be called the field of communications
is being done continually by sociologists, psychologists, and
political scientists drawn to the study; but up to this time few
reliable conclusions have been drawn. Most published studies
begin or end with the reiterated lament that too little is known
and that more study should be done. Wilbur Schramm, in
acknowledging and assaying work done by investigators to the
end of 1949, could say only that "The present trend of thinking
about the study of communications effects is to recognize the
full complexity of the problem, and also to recognize that it
cannot be solved by any simple and direct attack, but only by
analyzing the whole situation minutely and painstakingly, bringing to bear on it all potential evidence from the different social
sciences, and then whittling away at the unknown area by means
of carefully controlled experiments." [4]   Carl I. Hovland, after
reviewing studies available five years later, could only repeat
in 1954 that some writers thought mass communications were
all-powerful while others minimized their effects.[5]

[4] "The Effects of Mass Communications: A Review," *Journalism
Quarterly*, XXVI (Dec., 1949), No. 4.
[5] "Effects of the Mass Media of Communications," in *Handbook of Social
Psychology*, Vol. II, *Special Fields and Applications* (Cambridge, Mass.:
Addison-Wesley Publishing Co., 1954). The chapter contains a useful
bibliography, pp. 1100–3. Containing, as it does, some of the work of Paul
F. Lazarsfeld, Walter Lippmann, Bernard Berelson, Hadley Cantril, Douglas

One difficulty which plagues researchers into communications effects is that people must form the basis of their study. If the proper study of mankind is man, as Alexander Pope insisted, he is also the most difficult subject of study. Usually he cannot answer questions accurately about his beliefs and behavior, simply because he does not know. His observed actions, even when controlled under laboratory conditions, are apt to be disconcerting and of small help in reaching valid generalizations. The student of communications must give much of his time and energy to the establishing of study techniques, borrowed many times from marketing research or the pollsters; and, as often as not, he gets lost in the process.

Little of the communications research done thus far has been done specifically on magazines. Magazine publishers make studies continually on the size and composition by age, sex, income, and other social factors of their reading audiences, but these are usually for the purpose of proving to advertisers and potential advertisers that their magazines reach an interested group of customers and prospects. Such studies are not concerned with the effects of a magazine's editorial content upon its readers. Though they were talking of reading of all kinds of printed media, what Waples, Berelson, and Bradshaw pointed out in 1940 can be applied to magazines. They indicated that people read for information to apply to personal problems, to enhance their self-esteem by reading what praises the group to which they belong, to reinforce positions already taken on controversial issues, and for respite or escape. Their aesthetic experience is usually enriched in some way in the process.[6]

These authors contend, and sensibly, that the effects of reading depend on two forces: the content of the publication and the predispositions of the reader, both of them compounded of

Waples, and other investigators, *Mass Communications* edited by Wilbur Schramm (Urbana, Ill.: University of Illinois Press) is a good indication of the present status of the general study.

[6] D. Waples, B. Berelson, and F. R. Bradshaw, *What Reading Does to People* (Chicago: University of Chicago Press, 1940).

many elements, few of which are easily isolated. Joseph T. Klapper in *The Effects of Mass Media* makes the further point that people select material to satisfy already established tastes, and that all the mass media tend to re-expose their audiences to the kind of material which their patrons already like best.[7]

One of the generally accepted opinions resulting from communications study is that radio and television tend to reach all ages and income and cultural levels, while reading is correlated with education. It would seem apparent then that radio and television have become by and large the mass media, while magazines tend to reach a selective audience. Radio and television are "mass" while magazines are "class" from the point of view of editorial appeal as well as from the point of view of the advertiser.

In magazine circles there has been discussion in recent years of "impact." Subjectively, the existence of magazine impact is acknowledged. A given periodical does have distinctive characteristics and does awaken particular responses in its readers. Objectively, impact is difficult to prove, difficult even to describe. Some "impact" is measurable; most of it is not.

We speak of the impact of a man's personality, meaning the effect of his physical presence, the sound of his voice, the color and texture of his clothes and how he wears them, what we know of his past or his present or his possibilities—and meaning also our own prejudices, how what we knew of him previously or suspect of him measures against whatever standards and beliefs we have amassed from our own total experience.

Impact is pleasant to the one affected and favorable to the object which provides it, if our previous experience with it has been satisfactory from our own viewpoint. This is true whether the object creating the impact is a man, a circumstance, or a magazine. The impact of a given magazine is a possibility made of a thousand related and diverse impressions. The magazine, in the past, has pleased us by its cover pictures and what

[7] Klapper, *op. cit.*

it has said about cancer, aspects of St. Paul, Minnesota, the habits of polar bears, or the Formosan situation. It has seemed credible and reliable or has jibed with what we wish to believe. The type and layout, the general makeup, were aesthetically pleasing or, at least, did not annoy. The illustrations were romantic or their colors did not jar. It took very little mental effort to understand what was said about cancer, Formosa, polar bears, or the advisability of buying a particular brand of motor oil. We read the magazine after a good dinner. It pleased, and we assume that it will please again. We have been made receptive. Succeeding issues of the magazine will have impact—they will reach us equipped with the possibility of arousing a favorable response.

This can work the other way, and still be "impact." We distrusted and detested what the magazine said about cancer, Formosa, and the motor lubricant. The periodical has established an effect of annoyance and displeasure. We will not believe what it may say of the Aleutians, tuberculosis, or any motor oil of any kind.

The probability, though, is against the second reaction. The magazine has long been a familiar part of the American scene. It has been able to become so because it has impressed millions, even billions, of its total audience favorably for generations. The probability is that the individual reader is enough like those millions that he too will be receptive to the carefully concocted allure of the periodical. The force of every issue which was ever published, of the fact that the magazine has been around all his life, that his father used to read it, perhaps his grandfather, that it has slick pictures of expensive automobiles and that he can remember poring over them in 1923 or 1930 or 1940, all help.

Because of all these things or things like them, a magazine has impact, the capacity to create an effect. The impact of various magazines, because of the reader's experience with them, is different. The sight of one arouses warm, friendly, reassuring feelings; another, the idea of excitement, cleverness; another

stirs troubled feelings of unsolved problems and perplexing issues, though there may be a kind of admiration intermingled
with the reader's unease. He makes his choice on the basis of
his feelings and his mood of the moment.

There may also be an unconscious element of despair in the
reader's choice. "The fact is," Nathaniel Hawthorne wrote in
his notebook in 1855, when he was American Consul in Liver-
pool, "the world is accumulating too many materials for
knowledge." The confusion which Hawthorne found perplexing more than a hundred years ago has multiplied until modern
man finds it and himself many times worse confounded. Experts
and specialists in thousands of fields and the boggy corners of
these fields have sprung up in increasing numbers because few
can cope with, understand, or attempt even to gather the materials for understanding much of the larger social, political,
economic, scientific, and what-else world we live in. Most of
us cannot form usable judgments on myriads of subjects that
touch us because we have not bases on which to form them and
cannot hope to accumulate enough of the pertinent facts to provide them. It is part of modern man's dilemma. It is also part
of the reason why he seizes avidly on magazine digests and
condensations; why he spends so much time seeking escape in
entertainment; why he gladly reads a superficial journalistic
foray into some subject he knows influences his world and
which he would like, if possible, to know a little about.

Chapter 22

MAGAZINES IN A WORLD AT WAR

Mᴏᴅᴇʀɴ war, which calls for intensified effort of every kind in industry, in agriculture, and in every department of the embattled community as well as by its military and naval forces, makes extraordinary demands on all the media of public communication. *The Atlantic Monthly, The Saturday Evening Post,* and many of the other magazines in the nineteenth century could virtually ignore the Civil War, leaving it to *Harper's Weekly* to cover it vividly with text and pictures; but today's magazines can no longer remain aloof from a war while it is being fought. Modern war is total war, fought with ideas as well as with armament. The newspaper press, the magazines, and now the motion pictures, radio, and television have to assume and carry out a dual responsibility.

Acting in their primary role as observers, the forces of communication must report the war, making its actualities real to the noncombatant public which, as always, is dependent upon them for all of its information. Acting as combatants in the larger wars of which the armed conflict is only a part, though the most compelling part and finally the most decisive, these forces must—as democracies are organized and as wars are fought by democratic countries—fight the propaganda war with publicity, persuasion, explanation, argument. Propaganda directed to building and maintaining the heightened sense of national unity and national purpose, and to producing increased national effort, has become a necessary and powerful implement as wars have developed from chivalric jousts between small, professional armies to cosmic disputes which can result in the annihilation of a whole people. In both roles, as observers and reporters and as combatants, magazines have proved their effectiveness in two world wars; and World War II, in particular, brought about marked changes in magazines.

Because public opinion had come to its decisions well before governmental action was taken, magazines did not wait until the actual entry of the United States into World War I in April, 1917, before offering their resources to the government. Quickly they made themselves powerful engines for publicizing the war in its many phases, for stirring patriotic emotions, and for keeping their audiences informed of wartime activities urged by the authorities. They began, in fact, to apply effectively some of the devices of organized propaganda before that term was in general usage, and long before its still loosely defined principles were generally understood or its force as a weapon was fully recognized.

Public figures appointed to head various programs turned to the magazines to get their messages before the public. Ex-President William Howard Taft used the magazines to publicize the activities of the American Red Cross. Herbert Hoover's plans as Food Administrator were first announced in the magazines. Assistant Secretary of the Navy Franklin D. Roosevelt wrote "What the Navy Can Do for Your Boy" for one of the women's magazines in order to stimulate Navy recruiting. "The Y.M.C.A. in the War" became a monthly magazine feature edited by John R. Mott.

Inspirational stories, articles, and pictures with patriotic themes were rife in the magazines. Patriotism was stressed as a compelling motif in World War I. But there was more factual coverage, too, of the war. The actual progress of the conflict in Europe was reported by such correspondents as Irvin Cobb, Mary Roberts Rinehart, George Pattullo, and Will Irwin. The war news from Washington was reported along with the biographies and comment about the war leaders: Wilson and his cabinet members, Bernard Baruch, R. S. Lovett, Charles Norton, and others who were members of the Advisory Committee of National Defense or were in other ways active in the prosecution of the war on the political and industrial fronts.

The *Literary Digest* practically transformed itself into a war journal in 1917 and 1918. Its pages were crammed with feature articles about the war, with war comment extracted from the newspapers, with war cartoons, and with maps outlining from week to week the progress of the Allies against Germany. A greatly increased number of readers looked to the *Digest,* the only news weekly during World War I, for accurate and authentic war information. *The National Geographic Magazine* issued maps of the western front so that its readers could follow the Allied armies over known terrain and, in issue after issue, concentrated on the geography of the countries at war.

The women's service magazines aided Herbert Hoover's food-saving campaigns by publishing practical explanations and illustrations of how to save flour, how to make bread of whole wheat, bran, Graham flour, and other substitutes for the refined white flour housewives were accustomed to use in their baking. They printed photographs of women in their new wartime occupations as farmerettes, factory workers, street-car operators, and the like, in order to stimulate more women to replace men in occupations which, until the war, had been considered wholly masculine. They told how to knit socks, sweaters, mufflers, mittens, and even "the new aviator's helmets" for men in the armed forces.

Their contents filled with war news, the general popular weeklies, such as *Collier's* and *The Saturday Evening Post,* carried covers displaying men in uniform, Red Cross girls, aviatrixes, and World War I planes in battle. A few advertisers were reproducing recruiting posters in their paid magazine space.

Earnest and effective as they were, the reporting and the propaganda effort of the magazines in World War I seem amateurish by comparison with the expert handling of their job by the magazines, as well as by the other press media, during World War II. This was a larger and a different war. The ideological conflicts behind the national differences were more apparent. The destruction was greater, and it was realized that this destruction could be made complete enough to extinguish whole peoples, whole countries, and whole ideas, whole ways of living. There was little inspirational idealism in the air. No one seemed able to state national war aims in understandable terms. It was accepted that not to win was not to survive nationally or politically.

No war in history has been as thoroughly recorded, documented, and covered in news, story, and pictures as World War II. The importance of such complete coverage was understood from the beginning. So was the increased wartime importance of all communications media. The attention of the magazines, the newspapers, and the radio was immediately focused on the war as the one subject of consuming interest; and all of them were immediately utilized for morale purposes and for the dissemination of war doctrine to produce concerted national action. Again, both as reporters and as instruments of psychological and propaganda warfare the magazines performed efficiently.

The position of the magazines in relation to the other media was somewhat changed by the time of the second major conflict of the twentieth century from what it had been a quarter century earlier. The radio was available for the rapid transmission of the highlights of the news. The magazines, especially the news weeklies and the pictorial magazines founded after the first of the two wars, could supplement and augment the radio and the newspaper by fuller coverage of the war news itself, but the chief magazine coverage, in the new type magazines as well as in the older magazines, was in articles that discussed as well as reported in greater detail than radio and newspapers could report. Scores of magazine correspondents with the armies and naval forces of the United States and with the fighting units of the other United Nations reported battle action from every theater of operation. With no sharp deadlines to meet, these writers could cover their subjects in greater detail than could representatives of radio and the daily press who had to meet the demands for spot news. American magazine readers followed the course of the warfare in Africa, Europe, and the Pacific in the word and photographic reporting of the magazines which at the same time could analyze and discuss the news they offered. *Life*'s photographs, *Time*'s comments, *The New Yorker*'s observations, and thoughtful articles in the general weeklies and monthlies merged to form the magazine picture of the war and to describe its progress.

The propaganda force of the magazines, better understood in World War II than in World War I, was utilized fully by the national government, and skillfully channeled by the magazines themselves. There was less exalted patriotism this second time. As there were fewer military bands, fewer parades, fewer emotional appeals generally, there was less flag-waving and sentimentality in the magazines. Instead there was the effort to present the facts clearly and to give thoughtful interpretations of what the facts, as they were seen at the time, seemed to mean. The magazines addressed their material to an audience whose war consciousness was not aroused by slogans but, increasingly, and largely through the efforts of the magazines, by an understanding of the conflicting political and social concepts which were largely responsible for the war. In this way, the reportorial and propaganda forces of the magazines were joined.

Articles in American magazines discussed the issues involved in the war, the causes for which the United Nations fought. Other articles described the German and Japanese enemy, analyzing the nature of our adversaries, their political beliefs, social institutions, and the character generally of the Germans and Japanese as individuals and national groups. The governments and the peoples of the various members of the United Nations were explained to American readers in hundreds of magazine articles. Other articles stressed the importance of American industrial production; literally thousands of news stories and articles were devoted to publicizing every aspect of life in the armed forces in training and in action. Within a year after Pearl Harbor national magazines had printed fifteen hundred stories and articles containing war information.

The national magazine became during the war years a forum, attended by the population of the country, for the exposition of the government's wartime policies and programs. It gave the facts of each problem—industrial, agricultural, social, and sometimes military—that the nation had to meet and solve, explained the significance of the facts, urged on every reader again and again the importance of each element in the complete war picture. Articles explained the need for price control as a war measure, and its functioning. Others gave repeated warnings of the dangers of inflation and showed what inflation would mean; or reported our mammoth plane production or showed to what use Russia put the American war equipment it received. Practical advice on how to live under rationing, how to conserve on tires, or how to get the most out of home-heating when fuel was scarce was run alongside explanations of Lend-Lease and descriptions of operations in Attu, at Kwajalein, in England, over Schweinfurt, on Omaha Beach in Normandy, at Anzio, and at Cassino.

One illustration may serve to indicate the extent to which the American people came to look upon magazines as national newspapers during the war, how far magazines influenced public opinion on war subjects, and how far this situation was recognized. *The Saturday Evening Post* published in two parts, May 13, and May 20, 1945, an article by Forrest Davis entitled "What Really Happened at Teheran." Until its publication almost nothing had been disclosed of what had transpired when Roosevelt, Stalin, and Churchill met for the last time as the leaders of the United States, Russia, and England, to plot the final strategy of the war. It was from the *Post* that the public learned something of the conversations that had been held and the decisions that would affect not only the conduct of the last part of the war but also the world's postwar future. Columnists and commentators were quick to remark the appearance of this information in the *Post* and to comment on the significance of its appearance there. Two stated that the articles were supposed to have been initialed in advance by the President. Another noted that the *Post* "told far more of the President's intentions in the post-war world than had been disclosed to the senators in the course of the discussions." The remarks of a fourth pointed squarely to the stature which the magazine had attained in the eyes of government as an effective medium of nationwide communication. He saw publication in the *Post* of "What Really Happened at Teheran" as a deliberate device used more than once by the President and the State Department; that of letting a magazine of national circulation tell the inside story to the people.

Outright publicity was used by the magazines, as over the radio and in motion picture theaters, to enlist support of the various wartime campaigns conducted among civilians: campaigns to sell War Bonds, to increase industrial and agricultural production, campaigns for blood donation, the United Service Organizations, the Red Cross, salvage, food conservation, and all of the other government-sponsored promotions designed to intensify war realization throughout the population and to mobilize all of the country's resources.

Magazine editorial space was devoted to these subjects, but much of this work, significantly, was done through magazine advertising. It was directed by the War Advertising Council, an association formed by advertisers, advertising agencies, and advertising media. By December 7, 1944, three years after Pearl Harbor, nearly a billion dollars' worth of advertising, much of it run in magazines, was thus used for the promotion of such programs.

Advertisers filled their space with the kind of vigorously written copy and forceful art work that would aid in recruiting WACs and nurses, emphasize the necessity for security of information, fight waste, influence people to buy more and more War Bonds and to keep them, combat absenteeism in war plants, get more women to take jobs left by men drafted into the armed services, and support the National War Fund. Magazines and magazine advertisers devoted over $15,000,000 in space to the promotion of War Bond sales alone. Full pages of space in 828 magazines with a combined circulation of 109,000,000 were used from August, 1943, to November, 1945, to warn Americans of the dangers of inflation and to promote conservation.

Wartime activities of these kinds wrought what seem to be permanent changes in American magazines. Wartime factual reporting and discussions of economic, political, and social issues, of scientific advances and possibilities, and of ideas previously handled only in the more pretentious periodicals accustomed popular magazine audiences to more serious treatment of serious subjects. The proportion of factual over fictional material in magazines mounted during the war. It has not lessened in the first postwar years. Standards and precedents set for themselves by the magazines during the war years have been maintained. Generally they seem to contain less froth, more information.

Habits developed by magazine advertisers during the war years have also carried over into the years immediately subsequent. A guess is that these will not disappear but continue and develop. Magazine advertising was used during the war years to convey information, to publicize ideas, and to persuade to social action. Since the war a considerable number of advertisers have continued to use paid magazine space for these same purposes, running copy and displays meant not primarily to sell their wares but to sell ideas that will affect thought and social action. Some of this advertising is basically informational in character; some of it is argument. Other advertisements are designed to influence public opinion favorably toward an industry, to defend a business or business generally, to explain an economic or social situation, and to state the viewpoints of an industrial institution or an organization.

Stories, articles, and reminiscences of World War II have been a magazine staple ever since that war ended. It is a poor general or upper-echelon wartime politician whose memoirs have not been serialized in one or another of the popular magazines. Land, naval, and air campaigns have been refought by observers or participants and intelligence secrets hidden under wartime security divulged in exciting accounts. One issue of *Reader's Digest,* that of November, 1953, ran two such British intelligence thrillers, "The Corpse That Hoaxed the Axis," a condensation of *The Man Who Never Was* by Ewen Edward Samuel Montagu, and a much longer tale, "The Man Who Wouldn't Talk" by Quentin Reynolds. It was the fault neither of the writer nor the magazine that the second story, purported war experience of a Canadian spy captured and brutalized by the Nazis, proved to be the greater hoax of the two.

Whether or not World War III ever materializes, war and rumors of war have been an actuality in the magazine press almost since the close of World War II. The unpleasant possibilities of atomic warfare have been explored in article after article, notably in a *Collier's* issue wholly devoted to World War III; and the so-called cold war between Russia and the United States, between world communism and western democracy, has been waged hotly and dramatically. Early in 1947 *The Saturday Evening Post* published two articles telling how Russia spied on her wartime allies to obtain atomic secrets. This was before Russia's attitude and purposes were generally recognized. Since that time the *Post, Life, Reader's Digest,* and virtually all of the popular magazines have carried both sober appraisals of Russian life and political action and pieces by escaped political prisoners, men released from slave labor in Siberian mines, American correspondents and businessmen imprisoned and mistreated, and other stories illustrating the temper and characteristics of the acknowledged antagonist.

Geared to war coverage, the large-circulation weekly magazines went into action quickly when the Korean War broke in June, 1950. A *Life* photographer was shooting pictures of the fighting two days after the war began. A *Saturday Evening Post* correspondent accompanied United Nations troops to the first fighting, and the *Post* was soon printing his stories of the exploits of Brigadier General, then Lieutenant-Colonel, Mike Michaelis and the Twenty-seventh Division. Harold H. Martin was joined by Nora Waln, Demaree Bess, William L. Worden, and later *Herald Tribune* correspondent Marguerite Higgins in covering the Korean War for the *Post*. Robert Sherrod, made managing editor of the magazine in 1955, served as chief correspondent for the *Post* in the Korean War area. *Life's* first man on the scene was joined by eleven other photographers and ten correspondents in reporting the Korean War. One *Time-Life* correspondent was killed in ambush early in the conflict, and three others were injured in Korea. During the 157 weeks of its duration *Life* published 454 pages of pictures of the Korean War. In its issue of July 6, 1953, it ran complete *The Bridges at Toko-Ri,* a novel by James Michener based on American naval fighting in Korea.

Time, in its issue of June 26, 1950, the day before the Korean outbreak, had carried nothing on Korea, but it had warned in its June 5th issue: ". . . South Korea can be made a sound political and economic unit. . . . Withdrawal now would leave not only a shattered and broken nation, but a broken moral obligation as well. Failure in Korea would cost America priceless prestige and augur American failure elsewhere in Asia." By July 11th, *Time* carried a cover picture of General Douglas MacArthur ("His Job to Police the Boundaries of Chaos") and a ten-page lead story on "War In Asia." "War In Asia" was retained as a regular department of *Time* until the issue of

IN THIS ISSUE: TWO SIDES OF A GREAT DISPUTE

LIFE

BY HARRY S. TRUMAN
'MacARTHUR LEFT ME NO CHOICE'

BY DOUGLAS MacARTHUR
'IT WAS A VENGEFUL REPRISAL'

TRUMAN AND MacARTHUR AT WAKE ISLAND

REG. U. S. PAT. OFF.

20 CENTS

FEBRUARY 13, 1956

Then President Harry S. Truman and General Douglas MacArthur shake hands at Wake Island before their controversy which resulted in the recall of the Far Eastern commander. *Life* published both their stories.

321

July 20, 1953. *Newsweek,* which featured Gloria Swanson on its June 26, 1950, cover ("The Great Comeback"), had nothing about Korea under its Foreign Affairs department. Soon, "Korean War," often in the lead position, was an established feature for the duration. *U. S. News and World Report,* given always to blacker and bolder type in startling heads, covered the war with more "exclusives," "inside information," and "reasons behind." In their Korean War coverage magazines not only gave chill reality to a particularly bloody war, conveying thoroughly the bitterness of the conflict, but strove to make clear the war's significance in the larger struggle for world power. The political implications of the whole were recognized in magazine articles as well as the narrative and drama of battle, Truman's abrupt removal of General Douglas MacArthur from command, the armistice negotiations which the communists dragged out for two years, prisoner repatriation, and the general aftermath of the war.

Early in 1956 two magazine articles in the general field of war and international affairs, published in the same week, brought renewed and unexpected proof of the vitality and effectiveness of the magazine in public communication. *Life* for January 16 carried an article by James Shepley, chief of the magazine's Washington Bureau, entitled "How Dulles Averted War." The article quoted the Secretary of State as claiming he had three times brought the United States to the brink of war—in Korea in June, 1953, in Indochina in April, 1954, in the Formosa Strait in January, 1955. As the article read, the Secretary defended such action as part of the strategy of foreign policy called for by a tense world situation. He spoke of it as the "necessary art" of risking war to maintain peace.

The article caused an immediate furor. The Secretary of State was berated. The President of the United States found it necessary to comment and explain in press conference. The Secretary of Defense became embroiled. Senators and Congressmen of the opposition party used the article to attack the administration's conduct of foreign affairs. *Life's* publisher issued a press statement defending and explaining the article.

On January 21 *The Saturday Evening Post* published the first installment of a six-part article by General Matthew B. Ridgway (as told to Harold H. Martin). In this initial piece entitled "Conflict in the Pentagon," General Ridgway charged that while he was army Chief of Staff military decisions were made on a basis of political expediency. Ridgway, who was outspoken in his criticisms, said in part: "I quickly learned that . . . the decisions of the Defense Department were based on . . . the advantages to be gained in the field of domestic politics by drastic reduction in military expenditures. I learned too, with a certain sense of shock, that sometimes I was not expected to present my reasoned military judgment to Secretary of Defense Charles E. Wilson. . . . I do not recall that I ever felt a greater sense of shock than when I read in President Eisenhower's State of the Union message in 1954 that: 'The defense program recommended for 1955 is based on a new program *unanimously recommended* by the Joint Chiefs of Staff.'" Most emphatically, Ridgway said, he had not concurred in the recommendation.

This forthright statement caused a second imbroglio. It gave the Democratic Party further ammunition to direct against the administration in a presidential election year. Opposition Senators demanded explanation. The Secretary of Defense and other Pentagon officials issued hurried statements and explanations. Public opinion was aroused for and against the disputants and the issues involved.

In both cases, as usually it does, the furor died away without resolving points of who said, did, or meant what; who was right, wrong, or indiscreet. The point demonstrated was the impact of the articles appearing in two powerful American magazines.

Chapter 23

MAGAZINE PUBLISHING TODAY

' Though it will not compare to basic industry, the national magazine today is big business. No current figure on the total gross or net income of the periodical publishing industry as a whole is available, but as long ago as 1945, the estimated total gross receipts from magazine publishing before deduction of any items of cost was $739,000,000.[1] The president of the National Association of Magazine Publishers estimated in 1947 that total magazine income would approximate or exceed one billion dollars yearly within a few years' time. It has probably done so. About a quarter of a million people, according to the NAMP president, are directly supported by the magazine industry, while two million depend on it in whole or in part for their livelihood.

There are 23 national magazines with circulations of 2 million or more, 53 with circulations exceeding 1 million.[2] More than 3¾ billion copies of magazines are sold every year. In 1955 the total per issue circulation of all the 267 members of the Audit Bureau of Circulations was 166 million. This contrasts with a figure of less than 18 million copies per issue in 1914, when the A. B. C. was founded with 54 general and farm magazines reporting. During and since World War II magazine circulation has increased 62 per cent, and magazine advertising has mounted year by year. Over $653,400,000 was spent for national advertising in magazines in 1955.[3] The number

[1] "The Magazine Publishing Industry in the United States, 1945," Bureau of the Census, Department of Commerce, October 6, 1947.

[2] Farm magazines included; comics excluded. A. B. C. figures.

[3] Leading National Advertisers, Inc.

of large advertisers has also risen; in 1954, 2,163 advertisers spent more than $25,000 each for advertising in magazines.[4]

Despite these increases in circulation and in advertising revenue, magazine profits have fallen as a result of mounting production and distribution costs. Second-class postal rates, accorded newspapers and magazines by the Postal Act of 1879, have been increased by Congressional legislation; rates now are almost one-third higher than in 1951; and there is pressure, fought by the magazine publishers, for further increases. Subscription and single-copy prices of magazines and the rates charged for magazine advertising space have not increased in proportion to magazine publishing expenses or in ratio with the price advance of most other commodities. Magazine net profit, profit after taxes as a percentage of sales, stood at about 6.7 per cent in the middle 1930's. This figure climbed during the war years, profitable years for magazines, to 8.3 per cent in 1946. It has gradually declined since that time. Although a few publishers are earning more, magazine net profits averaged 2.8 per cent in 1954.[5]

The number of magazines stays constant at over 7,000, though the mass periodicals are concentrated in the hands of a relatively few large publishers. The Curtis Publishing Company covers the general weekly, the women's, the recreational, and the children's field with *The Saturday Evening Post, Ladies' Home Journal, Holiday,* and *Jack and Jill.* Its subsidiary, the Curtis Circulation Company, distributes an additional fourteen magazines, including *Harper's,* the *Atlantic, Look, Esquire, Coronet, American Home,* and *Field and Stream.* Time, Inc. has *Time, Life, Fortune, Architectural Forum, House and Home,* and *Sports Illustrated.* The Crowell-Collier Publishing Company has a general biweekly and a general monthly as well as a woman's monthly: *Collier's, The American Magazine,* and *Woman's Home Companion.* Hearst

---

[4] *Sales Management,* October 15, 1955.
[5] Magazine Publishers Association.

Magazines, Inc., has *Good Housekeeping, Harper's Bazaar, House Beautiful, Cosmopolitan,* and *Town and Country;* while the McCall Corporation publishes *Redbook* in addition to *Mc-Call's Magazine;* and Meredith Publishing Company puts out *Successful Farming* and *Better Homes and Gardens. Reader's Digest,* biggest of them all, *Farm Journal* and *Town Journal,* the farm periodicals of Capper Publications, the publications of Esquire, Inc., and the large Macfadden group (detective story magazines, magazines retailing true life stories, and their ilk) must be added to the list of magazines and publishers reaching very large circulations.

It is a far cry from the days when a magazine editor and publisher could almost count, as could Noah Webster, on the early financial failure of his venture. It is a far cry, too, from the days when magazine contributors were unpaid, or the days, a little later, when Edgar Allan Poe was paid ten dollars for "The Raven" by the *American Review.* Longfellow sometimes received twenty dollars a poem from *Graham's,* and Lowell got ten dollars at first, more somewhat later. When Lowell himself became an editor, he paid such contributors as Emerson, Longfellow, and Bryant about five dollars a page for their work in the *Atlantic.* "Couldn't you," he wrote in 1864, as editor of *The North American Review,* to John Lothrop Motley, who was then minister to Austria, "write on the natural history of the diplomatic cuttlefish of Schleswig-Holstein without forfeiting your ministerial equanimity?" Again he offered five dollars a page.

Today the mass magazines compete with each other in purchasing manuscripts, usually the memoirs of public men, at announced prices running into the hundreds of thousands of dollars. A magazine paid $60,000 for "Admiral Halsey Tells His Story," $175,000 for the war diary of General Eisenhower, and $102,000 to another general and his collaborator for their series of six articles on World War II. Though no price was announced, *Life, The New York Times,* and a book publisher are reported to have paid $1,000,000 for Winston Churchill's war memoirs. *The Saturday Evening Post* paid $100,000 for Lindbergh's "33 Hours to Paris," and $75,000 for Bing Crosby's "Call Me Lucky." Press reports stated that ex-President Truman was paid about $600,000 for his memoirs which were published in *Life*.

The larger magazines pay from a few hundred dollars up to $1,500 for a single story or article, and up to $2,500 for a cover painting. *The New Yorker*, though it has a comparatively small circulation, pays regular contributors fifteen to thirty cents a word, half as much again for pieces of less than 2,000 words, and an additional bonus of 25 per cent to writers placing six or more pieces with the magazine in the same year. The *Post* pays $750 for the first article accepted from a writer; $850 for the first short story. *Reader's Digest* pays writers of articles condensed from other magazines a minimum of $200 a *Digest* page. After a free-lance writer has sold the *Digest* five articles, he gets an additional $500 bonus on every article he sells the magazine. *Ladies' Home Journal* pays a minimum of $850 for short stories.

Rufus Wilmot Griswold's salary as editor of *Graham's* was $1,000 a year. James Russell Lowell received what was at the time the very large salary of $2,500 as editor of *The Atlantic Monthly*. The salary proved more than the magazine could support. A chief reason for supplanting Lowell with James T. Fields, a member of the firm which then published the *Atlantic*, was to save this salary. The successful editors of the modern national magazines receive salaries reputed to be somewhat larger. According to a fact sheet released by *The Saturday Evening Post* in 1954, "Editorial pay ranges downward from the editor's salary of more than $100,000 a year." Top editors of *The Reader's Digest* get both large salaries and large bonuses. Roving editors get $10,000 to $20,000 a year, travel expenses, and a minimum of $1,200 for each piece accepted.

The product put forth by an industry of this size cannot be manufactured by hit-or-miss methods. Every device is used to insure a product which will be approved by the mass public which it serves and which supports it. Modern means of assistance to editorial judgment are in use throughout magazine activity. National sample surveys are used to measure public reaction to magazine contents. The purpose of these interviews, conducted through personal interrogation and by mail, is to discover what stories, articles, and features are read, how closely they are read, and by what kinds of people. Editors use the findings to help them decide what new departments to inaugurate or what old ones to drop, and what types of fiction and articles will be most widely and appreciatively read. Through reader research, now in use by almost all the larger magazines, the editors can discover what magazine covers their audience likes best, what stories men prefer, which women like best, and a hundred other things; and the knowledge thus gained serves as a guide in the selection of new material for publication. Each month *Reader's Digest* queries 4,000 of its subscribers on their likes and dislikes in a current issue. Personal interviews are conducted among a sample of the magazine's readers every month on *The Saturday Evening Post*. Several of the women's magazines have used this poll and sampling technique to discover what women think about subjects often avoided in magazine discussion—divorce, moral standards, birth control—and to find out what material, outside the purely domestic sphere, women wish to read. Months of such research into the probable audience and market go into the planning before any new large magazine is inaugurated. Painstaking work of this type was done before *Holiday* began publication in 1946. Research is done monthly on every *Holiday* issue. "Reader research," the executive editor of a weekly magazine remarked somewhat ruefully, "has become a great leveler among editors."

With such a research device at their disposal, it might be thought that editors now can put out their magazines by slide rule and tabulating machine, avoiding by simple arithmetic the possibility of serious errors in editorial judgment. It is conceivable that they could. It is fortunate that they do not, for the tendency would undoubtedly be to level downward to the lowest common denominator and to publish only writing of some kind approved in the past, as there is yet no reliable way of estimating the potential readership of new material.

Editors accept or reject the findings of reader research in the light of their experience and editorial judgment. They will deliberately publish a story or an article whose value they recognize, despite foreknowledge that it will have a low readership. In doing so they are motivated not so much by an altruistic desire to raise the public taste as by an intent to maintain and improve the editorial quality of their individual magazines. Competition among magazines for vital material in itself obviates the possibility of dependence upon mechanical editing. The modern magazine editor practices what is still very much an art and not an exact science. Reader research is an aid to editorial judgment, not a substitute; but it is an aid which the editor is finding helpful as a quick and useful check on features and qualities of his periodical.

When he visited the United States in 1908, Lord Northcliffe, originator of the tabloid, astute publisher of the *London Daily Mail* and *The Times* [London], was outspoken in his opinion that even then American magazines were "infinitely better than those of England." The next great advance in American magazine production, he prophesied, would take place when some method of printing photographs accurately in color could be devised. His prophecy was correct. The increased use of full color, the increased emphasis on graphics generally, is one of the most noticeable changes in the modern magazine. Not only the picture magazines like *Life* and *Look* but the general weeklies and monthlies, the women's magazines, the shelter magazines, and the fashion magazines are using more and more photographs both in black and white and in color. In all of these magazines, color photography has become not an added decoration but an essential editorial element. The increased use of photographs and more profuse use of illustration have been accompanied by a general streamlining and refurbishing of the mass magazines. Type faces have been modernized, new logotypes devised to replace older ones. Margins have disappeared with the increased use of bleed for color and picture pages.[6] Physically the national magazine has been made as attractive as expert photography and reproduction, expert makeup and printing, expert styling, and capable art work, done for both editorial and advertising use by the country's finest illustrators, can make it.

The change is more than superficial. All the sensuous appeal of color and art work is being used by the magazine, used skillfully and with psychological knowledge carefully applied. The whole appeal of the mass magazines has become one of speed. Articles have been shortened to balance the quickness of impression provided by pictures. Magazine fiction, too, has been shortened. The ratio of articles to fiction has been increased. Clarity, brevity, and sharpness have been substituted for prolixity, in some cases for thoroughness. A greater variety of short features, cartoons, quips, puzzles, has been introduced, and the accent on timeliness has been stressed.

The American public has proved that it will read, at least tolerate and support, a great variety of magazines. It has shown its favor to long-established periodicals, to certain relatively new magazines, and to some so changed in content and format as to

---

[6] Too often page numbers seem also to have disappeared. Full bleed pages are not numbered, nor are full pages in four-color. On other type pages, numbers are shifted from the upper outside corner to the bottom middle of the page, or to some other position where they are almost impossible to detect. There are mechanical reasons for this annoyance, but it often seems as though a magazine has been made up by someone careless of arithmetic or by a layout editor who just does not like people.

seem new. It accepts the pretentious, the cultural, and at the other extreme, the crudest of periodical publications. There is the simple fact that the United States population is far larger than it was, and is growing rapidly. It is affluent and can afford to indulge its fancies. The spread and dilution of education has at least made more people susceptible to print and pictures in pleasing format. Acceptance of certain of these magazines by at least a substantial segment of the population that reads at all reflects something of our changing social interests. The response to others reflects the perennial appeal of other subject matter to basic humankind.

One of the most outstanding of the post-World War II magazines is *Holiday,* founded in 1946. Calling itself a "class-mass" magazine, it steadily maintains a substantial circulation of about 850,000. *Holiday,* the elaborate, lushly dressed, fifty-cent, Curtis-owned magazine, is difficult to classify. It is not a fashion magazine, a travel magazine, a shelter book, or a literary monthly, though it shows some of the aspects of all of these. It has some of the glamour of *Vogue,* some of the substance of *National Geographic,* some, though it is worn unsurely, of *The New Yorker*'s urbanity. It falls into none of the established magazine categories. In part, this may be because *Holday* is devoted not to a particular subject or directed to a specific audience, but is based on a practically indefinable concept, the concept of leisure and recreation. It is published on the factual premise that the mid–twentieth century American has an increased and increasing amount of leisure time, and edited with the conviction that there are certain ways in which he can be taught to use it gracefully.

Holiday describes itself as "the magazine of creative leisure." Its purpose is to instruct people how best to use the new leisure with which they are blessed or confounded. In the words of Ted Patrick, its editor, "Creative use of leisure time includes travel, but also other activities . . . all sports, the theater, movies, television and radio, music, painting or writing indulged

A mounted trooper of the Blues stands guard over an issue of *Holiday* devoted entirely to London—London scenes, shops, royalty, restaurants, hotels, clubs, and crime. *Holiday*'s dominant theme is "The New Leisure."

From its blue-tile skyscraper on West Forty-second Street, New York, the McGraw-Hill Publishing Company issues a wide variety of industry and business magazines, whose total circulation exceeds one million.

in as a pastime, the reading of good books, the preparation and pursuit of food, party-giving and attending, the fixing of one's home to make it more rewarding and relaxing to live in, and the making or acquisition of the clothing best designed for any of these activities."

This description about fits the *Holiday* menu. Served for the aspiring epicure and *bon vivant,* the correctly attired lawn or field sportsman, the self-conscious cosmopolitan, and the suburbanite who would be socially sophisticated, the menu offers caviar, the approved wines, and some more substantial fare, usually in a night-club setting.

Place articles are the *Holiday pièces de résistance.* They are full, informative, sometimes charming, sometimes pretentious, often seductive—objective and subjective descriptions of Atlanta or Rome, café and resort society in Philadelphia or on Capri, the romance of Africa, Asia, Indianapolis, or Kansas City. Most of these pieces are pleasantly and skillfully written. Some are superficial and brilliant; others, like the E. B. White piece on New York (April, 1949), J. B. Marquand on Boston (November, 1953), and Frank O'Connor on Ireland (December, 1949), have greater depth, strength, and virtue.

Holiday standards of writing are high, and the magazine uses some of the best and best-known writers of the day: Faulkner, Dunsany, Hemingway, Steinbeck, O'Faolain, Joyce Cary. More characteristic of the magazine's tone and attempt are Bemelmans, Perelman, Fadiman, Lucius Beebe, Stong, Michener, Guthrie, Schulberg, Wechsberg, and Jerome Weidman. *Holiday* has published notable issues on Paris (April, 1953), on Italy (April, 1955), on London (April, 1956). From the standpoint of layout, illustration, and reproduction, every issue of *Holiday* is attractive. Photographically, *Holiday* compares favorably with the best of its competitors.

The McGraw-Hill Publishing Company, founded in 1917 by the merger of two older organizations, is a unique and greatly influential periodical publishing enterprise, the country's largest publisher of technical, scientific, and business magazines. Through a subsidiary company, the McGraw-Hill Book Company, which has over 3,500 active titles and publishes perhaps 300 new books a year, it is also one of the country's largest book publishers. Currently McGraw-Hill issues twenty-nine industrial, trade, and technical magazines, most of them the best-known publications in the fields they cover. *American Machinist, Chemical Engineering, Electrical Merchandising, Electrical World, Engineering News-Record, Engineering and Mining Journal, Textile World,* and a few of the others are old and highly respected magazines with reputations transcending their immediate fields of interest. McGraw-Hill can well claim to have kept pace with, and perhaps even assisted, the advance of technology, engineering, and business in the United States.

In 1929 McGraw-Hill established *Business Week*. The company's other magazines deal with specific management, engineering, production, maintenance, and selling functions in business. They are intended as vehicles to communicate applicable information to men at work within given industries or professions. *Business Week,* described by its publishers as "essentially a news service," has by the nature of its coverage a wider appeal. Because business in some form is the primary American occupation and preoccupation, the magazine's emphasis on business and its handling of most subjects from an economic viewpoint makes it function in some degrees as an important news weekly.[7] Timely, accurate, authoritative, *Business Week* covers production, finance, labor, and marketing. It gives, in what has become the standard telegraphic inset form, used early by *U. S. News,* "Washington News," "International Outlook," and "Business Outlook." The American businessman seems to thirst always for forecasts, tips, and the interpretations of portents; he wants the news of the day after tomorrow, of the month after next if he can get it and anything that gives

---

[7] Standard Rate and Data service lists *Business Week* as a consumer magazine, as well as listing it among business publications.

him the impression he is "in the know." *Business Week's* "Personal Outlook" is chatty in content despite the flash form which it also wears: "Your morning grapefruit will have 10% more juice this year. . . . Note for football fans: At your bookstore now is one of the more vivid histories of the game's development. . . . Try daffodils for an effective display on sloping lawns. . . . Tip for your wife. Here are a few hints to help avoid unscrupulous salesmen. . . ."

Featured articles in *Business Week,* whether on automation, television, or the crowded Ohio River (illustrated in full color), are full and informative. In terms of advertising revenue, which was estimated at over $14.5 million for 1954, *Business Week* has become by far the largest business magazine in the United States.[8]

Business Week does well at one pole of American interest, the office, the plant, the job. Another magazine, its success renowned in the trade, does as well at the other pole of American interest, the home.

There are a number of handsome "shelter" magazines. Some are older and more pretentious, affect a more patrician pose and appeal. None has achieved greater popular success in recent years than *Better Homes & Gardens,* founded 1922 and published in Des Moines by the Meredith Publishing Company. Heavy, thick with advertising, diversified in skillfully chosen editorial content, *Better Homes & Gardens* has a monthly circulation of well over 4,000,000.

Since World War II the United States has been building houses at an unprecedented rate. Through G. I. loans purchase was made easy for ex-servicemen. Small down payments and small monthly charges have brought new houses within the range of most people. Home ownership has become the rule even among people of an age and income scale which previously would have caused delay in the acquisition of a new house.

[8] "McGraw-Hill," *Barron's,* February 7, 1955. *Barron's* called *Business Week* "the workhorse of the [McGraw-Hill] company."

Social conditions are such that an attractive and practical magazine about the home appeals to a wide audience. Founded by E. T. Meredith, who had been Wilson's Secretary of Agriculture, with idealistic pronouncements about the home and its place in American life, *Better Homes & Gardens* is a very practical success.

When the magazine was twenty-five years old it printed a folksy editorial statement in which it could claim that for years it had printed more about food than any other magazine in the world, that one out of four subscribers clipped and saved its recipes—560,000,000 clipped recipes in ten years. A study had found it the magazine gardeners most often turned to for help. It was the magazine most read by families building new homes. More than a million families had used the complete home-planning centers set up by the magazine with department stores in various cities. Five to six thousand people wrote the magazine monthly "for help on anything from smoky fireplaces to keeping frogs through the winter." [9] Every month *Better Homes* describes in detail a "Five Star" home. Complete plans and specifications after designs by leading architects are offered for $7.50. Hundreds of thousands of these plans have been sold. Most popular of all was Number 2001, published in January, 1950. By March, 1955, 28,982 sets of plans for this house had been sold. This one house plan has accounted for the building of almost 6,000 homes for a total building cost of nearly $120,000,000. Some 3,600 families still planned to build Number 2001 at a future estimated building cost of another $73,-000,000.

Hundreds of homes have been remodeled, miles of landscaping have been done, scores of community beautification projects have been undertaken and completed, thousands of shrubs and trees have been planted as a result of *Better Homes* contests, advice, and suggestions. The magazine, which does a thorough job of reader and marketing research as a continuing program,

[9] *Better Homes & Gardens,* September, 1947.

gives its readers plenty of luscious illustrations, plenty of how-to-do-it hints, plenty of practical home remodeling ideas, plenty of articles on family problems, plenty of green-thumb tips on bulbs, perennials, parasites, and sprays, and takes in plenty of profitable advertising. *Better Homes* holds first place in advertising revenue among all monthly magazines.

Two other magazines, one new, the other revamped, are comparable neither in size, focal interest, nor influence on things material to those just discussed. They do not tell anybody how to do anything, not even how to succeed. They do not read the future. One carries no advertising; the other, little. The point is that the American public will respond to other appeals besides those of play, work, and home. It will patronize, if not extravagantly, publications of a very different kind from *Holiday, Newsweek,* and *Better Homes & Gardens.*

From 1920 to 1924 Yale professor of English Henry Seidel Canby edited the Saturday night *Literary Review,* a supplement of the *New York Evening Post.* On the staff of the *Post,* writing a column called "The Bowling Green," was Christopher Morley. In 1924 the *Literary Review* broke away from the *Post* and became *The Saturday Review of Literature* with Henry Seidel Canby as editor and Christopher Morley and William Rose Benét as associates. Under Canby, who retired as editor in 1936 but is still chairman of the magazine's editorial board, *The Saturday Review of Literature,* which had a difficult time financially for some years, was a thin, scholarly paper, on newsprint, primarily a collection of book reviews. Bernard De Voto succeeded Canby as editor. In 1942 the editorship went to Norman Cousins, who for two years had been the magazine's executive editor and before that managing editor of *Current History.* Since that time *The Saturday Review* has dropped "of Literature" from its title and bravely has taken all culture within reach for its province.

The Saturday Review covers travel, music, recordings, television, and movies as well as the new books. It has liberal

opinions. It fights for causes. It seems to consider its mission
the dispensation of knowledge and the generation of ideas.
It is still very literary but seems more vital. Page size cut down,
slick paper front and back, illustrated with line cuts and half-
tones, it looks more like a magazine than the supplement from
which it stemmed. Popular opinion used to link *The Saturday
Review* with the Sunday *Herald Tribune* "Books" and *The
New York Times Book Review*. *The Saturday Review* has left
this group to become a periodical entity. It carries signed articles as well as reviews, the humor of Bennett Cerf, anagrams,
cryptograms, the mellow conversation of bibliophiles, and pieces
which its table of contents lists proudly as "SR Ideas." Even
its book reviews are not merely reviews. *The Saturday Review*
takes literary criticism seriously as an art in itself. The "personals" in its classified advertising columns, long the warmest
and most amusing page of the publication, seem less colorful.
The magazine calls itself now a "magazine of ideas, entertainment, and the arts." *Time* has called it a bookworm that turned
and described it as "a sort of last haven for the sprightly American essay." [10] Like the *Atlantic* and *Harper's* (and it is not far
behind the older monthlies in its weekly circulation), *The Saturday Review* carries a kind of hallmark of prestige for readers
who take their culture seriously in conversation. A point at
issue when Henry Seidel Canby and his fellows started what
used to be referred to affectionately as the *SRL* was to see
whether the United States would support a purely literary
weekly. The answer, apparent in the revamped magazine, is
that it can and does; in moderation, of course. It is in great
moderation that nationally circulated magazines of literature,
ideas, and the arts are tolerated in mid–twentieth century
United States. The *Atlantic, Harper's,* and *The Saturday Review* are about all there is, where a generation ago there were

[10] "A Bookworm Turned," August 1, 1949. The bookworm has really
not turned much.

also *Scribner's, The North American Review, The Dial,* the *Forum,* and the *Century.*

In December, 1954, appeared the first handsome issue of *American Heritage,* a bimonthly magazine between hard covers, with full color illustrations, no advertising, and a subscription price of $12 a year; single copies, $2.95. *American Heritage* had been founded in 1949 by the American Association for State and Local History. About to founder, it was combined with a projected magazine called *History,* planned as organ of the Society of American Historians. Backed by both organizations, the new *American Heritage* is dedicated to history. Its editor, Bruce Catton, Civil War historian, said in a preface to the first issue that it was published in ". . . the belief that our heritage is best understood by a study of things that the ordinary folk of America have done and thought and dreamed since they first began to live here. Our beat is . . . anything that ever happened in America."

Contributors to *American Heritage* are popular historians, commentators on American manners and mores, novelists, and politicians: Allan Nevins, Carl Carmer, Paul Horgan, Adlai Stevenson, Mark Van Doren, Bernard De Voto. History here is dramatized as colorful narrative and incident. During its first year the magazine described the boyhood and youth of Alexander Hamilton, gave a previously unknown account of the death of John Brown, a medical report on George Washington, a Civil War correspondent's story of an off-duty Grant during the siege of Vicksburg, and published Albert Lasker's account of his life in advertising. Unlikely as it seems, public response to an expensive magazine of limited appeal made the venture a quick success. The print order for *American Heritage* sold in bookstores as well as through subscription, went from 55,000 for the first issue to 115,500 a year later.

Another large group of magazines does better than that. If the circulation they have attained and the hold they have on their addicts is reasonable evidence, they reflect even more of what the United States approves and prefers to read than *Holiday, Newsweek, Better Homes & Gardens, The Saturday Review,* and *American Heritage* combined. Harried and bedeviled, attacked as depraved, violent, sadistic, obscene, accused of fomenting juvenile delinquency, preying on the immaturity of adults, and pandering to the lowest instincts and impulses of the human animal, the so-called "comic books" sell at the rate of 60 to 90 million copies a month.[11]

The comic magazines are an offshoot of the newspaper comic strips and pages which began late in the last century in the New York *World* with R. F. Outcault's "Yellow Kid." He took the Kid to the *New York Journal,* later developed the famous Buster Brown for the *New York Herald.* Today's Superman, L'il Abner, Blondie, Orphan Annie, *et al.* are direct descendants of Buster Brown, Foxy Grandpa, Happy Hooligan, and the rest. The comics have been powerful circulation builders for the newspapers for a long time. The comic monthly magazine originated in the 1930's when the Eastern Color Printing Company in New York, printers of Sunday newspaper comic supplements, conceived the idea of printing comics in book form in small page size. They successfully published *Funnies on Parade,* and followed that with *Famous Funnies,* issued for distribution through variety stories. The book proved so popular that the publishers began to put it out monthly. Then came the deluge. By 1950 a Fawcett Comics Group advertisement could be headlined in true comic book style: "The comic magazines bought each month laid end to end would reach 1/25th the space from the earth to the moon." [12]

The agitation against the worst of the comic books started

---

[11] *Barron's,* January 17, 1955. *Time,* September 27, 1954, said 80 million; the New York *Herald Tribune,* December 29, 1954, said 60 million. Accurate circulation figures are available only for those comic magazine publishers reporting to the Audit Bureau of Circulations.

[12] Advertisement in *Advertising Age,* May 8, 1950.

in magazines.[13] Horror and crime comics have been condemned in the newspaper press. Parents' groups rose in protest against them. The comics have been legislated against in a dozen states, banned from the newsstands of some large cities, policed in others. Leading comic book publishers were quizzed by a Senate subcommittee on juvenile delinquency. Under fire and complaining bitterly that their attackers did not discriminate between good and bad comic magazines, they formed the Comics Magazine Association of America and appointed a New York magistrate, who had specialized in juvenile delinquency, to act as czar and censor for the industry.

As a result of all this agitation by outraged public opinion, some of the worst of the horror comics ceased publication. Others edited out some of their more offensive material. In England, where millions of copies of American comic magazines had been reprinted each month, the activity came to an end.[14] There has been a considerable reduction in the number of comic book titles reaching the newsstands. There had been overproduction, anyway, both in number of titles—as many as 350 in one month—and in number of copies of a title printed. The newsstands could not handle them all.

The comics have been seriously defended as a new kind of

[13] "What Parents Don't Know About Comic Books," by Frederic Wertham, M.D., *Ladies' Home Journal,* November, 1953. The article came out in book form as *Seduction of the Innocent* and was condensed by *Reader's Digest,* May, 1954. The *Digest* also published another exposé, "The Face of Violence" by T. E. Murphy, in November, 1954. In the horror comics, magazines have an example of magazine influence which they would gladly disavow. Reputable and responsible magazines have done their best to correct an abuse of the power of the periodical press.

[14] One of the two big English publishers of comic magazines said the outcry against his wares had made it so difficult to get comics printed and distributed that his costs had become prohibitive. He pointed out that the comic magazines were not intended for children anyway. Among his customers, he said, were two army colonels, some majors, and a number of people in public life. "An analysis of my sales would almost certainly reveal that the main readers are young married women with too much time on their hands." "Britons Drop Publication of Horror Comics," *Advertising Age,* December 6, 1954.

American folklore, as a survival of primitive adventure narrative. They have been looked upon as inheritors of the tradition of the dime novel, now sanctified in wreaths of nostalgia. The comic technique has been praised for its educational uses. The comic magazine idea has been used as a teaching device by both the army and the navy and for purposes of government propaganda. Literary classics and Bible stories are presented in comic magazines. Used in these ways, the comics have been defended as exerting a benevolent social force.[15] As it usually is when censorship is applied or threatened, "the freedom of the press" has been invoked, this time by the indignant publishers of "good" comic books. The one thing which, in all the dispute, no one has called the comic magazines is comical. Humor is seldom their intent.

The comic books provide breathtaking, fantastic adventure, prolonging suspense until the hero finally triumphs over a long, long series of obstacles. The comics, a psychologist explains, are picture-story fantasies appealing directly to human desires and aspirations, to wish fulfillment. "Superman and his innumerable followers satisfy the universal human longing to be stronger than all opposing obstacles . . . to experience vicariously the supreme gratification of the *deus ex machina* who accomplishes these monthly miracles of right triumphing over not-so-mighty might.[16] It all depends, the moralist might add, on what kinds of wishes are to be fulfilled and what kinds of obstacles overcome.

Whatever the ethical, moral, or civic solution to the problem, the comic magazines prevail. Dell, the largest publisher, has a circulation of over 9,000,000 for its group, which includes: *Gene Autry, Tom and Jerry, Little Lulu, Mickey Mouse, Donald Duck, Lone Ranger, Roy Rogers,* and *Tarzan*—all very respectable characters. National Comics, which issues 49 titles,

[15] Sidonie Matsner Gruenberg, "The Comics as a Social Force," *The Journal of Educational Sociology,* December, 1944.

[16] William Moulton Marston, "Why 100,000,000 Americans Read Comics," *The American Scholar,* Winter 1943–44.

has a circulation of over 6,000,000. *Bob Hope, Nutsy Squirrel, Martin and Lewis,* and *Mr. District Attorney* are all in the National Comics stable. Marvel Comics, with 59 titles, among them *Annie Oakley, Black Rider, My Friend Irma,* and *Cowboy Action,* has a circulation of nearly 5,000,000. Harvey Comics, with *Joe Palooka, Little Audrey, Dick Tracy, Blondie, Dagwood, Ripley's Believe It Or Not,* and 20 other titles, go to over 4,000,000 buyers for each issue.

Whether the comic magazines are the textbooks in crime and depravity many think them or educational periodicals with traditions going back to paleolithic times, as their admirers claim, they are read. Seemingly, at this stage in the cultural development of the United States these crudely written, crudely illustrated and reproduced magazines gratify the literary and artistic tastes of a large part of the population. In 1946 Professor Harvey Zorbaugh of the School of Education, New York University, stated that at post exchanges during World War II comic books outsold *The Saturday Evening Post, Life,* and *Reader's Digest* combined by ten to one. A study done by *Puck* in 1948 showed that four out of five American adults read comics. No more than in England are comic magazines read only by children and adolescents, though one study by Marvel Comics showed over 90 per cent readership for boys and girls aged eight to sixteen. According to survey results released by the Bureau of Public Administration of the University of California in 1955, about $100 million is spent yearly for about one billion copies of comic magazines. They are read by one quarter of American high school graduates, 16 per cent of the country's college graduates, and 12 per cent of its teachers.[17]

Magazine publishing today is larger than ever it was. Profits have fallen, but the industry's product is diversified, pervasive, and influential; and like any other commodity, it is accepted in proportion to its ability to please the many or the few.

[17] Survey findings reported in *Time,* March 1, 1955, and *The Reader's Digest,* June 1955.

Chapter 24

SOME CHANGES IN THE NATIONAL
MAGAZINE; THE "LITTLE MAGAZINES"

No OBJECTIVE SCRUTINY of magazines can pretend that all that magazines publish is of equal worth by any standard of judgment, that all of it is of social significance, or that in every direction and at all times the social force of magazines is wisely and usefully applied with resultant good for American society as a whole. It is an easily understood anomaly that the very circumstance of mass circulation which has widened and strengthened the social force of magazines still operates to some extent to limit its scope.

In 1936, in an address at the University of Virginia, William Ludlow Chenery, then editor, later publisher, of *Collier's,* pointed out that from the very beginning magazines were founded, published, and edited by men intensely concerned with public affairs and public good: "The desire to serve the public interest or participate in public affairs is warp and woof of magazine history." The history of Chenery's own magazine can be used to prove this point.

Under Norman Hapgood *Collier's* had been one of the powerful muckraking weeklies. Hapgood boasted that it stood first in influence with the public. Mark Sullivan, Hapgood's associate on *Collier's* and then his successor as editor, said much the same thing in 1938, calling the *Collier's* of that period the most influential magazine in the country and one of the most distinguished. The achievements of *Collier's* in the magazine fight against the patent-medicine industry and against the foisting of adulterated food on the public have been noted. Finley

Peter Dunne was the magazine's last editor under the management of Robert Collier.

In 1919 the Crowell Publishing Company purchased control of *Collier's*, which was in difficulties as a business venture, for about $1,750,000. As Cyrus Curtis had poured *Ladies' Home Journal* money into establishing *The Saturday Evening Post*, the Crowell Company in promoting *Collier's* spent about $15,000,000 earned by the *Woman's Home Companion*, highly successful under the veteran Gertrude Battles Lane, and by the *American Magazine*, which was thriving with John Siddall as editor and Bruce Barton as chief writer of the success stories and inspirational articles it purveyed under the slogan "Not Literature But Life." William Ludlow Chenery, a Virginia newspaperman, was made *Collier's* editor in 1925, and quickly brought to the magazine a staff of first-line writers and reporters, including William G. Shepherd, William B. Courtney, John B. Kennedy, and Walter Davenport. More writers, whose names are now well known, were added to the *Collier's* staff: Quentin Reynolds to write reports; Kyle Crichton to do the theater and the motion pictures; other men to cover Washington, Europe, and the Orient.

The reinvigorated *Collier's* attacked the Ku Klux Klan when that organization was growing in power as a dangerous threat to the civilized community. It reported fully on the activities of Huey Long, attacking his fascistic ideas and operations. *Collier's* had originally supported Prohibition. When thorough investigation around the United States by its reporters showed that Prohibition was not only not working, but was also creating a situation worse than that which it had been designed to cure, *Collier's* began to fight for its repeal. It even drafted a model constitutional amendment which would abolish it. *Collier's* lost 3,000 angered subscribers as a result of its attack on Prohibition. It gained 400,000 new ones.

Some of these social achievements of his magazine Chenery reviewed. He also pointed honestly and accurately to the limitations which large circulation then imposed on the national magazine:

> Many conditions of great importance are . . . outside the scope of a national magazine. To be magazine material it must be possible without violence to the facts to contrive an interesting and, therefore, a dramatic story. . . . It [the national magazine] is not an endowed educational institution. It is a business operated primarily for profit. If it does not interest its readers, it cannot endure.[1]

There is no gainsaying the truth of this statement, but the limitations on the force of a national magazine in influencing public opinion are less today than they were in 1936. Because magazines are continually educating their readers to look for comprehensive and intelligent articles on the greater variety of world subjects in which the individual must be interested today, magazines today can and do present material that might not have been considered dramatic and exciting enough for their readers more than a decade ago.

Collier's itself has undergone many and rapid changes in recent years. It is no longer the muckraking, strident reform magazine it once was. For a time after William Chenery ceased to be either editor or publisher—he resigned in March, 1949—the magazine, though straining to increase its stature, seemed to lack coordinated planning and direction. *Collier's* looked to be wavering and slipping. It suffered both circulation and advertising losses and apparently was declining in public favor. A succession of editors and publishers strove, each by various means, to relieve the situation. After weaving, wavering, and pitching, *Collier's* has come a long way toward righting itself again.

Despite all the surface agitation the essential *Collier's* was there. With a mixture of defensiveness and self-congratulation, it said of itself in 1949 that it was a popular magazine, its chief

---

[1] William L. Chenery, "The Magazine and Public Opinion," *Vital Speeches,* August 15, 1936.

function to entertain, and that it intended to remain just that; but it pointed out also that it intended to face up to the facts of our day, stating the problems that confront people, even if it did not have all the answers.[2]

About this time, though the magazine had said it was not interested in sensation for sensation's sake, *Collier's* began to run many sensational articles. "An Exposé an Issue" was the slogan attributed to its editor from 1949 to 1952. Much of this was done in an obvious effort to bolster circulation.

Most sensational of all during this period was the October 29, 1951, issue which was devoted wholly to a "Preview of the War We Do Not Want." This was a detailed account of an imagined World War III in articles, all on aspects of the same subject, by many big-name contributors. Vividly described and illustrated were the atomic bombing of New York, Washington, and Moscow, the disappearance of Stalin, the defeat of Russia, and the occupation of that country by the Western allies. The spectacular offering was noisily ballyhooed in advance. "This issue . . . may change the course of history." *Collier's* is reported to have spent an additional $40,000 for editorial costs. The issue proved the sensation that was planned. A press run of 3,900,000 copies was a quick sell-out.

The issue attracted the attention it clamored for, but much of the comment was unfavorable. *Collier's* was accused of warmongering, irresponsibility, disturbing the delicate international situation, and of other peccadilloes. Greatly hurt, it found itself having to defend an attempt which it felt had been misunderstood and misinterpreted. Reader opinion was sampled. Seventy-one per cent, *Collier's* reported, thought the issue a "good idea." So did Henry Luce, publisher of *Time* and *Life,* who wrote *Collier's* editor, "There is no question that you made a great impact with that issue and, in my personal opinion, a useful one." [3]

[2] "What *Collier's* Stands For," *Collier's,* June 18, 1949.
[3] "Time Out of Mind," *Collier's,* February 10, 1952.

The most drastic change in *Collier's* policy and operation was announced May 7, 1953. With the issue of August 7, 1953, *Collier's*, a weekly magazine for sixty-five years, would become a biweekly. Throughout the newspaper and trade press, the magazine's publishers were quoted as blaming television for necessitating the change.[4] *Collier's* publishers quickly denied what was reported. The real reason for their decision, they said, was that *Collier's* had been losing circulation, advertising, thus money.[5] The change to biweekly publication would take the magazine out of direct competition as an advertising medium with the long firmly entrenched *Saturday Evening Post* in the general weekly field and place it in competition with *Look*. A biweekly has a longer on-sale period and, because it is current longer, has that much more chance of being read by more people. The new *Collier's* would be launched with a guarantee of at least 112 pages in each issue and a circulation guarantee of 3,500,000.

The biweekly *Collier's* was planned to reverse one trend apparent in most of the general mass magazines. It would run more, rather than less, fiction and would restore the practice, dropped some time previously, of publishing serialized fiction. Deliberately, many of these stories would be slanted to appeal to women readers. To accomplish this, a male fiction editor was replaced by a woman.

When the August 7, 1953, issue of *Collier's* appeared, it proved to be 50 per cent larger than previous weekly issues. It contained a substantial number of advertising pages, most advertisers in the weekly issue continuing their schedules. An editorial reaffirmed, verbatim, the *Collier's* policy stated in 1949:

[4] *The New York Times* said, May 8, 1953: "The publishers of *Collier's* announced yesterday that the magazine would be published every other week in a move made necessary by television's inroads on the reading audience."

[5] *Collier's* was losing $400,000 a week in April, 1953. Its loss for the year was over $4 million ("Can *Collier's* Come Back?" *Forbes*, September 15, 1955).

Collier's is a popular magazine, first and last, and it means to remain one. It knows that a major function of a popular magazine is to entertain. All of us have to have some escape in these troubled times. . . .

But we must also face up to the facts.

Collier's intends to face the facts and to state the problems that confront us, even if it doesn't have all the answers. It is not interested in sensation for sensation's sake. . . . *Collier's* believes in change, but only within the framework of American institutions and traditions. . . .

Collier's is not buying any new political systems. . . . It is allergic to stuffiness. . . . It believes there are times when kidding can be more effective than crusading. . . .

Collier's believes that it is just as important to appreciate and perpetuate all that is good in our national life as it is to correct what is wrong.[6]

The first biweekly *Collier's* carried on the cover a cartoon treatment in color of William O'Dwyer, ex-mayor of New York and ex-ambassador to Mexico. Its lead story was on "William O'Dwyer—The Man Who Won't Come Home," a description of the private life of a mysterious and controversial expatriate. The issue featured "the dramatic story of Saint Paul" from a new religious book by the late Fulton Oursler, and a love story by Pearl Buck. A lively article described Frank Sinatra in a new role as a dramatic actor in "From Here to Eternity"; another, with vivid photographic illustrations in color, was "Forest Fire." There was plenty of light fiction, the beginning of a new serial and a short-short story, a literary form which *Collier's* can claim to have originated. These, together with such standard *Collier's* features as *"Collier's* Credits" (item about contributors), Walter Davenport's "48 States of Mind," and a plenitude of *Collier's* popular cartoons, set the pace for the changed magazine. It has retained much the same tone and content since then—articles, special pieces, short stories, serials, and continuing features, adding such regular

[6] "A Restatement of What *Collier's* Stands For," *Collier's,* August 7, 1953.

departments as "Appointment with O'Hara," chatty columnist material, and titling its last-page editorial *"Collier's* Comment."

People, behind-the-scenes articles, adventure and romantic stories, and sensational exposés are the *Collier's* staples, as, to a large extent, they have been for many years. Big-name writers, many of whom *Collier's* developed over the years, appear often. The magazine carries solid fiction by writers as good as John Steinbeck, and as popular as Erich Maria Remarque, as well as Ellery Queen mysteries and Luke Short westerns. Yet, through all its changes and with its avowed purpose of entertaining as a popular magazine, *Collier's* has retained its position as a national weekly of serious intent. For journalistic purposes, its presentations are usually more flamboyant than those of its long-time rival, *The Saturday Evening Post,* for its appeal is, generally, to the man in the street and the middle-class man and woman at home. Yet *Collier's* still exerts its influence strongly on public opinion. It made no immoderate claims, one year-end editorial said, yet the magazine's part in some causes and effects was more than coincidence. It pointed out that it had revealed the connections between remnants of the Capone gangs and politicians, had exposed gambling and gangsterism before Marcantonio's defeat when he ran for re-election from New York, and that certain pertinent articles had preceded Robert Taft's re-election to the Senate in 1950.[7] *Collier's* might have pointed to many more examples of its keeping ahead of public opinion as well as reflecting it.

It has spoken out forthrightly on public questions, on big business, its responsibilities, dangers, and value to the country; it has treated race problems and the problems of minority groups courageously. It attacked Prohibition when the abuses which flourished under it had become manifest. Its articles on the conservation of natural resources from 1910 through 1955 have been informative and effective. It has paid its share of attention and had its share of influence on national and inter-

[7] "Causes and Effects," *Collier's,* December 30, 1950.

national affairs. *Collier's* circulation was 3,776,538 average per issue for the second six months of 1955.

In 1941 Frederick Lewis Allen commented on the revolution that had taken place in magazine publishing within fifty years. In 1891 a small group of monthly magazines, all with circulations of between 100,000 and 200,000 were dominant. Only two of them, *The Atlantic Monthly* and *Harper's,* survive, and these partly because they have imitated the national magazines which took over the leadership by inserting more information on vital subjects and more human interest material in their pages. Commenting on the changes between 1891 and 1941, Allen said:

> The revolution of which I have been speaking has undoubtedly had its bad side. It has brought us much vulgarity and evasion. It has brought us too much pseudo-information, pellets of half-truths designed to be consumed on the run. . . . Yet the existence of this mass reading public offers more than a gigantic demonstration of the bare literacy of the American public, or of its wish for easy entertainment. It offers a demonstration also of the American appetite for information—practical information—for tips on how to do one's job better, on how other people have succeeded at the same sort of job, on what is going on in the community and beyond its borders. These innumerable magazines of ours appeal to—and satisfy—a tremendous and undying urge to get on, to escape from provincial limitations, to acquire a sense of taste and style and at least outward distinction, to widen the horizon, to become . . . in some degree citizens of the world. In that sense our American magazines of today, considered as a broad group, give us a very impressive exhibit of democracy working.[8]

The social force of magazines is expressed not only in legislative reforms following magazine campaigns fought to bring them about, but also in what we eat, what we wear, what we plant in the garden or buy from the automobile dealer and the refrigerator manufacturer, what we think about foreign and domestic affairs, and how we judge our neighbors. We measure

[8] Frederick Lewis Allen, "American Magazines, 1741–1941," *Bulletin of The New York Public Library,* June, 1941.

our own accomplishments by those of men whose life and actions are described in magazine articles; we desire and buy the necessities and gadgets artfully presented in magazine advertisements; we store the facts of current happenings as these are given in magazine accounts, and even react approvingly or disapprovingly to the visual and tactile stimuli offered by the physical properties of the periodical. Magazines are a continuous and almost inescapable pressure exerted on our minds and our emotions.

Fiction as well as fact is the province of the national magazines. If these magazines were informative merely, they probably would not be read. Their purpose is to attract and entertain, as well as to report, analyze, and discuss. In 1902 William Dean Howells, one of the greatest of American realistic novelists, was able to write in *Literature and Life* that "most of the best literature now sees the light in the magazines, and most of the second-best appears first in book form." What was true when Howells wrote, and was true for a number of years afterward, is not true of popular magazine fiction now. This is a general and, from the purist viewpoint, a legitimate complaint. Those magazines of large circulation which publish short stories and novels print, for the most part, "escape" fiction.

There is something to be said in favor of stories that take the reader out of the familiar and sometimes drab actualities of his own life into a more romantic and alluring scene where all women are beautiful, all men handsome, and good fortune is assured after exciting interplay of plot and glamorous characters. There is more to be said in favor of fiction that uses recognizable people for characters, something resembling occurrences in life as plot, and which, as Howells' fiction did, serves in some degree and in some way as a representation and criticism of real life. Though there have been some notable exceptions, the mass magazines ignore much of the better fiction which, if it appears at all before publication in book form, must find publication now in the so-called "little magazines."

The little magazines are a numerous and varied group of periodicals. With new ones appearing as fast as older ones, their funds exhausted or their motivating ideas abandoned, cease publication, they perform a service for letters which the national magazines cannot, at least do not, attempt. Subsidized in some way, controlled usually by a group interested in experimental writing of some kind, the typical little magazine can be published without regard to the tastes of a large reading audience or the necessity of providing an effective vehicle for advertisers. It is used solely as a medium of expression for the linguistic, poetic, critical, and sometimes political ideas of the group controlling it. It pays nothing to its contributors, or gives only token payments. Its real service is in providing publication for writers who would otherwise find it difficult or impossible to get their work before any public. Many of the little magazines exhibit an unmistakable vanity and snobbishness. They parade eccentricities and deliberate variations from the accepted norms in subject matter and style. Specific little magazines are annoying and often unintelligible to the lay reader, who suspects affectation for the sake of affectation. Their editors and writers would be displeased if they were understood by the vulgar. The best of them have a more serious intent, and the little magazines as a whole have amassed a record of reputable accomplishment.

In 1946 three investigators who looked thoroughly into the little magazines came to the conclusion that these unsung periodicals had discovered and sponsored about 80 per cent of the important novelists, poets, and critics who began to write after 1912, and that they not only introduced but also remained the basic magazines to publish 95 per cent of the poets of this period.[9] Poetry has little or no commercial value. The larger magazines want little or none of it. It is probably not too much of an exaggeration to say that the renascence of poetry in the

---

[9] Frederick J. Hoffman, Charles Allen, and Carolyn F. Ulrich, *The Little Magazine, A History and a Bibliography* (Princeton, N. J.: Princeton University Press, 1946), p. 8.

United States after the close of World War I could not have occurred without the help of the little magazines. The reputations of Robert Frost, Edwin Arlington Robinson, Carl Sandburg, Vachel Lindsay, and John Gould Fletcher were established in part through the appearance of their verse in the little magazines. The little magazines published many of the poets whose work is now recognized as some of the best of our poetic production in the twentieth century at a time when these writers were being ignored by the larger literary monthlies, such as *Harper's* and the *Atlantic,* which might have been expected to encourage them. Novelists such as Erskine Caldwell, Albert Halper, and James Farrell, all used the little magazines to get started on their careers. The *Double Dealer* in New Orleans gave early publication to Hart Crane and introduced Ernest Hemingway, probably the most successful commercially of any of the novelists to emerge from the little magazine movement, in 1922. The same *Double Dealer* printed the early work of the critic Edmund Wilson and of the prize-winning novelist Robert Penn Warren. Warren's verse is still published in little magazines, as is the work of William Carlos Williams.

The expatriate T. S. Eliot, whose long poem of poetic despair, *The Waste Land* (1922), made him the poet of the "lost generation," as Hemingway was its novelist, edited a little magazine, *Criterion,* in England. In it he published the poetry on which his fame depends. Ezra Pound, expatriate poet of the most advanced school, who made a cult of obscurity, and whose ideas in other directions brought him a new notoriety in World War II, emerged from the little magazines. Richard Aldington, English poet and novelist, and Wyndham Lewis, refreshingly individualistic literary critic, came up through the little magazines. Max Eastman, now (so greatly have ideas and people changed) an editor of *The Reader's Digest,* was once, with Floyd Dell, an editor of the left-wing little magazine *The Masses.* Many more of our best writers had to obtain periodical publication in one or another of the little magazines.

Poetry: A Magazine of Verse, founded in Chicago by Harriet Monroe in 1912 and still extant, published now by the University of Chicago Press, had more to do with the rise of modern poetry in this country than any other magazine, large or small. *Poetry* was near extinction for lack of operating funds in 1955. In November a fifty-dollars-a-plate banquet and an auction of rare books and manuscripts was held in the Blackstone Theatre in Chicago as a benefit for the magazine. Robert Frost, whose first poem appeared in *Poetry* in 1949, recited some of his verse. A rare edition of one of Siegfried Sassoon's volumes of poetry was auctioned off. The benefit netted about $30,000, which was enough to float the magazine another year. *The Little Review,* published first in Chicago, but for most of its life, 1912–1929, in New York, ran James Joyce's *Ulysses* in installments for three years. For introducing American readers to one of the literary classics of the twentieth century, the magazine was prosecuted on the grounds of circulating obscene material. In Paris, *transition,* founded in 1927, published parts of Joyce's *Finnegans Wake* as "Work in Progress," and published also Gertrude Stein, Hemingway, and William Carlos Williams. This famous little magazine was discontinued in 1930 because, as one of its editors said, it "threatened to become a mercantile success." Publication was later resumed at Mt. Vernon, Iowa. The *Partisan Review,* now a bimonthly of literature and politics, was associated with the Communist Party at its 1934 founding but has been independent and anti-Communist since 1938. A proponent of intellectual freedom, it opposes regimentation of any kind, is generally liberal and critical in tone. The *Review,* which features modern short stories, essays, poems, and sound, clear-headed literary criticism, has published T. S. Eliot, John Dos Passos, Archibald MacLeish, William Carlos Williams, and Edmund Wilson at one time and another. Such comparable writers as Conrad Aiken, Cyril Connolly, Andre Malraux, and John Crowe Ransom still appear in its pages. Many of the little magazines, their purpose served, have disappeared. Printing and paper costs make them an insupportable luxury today. Their nearest equivalents as magazines of arts and letters are the subsidized academic quarterlies like the *Yale Review, Sewanee Review, Kenyon Review,* and Phi Beta Kappa's *American Scholar.*

Novelists who have had to find periodical publication in the little magazines have had their work accepted and acclaimed by the larger public when it appeared in book form. There is just cause, then, for the unfavorable criticism leveled at the popular magazines for their failure to print more serious fiction. Justification for the mass magazine's attitude toward some of the best short stories and novels being written today can lie only in the editorial belief, substantiated by reader research, that the mass public will not accept serious fiction. That they publish light fiction which millions enjoy is fact. That these magazines once published the best fiction, verse, and essays that the country's writers could produce, and that they still publish at least some of the best is also fact.

Chapter 25

CONCLUSION

THOUGH "magazine" or "the American magazine" has been used as a term of convenient reference often in this discussion, the actuality does not exist. There is no such composite entity, any more than there is a normal man or a typical book. The infinite variety of the more than 7,000 American magazines includes trade, vocational, and hobby periodicals, professional journals, magazines for chess players, for chain-store managers, for numismatists, obstetricians, orthodontists, and embalmers. American magazines range from the publications of learned societies, their contents intelligible only to a highly restricted group of initiated readers, to pulp magazines whose stories and comic strip sequences are intelligible to most. Specialized periodicals have not been taken into account here, nor, except in the case of the comic books, have the subliterate been considered. "Magazine," with few exceptions, has been used to mean general periodical publications of large national circulation. Even here there is variety enough, but there are basic similarities, and the differences are not as sharply defined as once they were.

Brevity and sharpness characterize today's magazine. They are timed to twentieth-century nervousness and hurry, styled to modern conceptions of swift design. More and more their appeal is visual. Increasingly they deal with the pressing social and economic problems of the day. The format, typography, and editorial style of some of the leaders are imitated by their competitors, but the similarity goes beyond mere imitation. Edward Bok once remarked that a picture is as good as a page

359

of text. Others have made the same remark with the same air of discovery and finality. But a picture has certain limitations. It can arrest the reader's attention; it can dramatize, convey static reality, give heightened color to a written account, sometimes, in a very limited sense, tell a story; but it cannot discuss or explain. Realizing the values of pictures, editors of the general magazines have used them more and more, but have continued to place their chief reliance on words to convey ideas. The pictorial magazines, given over almost entirely to pictures at first, have used an ever greater proportion of text. *Life* now is far from being a purely pictorial magazine. The amount of writing has increased as the thoughtful content of the magazine has mounted.

The women's general and service magazines, all of them good when judged by the standards they have set for themselves, are scarcely distinguishable in purpose or type of contents. The pattern for these magazines was set by Louis Godey and Sarah Josepha Hale in *Godey's Lady's Book* in the nineteenth century. Edward Bok enlarged and vastly improved the contents of all women's magazines through the influence of the *Ladies' Home Journal,* but he did not change the basic pattern. Editors of women's magazines since Bok's time have added more material of general interest to their pages, keeping pace with women's widened social and political interest in the twentieth century, but have retained the *Godey's* pattern built around fashions, home decoration, recipes, house plans, hints on decorum and etiquette, and all the rest. Today's so-called shelter magazines, with their full-color pictures of the beautiful interiors and the beautiful exteriors of beautiful homes, seem all cut from the same bolt of glitter. The same terse news item, or the same magnificent or subtle advertisement, appears in an urban weekly, a small-town news magazine, or a rural monthly. The World War II diary of an American general or a statesman's views on world politics is as apt to appear in one of the women's magazines as in one of the pictorial magazines or in one of the general weeklies. Such articles have, in fact, appeared in all three. No magazine, no group of magazines, now has a monopoly on significant material. The memoirs or biographies of men whose decisions and actions influenced history in a period of world crisis—Henry L. Stimson, General Dwight Eisenhower, James Farley, Harold Ickes, Harry Hopkins, Admiral William Halsey, General Joseph Stilwell, Franklin D. Roosevelt, and Winston Churchill—have appeared in a diverse group of periodicals—*Life, Look, The Saturday Evening Post, Collier's,* and *Ladies' Home Journal.*

Since 1888, when the National Geographic Society was founded at a meeting in the Cosmos Club in Washington, *The National Geographic Magazine* has been the teacher of geography to the nation. There is no need to stress the educational influence exerted by this magazine, which, each issue containing six to ten articles on travel, exploration, and natural history, each replete with pictures in color and in black and white, has carried contributions by Robert E. Peary, Roald Amundsen, Theodore Roosevelt as African explorer, Vilhjalmur Stefansson, Sir Ernest Shackleton, Charles A. Lindbergh, and many lesser-known travelers and explorers.[1] The magazine, a favorite with educators, has made world travelers and explorers of its readers. It has done much more. The magazine has no actual subscribers as such. It goes each month to members of the National Geographic Society as part of their membership privileges. When Gilbert Grosvenor, now Chairman of the Board of Trustees of the Society, became its editor before the turn of the twentieth century, the membership was so small that he said he could carry an entire month's edition on his back.

[1] Alexander Graham Bell succeeded his father-in-law, Gardiner G. Hubbard, as president of the National Geographic Society on the death of the Society's first president in 1897. In the same year he appointed Gilbert Grosvenor, who later became his son-in-law, to the editorship of the *National Geographic Magazine.* Gilbert Grosvenor and Oliver LaGorce, who joined him in 1905 as editor and associate editor, built the magazine to its present eminence in its special field. *National Geographic* maps proved invaluable in two world wars.

Skillfully promoted as it has been through the membership device, *The National Geographic Magazine* now goes to over two million members for the "increase and diffusion of geographic knowledge."

Grosvenor during his long editorship decided that the publication would have absolute accuracy, an abundance of illustration. Its articles would have permanent value. The magazine would discuss nothing of a controversial or partisan nature; it would always speak kindly of nations and peoples. *The National Geographic* has consistently and successfully observed these rules for more than half a century. It has been and is an advertising as well as an editorial success, and the National Geographic Society has long been able to sponsor explorations and expeditions to many parts of the globe, reporting the experiences of its travelers and the findings of geographic and scientific importance made by its explorers and writers in articles long respected for their authenticity and admired for their illustrations in color. There can be no doubt of the pre-eminence of *The National Geographic* as a travel magazine, yet today informative and attractive articles on travel appear in *Holiday* and in many other magazines, *The Saturday Review,* for instance, in which travel has only lately become an established editorial feature. *Holiday* certainly has not the same serious cultural and educational aim as *The National Geographic,* yet its pictures and articles about various sections of the United States and about foreign countries, its travel stories, its maps, and its cartographs have a kindred educational value.

The Reader's Digest can find the vital, lively, or innocuous material it wants as readily in one of the literary monthlies as in one of the powerful general weeklies or in the feature sections of the metropolitan newspapers. It has found and reprinted articles from them all. The *Digest* has functioned as a great leveler among magazines.

If a capably written and informative article on national or

international affairs, or an illuminating discussion of social problems were taken out of its magazine context, a reader would find it difficult to determine whether the article had appeared in *Life, The Saturday Evening Post,* the *Yale Review, Fortune, Collier's,* or *The Atlantic Monthly.* The staid *Atlantic,* not the *Woman's Home Companion,* published Betty MacDonald's entertaining light novel, *The Egg and I,* just as *The Saturday Evening Post,* not one of the literary monthlies, published *The Pit* and *The Octopus* by Frank Norris, and, years later, J. P. Marquand's *The Late George Apley. The New Yorker,* and not one of the country's more ostensibly serious magazines, devoted an entire issue to John Hersey's 30,000-word account of the devastation wrought at Hiroshima by the atom bomb.

The first full news of the discovery of atomic power and an appraisal of the significance of the discovery reached the public through two contrasting magazines. Only a few days after newspaper announcements that atomic fission had been effected, *Harper's Magazine* published in its issue of June, 1940, "Enter Atomic Power" by J. J. O'Neill. *The Saturday Evening Post,* September 9, 1940, published "The Atom Gives Up" by William L. Laurence, the same writer on scientific subjects who was later selected to write the official War Department releases when Hiroshima was bombed in August, 1945, and announcements of atom bomb experiments in New Mexico were made. "The Atom Gives Up" described in detail the discovery of U-235. It told of the work of Professor Arthur J. Dempster at the University of Chicago, of Professor Enrico Fermi's work first in Italy, then at Columbia, of the investigations of Lise Meitner and Dr. Otto Hahn in Germany, and of the contribution of other nuclear scientists to the ultimate discovery. The splitting of the uranium atom and the release of atomic power were fully described; so was the power of the force newly released. One pound of pure U-235, wrote William Laurence, would have the explosive power of 15,000 tons of

TNT, or 300 carloads of fifty tons each.[2] So important and so revealing was this article considered that during World War II the Federal Bureau of Investigation forbade *The Saturday Evening Post* to send out reprints of the article or any copies of the issue containing it. The names of people requesting it had to be turned over to the War Department.

In February, 1947, *Harper's Magazine* published former Secretary of War Henry L. Stimson's statement on why the United States had used the atom bomb in the war with Japan, a document that was both major news and a record important in world history. Knowledge of the newly discovered atomic force, and realization of what its influence on their lives and on the future of the world might be, thus came first and most fully to the public, couched in terms understandable to the lay reader, through America's magazines.

Magazine influence in the United States is pervasive. It is a continuous pressure, constantly moulding the ideas of many millions, both the leaders of public opinion and the followers. Although this influence is difficult to isolate and to prove, cause and effect are discernible in given instances. In 1928 *Harper's Magazine* printed an article on "The Possibilities of Large Telescopes" by George Ellery Hale. The article led directly to the construction and erection of the 200-inch telescope on Mount Palomar in California.

Alva Johnston, who had earlier written *New Yorker* "Profiles," first introduced Wendell Willkie to a national audience when he wrote "The Man Who Talked Back" for *The Saturday Evening Post* of February 25, 1939. This was a biography of Willkie as president of the Commonwealth and Southern Corporation, a private utilities company, and as an opponent of the Tennessee Valley Authority. Wendell Willkie himself wrote "Idle Money—Idle Men" for the *Post* of June 17, 1939. A poll taken by George Gallup's American Institute of Public Opinion

[2] The article ventured a prophecy that, unfortunately, was incorrect: ". . . such a substance would not be likely to be wasted on explosives."

in March, 1940, disclosed that Willkie was well enough and favorably enough known to be mentioned in answer to the question, "Whom would you like to see elected President this year?" But Willkie, then, was named by fewer than 1 per cent of those answering the question. Three days before the opening of the Republican national convention in 1940, a second Gallup poll showed 29 per cent favoring Wendell Willkie for the Republican nomination for President. Two days later *The Saturday Evening Post* of June 22, 1940, was published. Its two lead articles were "Five Minutes to Midnight" by Wendell L. Willkie and "I Am Not Nominating Him" by General Hugh S. Johnson, an early and enthusiastic Willkie supporter. Eight days after the appearance of these articles, with the convention still in session, a third poll by the American Institute of Public Opinion showed that 44 per cent of Republican voters wished Willkie to receive the nomination. These widely read magazine articles undoubtedly contributed greatly to Willkie's growing popularity.

Sumner Blossom, when he became editor of the *American Magazine* in 1929, is said to have written a memorandum to his staff: "Horatio Alger doesn't work here any more." Yet the national magazines of mass circulation still purvey success stories and enough of the same kind of inspirational material they found popular a quarter century ago. Social and economic conditions may have changed. There may, obviously, be fewer opportunities for the individual to attain an Alger-like success now than there were in 1870 or even in 1900, but editors seem unwilling to concede the point. Few of the mass magazines go to the same extreme as *Reader's Digest,* but they all print such material. Whether it is a *Saturday Evening Post* story of a small-town banker or a *Life* story of the small-town girl who becomes a successful model in New York, their appeal is the same. Even *New Yorker* "Profiles" are based on this same universal human interest in people who have succeeded in becoming celebrities of one kind or another.

Perhaps there is no real reason why hope, though it is more often joined by a thin thread to possibility than firmly anchored in the probable, should be permanently and completely withdrawn from circulation. The human spirit has always responded to the story of from rags to riches. From log cabin to White House is a variant particularly beloved by Americans. Again, though it is clothed in the more pretentious language of economics and politics, the twentieth century's intensive drive toward social gains is only a strong attempt to realize such dreams for everyone.

Certain formulas of magazine journalism persist. Yet despite the success stories, the slick fiction, and the glib superficiality of some of their articles, today's magazines are compact of a marked seriousness, evident in purpose and performance. Editors of the larger magazines are fully aware of the powers they exercise, of their responsibility in selecting material from the whole range of human interests, and in presenting the interpretations of their writers to a wide public whose thinking, inevitably, will be guided by what they read in magazines whose integrity they have learned to trust.

Some magazines, and other magazines in some issues, seem unable to check a strained attempt to embrace and explain the scientific, the economic, the political, the sublime and the less sublime in one gasping issue which will, at the same time, acknowledge art, literature, and all of history. The result is usually startling, and as confusing as the attempt is admirable. Other magazines sometimes smother their real substance with so much froth that the sterner stuff goes unnoticed.

Every national general magazine must entertain as well as inform. If it does not, it is not read. If it is not read, its influence, its force of any kind, is nil. If it continues to go unread, the magazine is soon extinct. The larger the audience at which a magazine is directed, the greater the concessions which must be made, but the more thoughtful as well as the more spectacular magazines must observe this fact. Men and women are under no compulsion to read America's magazines. They read magazines, on their own declaration, to amuse themselves and "to keep well informed." As part of an elaborate pilot study made in 1944 to determine the feasibility of launching a new magazine, a survey was made in an east coast city. The sample of magazine readers questioned answered that they read magazines for these reasons in this order: entertainment, increase in knowledge, conversational material, escape, practical information, inspiration.[3]

Every issue of one of the larger magazines must be a compromise. To reach its audience and continue to be acceptable to that audience, it must please as well as educate. The only reading animal has emotions as well as a mind. He seeks pleasure and relaxation, as well as information and intellectual stimulus, from his magazine reading. The story is perhaps apocryphal, but the point is fundamental in magazine editing: When an overenthusiastic constant reader told Cyrus H. K. Curtis that he read every issue of *The Saturday Evening Post* from cover to cover and liked everything in it, the publisher replied that he would have to check on his editors. If they were so perfectly matching the tastes and interests of this one reader, it was obvious that they were not putting a sufficient variety of interests into the magazines.

There must be variety in mood, variety in the writing, and variety in the kind and extent of mental effort exacted of the reader. It was in part because the popular magazines which arose in the late nineteenth century learned quickly to provide it that they attained the success which enabled them to obtain the writers, editors, and artists with the skill to attract great audiences. Of the great literary monthlies dominant in the last quarter of the nineteenth century—magazines written by edu-

---

[3] The projected magazine was not launched. *Holiday* and *Sports Illustrated* are the only major magazines started since the close of World War II, whereas important new magazines of important new types were founded soon after World War I.

cated, intelligent, intellectual men and women for the literate, educated minority—only *Harper's Magazine* and *The Atlantic Monthly* survive. They retain their prestige and influence today, in large part, because, while fully maintaining their editorial integrity, they began to present more diversified material in more lively fashion.[4]

As already intimated, there can be no doubt that tremendous circulations still limit to some extent the kinds of subjects that can be treated in a mass magazine and the ways in which admitted subjects can be handled. The same consideration dictates the inclusion of other material. Sex in its most glamorous aspects, violence which by superb photography and fine reproduction is made to appear more romantic and exciting than cruel and painful, saccharine optimism, pretense of intellectuality where there is only glibness, articles shining with a polished mediocrity, and dishonest fiction—all these appear in some of

[4] *Harper's* is the more vigorous, worldly, and varied of the two, the more practical, alert, and amusing. *The Atlantic,* despite its "Atlantic Report on the World Today," with is pages devoted to Washington and other capitals after the manner of a news weekly, is still the more genteel-literary, the more Boston–Harvard Square–Anglophilic parochial. As prestige, "class" magazines, both command the occasional serious work of distinguished writers whose more popular work appears in the mass media. They also command attention far beyond the reading audience suggested by their small circulations. *Harper's* does not shrink from controversial subjects. In October, 1954, it ran a very long piece, five times the length of an ordinary *Harper's* article, "The Case of J. Robert Oppenheimer" by Joseph and Stewart Alsop. In December, 1955, *Harper's* published "Pay by the Year: Can the Unions Afford It?" by a businessman who had earlier been a CIO economist. In January, 1956, the magazine published a piece it had deliberately sought out, "The Southern Case Against Desegregation" by Thomas R. Waring, editor of the Charleston *News and Courier.* "One of the duties of an independent magazine, allied to no party or interest group, is to give a hearing to significant bodies of opinion which cannot find expression elsewhere—even when the editors disagree," an editorial note explained. *Harper's* for February, 1956, contained even more explosive matter, a brief letter in which the Secretary of Agriculture commended as excellent a December, 1955, article by *Harper's* editor-in-chief, "The Country Slicker Takes Us Again." The article had described the American farmer as a pampered tyrant. Segments of public opinion did not believe the Secretary should agree with such a description of his charges, and the dispute was front-page controversy before the Secretary could hastily explain that his commendation was all a mistake.

our best and best-known magazines, though not all of these in any one of them. Side by side with them is much of the best that is being thought and written in our day. Yet the standard of the editorial contents in the national magazine is far higher than it was twenty-five and even ten years ago. Several forces have operated to bring this about, the same basic forces which have made today's magazines more and more alike.

More and more the magazines of the United States have become what Colonel George Harvey called them in 1910, the country's "national newspapers." Many of the country's best newspapers have disappeared. Some have been discontinued; others, bought by competitors and merged with other newspapers, have had their once strong individualities submerged in the newspaper chains of which they have become a part. Excellent as many of them are, they suffer from a monotonous uniformity. Front pages across the country are made up of news off the various wire services. Local news, and in many cases it is the local news alone which is specifically prepared for the paper in which it appears, is run among the many pages of department store and other local advertising which fills the inside pages. Solid columns of syndicated material, stories, gossip columns, estimates of the national or international situation by journalist commentators—essentially magazine material—give these newspapers what distinctiveness and influence on public opinion they retain. By virtue of their prestige and influence, certain of the country's great metropolitan newspapers, as in New York, Washington, and Chicago, are "national newspapers," though their circulations are almost entirely limited to the cities in which they are published and nearby areas. This is far from true of the newspapers across the country, and the position of the newspaper press in too many of our largest cities is very weak.

Early in this century American magazines, led by the muckrakers, took over what had been until then the function of the newspaper editorial in guiding public opinion. Recently, magazines have assumed much of the more basic characteristic of the newspaper. The weekly news magazines like *Time* and *Newsweek* are definitely in competition with the daily newspapers in the gathering and dissemination of the news. They supplement and, for some of their readers, supplant the newspapers. The general weekly and monthly magazines, all of them publishing an increasing proportion of informative material, are also dealing with what is essentially news in their expanded and considered discussion of national and world events.

A second and even more significant force has resulted in the betterment of magazines' contents generally and in the raising of the editorial standards of the national magazines to a level not previously possible. The wide and rapid spread of education in the United States has brought the majority of magazine readers to acceptance of more thoughtful, better written material. The educational and intellectual level of the population has been raised to the point where the large general magazines can and must present subjects and treatments of these subjects which their audience would have rejected as boring, unnecessary, or highbrow a few years ago. The magazines of the mid–twentieth century can hold their huge circulations with serious discussions which would not have been tolerated by the magazine audience of 1910 or even 1930. It is a more critical audience, less easily deluded, less apt to be hypnotized by phrases, or content with standardized, colorless treatment of vital subjects. It is a fact-hungry audience which has learned to evaluate facts and their significance, to form its own opinions, and to judge those proffered by magazine writers. As the national educational level continues to rise, the magazines must print continually better material for readers who have been taught to be more discriminating.

This is true only in part. As education has spread, it has also spread thin. It has been said often enough that more people can read today but fewer can think. A literate population does not constitute a critically intelligent one. The tolerance of most mass magazine readers for thoughtful material is low. They read mostly to be amused; they do not wish to be shocked or made unhappily aware of unpleasant facts when what they are seeking is the kind of escape they have gone to popular magazines to find. These magazines can run substantial material in many instances only if they treat it lightly, make it diverting, avoid taboos, and sweeten the material sufficiently to make it palatable. Television came into being as a communications medium with astounding swiftness. As quickly as it came it conditioned its vast audience to undiluted light entertainment, little of better than mediocre quality. The continuing appeal of the comic books is reassuring guarantee that American magazines have not, and cannot if they wish to maintain and enlarge their circulations, become too serious and informative. Yet they have, as a whole noticeably improved.

Two world conflicts have wrought permanent improvements in the editorial contents of American magazines. World War I forced readers into awareness of people, places, and ideas beyond Sandy Hook and the Golden Gate. World War II enabled the magazines, and they made the most of their opportunity, to present explanation and discussion of political, geographical, economic, ideological, and a myriad of other subjects which they could not have published successfully earlier. Since the end of the last war the magazines have been compelled to maintain the high reportorial and educational standards they reached between 1939 and 1945, when, incidentally, their circulations multiplied.[5]

Magazines were the favorite reading of millions of men and women in the armed forces; often they were the only reading matter available. These men and women, their knowledge of

[5] Average circulation per issue of magazines reporting to the Audit Bureau of Circulations rose from 96.8 million in 1939 to 147.8 million in 1945. Circulations have continued to climb since the end of the war, to 161 million in 1946, to 166,286,858 ten years later.

the war limited to what was happening in their own sectors or at their own posts, read primarily for information about the progress of the war and the kind of peace that might be expected to follow, and secondly for recreation. Often, in Europe and in the South Pacific, magazines were the most typically American product obtainable. Their contents were devoured. Sight and feel of the magazines themselves provided comfort and reassurance. In this country, their publishers hampered by paper shortages, magazines were at a premium. Copies of new issues of the large magazines disappeared from the newsstands in a matter of minutes. American dependence on magazines increased greatly during World War II.

The tense world situation following World War II, and, equally, the serious purpose of American magazine editors to keep their readers informed, have resulted in continued emphasis on international affairs, on political and social movements at home and abroad, on economic subjects and diplomatic maneuvering. There is lighter material about people and places, but serious discussions of these subjects still predominate in our magazines. Present magazine preoccupation with economics and international politics may give way to other interests if the world situation changes and other subjects loom in importance, but the magazines will continue to give serious treatment to matters affecting the individual and the social group. Most editors of today's influential magazines are fully aware of their responsibilities and the responsibilities of their magazines to society, but even if they were totally without such an awareness they would be forced to print such material. The standards which the magazines have established for themselves, the strong competition among magazines—always an unrelenting pressure making for improvement in magazine editorial content—and the demands of the public for accurate information and considered opinion, make performance of the obligation inescapable.

A magazine is a perishable product. It has to do with the contemporary; it is meant for ready and relatively quick perusal. For planned study the serious student goes to books, many of which have been developed from material first printed in magazines. The general reader also turns to books, many of which have likewise first appeared in magazines, for lasting literary enjoyment. A book is produced as a durable article which it is expected will be kept for some time. The newspaper is printed to be discarded after it has been read or scanned.

The magazine, essentially a compromise between the newspaper and the book, lacks the permanence of the book but has much more than the highly transient value of the newspapers. Normally it is kept for some time after purchase and original reading. Usually it is read by the entire family, picked up and read by visitors to the household, often passed on to friends. Its influence, its potential as a social and economic force, is not limited to the subscriber or newsstand purchaser. The active life of one issue of a periodical, the duration of its spreading influence, may well be a matter of weeks, months, or even years. The time varies with the periodical and the contents of a particular issue. A news magazine may well be discarded after a week, whereas a fashion magazine may be of use for an entire season. Some magazine material has proved its timelessness. Henry Thoreau's *Ktaadn,* which appeared in the *Union Magazine* in 1848, was the subject of magazine articles a hundred years later. It is still read and enjoyed. What were originally the contents of the first few years of *The Atlantic Monthly,* the work of Emerson, Holmes, Longfellow, Lowell, and their contemporaries, affect new readers every year. A few of the pieces appearing in our magazines today may prove as lasting.

Today's magazine is shiny and brightly colored to attract the attention of men and women who have other sources of information and amusement competing for their attention. Their surface glitter attracts, but it takes substance to hold. Most adults have had the experience of buying a magazine at a railroad station, expecting its contents to interest for most of a journey of several hours, then found they had exhausted its possibilities in ten minutes and had to stare out of the train window, usually at the unkempt back yards of discouraged looking houses, for the rest of their journey. This is not always the fault of the magazine. It can be the state of the reader's mind or body. But in one short trip I have seen the same new copy of a very popular magazine discarded by its businessman purchaser after a brief and obviously unsatisfactory perusal, likewise discarded by a bored sailor, then scanned for only a few minutes by the housewife who took the seat after the sailor got off the train. The magazine was finally utilized by a small child, who, staggering up the aisle of the swaying coach, espied the magazine and enthusiastically tore out most of the pages. It ate one.

More often the magazine is read, read by more than one person; then, whether that copy is kept for a day or five years, it becomes an important part of the written record of American civilization. The bound files of magazines maintained by libraries throughout the United States are invaluable to the investigator into the tastes, manners, habits, interests, and achievements of any period of our history. The social historian has no richer source. He can discover and check facts in the newspapers of the time. For contemporary opinion of that time, for comment revealing how the news of the day appeared to those who made or were first affected by it, for discovery of what was approved in popular fiction and art, he must go to the magazines. Our present will some day be the quaint past at which possible survivors of future wars can be amused or aghast, but which they cannot neglect, in the pages of our magazines.

Probably every literate adult in the United States has read a magazine at one time or another, and usually more often than that. The statement is undoubtedly conservative. Everyone, whether he can read or not, is influenced, directly or indirectly, by what American magazines print. The influence is unavoidable, and though flagrant exceptions can be found, it is usually an influence making for public and private good.

Magazines, almost all of them and certainly all of the most influential from the standpoint of circulation, prestige, and accomplishment, are strong proponents of democracy as it is understood and practiced in the United States. They have attained their present dominant position under an economic system of free enterprise and under the traditional and constitutional democratic rights of free speech and a free press. It is natural that they should be firm upholders of free competition in business and defenders of the freedom of the individual within the framework of a democratic society.

The charge used to be made—it is heard less frequently now —that some magazines were controlled by their advertisers. The charge was always absurd. People buy and read a magazine primarily for its editorial contents. No honest or capable editor can permit dictation from the magazine's advertisers. Magazine advertising and circulation managers are equally aware of the danger. The editor, the business executives, and the advertising space salesman of a magazine run to suit the wishes of its advertisers would soon be out of jobs. Unless a magazine establishes and maintains an editorial integrity which the public recognizes and approves, that magazine is as useless as a vehicle for advertising as it is impotent as an editorial force.

Though they have become notably more liberal in recent years in their consideration of domestic, social, and industrial problems and in their treatment of international affairs, the magazines are basically conservative. They may criticize adversely what they see as inefficient, extravagant, and culpable in the conduct of business or government, but, like the more outspoken muckraking magazines in the first decade of this century, they are intent on improvement within the present structure, not on tearing it down. By opposing the trend toward collectivism manifest in the twentieth century, they act as a necessary corrective and restraining influence on thought and action in politics and government. Socialism and communism have had little support from American magazines. They have consistently fought all evidences of dictatorship and the undue expansion of bureaucratic powers, excessive government control of commerce and industry, and the tyrannical exercise of power over their fellows by any group within the population. As magazines are one of the most characteristic products of American democracy, they are also one of the strongest forces supporting it.

"The reading of magazines," wrote William B. Cairns in 1921, while he was professor of American literature at the University of Wisconsin, "has come to be far more common than the reading of books. Thousands of persons who would resent the imputation that they are lacking in culture read almost no books at all. . . . No home, however, in which there is pretense of intellectual interest is without magazines, which are usually read by all members of the family." [6] Since that time American magazines have made great gains in prestige and in influence on the social and economic life of the United States, but their force has been building up to its present strength for a much longer time and has been evident throughout the whole of magazine history and development.

For over 200 years American magazines have disseminated information and opinion. They have reported, commented, advised, entertained. Directly, through discussion of contemporary interests, and indirectly, through fiction and verse, they have influenced both the life of the nation and the lives of millions of individuals. Since 1741 the magazines have affected American social, political, and economic thought. They have made their

---

[6] *Cambridge History of American Literature* (New York: The Macmillan Co., 1943), Vol. II, p. 299. Used by permission of The Macmillan Company, publishers.

influence felt in government, commerce, and industry. They have stimulated the minds and imaginations of American readers, formed many of their ideas, affected their actions, fashioned their ethical and social concepts, as well as their clothes and their homes.

When the nascent United States was a handful of separated colonies scattered along the eastern seaboard, magazines gave it a consciousness of itself as a colonial entity. During and after the Revolution, they developed the hesitant national consciousness among the original states. Magazines were as potent a force in the abolition of slavery as in the lessening of sectionalism and insularity. Today they are perhaps the most powerful force at work in making the American recognize and realize the place of the United States in an international order.

By developing both writers and an audience for these writers, magazines have been and are a primary force in American literature. Through the national advertising, which alone makes financially possible the editorial content and force of American magazines, they have been helped to effect business expansion, mass production, and the possession by practically the whole population of those products of industry which have made the American standard of living materially the highest in the world. American magazines have proved themselves an effective weapon in two great wars, an aid to civilization, science, and the arts in times of peace.

Magazines have carried on planned crusades to correct social abuses. At the same time, through continual spreading of fact and through thoughtful interpretation of the events and ideas current at the time of their publication, they have exerted a strong positive force in the forming of public opinion on all matters of vital public concern.

The magazine today is not essentially different from the magazine in 1741. *The General Magazine and Historical Chronicle* then, and *Time, Life, The Saturday Evening Post,* and *Harper's* now, are recognizably the same in basic identity and function. The magazine is, as it has been, a vehicle for communication among people, a medium for the transmission of facts, ideas, and fancies. An improved vehicle now, it provides more efficient communication among more millions of people than it did over two centuries ago. It transmits more and different facts and more complicated ideas largely because the twentieth century has more of each to transmit than had the eighteenth century, and because people today wish and need more knowledge and information. Its social force is greater because it reaches more readers who through their education are more receptive to ideas in print and who have learned, largely through magazines, to live in an extended social, political, and economic environment.

A sharp-sighted and sharply spoken Englishwoman, exiled for three years in Cincinnati, made her famous comments on this country and its people in *Domestic Manners of the Americans*, first published in 1832. She saw even in that day the power of American magazines. General taste in this country she found execrable, and she knew where to place the blame. "The immense exhalation of periodical trash which penetrates into every cot and corner of the country, and which is greedily sucked up by all ranks, is unquestionably one great cause of its inferiority."

Could Mrs. Trollope make a return visit to the United States she would find the country's magazines far more influential than they were a century and a quarter ago. It is to be hoped that even so severe a critic would decide that their influence is producing happier results.

American magazines have flaws, a few of which have been noted in this discussion. They have not yet attained idealized perfection, and it is unlikely that they ever will. They do an imperfect but a useful job, and they have been doing it, continually better, for a long time.

SELECTED BIBLIOGRAPHY

Books and Pamphlets

ALDEN, HENRY MILLS. *Magazine Writing and the New Literature.* New York: Harper & Bros., 1908.

ALLEN, FREDERICK L. *Harper's Magazine, 1850–1950.* New York: The Newcomen Society in North America, 1950.

ATKINSON, WILMER. *An Autobiography.* Philadelphia: Wilmer Atkinson Co., 1920.

BAINBRIDGE, JOHN. *Little Wonder and How It Grew.* New York: Reynal & Hitchcock, 1946.

BAKER, RAY STANNARD. *American Chronicle.* New York: Charles Scribner's Sons, 1945.

BOK, EDWARD. *The Americanization of Edward Bok.* New York: Charles Scribner's Sons, 1920.

————. *A Man from Maine.* New York: Charles Scribner's Sons, 1923.

BORDEN, NEIL H. *The Economic Effects of Advertising.* Chicago: Richard D. Irwin, Inc., 1942.

Country Gentleman, A Brief History of. Philadelphia: The Curtis Publishing Co., 1954.

DREWRY, JOHN E. *Some Magazines and Their Makers.* Boston: The Stratford Co., 1924.

ELLIS, HAROLD MILTON. *Joseph Dennie and His Circle.* Austin, Texas: Bulletin of the University of Texas, No. 40, 1915.

FAULKNER, HAROLD UNDERWOOD. *The Quest for Social Justice, 1898–1914.* (*A History of American Life,* Vol. XI.) New York: The Macmillan Co., 1931.

HARPER, J. HENRY. *The House of Harper.* New York: Harper & Bros., 1912.

HODGINS, ERIC. *The Span of Time* (Reprint of a Speech delivered at the Chautauqua Institution). New York, 1946.

HOFFMAN, FREDERIC J., CHARLES ALLEN, and CAROLYN F. ULRICH. *The Little Magazine, A History and a Bibliography.* Princeton, N. J.: Princeton University Press, 1946.

HOWE, M. A. DEWOLFE. *The Atlantic Monthly and Its Makers.* Boston: Atlantic Monthly Press, 1919.

HOWER, RALPH M. *The History of an Advertising Agency, N. W.*

379

Ayer & Son at Work. Cambridge, Mass.: Harvard University Press, 1939.

JOHNSON, WALTER. *William Allen White's America*. New York: Henry Holt & Co., 1947.

KLAPPER, JOSEPH T. *The Effects of Mass Media*. New York: Bureau of Applied Social Research, Columbia University, 1949.

KLEPPNER, OTTO. *Advertising Procedure*. 4th ed. New York: Prentice-Hall, Inc., 1950.

LYNCH, DENIS T. *Boss Tweed*. New York: Boni and Liveright, 1927.

MORRIS, LLOYD. *Postscript to Yesterday*. New York: Random House, 1947.

MOTT, FRANK LUTHER. *American Journalism, A History of Newspapers in the United States*. New York: The Macmillan Co., 1942.

———. *A History of American Magazines, 1741–1885*. 3 vols. New York: Appleton-Century-Crofts, Inc., 1930, and Cambridge, Mass.: Harvard University Press, 1938–1939.

NOEL, MARY. *Villains Galore—The Heyday of the Popular Story Weekly*. New York: The Macmillan Co., 1954.

PATTEE, FRED LEWIS. *The First Century of American Literature, 1770–1870*. New York: Appleton-Century-Crofts, Inc., 1935.

Printers' Ink, Fifty Years: 1888 to 1938. New York: Printers' Ink Publishing Co., 1938.

RICHARDSON, LYON. *A History of Early American Magazines*. New York: Thomas Nelson and Sons, 1931.

ROWELL, GEORGE P. *Forty Years an Advertising Agent*. New York: Franklin Publishing Co., 1926.

Saturday Evening Post, A Short History of The. Philadelphia: The Curtis Publishing Co., 1949.

SCHLESINGER, ARTHUR MEIER. *Political and Social Growth of the American People, 1865–1940*. New York: The Macmillan Co., 1941.

———. *Political and Social History of the United States. 1829–1925*. New York: The Macmillan Co., 1925.

SCHRAMM, WILBUR (ed.). *Mass Communications*. Urbana, Ill.: The University of Illinois Press, 1949.

SEDGWICK, ELLERY. *The Happy Profession*. Boston: Little Brown & Co., 1946.

SELDES, GILBERT. *The Great Audience*. New York: The Viking Press, 1950.

SLOSSON, WILLIAM PRESTON. *The Great Crusade and After, 1914–1928*. (*A History of American Life*, Vol. XII.) New York: The Macmillan Co., 1930.

SMYTH, ALBERT H. *Philadelphia Magazines and Their Contributors, 1741–1850*. Philadelphia: Robert M. Lindsay, 1892.

STEPHENS, ETHEL A. (comp.). *American Popular Magazines, A Bibliography.* Boston: The Boston Book Co., 1916.

STODDARD, HENRY LUTHER. *Horace Greeley, Printer, Editor, Crusader.* New York: G. P. Putnam's Sons, 1946.

Story of an Experiment, The. New York: Time, Inc., 1948.

SULLIVAN, MARK. *The Education of an American.* New York: Doubleday, Doran & Co., 1928.

———. *Our Times.* Vol. I, *The Turn of the Century,* and Vol. II, *America Finding Herself.* New York: Charles Scribner's Sons, 1926, 1927.

TARBELL, IDA. *The Nationalizing of Business, 1878–1898.* (*A History of American Life,* Vol. IX.) New York: The Macmillan Co., 1944.

TASSIN, ALGERNON. *The Magazine in America.* New York: Dodd, Mead & Co., 1916.

TEBBEL, JOHN. *George Horace Lorimer and The Saturday Evening Post.* Garden City, N. Y.: Doubleday & Co., Inc., 1948.

TOOKER, L. FRANK. *The Joys and Tribulations of an Editor.* New York: Appleton-Century-Crofts, Inc., 1920.

TRENT, W. P., SHERMAN ERSKINE, and CARL VAN DOREN (eds.). *Cambridge History of American Literature.* New York: The Macmillan Co., 1943.

WAPLES, DOUGLAS, BERNARD BERELSON, and FRANKLIN BRADSHAW. *What Reading Does to People.* Chicago: University of Chicago Press, 1940.

WARD, A. W., and A. R. WALLER (eds). *The Cambridge History of English Literature,* Vols. IX and X. New York: G. P. Putnam's Sons, 1913.

What Makes Time Tick. New York: Time, Inc., n.d.

WHITE, WILLIAM ALLEN. *Autobiography.* New York: The Macmillan Co., 1946.

WOLSELEY, ROLAND E. *The Magazine World.* New York: Prentice-Hall, Inc., 1951.

MAGAZINE ARTICLES

ALLEN, FREDERICK LEWIS. "American Magazines, 1741–1941," *Bulletin of The New York Public Library,* XLV, No. 5 (June, 1941).

———. "The American Magazine Grows Up," *The Atlantic Monthly,* November, 1947.

"American Magazine—Literature of the Last Century," *The Atlantic Monthly.* April, 1860.

"American Men of Letters and Periodical Literature," *Harper's Magazine,* April, 1907.

BUTTERFIELD, ROGER. "What Pocket Magazines Feed On," *The Saturday Review of Literature,* March 9, 1946.

CALKINS, ERNEST ELMO. "Fifty Years of Advertising," *Printers' Ink,* October 10, 1947.

CHENERY, WILLIAM L. "American Magazines, 1741–1941," *Bulletin of The New York Public Library,* June, 1941.

——. "Magazines and Public Opinion," *Vital Speeches,* August 15, 1936.

CHURCHILL, ALLEN. "Harold Ross, Editor of The New Yorker," *Cosmopolitan,* May, 1948.

"Crowell," *Fortune,* August, 1937.

EDWARDS, JACKSON. "One Every Minute; The Picture Magazines," *Scribner's Magazine,* May, 1938.

ELLISON, JEROME. "Selling Dreams in Marble Halls," *The New Republic,* October 13, 1947.

FRANCIS, C. M. "Fighting Magazines," *Bookman,* July, 1910.

"Freedom of the Press," *Survey,* June 4, 1910.

GIBBS, WOLCOTT. "Time . . . Fortune . . . Life . . . Luce," *The New Yorker,* November 28, 1936.

GILDER, RICHARD WATSON. "Century's Twentieth Anniversary," *Century Magazine,* November, 1890.

"Glance at the World's Periodicals," *Review of Reviews,* January, 1911.

HARMSWORTH, ALFRED (Lord Northcliffe). "The Future of Magazines," *The Independent,* November 19, 1908.

HARRIMAN, MARGARET CASE. "The Candor Kid," *The New Yorker,* January 4 and 11, 1941.

HARTMAN, E. P. "Magazines; Moulders of Opinion," *Wilson Library Bulletin,* April, 1947.

HARVEY, GEORGE. "Magazines in Journalism," *Harper's Weekly,* March 19, 1910.

HAVILAND, THOMAS P. "Franklin's General Magazine," *General Magazine and Historical Chronicle* (University of Pennsylvania), Winter, 1946.

HICKMAN, POWELL. "Collier's," *Scribner's Magazine,* May, 1939.

"History of a Publishing House, The," *Scribner's Magazine,* December, 1894.

HUGHES, LAWRENCE M. "North American Steppes Yield Gold to Mr. Tilley," *Advertising Age,* December 1, 1947.

KERR, W. A., and H. H. REMMERS. "Cultural Value of 100 Representative American Magazines," *School and Society,* November 22, 1941.

"Literature of Business," *The Nation,* November 15, 1906.

LYDGATE, WILLIAM A. "Romantic Business," *Scribner's Magazine,* September, 1938.

"Magazine Literature," *Harper's Magazine,* February, 1903.

"Magazines, Their Scope and Influence," *The Independent,* October 1, 1908.

MANCHESTER, HARLAND. "Farm Magazines," *Scribner's Magazine,* October, 1938.

MILLER, MERLE. "Freedom to Read; Magazines," *Survey Graphic,* December, 1946.

MULLER, EDWIN. "Radio versus Reading," *The New Republic,* February 19, 1940.

"New Yorker, The," *Fortune,* August, 1934.

"Norman Hapgood and Collier's Weekly," *Outlook,* November 2, 1912.

OURSLER, FULTON. "American Magazines, 1741–1941," *Bulletin of The New York Public Library,* June, 1941.

PRINGLE, HENRY F. "High Hat; The Luxury Magazines," *Scribner's Magazine,* July, 1938.

———. "Ross of The New Yorker," *'48,* March and April, 1948.

REPPLIER, AGNES. "American Magazines," *Yale Review,* XVI (1926–1927).

ROSS, ISHBEL. "Geography, Inc.," *Scribner's Magazine,* June, 1938.

"Story of an Experiment, The." *Time,* March 8, 1948.

"Strangling the Magazines," *The Nation,* May 2, 1912.

TARBELL, I. M. "Sarah Josepha Hale," *American Magazine,* March, 1910.

WHIPPLE, LEON. "SatEvePost," *Survey,* March 1, 1928.

INDEX

Adams, Charles Francis (1807–1886), 44

Adams, Charles Francis (1835–1915), 44, 45, 131, 184

Adams, Henry, 44, 45, 184

Adams, John Quincy, 28ff., 148

Addison, Joseph, 5, 6, 9

Advertising, 270–90
  agencies, 287–89
  costs, 284–85, 289–90
  Curtis Code, 282
  in farm magazines, 169
  in fashion magazines, 129–30
  in *Ladies' Home Journal,* 107–8
  in *McClure's Magazine,* 137, 276
  in store-distributed magazines, 257ff.
  of *The New York Ledger,* 86–89
  in *The New Yorker,* 242, 254
  patent medicine, 115–17
  in *The Reader's Digest,* 228–30, 254
  rise of, 75
  in *The Saturday Evening Post,* 155–56

Alden, Henry Mills, 42, 75, 78

Allen, Frederick Lewis, 80, 104, 353

American Agriculturist, 178

American Heritage, 341

American Magazine (1906–   ), 141, 184

American Magazine, or a Monthly View of the Political State of the British Colonies, 10, 12–13

American Magazine, The (1787–1788), 22

American Magazine of Useful and Entertaining Knowledge, 67

American Mercury, The, 190, 193–96

American Museum, The, 17, 19–20

American Notes, 60, 61

"— And Sudden Death," 230, 298

Anti-Slavery Examiner, 74

Anti-Slavery Record, 74

Anti-Slavery Reporter, 74

Architectural Forum, 214

Atkinson, Wilmer, 172–73, 174

Atlantic Monthly, The, 36, 59, 66–68, 80–84, 368

Baker, Ray Stannard, 132, 134, 142–43

Ballyhoo, 214

Belknap, Jeremy, 17, 18, 19, 26

Better Homes and Gardens, 327, 337–39

Better Living, 267

Blossom, Sumner, 365

Bok, Edward, 75, 106–20, 282, 300, 360

Bonner, Robert, 86ff.

Bradford, Andrew, 10, 12–13, 14, 271

Brown, Charles Brockden, 14, 23, 26, 32, 36–38

Bryan, Clark W., 122

Bryant, William Cullen, 39, 46, 50, 53, 67, 87, 97, 327

Business Week, 336–37

Cairns, William B., 376

Canby, Henry Seidel, 339

Capper's Farmer, 103, 180–81

Catton, Bruce, 341

Century, The, 83, 129, 134, 143, 272

Charm, 130

Chenery, William Ludlow, 346, 347–48

Circulation; *see also individual titles of magazines*
  average per issue, 198, 323
  before 1800, 25

385